FEMINISM
IN OUR TIME

FEMINISM IN OUR TIME

The Essential Writings, World War II to the Present

Edited with an introduction and commentaries by

MIRIAM SCHNEIR

Vintage Books

A Division of Random House, Inc. / New York

A VINTAGE ORIGINAL, JULY 1994

FIRST EDITION

Introduction, commentary, and compilation copyright © 1994 by Miriam Schneir

Library of Congress Cataloging-in-Publication Data
Feminism in our time: the essential writings, World War II to the present / edited
and with an introduction and commentaries by Miriam Schneir.
     p.   cm.
"A Vintage original."
ISBN 0-679-74508-4
1. Feminism—United States—History.   2. Women—United States—
History. I. Schneir, Miriam.
HQ1420.F38   1994
305.42'0973—dc20 93-46391
CIP

COVER PHOTOGRAPHY:
Simone de Beauvoir by Elliott Erwitt/Magnum;
Betty Friedan by Philippe Halsman;
Germaine Greer by Jerry Bauer;
Doris Lessing by Peter Lessing;
Audre Lorde by Dagmar Schultz;
Cynthia Ozick by Julius Ozick;
Adrienne Rich by Jason Langer;
Anne Sexton by Rollie McKenna.

Manufactured in the United States of America

10 9 8 7

CONTENTS

IV "WE CANNOT RELY ON EXISTING IDEOLOGIES"

INTRODUCTION

This anthology brings together the major literature and documents that inspired and shaped modern feminism. The writings cover a period of more than forty years—from 1949, when Simone de Beauvoir's *The Second Sex* was published in France, to 1993, when Ruth Bader Ginsburg responded to her nomination to the U.S. Supreme Court.

The feminism of the post–World War II decades profoundly transformed the lives of women in the United States and throughout the world. It brought about upheavals in law and the customs of everyday life, and altered the consciousness of women themselves. Obviously, such momentous changes did not spring from unprepared ground. In an earlier volume, *Feminism: The Essential Historical Writings*, I collected works by the women whose seventy-year struggle—from the mid–nineteenth century to the 1920s—created the conditions that made modern feminism possible.

The world's first organized movement in behalf of women was inaugurated in 1848 at a small chapel in the sleepy village of Seneca Falls, New York. There the thirty-two-year-old Elizabeth Cady Stanton delivered what she described as her first public speech, confessing that she was "nerved" for the ordeal only by her conviction that the time had come for "the question of woman's wrongs to be laid before the public" and by her belief "that woman herself must do this work; for woman alone can understand the height, the depth, the length, and the breadth of her own degradation."

Stanton's statement was not hyperbole. Women in the United

States at that time were barred from attending all but a few institutions of higher education, from voting in elections, from participating in legislative bodies, or from serving as jurors. They lived under a double standard that tolerated a high degree of sexual freedom for males but none for females. Married women were obliged to obey husbands, who had almost unlimited control over their wives' activities and finances—for example, a wife's inheritance and even the wages she earned could be claimed by her spouse. In case of divorce, women had few legal rights and usually lost custody of their children. Single women, excluded from well-paid employment that could provide economic independence, were frequently forced to live as unwelcome dependents in the homes of fathers or brothers.

The campaign waged by Stanton and her comrades met with belligerence and ridicule from journalists, politicians, and churchmen alike. Sentiment seemed overwhelmingly hostile. Nonetheless, the women persevered, calling conferences, delivering speeches, circulating petitions, and making arduous journeys to far-flung towns and rural districts to address small groups in churches, halls, and even barns. By 1860, at a national woman's rights convention, Ernestine Rose, a movement activist, reported that the first favorable shifts in public opinion had been brought about by their hard work. "Freedom, my friends," she declared, "does not come from the clouds, like a meteor; it does not bloom in one night; it does not come without great efforts and great sacrifices; all who love liberty, have to labor for it." And labor they did. Soon the cause of women was taken up in western Europe, too, and feminists on both sides of the Atlantic followed one another's activities and eventually formed international alliances.

Elizabeth Cady Stanton lived until 1902, and her chief collaborator, Susan B. Anthony, to 1906—long enough to see the next generation of women endowed with what must have seemed to the pioneers a dazzling array of opportunities. During the lifetimes of Stanton and Anthony, women's legal and property rights were enlarged, new employment options opened, and access to higher education improved. It was advances such as these that afforded feminists in the 1960s a securer base from which to launch their activities and enabled them to move ahead with a speed and effectiveness that would have amazed their predecessors.

In 1920 the American women's movement achieved the goal toward which its energy had been directed since the turn of the century—a constitutional amendment giving women the right to vote. But although suffrage was an outstanding victory, the great expectations held for it were not realized, since few female candidates ran for political office and no separate woman's vote developed. Moreover, soon after 1920, the main women's organizations disintegrated, and feminism entered a long period of dormancy. Several important feminist books were published during those dark ages—notably works by Virginia Woolf and Mary Beard—and clusters of women here and there continued to carry on the fight. But as a serious topic of discussion or study, feminism all but disappeared. Feminist leaders vanished into virtual oblivion, their struggle nearly forgotten. My own experience was typical: Neither in high school nor in college in the fifties was I exposed to the literature or history of feminist protest, although the college I attended, Antioch, was one of the first schools of higher education in the United States to admit female students. And in the early seventies, when I was assembling the essential historical writings of feminism, I found that many key documents were out of print and unavailable in most libraries, while others had been reissued in just the previous year or two.

The disappearance of feminism from the stage of history for several decades meant that the emerging women of the sixties had to rediscover basic truths about the oppression of women for themselves. One young activist noted that after reading the works of a forgotten feminist of the nineteenth century, she had been "shocked that this perceptive and powerful analysis of society should have been formulated a century ago and not built upon, shocked that in the late 1960s we had to begin again without benefit of these valuable insights . . . forged over a lifetime." She asked bitterly, "How many times does women's history have to repeat itself?"[1]

The first indications of a feminist reawakening appeared after World War II. Initially, the stirrings were so slight as to be almost imperceptible: The United Nations affirmed "the equal rights of men and women" in its 1945 charter and a few years later established the U.N. Commission on the Status of Women to advance this ideal. Woman suffrage was granted or extended in France, Belgium, Italy, Venezuela, Japan, Korea, and other nations.[2] *The Second Sex* appeared and was read and discussed by women everywhere. Then gradually the pace quickened. In the United States, the ranks of women employed outside the home grew steadily. President John F. Kennedy authorized an official governmental commission to study the status of American women. Betty Friedan's *The Feminine Mystique* was published. Finally, in the late sixties, a vigorous feminist movement arose in the United States and rapidly spread to other countries. It was not really sudden, but it seemed so to those who had not been listening.

The feminists of the sixties set out on two separate paths. Business and professional women, dissatisfied with their lack of opportunity, joined together in traditional-style associations, like the National Organization for Women, to campaign for equality with men in employment, law, education, and politics. Other women—most of them young veterans of the sixties' antiwar and civil rights movements—eschewed formal structure or leadership and worked in loosely organized groups that were well suited to the "zap" actions they preferred. They adopted the larger goals of liberating women from sex-role stereotypes and reshaping sexist institutions. It was their vitality, daring, and creativity that gave feminism in our time its distinctive style and character—and, incidentally, its media image.

The dichotomy that marked the beginnings of second-wave

[1]Lynne Spender, "Matilda Joslyn Gage: Active Intellectual," in *Feminist Theorists*, ed. Dale Spender (New York: Pantheon, 1983), p. 143.

[2]*The World's Women, 1970–1990: Trends and Statistics* (New York: United Nations, 1991); referring to the years 1945–1948 from table, "Indicators on Women in Public Life," pp. 39–42.

feminism did not last. Eventually the tendencies merged, with a blending of goals and tactics. The resulting diversity is a strength, but it makes it difficult to generalize about the movement's distinctive characteristics. However, a comparison of today's movement with that of a century ago can bring several features of modern feminism into sharper relief.

The women of the Stanton-Anthony generation were educated at home or at inferior female academies; they had few opportunities for meaningful work or financial independence. Among the nineteenth-century female authors in my historical anthology, only one, Lucy Stone, had the advantage of a higher education. In contrast, nearly all the writers in the present volume are college graduates, and many have advanced degrees; five are attorneys, and over a dozen are university professors.

The historical anthology includes several male authors and has a section titled "Men as Feminists," with excerpts from fundamental writings in the literature of feminism by John Stuart Mill, Friedrich Engels, Henrik Ibsen, and other men. It was not unusual then for men to speak for women; at the Seneca Falls meeting the proceedings were chaired by a man. But the present book has only one selection attributed to a male author—the Supreme Court majority opinion in *Roe v. Wade,* by Justice Harry A. Blackmun.

The historical anthology contains only two African-American writers: Frederick Douglass and Sojourner Truth, both former slaves. The modern collection has many African-American voices, documenting a growing commitment to feminist goals among black women. Moreover, as the contemporary movement enlarges its agenda to encompass a wider range of issues, it is certain to attract a broader constituency; we can anticipate valuable new feminist insights from Asian-American women and Latinas in the coming years.

The psychological consequences for women of gender discrimination were not examined in much depth by early feminism. But second-wave feminists, while discarding a great deal of psychological and psychoanalytic dogma on women, nevertheless insisted on the central importance to female liberation of women's consciousness. They developed the innovative technique of consciousness raising, by means of which women could help one another overcome negative feelings about themselves and their place in the world.

None of the nineteenth-century documents in the historical anthology deals with childbirth, abortion, homosexuality, or rape, and only one discusses female sexuality with any specificity (it was written by Victoria Woodhull, who was notorious for her disregard of proprieties). The present collection, in contrast, contains references throughout to many formerly taboo topics and has a separate section titled "Our Bodies." The revolution in sexual mores that began in the early twentieth century—aided and abetted by such social rebels as anarchist Emma Goldman, poet Edna St. Vincent Millay, birth control advocate Margaret Sanger, and hosts of spirited, scantily clothed flappers—freed modern feminists to explore sexual subjects with unprecedented openness and honesty.

The early feminists were internationalists, but their contacts were confined to developed regions of the world. The perspective of today's feminists is global. It includes areas where women disproportionately suffer from poverty and hunger, where conception is uncontrolled and childbirth dangerous, where wives and daughters are virtual chattels of husbands and fathers, where female illiteracy is widespread, and where genital mutilation is practiced. Communication among the worldwide family of woman was furthered by conferences sponsored by the United Nations Decade for Women—in Mexico City (1975), Copenhagen (1980), and Nairobi (1985).

The many contrasts noted between first- and second-wave feminism are not surprising, since the modern movement is being enacted in a historical and technological setting entirely different from that which existed in the previous century. Still, there is a fundamental question that spans the generations, linking the new movement with the old. It is a question that has long haunted feminism: What is the essential nature of woman? it asks. What are her immutable attributes, abilities, and predilections? The problem was enunciated by Elizabeth Cady Stanton in 1888, at the age of seventy-two, in an address to the International Council of Women. "Thus far," she said, "women have been the mere echoes of men. Our laws and constitutions, our creeds and codes, and the customs of social life are all of masculine origin. The true woman is as yet a dream of the future."

The mystery of "the true woman" has sparked a debate among contemporary feminists. At issue is whether the sexes basically think, behave, and speak differently from each other. The claims of "difference" proponents have taken various forms: women have a closer relation to the earth and to natural phenomena; women are less aggressive and more peace loving; women have a different understanding of ethical dilemmas. And some antipornography activists apparently assume that women are sexually purer than men. But no definitive statement on the true nature of woman is yet possible, for reasons psychologist Naomi Weisstein expressed succinctly years ago: "I don't know what immutable differences exist between men and women apart from differences in their genitalia; perhaps there are some other unchangeable differences. . . . But it is clear that until social expectations for men and women are equal, until we provide equal respect for both men and women, our answers to this question will simply reflect our prejudices."[3]

The readings in this volume are arranged chronologically within sections, with the sections reflecting the lines of development of the modern women's movement. Preceding each selection is a headnote that places it in historical context and offers interpretative commentary along with a thumbnail sketch of the author, where useful. In some cases only a part of a long work is reprinted; the reader is urged to regard the anthology as a sampler and to obtain the full text of writings that intrigue. (The list of sources of selections at the end of the book cites currently available editions.)

The literature of second-wave feminism is varied and plentiful. To keep this volume to a reasonable size, it was necessary for me to omit specialized studies in history, sociology, or other academic disciplines; all fiction except for Doris Lessing's *The Golden Notebook*, which was unique in its impact; and writ-

---

[3]Naomi Weisstein, "Psychology Constructs the Female," *Social Education*, April 1971, p. 373.

ings, however excellent, that treat an idea or viewpoint already represented. A handful of poems were chosen as exemplars of the remarkable renaissance in women's poetry that has occurred during these years.

Here then are the essential writings of feminism in our time. To those who participated in the adventure of the sixties and seventies, many of these readings will be familiar. When first encountered, they were revelatory. They opened doors to new possibilities and provided road maps to a future that suddenly held unexpected promise. Some were best-sellers, some were passed hand-to-hand in mimeographed form. Either way, these were texts that women took to heart, finding in them expression of their inchoate feelings and uncannily accurate analysis of their own life situations.

Readers today, whether discovering or rediscovering these writings, do so in a period when all who embrace feminism would do well not to underestimate the strong social forces that oppose it. Several decades from now women will perhaps look back on this moment as a midpoint from which continued and abundant progress has been made. Or the present may be seen in retrospect as a high-water mark at which the gains of feminism stagnated or receded. The outcome cannot be predicted, but it will be determined by the actions of women themselves. The writings in this volume are a legacy from feminists of the recent past, to arm our vision for the inevitable struggles ahead.

FEMINISM
IN OUR TIME

I

Reawakening

SIMONE DE BEAUVOIR

The Second Sex

Soon after 1920, when woman suffrage was won in the United States, the movement that had brought it about faltered, then came to a standstill. Over the following decades of global economic collapse and war, feminism itself seemed drained of energy, an issue without gravity or relevance. It was left to small networks of dedicated women to keep remnants of the cause alive. Yet despite the quiescence of feminism as a broad-based movement, in 1949, only four years after the conclusion of World War II, one of the most important books ever written about the oppression of women—*The Second Sex*—was published in France.

The author, Simone de Beauvoir (1908–1986), was already internationally known as an existentialist philosopher, a left-wing political activist, and a writer of both fiction and nonfiction. But she was not then a feminist, according to her own declaration. A weighty book about women—in a period when womanhood was not considered an interesting, much less a serious, topic—was an unexpected turn in her career. Although widely read and debated at the time—an English translation appeared in 1953—the book was not elevated to its position as basic to the feminist canon for many years.

The Second Sex is large in scope, grand in design and purpose. Its goal was no less than to describe the creation of woman, for de Beauvoir insisted that womanhood as we know it is a social construct; that is, that the subordination of female to male does not represent an immutable state of nature, but is the result of various social forces. "One is not born, but rather becomes, a woman," she wrote.

Exposing this puzzling construct—woman—to searching inquiry, turning it this way and that, examining various facets of the surface, she tried to fathom what lay beneath. Biology was basic: "Woman is weaker than man . . . she cannot stand up to him in a fight," she wrote; and of woman's reproductive function: "The female is the victim of the species." But biology was only the beginning. What insights could psychology, anthropology, history, and economics offer? How have art, literature, myth, and religion depicted and explained woman?

De Beauvoir concluded that civilization—all of it: culture, knowledge, art, values—was of man's making. Men are normative human beings, "the One"; women are "the Other." Men are active, transcendent, able to transform their environment; women are passive and "immanent," that is, existing within themselves, with little capacity to affect outside society. Men are the "subjects" of their own lives, the actors; women are "objects," the acted upon. This is the way the world has always been.

However, if de Beauvoir held a gloomy view of woman's past, she was optimistic about the future. With modern technology—including contraception and abortion—women could surmount their physical disadvantages; with the advent of socialism, their secondary social and economic status would be overcome. Signs of improvement already were noticeable among a small group of emancipated women who constituted a vanguard striving to live as independent, self-defined people. She counted herself as one of this number.

To the emerging activists of the European women's movement, *The Second Sex* was—in the words of one of them—a "beacon which Simone de Beauvoir lit to show women in the second half of this century the way."[1] And in the United States, de Beauvoir was mentor to those who arrived at feminism via the sixties student movements for social change; a collection of writings by some of these young women was dedicated "to Simone de Beauvoir," who "gave us our feminism."[2]

[1] Alice Schwarzer, *After The Second Sex: Conversations with Simone de Beauvoir,* trans. Marianne Howarth (New York: Pantheon, 1984), pp. 12–13.

[2] Redstockings, *Feminist Revolution* (New York: Random House, 1975, 1978).

De Beauvoir's private life came to be admired almost equally with her work. She chose never to marry or set up a joint home with the man who was her lover and lifelong comrade—writer-philosopher Jean-Paul Sartre. She never bore a child. Without domestic entanglements, she was free to earn an advanced academic degree, travel, write, teach, join political causes, take lovers. Although a biography that appeared after her death showed that her relationship with Sartre was more dependent, both personally and professionally, than outsiders had imagined, few people at the time realized this.[3] Many contemporaries saw her as a model of the liberated woman, a symbol of the possibility that a woman might live as she wished, ignoring convention.

In the years since the publication of *The Second Sex*, a few of de Beauvoir's key ideas have been criticized by feminists. One of the first to do so was eminent historian Mary Beard, a veteran activist in behalf of women's rights. Beard commented in 1953 that de Beauvoir was wrong in stating that the female sex had been subordinate throughout time; Beard believed that women had played an essential part in the making of civilization and had been a force in all human history. As for de Beauvoir's views on the female body and maternity, some later feminists saw strength and potency where the French theorist had seen weakness and incapacity.

Eventually de Beauvoir joined the campaign for women's liberation in France. In 1971 she signed a petition for legalized abortion with 343 other Frenchwomen who publicly declared that they had had abortions. And when abortion activists in France went on to set up an illegal abortion network, in which abortions were performed in the apartments of public figures to lessen the likelihood of reprisals, she unhesitatingly made her own apartment available.[4] De Beauvoir announced in 1972 that she now considered herself a feminist. She had come to realize that "we must fight for the situation of women, here and now, before our dreams of socialism come true" and that "even in

[3]Deirdre Bair, *Simone de Beauvoir, A Biography* (New York: Summit, 1990).
[4]Schwarzer, *After The Second Sex*, pp. 13, 14.

socialist countries, equality between men and women has not been achieved."[5]

The following excerpts from *The Second Sex* come from the introduction and the last chapter, "The Independent Woman." They provide a sample of de Beauvoir's style and wide-ranging interests, and they present her principal thesis.

Introduction

FIRST WE MUST ASK: WHAT IS A WOMAN? "*Tota mulier in utero,*" says one, "woman is a womb." But in speaking of certain women, connoisseurs declare that they are not women, although they are equipped with a uterus like the rest. All agree in recognizing the fact that females exist in the human species; today as always they make up about one half of humanity. And yet we are told that femininity is in danger; we are exhorted to be women, remain women, become women. It would appear, then, that every female human being is not necessarily a woman; to be so considered she must share in that mysterious and threatened reality known as femininity. Is this attribute something secreted by the ovaries? Or is it a Platonic essence, a product of the philosophic imagination? Is a rustling petticoat enough to bring it down to earth? Although some women try zealously to incarnate this essence, it is hardly patentable. It is frequently described in vague and dazzling terms that seem to have been borrowed from the vocabulary of the seers, and indeed in the times of St. Thomas it was considered an essence as certainly defined as the somniferous virtue of the poppy. . . .

In truth, to go for a walk with one's eyes open is enough to demonstrate that humanity is divided into two classes of individuals whose clothes, faces, bodies, smiles, gaits, interests, and occupations are manifestly different. Perhaps these differences

[5]Ibid., p. 32.

are superficial, perhaps they are destined to disappear. What is certain is that right now they do most obviously exist.

If her functioning as a female is not enough to define woman, if we decline also to explain her through "the eternal feminine," and if nevertheless we admit, provisionally, that women do exist, then we must face the question: What is a woman?

To state the question is, to me, to suggest, at once, a preliminary answer. The fact that I ask it is in itself significant. A man would never get the notion of writing a book on the peculiar situation of the human male. But if I wish to define myself, I must first of all say: "I am a woman"; on this truth must be based all further discussion. A man never begins by presenting himself as an individual of a certain sex; it goes without saying that he is a man. The terms *masculine* and *feminine* are used symmetrically only as a matter of form, as on legal papers. In actuality the relation of the two sexes is not quite like that of two electrical poles, for man represents both the positive and the neutral, as is indicated by the common use of *man* to designate human beings in general; whereas woman represents only the negative, defined by limiting criteria, without reciprocity. In the midst of an abstract discussion it is vexing to hear a man say: "You think thus and so because you are a woman"; but I know that my only defense is to reply: "I think thus and so because it is true," thereby removing my subjective self from the argument. It would be out of the question to reply: "And you think the contrary because you are a man," for it is understood that the fact of being a man is no peculiarity. A man is in the right in being a man; it is the woman who is in the wrong. It amounts to this: just as for the ancients there was an absolute vertical with reference to which the oblique was defined, so there is an absolute human type, the masculine. Woman has ovaries, a uterus; these peculiarities imprison her in her subjectivity, circumscribe her within the limits of her own nature. It is often said that she thinks with her glands. Man superbly ignores the fact that his anatomy also includes glands, such as the testicles, and that they secrete hormones. He thinks of his body as a direct and normal connection with the world, which he believes he apprehends objectively, whereas he regards the body of woman as a hindrance, a prison, weighed down by every-thing peculiar to it. "The female is a female by virtue of a certain *lack* of qualities," said Aristotle; "we should regard the female nature as afflicted with a natural defectiveness." And St. Thomas for his part pronounced woman to be an "imperfect man," an "incidental" being. This is symbolized in Genesis where Eve is depicted as made from what Bossuet[6] called "a supernumerary bone" of Adam.

Thus humanity is male and man defines woman not in herself but as relative to him; she is not regarded as an autonomous being. . . . She is simply what man decrees; thus she is called "the sex," by which is meant that she appears essentially to the male as a sexual being. For him she is sex—absolute sex, no less. She is defined and differentiated with reference to man and not he with reference to her; she is the incidental, the inessential as opposed to the essential. He is the Subject, he is the Absolute—she is the Other.

The category of the *Other* is as primordial as consciousness itself. In the most primitive societies, in the most ancient mythologies, one finds the expression of a duality—that of the Self and the Other. This duality was not originally attached to the division of the sexes; it was not dependent upon any empirical facts. . . . The feminine element was at first no more involved in such pairs as Varuna-Mitra, Uranus-Zeus, Sun-Moon, and Day-Night than it was in the contrasts between Good and Evil, lucky and unlucky auspices, right and left, God and Lucifer. Otherness is a fundamental category of human thought.

Thus it is that no group ever sets itself up as the One without at once setting up the Other over against itself. If three travelers chance to occupy the same compartment, that is enough to make vaguely hostile "others" out of all the rest of the passengers on the train. In small-town eyes all persons not belonging to the village are "strangers" and suspect; to the native of a country all who inhabit other countries are "foreigners"; Jews are "different" for the anti-Semite, Negroes are "inferior" for

---

[6]Jacques Bénigne Bossuet (1627–1704), French religious leader and historian.—*Ed.*

American racists, aborigines are "natives" for colonists, proletarians are the "lower class" for the privileged. . . .

The subject can be posed in being opposed—he sets himself up as the essential, as opposed to the other, the inessential, the object.

But the other consciousness, the other ego, sets up a reciprocal claim. The native traveling abroad is shocked to find himself in turn regarded as a "stranger" by the natives of neighboring countries. As a matter of fact, wars, festivals, trading, treaties, and contests among tribes, nations, and classes tend to deprive the concept *Other* of its absolute sense and to make manifest its relativity; willy-nilly, individuals and groups are forced to realize the reciprocity of their relations. How is it, then, that this reciprocity has not been recognized between the sexes, that one of the contrasting terms is set up as the sole essential, denying any relativity in regard to its correlative and defining the latter as pure otherness? Why is it that women do not dispute male sovereignty? No subject will readily volunteer to become the object, the inessential; it is not the Other who, in defining himself as the Other, establishes the One. The Other is posed as such by the One in defining himself as the One. But if the Other is not to regain the status of being the One, he must be submissive enough to accept this alien point of view. Whence comes this submission in the case of woman? . . .

The reason for this is that women lack concrete means for organizing themselves into a unit which can stand face to face with the correlative unit. They have no past, no history, no religion of their own; and they have no such solidarity of work and interest as that of the proletariat. They are not even promiscuously herded together in the way that creates community feeling among the American Negroes, the ghetto Jews, the workers of Saint-Denis, or the factory hands of Renault. They live dispersed among the males, attached through residence, housework, economic condition, and social standing to certain men—fathers or husbands—more firmly than they are to other women. If they belong to the bourgeoisie, they feel solidarity with men of that class, not with proletarian women; if they are white, their allegiance is to white men, not to Negro women. The proletariat

can propose to massacre the ruling class, and a sufficiently fa-
natical Jew or Negro might dream of getting sole possession of
the atomic bomb and making humanity wholly Jewish or black;
but woman cannot even dream of exterminating the males. The
bond that unites her to her oppressors is not comparable to any
other. The division of the sexes is a biological fact, not an event
in human history. Male and female stand opposed within a primordial *Mitsein*,[7] and woman has not broken it. The couple is a
fundamental unity with its two halves riveted together, and the
cleavage of society along the line of sex is impossible. Here is to
be found the basic trait of woman: she is the Other in a totality
of which the two components are necessary to one another.

One could suppose that this reciprocity might have facilitated
the liberation of woman. When Hercules sat at the feet of
Omphale and helped with her spinning, his desire for her held
him captive; but why did she fail to gain a lasting power? To revenge herself on Jason, Medea killed their children; and this
grim legend would seem to suggest that she might have obtained
a formidable influence over him through his love for his offspring. In *Lysistrata* Aristophanes gaily depicts a band of
women who joined forces to gain social ends through the sexual
needs of their men; but this is only a play. In the legend of the
Sabine women, the latter soon abandoned their plan of remaining sterile to punish their ravishers. In truth woman has not
been socially emancipated through man's need—sexual desire
and the desire for offspring—which makes the male dependent
for satisfaction upon the female.

Master and slave, also, are united by a reciprocal need, in this
case economic, which does not liberate the slave. In the relation
of master to slave the master does not make a point of the need
that he has for the other; he has in his grasp the power of satisfying this need through his own action; whereas the slave, in his
dependent condition, his hope and fear, is quite conscious of the
need he has for his master. Even if the need is at bottom equally
urgent for both, it always works in favor of the oppressor and

[7]Fellowship.—*Ed.*

against the oppressed. That is why the liberation of the working class, for example, has been slow.

Now, woman has always been man's dependent, if not his slave; the two sexes have never shared the world in equality. And even today woman is heavily handicapped, though her situation is beginning to change. Almost nowhere is her legal status the same as man's, and frequently it is much to her disadvantage. Even when her rights are legally recognized in the abstract, long-standing custom prevents their full expression in the mores. In the economic sphere men and women can almost be said to make up two castes; other things being equal, the former hold the better jobs, get higher wages, and have more opportunity for success than their new competitors. In industry and politics men have a great many more positions and they monopolize the most important posts. In addition to all this, they enjoy a traditional prestige that the education of children tends in every way to support, for the present enshrines the past—and in the past all history has been made by men. At the present time, when women are beginning to take part in the affairs of the world, it is still a world that belongs to men—they have no doubt of it at all and women have scarcely any. To decline to be the Other, to refuse to be a party to the deal—this would be for women to renounce all the advantages conferred upon them by their alliance with the superior caste. Man-the-sovereign will provide woman-the-liege with material protection and will undertake the moral justification of her existence; thus she can evade at once both economic risk and the metaphysical risk of a liberty in which ends and aims must be contrived without assistance. Indeed, along with the ethical urge of each individual to affirm his subjective existence, there is also the temptation to forgo liberty and become a thing. This is an inauspicious road, for he who takes it—passive, lost, ruined—becomes henceforth the creature of another's will, frustrated in his transcendence and deprived of every value. But it is an easy road; on it one avoids the strain involved in undertaking an authentic existence. When man makes of woman the *Other*, he may, then, expect her to manifest deep-seated tendencies toward complicity. Thus, woman may fail to lay claim to the status of subject because she lacks definite resources, because she feels the necessary bond that ties her to man regardless of reciprocity, and because she is often very well pleased with her role as the *Other*.

But it will be asked at once: how did all this begin? It is easy to see that the duality of the sexes, like any duality, gives rise to conflict. And doubtless the winner will assume the status of absolute. But why should man have won from the start? It seems possible that women could have won the victory; or that the outcome of the conflict might never have been decided. How is it that this world has always belonged to the men and that things have begun to change only recently? Is this change a good thing? Will it bring about an equal sharing of the world between men and women?

These questions are not new, and they have often been answered. But the very fact that woman *is the Other* tends to cast suspicion upon all the justifications that men have ever been able to provide for it. These have all too evidently been dictated by men's interest. A little-known feminist of the seventeenth century, Poulain de la Barre, put it this way: "All that has been written about women by men should be suspect, for the men are at once judge and party to the lawsuit." Everywhere, at all times, the males have displayed their satisfaction in feeling that they are the lords of creation. "Blessed be God . . . that He did not make me a woman," say the Jews in their morning prayers, while their wives pray on a note of resignation: "Blessed be the Lord, who created me according to His will." The first among the blessings for which Plato thanked the gods was that he had been created free, not enslaved; the second, a man, not a woman. But the males could not enjoy this privilege fully unless they believed it to be founded on the absolute and the eternal; they sought to make the fact of their supremacy into a right. "Being men, those who have made and compiled the laws have favored their own sex, and jurists have elevated these laws into principles," to quote Poulain de la Barre once more.

Legislators, priests, philosophers, writers, and scientists have striven to show that the subordinate position of woman is willed in heaven and advantageous on earth. The religions invented by men reflect this wish for domination. In the legends of

Eve and Pandora, men have taken up arms against women. They have made use of philosophy and theology, as the quotations from Aristotle and St. Thomas have shown. Since ancient times satirists and moralists have delighted in showing up the weaknesses of women. We are familiar with the savage indictments hurled against women throughout French literature. Montherlant, for example, follows the tradition of Jean de Meung, though with less gusto. This hostility may at times be well founded, often it is gratuitous; but in truth it more or less successfully conceals a desire for self-justification. As Montaigne says, "It is easier to accuse one sex than to excuse the other." Sometimes what is going on is clear enough. For instance, the Roman law limiting the rights of woman cited "the imbecility, the instability of the sex" just when the weakening of family ties seemed to threaten the interests of male heirs. And in the effort to keep the married woman under guardianship, appeal was made in the sixteenth century to the authority of St. Augustine, who declared that "woman is a creature neither decisive nor constant," at a time when the single woman was thought capable of managing her property. Montaigne understood clearly how arbitrary and unjust was woman's appointed lot. . . . But he did not go so far as to champion their cause.

It was only later, in the eighteenth century, that genuinely democratic men began to view the matter objectively. Diderot, among others, strove to show that woman is, like man, a human being. Later John Stuart Mill came fervently to her defense. But these philosophers displayed unusual impartiality. In the nineteenth century the feminist quarrel became again a quarrel of partisans. One of the consequences of the industrial revolution was the entrance of women into productive labor, and it was just here that the claims of the feminists emerged from the realm of theory and acquired an economic basis, while their opponents became the more aggressive. Although landed property lost power to some extent, the bourgeoisie clung to the old morality that found the guarantee of private property in the solidity of the family. Woman was ordered back into the home the more harshly as her emancipation became a real menace. Even within the working class the men endeavored to restrain woman's liberation, because they began to see the women as dangerous competitors—the more so because they were accustomed to work for lower wages.

In proving woman's inferiority, the antifeminists then began to draw not only upon religion, philosophy, and theology, as before, but also upon science—biology, experimental psychology, etc. At most they were willing to grant "equality in difference" to the *other* sex. That profitable formula is most significant; it is precisely like the "equal but separate" formula of the Jim Crow laws aimed at the North American Negroes. As is well known, this so-called equalitarian segregation has resulted only in the most extreme discrimination. The similarity just noted is in no way due to chance, for whether it is a race, a caste, a class, or a sex that is reduced to a position of inferiority, the methods of justification are the same. "The eternal feminine" corresponds to "the black soul." . . . In both cases the former masters lavish more or less sincere eulogies, either on the virtues of "the good Negro" with his dormant, childish, merry soul—the submissive Negro—or on the merits of the woman who is "truly feminine"—that is, frivolous, infantile, irresponsible—the submissive woman. In both cases the dominant class bases its argument on a state of affairs that it has itself created. As George Bernard Shaw puts it, in substance, "The American white relegates the black to the rank of shoeshine boy; and he concludes from this that the black is good for nothing but shining shoes." This vicious circle is met with in all analogous circumstances; when an individual (or a group of individuals) is kept in a situation of inferiority, the fact is that he *is* inferior. But the significance of the verb *to be* must be rightly understood here; it is in bad faith to give it a static value when it really has the dynamic Hegelian sense of "to have become." Yes, women on the whole *are* today inferior to men; that is, their situation affords them fewer possibilities. The question is: should that state of affairs continue?

Many men hope that it will continue; not all have given up the battle. The conservative bourgeoisie still see in the emancipation of women a menace to their morality and their interests. . . .

Men profit in many . . . subtle ways from the otherness, the alterity of woman. Here is miraculous balm for those afflicted with an inferiority complex, and indeed no one is more arrogant toward women, more aggressive or scornful, than the man who is anxious about his virility. Those who are not fear-ridden in the presence of their fellow men are much more disposed to recognize a fellow creature in woman; but even to these the myth of Woman, the Other, is precious for many reasons. They cannot be blamed for not cheerfully relinquishing all the benefits they derive from the myth, for they realize what they would lose in relinquishing woman as they fancy her to be, while they fail to realize what they have to gain from the woman of tomorrow. Refusal to pose oneself as the Subject, unique and absolute, requires great self-denial. Furthermore, the vast majority of men make no such claim explicitly. They do not *postulate* woman as inferior, for today they are too thoroughly imbued with the ideal of democracy not to recognize all human beings as equals.

In the bosom of the family, woman seems in the eyes of childhood and youth to be clothed in the same social dignity as the adult males. Later on, the young man, desiring and loving, experiences the resistance, the independence of the woman desired and loved; in marriage, he respects woman as wife and mother, and in the concrete events of conjugal life she stands there before him as a free being. He can therefore feel that social subordination as between the sexes no longer exists and that on the whole, in spite of differences, woman is an equal. As, however, he observes some points of inferiority—the most important being unfitness for the professions—he attributes these to natural causes. When he is in a co-operative and benevolent relation with woman, his theme is the principle of abstract equality, and he does not base his attitude upon such inequality as may exist. But when he is in conflict with her, the situation is reversed: his theme will be the existing inequality, and he will even take it as justification for denying abstract equality.

So it is that many men will affirm as if in good faith that women *are* the equals of man and that they have nothing to clamor for, while *at the same time* they will say that women can never be the equals of man and that their demands are in vain. It is, in point of fact, a difficult matter for man to realize the

extreme importance of social discriminations which seem outwardly insignificant but which produce in woman moral and intellectual effects so profound that they appear to spring from
her original nature. The most sympathetic of men never fully
comprehend woman's concrete situation. And there is no reason
to put much trust in the men when they rush to the defense of
privileges whose full extent they can hardly measure. We shall
not, then, permit ourselves to be intimidated by the number and
violence of the attacks launched against women, nor to be en-
trapped by the self-seeking eulogies bestowed on the "true
woman," nor to profit by the enthusiasm for woman's destiny
manifested by men who would not for the world have any part
of it. . . .

The women of today are in a fair way to dethrone the myth
of femininity; they are beginning to affirm their independence in
concrete ways; but they do not easily succeed in living completely the life of a human being. Reared by women within a
feminine world, their normal destiny is marriage, which still
means practically subordination to man; for masculine prestige
is far from extinction, resting still upon solid economic and social foundations.

The Independent Woman

THERE ARE . . . A FAIRLY LARGE NUMBER of privileged women who
find in their professions a means of economic and social autonomy. These come to mind when one considers woman's possibilities and her future. This is the reason why it is especially
interesting to make a close study of their situation, even though
they constitute as yet only a minority; they continue to be a subject of debate between feminists and antifeminists. The latter assert that the emancipated women of today succeed in doing
nothing of importance in the world and that furthermore they
have difficulty in achieving their own inner equilibrium. The
former exaggerate the results obtained by professional women
and are blind to their inner confusion. There is no good reason,
as a matter of fact, to say they are on the wrong road; and still it

is certain that they are not tranquilly installed in their new realm: as yet they are only halfway there. The woman who is economically emancipated from man is not for all that in a moral, social, and psychological situation identical with that of man. The way she carries on her profession and her devotion to it depend on the context supplied by the total pattern of her life. For when she begins her adult life she does not have behind her the same past as does a boy; she is not viewed by society in the same way; the universe presents itself to her in a different perspective. The fact of being a woman today poses peculiar problems for an independent human individual.

The advantage man enjoys, which makes itself felt from his childhood, is that his vocation as a human being in no way runs counter to his destiny as a male. Through the identification of phallus and transcendence, it turns out that his social and spiritual successes endow him with a virile prestige. He is not divided. Whereas it is required of woman that in order to realize her femininity she must make herself object and prey, which is to say that she must renounce her claims as sovereign subject. It is this conflict that especially marks the situation of the emancipated woman. She refuses to confine herself to her role as a female, because she will not accept mutilation; but it would also be a mutilation to repudiate her sex. Man is a human being with sexuality; woman is a complete individual, equal to the male, only if she too is a human being with sexuality. To renounce her femininity is to renounce a part of her humanity. . . .

The . . . difficulties that beset a life of freedom urge woman toward monogamy. Liaison or marriage, however, can be reconciled with a career much less easily for her than for man. Sometimes her lover or husband asks her to renounce it: she hesitates, like Colette's Vagabonde, who ardently desires the warm presence of a man at her side but dreads the fetters of marriage. If she yields, she is once more a vassal; if she refuses, she condemns herself to a withering solitude. Today a man is usually willing to have his companion continue her work; . . . living together is an enrichment for two free beings, and each finds security for his or her own independence in the occupation of the mate. The self-supporting wife emancipates her husband from the conjugal slavery that was the price of hers. If the man is scrupulously well-intentioned, such lovers and married couples attain in undemanding generosity a condition of perfect equality. It may even be the man that acts as devoted servant; thus, for George Eliot, Lewes created the favorable atmosphere that the wife usually creates around the husband-overlord. But for the most part it is still the woman who bears the cost of domestic harmony.

To a man it seems natural that it should be the wife who does the housework and assumes alone the care and bringing up of the children. The independent woman herself considers that in marrying she has assumed duties from which her personal life does not exempt her. She does not want to feel that her husband is deprived of advantages he would have obtained if he had married a "true woman"; she wants to be presentable, a good housekeeper, a devoted mother, such as wives traditionally are. This is a task that easily becomes overwhelming. She assumes it through regard for her partner and out of fidelity to herself also, for she intends . . . to be in no way unfaithful to her destiny as a woman. . . .

There is one feminine function that is actually almost impossible to perform in complete liberty. It is maternity. In England and America and some other countries a woman can at least decline maternity at will, thanks to contraceptive techniques. . . . In France she is often driven to painful and costly abortion; or she frequently finds herself responsible for an unwanted child that can ruin her professional life. If this is a heavy charge, it is because, inversely, custom does not allow a woman to procreate when she pleases. The unwed mother is a scandal to the community, and illegitimate birth is a stain on the child; only rarely is it possible to become a mother without accepting the chains of marriage or losing caste. If the idea of artificial insemination interests many women, it is not because they wish to avoid intercourse with a male; it is because they hope that freedom of maternity is going to be accepted by society at last. It must be said in addition that in spite of convenient day nurseries and kindergartens, having a child is enough to paralyze a woman's activity entirely; she can go on working only if she abandons it to relatives, friends, or servants. She is forced to choose between sterility, which is often felt as a painful frustration, and burdens hardly compatible with a career.

Thus the independent woman of today is torn between her professional interests and the problems of her sexual life; it is difficult for her to strike a balance between the two; if she does, it is at the price of concessions, sacrifices, acrobatics, which require her to be in a constant state of tension. . . .

There is one category of women to whom these remarks do not apply because their careers, far from hindering the affirmation of their femininity, reinforce it. These are women who seek through artistic expression to transcend their given characteristics; they are the actresses, dancers, and singers. For three centuries they have been almost the only women to maintain a concrete independence in the midst of society, and at the present time they still occupy a privileged place in it. Formerly actresses were anathema to the Church, and the very excessiveness of that severity has always authorized a great freedom of behavior on their part. They often skirt the sphere of gallantry and, like courtesans, they spend a great deal of their time in the company of men; but making their own living and finding the meaning of their lives in their work, they escape the yoke of men. Their great advantage is that their professional successes—like those of men—contribute to their sexual valuation; in their self-realization, their validation of themselves as human beings, they find self-fulfillment as women: they are not torn between contradictory aspirations. . . .

These are rare advantages, but they also hide traps: instead of integrating her narcissistic self-indulgence and her sexual liberty with her artistic life, the actress very often sinks into self-worship or into gallantry; . . . [some] seek in the movies or in the theater only to make a name for themselves that represents capital to exploit in men's arms. The conveniences of masculine support are very tempting in comparison with the risks of a career and with the discipline implied by all real work. Desire for a feminine destiny—husband, home, children—and the enchantment of love are not always easy to reconcile with the will to succeed. . . .

• • •

The free woman is just being born; when she has won possession of herself perhaps Rimbaud's prophecy will be fulfilled:
"There shall be poets! When woman's unmeasured bondage
shall be broken, when she shall live for and through herself,
man—hitherto detestable—having let her go, she, too, will be
poet! Woman will find the unknown! Will her ideational worlds
be different from ours? She will come upon strange, unfath-
omable, repellent, delightful things; we shall take them, we shall
comprehend them."[8] It is not sure that her "ideational worlds"
will be different from those of men, since it will be through at-
taining the same situation as theirs that she will find emancipation; to say in what degree she will remain different, in what
degree these differences will retain their importance—this would
be to hazard bold predictions indeed. What is certain is that
hitherto woman's possibilities have been suppressed and lost to
humanity, and that it is high time she be permitted to take her
chances in her own interest and in the interest of all.

[8]In a letter to Pierre Demeny, May 15, 1871.

DORIS LESSING

The Golden Notebook

In 1991 the Women's Committee of the American Center of PEN, an international writers' organization, presented a series of panels in New York City titled "Thirty Years of Feminism: Literature and the Movement." The first event, called "Remembering the Source," featured *The Golden Notebook* by English novelist Doris Lessing (b. 1919 in Southern Rhodesia). One after another, the panelists, all well-known American writers, reflected on this book's singularly powerful impact on their personal and artistic development. Lessing, said the moderator, "began it all."[1]

When it appeared in 1962, *The Golden Notebook* quickly became one of those works of fiction that everyone was talking about—especially everyone young and female and ambitious. The book was startling in its frank discussion of previously taboo subjects such as menstruation, masturbation, and female orgasm, and also in its focus on two female characters, with no "hero." As one reviewer commented, women were reading Lessing not "to learn how to write a good novel or . . . admire a beautiful work of art" but because of what it could teach them about their own lives.[2] The novelist had divined modern women's aspirations and had uncovered their weaknesses and secret fears.

Lessing later complained that her book had been "instantly belittled, by friendly reviewers as well as by hostile ones, as

---

[1] The moderator was E. M. Broner. The panelists were Mary Gordon, Vivian Gornick, Elizabeth Janeway, and Margo Jefferson.

[2] Florence Howe, "Doris Lessing's Free Women," *Nation*, January 11, 1965, p. 37.

being about the sex war"—while the presumably larger themes that she herself found more interesting had been overlooked.[3] But the enduring legacy of *The Golden Notebook* remains its depiction of a particular transitional moment in the history of women, and its evocation of the feelings of women of that era: their desperate wish to create themselves as independent people and the intractable impediments they were encountering, especially within their own psyches.

Heroines in nineteenth-century fiction suffered for lack of rights: With no access to divorce, they were caught—like George Sand's Indiana—in intolerable marriages. Barred from training for most careers, they found themselves, if unmarried—like Charlotte Brontë's Jane Eyre—trapped in stifling jobs. And how different Anna Karenina's lot would have been if contraception or abortion had been available! But Doris Lessing's two principal female characters in *The Golden Notebook*, living in the 1950s, do not lack rights—or perhaps one should say that lack of rights is not at the heart of their problems. Each has been divorced and is raising a child on her own; each has economic independence and a career—Molly as an actress, Anna Wulf as a writer who has published one successful novel; and each takes lovers without suffering social ostracism or undue fear of pregnancy. Lessing labeled them free women—not without good reason, for clearly they enjoy many freedoms. But the label is ironic, tongue-in-cheek, as well, for Molly and Anna are far from being truly free. Their struggles call to mind the moral, social, and psychological quagmire of the emancipated women described by de Beauvoir in the last chapter of *The Second Sex*: "privileged women who find in their professions a means of economic and social autonomy" but are not as yet "tranquilly installed in their new realm."

Molly and Anna are Communists who, following Khrushchev's revelations about Stalin in 1956, are increasingly uncomfortable with their political allegiance. Both have been psychoanalyzed, but Anna, especially, is doubtful about the

---

[3]Introduction to a new edition of *The Golden Notebook* (New York: Bantam, 1973), p. viii.

value of the treatment. They cannot integrate their lives; they feel like failures in their work; most important, they seem powerless to overcome their dependence on men. It is through men's eyes that they see themselves; despite their best efforts, the approval of men remains essential to their self-esteem.

The first part of the following reading is from the opening scene of the book, in which Anna tries to talk to Molly about the doubts that torment her and her inability to "get over" the pain of having been "ditched" by her lover. The second part is from an incomplete autobiographical novel that Anna is writing in one of her notebooks, the yellow one. In it, she calls herself by the name of Ella. Ella, too, is struggling to recover from a long-term love affair that ended when the man rejected her.

Free Women

Anna meets her friend Molly in the summer
of 1957 after a separation

THE TWO WOMEN WERE ALONE in the London flat.

"The point is," said Anna, as her friend came back from the telephone on the landing, "the point is, that as far as I can see, everything's cracking up."

Molly was a woman much on the telephone. When it rang she had just inquired: "Well, what's the gossip?" Now she said, "That's Richard, and he's coming over. It seems today's his only free moment for the next month. Or so he insists."

"Well, I'm not leaving," said Anna.

"No, you stay just where you are." . . .

It had always been understood that Anna and Richard disliked each other; and before Anna had always left when Richard was expected. Now Molly said: "Actually I think he rather likes you, in his heart of hearts. The point is, he's committed to liking me, on principle—he's such a fool he's always got to either like or dislike someone, so all the dislike he won't admit he has for me gets pushed off on to you."

"It's a pleasure," said Anna. "But do you know something? I discovered while you were away that for a lot of people you and I are practically interchangeable." . . .

"When we're so different in every way," said Molly, "it's odd. I suppose because we both live the same kind of life—not getting married and so on. That's all they see."

"Free women," said Anna, wryly. She added, with an anger new to Molly, so that she earned [a] quick scrutinizing glance from her friend: "They still define us in terms of relationships with men, even the best of them."

"Well, *we* do, don't we?" said Molly, rather tart. "Well, it's awfully hard not to," she amended, hastily, because of the look of surprise Anna now gave her. There was a short pause, during which the women did not look at each other but reflected that a year apart was a long time, even for an old friendship.

Molly said at last, sighing: "Free. Do you know, when I was away, I was thinking about us, and I've decided that we're a completely new type of woman. We must be, surely?" . . .

"Michael came to see me," [said Anna]. "About a month ago." She had lived with Michael for five years. This affair had broken up three years ago, against her will.

"How was it?"

"Oh, in some ways, as if nothing had happened."

"Of course, when you know each other so well."

"But he was behaving—how shall I put it? I was a dear friend, you know. He drove me to some place I wanted to go. He was talking about a colleague of his. He said, 'Do you remember Dick?' Odd, don't you think, that he couldn't remember if I remembered Dick, since we saw a lot of him then. Dick's got a job in Ghana, he said. He took his wife. His mistress wanted to go too, said Michael. Very difficult these mistresses are, said Michael, and then he laughed. Quite genuinely, you know, the debonair touch. That was what was painful. Then he looked embarrassed, because he remembered that I had been his mistress, and went red and guilty."

Molly said nothing. She watched Anna closely.

"That's all, I suppose."

"A lot of swine they all are," said Molly cheerfully, deliberately striking the note that would make Anna laugh.

"Molly," said Anna painfully, in appeal.

"What? It's no good going on about it, is it?"

"Well, I've been thinking. You know, it's possible we made a mistake."

"What? Only one?"

But Anna would not laugh. "No. It's serious. Both of us are dedicated to the proposition that we're tough—no listen, I'm serious. I mean—a marriage breaks up, well, we say, our marriage was a failure, too bad. A man ditches us—too bad we say, it's not important. We bring up kids without men—nothing to it, we say, we can cope. We spend years in the communist party and then we say, Well, well, we made a mistake, too bad."

"What are you trying to say," said Molly, very cautious, and at a great distance from Anna.

"Well don't you think it's at least possible, just possible that things can happen to us so bad that we don't ever get over them? Because when I really face it I don't think I've really got over Michael. I think it's done for me. Oh I know, what I am supposed to say is, Well, well, he's ditched me—what's five years after all, on with the next thing."

"But it has to be, on with the next thing. . . . Oh, Anna! All this is simply because of Michael. And probably he'll come in again one of these days and you'll pick up where you left off."

The Yellow Notebook

IT WAS PATRICIA BRENT, EDITRESS, who suggested Ella should spend a week in Paris. Because it was Patricia, Ella's instinct was to refuse immediately. "Mustn't let them get us down," she had said, the "them" being men. In short, Patricia was over-eager to welcome Ella into the club of forlorn women; there was kindness in it, but also a private satisfaction. Ella said she thought it was a waste of time to go to Paris. The pretext was that she must interview the editor of a similar French magazine in order to buy the rights of a serial story for Britain. The story, Ella said, might be right for the housewives of Vaugirard; but it was wrong for the housewives of Brixton. "It's a free holiday," said Patricia, tart because she knew Ella was rejecting more than a Paris trip. After a few days Ella changed her mind. She had been reminded that it was over a year since Paul had left her and that everything she did, said, or felt, still referred to him. Her life was shaped around a man who would not return to her. She must liberate herself. This was an intellectual decision, un-backed by moral energy. She was listless and flat. It was as if Paul had taken with him, not only all her capacity for joy, but also her will. She said she would go to Paris, like a bad patient agreeing at last to take medicine, but insisting to the doctor that: "Of course it won't do me any good."

It was April, Paris, as always, charming; and Ella took a room in the modest hotel on the Left Bank she had last been in, two years before, with Paul. She fitted herself into the room, leaving space for him. It was only when she saw what she was doing that it occurred to her that she should not be in this hotel at all. But it seemed too much effort to leave it and find another. It was still early in the evening. Below her tall windows Paris was animated with greening trees and strolling people. It took Ella nearly an hour to get herself out of the room and into a restaurant to eat. She ate hastily, feeling exposed; and walked home with her eyes kept deliberately preoccupied. Nevertheless two men good-humoredly greeted her, and both times she froze into nervous an-noyance, and walked on with hastening steps. She got into her bedroom and locked the door as if against a danger. Then she sat at the window and thought that five years before, the dinner alone would have been pleasant because of its solitariness, and because of the possibilities of an encounter; and the walk home from the restaurant alone delightful. And she would certainly have had a cup of coffee or a drink with one or other of the two men. So what had happened to her? It was true that with Paul she had taught herself never to look at a man, even casually, be-cause of his jealousy; she was, with him, like a protected indoors woman from a Latin country. But she had imagined this was an outward conformity to save him from self-inflicted pain. Now she saw that her whole personality had changed.

For some time she sat, listless, at the window, watching the darkening but blossoming city, and told herself she should make herself walk through its streets, and force herself into talking to people; she should let herself be picked up and flirt a little. But she understood she was as incapable of walking down the hotel stairs, leaving her key at the desk and going into the streets, as if she had just served a prison sentence for four years in solitary confinement and then told to behave normally. She went to bed. She was unable to sleep. She put herself to sleep, as always, by thinking of Paul. She had never, since he had left her, been able to achieve a vaginal orgasm; she was able to reach the sharp violence of the exterior orgasm, her hand becoming Paul's hand, mourning as she did so, the loss of her real self. She slept, over-stimulated, nervous, exhausted, cheated. And by using Paul thus, brought close to her his "negative" self, the man full of self-distrust. The real man retreated further and further from her. It was becoming hard for her to remember the warmth of his eyes, the humor of his voice. She would sleep beside a ghost of defeat; and the ghost wore, even when she might wake, briefly, out of habit, to open her arms so that his head might come to her breast, or to lay her head on his shoulder, a small, bitter, self-derisive smile. Yet when she dreamed of him, asleep, he was always to be recognized in the various guises he chose, because his image was one of warmth, a calm masculinity. Paul, whom she had loved, she kept sleeping; awake she retained nothing but shapes of pain.

Next morning she slept too long, as she always did when away from her son. She woke thinking that [he] must have been up, dressed, and breakfasted hours ago . . . ; he would be nearing his lunchtime at school. Then she told herself she had not come to Paris to follow in her mind the stages of her son's day; she reminded herself that Paris lay waiting for her outside, under a light-hearted sun. And it was time for her to dress for her appointment with the editor.

The offices of *Femme et Foyer* were across the river and in

the heart of an ancient building that one must enter where once
carriages, and before then, troops of privately owned soldiers
had pressed under a noble carved archway. *Femme et Foyer* oc-
cupied a dozen soberly modern and expensive rooms in decay-
ing piles of masonry that smelt even now of the church, of
feudalism. Ella, expected, was shown into Monsieur Brun's office, and was received by Monsieur Brun, a large, well-kept, ox-
like young man who greeted her with an excess of good
manners which failed to conceal his lack of interest in Ella and
in the proposal deal. They were to go out for an apéritif. Robert
Brun announced to half a dozen pretty secretaries that since he
would be lunching with his fiancée he would not be back until
three and received a dozen congratulatory and understanding
smiles. Ella and Robert Brun passed through the venerable
courtyard, emerged from the ancient gateway, and set out for
the café, while Ella inquired politely about his projected marriage. She was informed in fluent and correct English that his fiancée was formidably pretty, intelligent and talented. He was to
marry her next month, and they were now engaged in preparing
their apartment. Elise (he spoke the name with an already practiced propriety, grave and formal) was at that very moment ne-
gotiating for a certain carpet they both coveted. She, Ella, would
have the privilege of seeing her for herself. Ella hastened to assure him that she would be delighted, and congratulated him
again. Meanwhile they had reached the patch of sun-shaded,
table-crowded pavement they were to patronize, had sat down,
and ordered pernods. This was the moment for business. Ella
was at a disadvantage. She knew that if she returned to Patricia
Brent with the rights of this serial *Comment J'ai fui un Grand
Amour,* that irrepressibly provincial matron would be delighted.
For her, the word *French* guaranteed a brand of excellence: dis-
creetly but authentically amorous, high-toned, cultivated. For
her, the phrase: by arrangement with the Paris *Femme et Foyer*
would exude precisely the same exclusive spiciness as an expensive French scent. Yet Ella knew that no sooner had Patricia actually read it (in translation—she did not read French) she
would agree, though reluctantly, that the story wouldn't do at
all. Ella could see herself, if she chose, as protecting Patricia

against her own weakness. But the fact was Ella had no intention of buying the story, had never had any intention of buying it; and therefore she was wasting this incredibly well-fed, well-washed and correct young man's time. She ought to feel guilty about it; she did not. If she had liked him, she would have been contrite: as it was, she saw him as a species of highly-trained middle-class animal, and was prepared to make use of him: she was unable, so weakened was she as an independent being, to enjoy sitting at a table publicly without a man's protection, and this man would do as well as another. For form's sake, she began explaining to Monsieur Brun how the story would have to be adapted for England. . . .

"You see," said Ella, "this is so French in flavor that we would have to have it re-written." . . .

His face, his full eyes, were momentarily immobilized with annoyed incomprehension. Then Ella saw his eyes move away and off in a glance along the pavement: the fiancée was overdue. He remarked: "I understood from Miss Brent's letter she had decided to buy the story." Ella said: "If we were to print it, we should have to re-write it." . . . He . . . understood that the story would not be bought; he did not care one way or the other; and his eyes had now focused themselves, for at the end of the pavement appeared a slight, pretty girl, in type rather like Ella, with a pale little pointed face and fluffy black hair. Ella was thinking: Well I may be his type, but he certainly isn't mine; as the girl approached, she waited for him to rise and greet his fiancée. But at the last moment he shifted his gaze and the girl passed. Then he returned to his inspection of the end of the pavement. Well, thought Ella; *well*—and sat watching his detailed, analytical, practically sensual appraisal of one woman after another, to the point where the woman in question would glance at him, annoyed or interested; when he would let his eyes move to one side.

Finally there appeared a woman who was ugly, yet attractive; sallow, lumpish in figure, yet made up with skill and very well dressed. This turned out to be the fiancée. They greeted each other with the licensed pleasure of the publicly linked couple. All eyes turned, as they had been intended to, towards the happy pair, and people smiled. Then Ella was introduced. Now the conversation continued in French. It was of the carpet, so much more expensive than either had expected. But it had been bought. Robert Brun grumbled and exclaimed; the future Madame Brun sighed and fluttered her lashes over dark black-rimmed eyes, and murmured with discreet lovingness that for him nothing was too good. Their hands met on a smile. His was complacent; hers pleased, and a trifle anxious. Before the hands had even parted, his eyes had escaped, out of habit, in a quick glance to the end of the pavement where a pretty girl appeared. He frowned as he collected himself. His future wife's smile froze, for a second, as she noted this. Smiling prettily, however, she sat back in her chair, and spoke prettily to Ella of the problems of furnishing in these hard times. Her glances at her fiancé reminded Ella of a prostitute she had seen late one night in the underground in London; just so had this woman caressed and invited a man with small, discreet, pretty glances of her eyes.

Ella contributed facts about furnishing from England, while she thought: now I'm odd-woman-out with an engaged couple. I feel isolated and excluded. I feel exposed again. In a minute they will get up and leave me. And I shall feel even more exposed. *What has happened to me?* And yet I would rather be dead than in this woman's shoes, and that's the truth.

The three remained together for another twenty minutes. The fiancée continued vivacious, feminine, arch, caressing towards her captive. The fiancé remained well-mannered and proprietary. His eyes alone betrayed him. And she, his captive, never for one moment forgot him—her eyes moved with his to note his earnest, minute (though now necessarily curtailed) inspection of the women who passed.

This situation was heartbreakingly clear to Ella; and she felt, surely, to anyone who examined the couple for as long as five minutes? They had been lovers over-long. She had money, and this was necessary to him. She was desperately, fearfully in love with him. He was fond of her, and already chafing at the bonds. The great well-groomed ox was uneasy before the noose had even tightened around his neck. In two years, three years, they would be Monsieur and Madame Brun, in a well-furnished apartment (the money provided by her) with a small child and perhaps a nurse-maid; and she would be caressing and gay and anxious still; and he would be politely good-humored, but sometimes bad-tempered when the demands of the home prevented his pleasures with his mistress.

And although every phase of this marriage was as clear to Ella as if it were in the past and she was being told of it; although she felt irritable with dislike of the whole situation, yet she dreaded the moment when the couple would rise and leave her. Which they did, with every allowance of their admirable French politeness, he so smoothly indifferently polite, she so anxiously polite, and with an eye on him which said: see how well I behave to your business friends. And Ella was left sitting at the table, at the hour for companionable eating, feeling as if a skin had been peeled off her. Instantly she protected herself by imagining that Paul would come to sit by her, where Robert Brun had sat. She was conscious that two men, now that she was alone, were weighing her up, weighing their chances. In a moment one of them would come over, and she would then *behave like a civilized person,* have a drink or two, enjoy the encounter, and return to her hotel fortified and freed from the ghost of Paul. She was sitting with her back to a low tub of greenery. The sunshade above her enclosed her in a warm yellow glow. She shut her eyes and thought: When I open my eyes perhaps I'll see Paul. (It suddenly seemed inconceivable that he should not be somewhere near, waiting to come and join her.) She thought: What did it mean, my saying I loved Paul—when his going has left me like a snail that has had her shell pecked off by a bird? I should have said that my being with Paul essentially meant I remained myself, remained independent and free. I asked nothing of him, certainly not marriage. And yet now I am in pieces. So it was all a fraud. In fact I was sheltering under him. . . . I am no better than Elise, future wife of Robert. . . . Elise is buying Robert. But I use the word love and think of myself as free, when the truth is . . . a voice, close to her, inquired if the place were free, and Ella opened her eyes to see a small, lively, vivacious Frenchman, in the act of seating himself. She told herself that he looked pleasant, and she would stay where she was; she smiled nervously, said she felt ill and had a headache, and got up and left, conscious that her manner had been that of a frightened schoolgirl.

And now she made a decision. She walked back to the hotel, across Paris, packed . . . and took the coach out to the airport. There was a free seat on an aircraft at nine o'clock, three hours from now. In the airport restaurant she ate at ease—feeling herself; a traveler has the right to be alone. She read a dozen French women's magazines, professionally, marking features and stories that might do for Patricia Brent. She did this work with half her mind; and found herself thinking: Well, the cure for the sort of condition I am in is work. . . .

What is terrible is that after every one of the phases of my life is finished, I am left with no more than some banal commonplace that everyone knows: in this case, that women's emotions are all still fitted for a kind of society that no longer exists. My deep emotions, my real ones, are to do with my relationship with a man. One man. But I don't live that kind of life, and I know few women who do. So what I feel is irrelevant and silly. . . . I am always coming to the conclusion that my real emotions are foolish, I am always having, as it were, to cancel myself out. I ought to be like a man, caring more for my work than for people; I ought to put my work first, and take men as they come, or find an ordinary comfortable man for bread and butter reasons—but I won't do it, I can't be like that.

SYLVIA PLATH

Purdah

The practice of purdah was observed by prosperous families in India for centuries. It required that women be secluded within a special section of the home, forbidden any contact with the outside world or with any man other than a chosen relative. For a young American poet in 1962 to choose purdah as the basis for a poem bespoke an unusual consciousness. Such a poet was Sylvia Plath (1932–1963).

Growing up in New England, Sylvia Plath seemed on the surface a typical young woman of the post–World War II era. She was pretty and popular; she apparently wanted to marry, be a housewife, have children—in short, to conform to that set of sex-role imperatives Betty Friedan would label for all time "the feminine mystique." But in a secret journal, Plath revealed depths of misery and vulnerability. Much as she longed for the love, social approbation, economic security, and sexual fulfillment that she was convinced a woman could acquire only through matrimony, she also dreaded becoming a wife, fearing that marriage would obliterate her identity and destroy her talent.

While a student at Smith College in the early fifties, Plath—aware of her literary gift (some would say genius)—vowed in her journal that she would never be "confined solely to home, other womenfolk, and community service, enclosed in the larger worldly circle of my mate."[1] She often recorded her bitterness about the limitations with which society surrounded females (the "sheath of impossibles" she called it in "Purdah"). "Being

---

[1] *The Journals of Sylvia Plath,* ed. Frances McCullough; Ted Hughes, consulting ed. (New York: Dial, 1982), p. 43.

born a woman is my awful tragedy," she wrote. "From the moment I was conceived I was doomed . . . to have my whole circle of action, thought and feeling rigidly circumscribed by my inescapable femininity." And "Most American males worship woman as a sex machine with rounded breasts and a convenient opening in the vagina, as a painted doll [see, in "Purdah," the image of a "small jeweled doll"] who shouldn't have a thought in her pretty head other than cooking a steak dinner and comforting him in bed." And "Some pale, hueless flicker of sensitivity is in me. God, must I lose it in cooking scrambled eggs for a man . . . hearing about life at second hand?"[2]

The second wave of feminism was still more than a decade away, and Plath felt totally isolated in her painful conflict.

In "Purdah," Plath imagined what it would be like to be a woman living under absolute patriarchal control. The woman in the poem sits cross-legged, smiles, speaks to us. She is enigmatic, seemingly cool and passive as a gemstone ("jade"). Calmly, she awaits the approach of her "bridegroom." She informs us that the least parts of her body are guarded: even her eyelash has its own attendant! But little by little the truth is unveiled. Beneath her smooth exterior, she is seething with rage. She is a lioness; she is plotting revenge, like the murderous Clytemnestra of classic Greek tragedy, who stabbed her husband, Agamemnon, in a bath.

"Purdah" was written just months before Plath's death by suicide at age thirty. At the time, she was separated from her husband of seven years, the British poet Ted Hughes, and was the mother of two young children. She left a group of recently composed poems—among them "Purdah"—all carefully arranged for a new collection, which she had titled *Ariel*. However, when *Ariel* was published in 1965, "Purdah" was omitted. It did not appear in print until 1971, in the compilation *Winter Trees*. The *Collected Poems* of Sylvia Plath, edited by Ted Hughes, was published in 1981 and won the Pulitzer Prize for poetry the following year.

[2]Ibid., pp. 21–22, 30, 33.

Her only novel, *The Bell Jar,* is set in the antifeminist, Cold War milieu of the early fifties. A barely disguised autobiographical account of an alienated young college student's breakdown and suicide attempt, the book first appeared under a pseudonym in England. Not until eight years after Plath's death was her novel published under her own name in the United States, where it became a best-seller. Volumes of her letters to her mother and excerpts from her journals have also been published.

Jade—
Stone of the side,
The agonized

Side of green Adam, I
Smile, cross-legged,
Enigmatical,

Shifting my clarities.
So valuable!
How the sun polishes this shoulder!

And should
The moon, my
Indefatigable cousin

Rise, with her cancerous pallors,
Dragging trees—
Little bushy polyps,

Little nets,
My visibilities hide.
I gleam like a mirror.

At this facet the bridegroom arrives
Lord of the mirrors!
It is himself he guides

In among these silk
Screens, these rustling appurtenances.
I breathe, and the mouth

Veil stirs its curtain
My eye
Veil is

A concatenation of rainbows.
I am his.
Even in his

Absence, I
Revolve in my
Sheath of impossibles,

Priceless and quiet
Among these parakeets, macaws!
O chatterers

Attendants of the eyelash!
I shall unloose
One feather, like the peacock.

Attendants of the lip!
I shall unloose
One note

Shattering
The chandelier
Of air that all day flies

Its crystals
A million ignorants.
Attendants!

Attendants!
And at his next step
I shall unloose

I shall unloose—
From the small jeweled
Doll he guards like a heart—

The lioness,
The shriek in the bath,
The cloak of holes.

THE REPORT OF THE PRESIDENT'S COMMISSION ON THE STATUS OF WOMEN

American Women

During World War II, millions of American women, dubbed Rosie the Riveters, entered the paid workforce, taking jobs formerly open only to men—usually at higher wages than they could earn doing traditional women's work. But with the end of the war, many women were laid off, and overall the number of workingwomen declined sharply for several years. Then a surprising reversal occurred. Starting in 1948, the percentage of women who worked outside the home—married as well as single, middle-aged as well as young—began a steady upward climb. This increase in female wage earners during peacetime signaled that momentous changes were quietly taking place among American women. By the presidential-election year of 1960, about 37 percent of all women were employed, though most were relegated to the lower rungs of the occupational ladder.

John F. Kennedy, then campaigning for the presidency, was invited to address a meeting of the National Council of Women of the United States, part of a federation that claimed a membership of 4 million. The candidate had been asked to speak on the topic "American Women, the Nation's Greatest Untapped Resource." However, he blatantly ignored the request and talked instead about foreign policy toward Africa. The head of the National Council of Women tactfully withheld criticism; she simply announced that she would give the next president a list of women well qualified for appointment to government and other jobs.[1]

When President Kennedy made his first 240 appointments,

---

[1] As reported in *The New York Times,* October 13, 1960, p. 26.

soon after his election, only 9 went to women. Eleanor Roosevelt was sufficiently disturbed by this poor showing to send him a three-page list of names of eligible women. But Kennedy remained insensitive to the problem. The following November a woman reporter at a White House news conference referred to the Democratic Party's platform promise to provide equal job opportunities and equal pay for women. "What have you done for women?" she asked the president. He evaded the question by quipping, "Well, I'm sure we have not done enough," prompting laughter from the mostly male press corps.[2]

A month later President Kennedy announced the creation of a commission to investigate the status of women, the first in the history of the nation. Undoubtedly the president hoped by this move to impress female voters with his good intentions. But whatever his political motives, his gesture was in keeping with the times. For as the sixties began, people everywhere were showing increased concern about violations of human rights. In Canada, for example, a bill of rights that prohibited discrimination on the basis of race, religion, national origin, *or sex* was enacted; the United Nations Commission on the Status of Women (founded in 1946) was circulating an international treaty on equal rights in marriage; and in the American South, men and women were conducting sit-ins to bring an end to racial segregation. Now the president had decreed that gender discrimination in American society was to be aired in a national forum.

Among the fifteen women and eleven men appointed to serve on the President's Commission on the Status of Women were cabinet officers and members of Congress, as well as labor, business, educational, professional, religious, and ethnic leaders. Eleanor Roosevelt was named chairman [*sic*] but died before the group's work was completed. The strongest individual force behind the commission was its executive vice chairman, Esther Peterson, an assistant secretary of labor and head of the department's Women's Bureau.

Kennedy's order setting up the commission stated that "prejudices and outmoded customs act as barriers to the full

[2]*The New York Times,* November 19, 1961, p. 14.

realization of women's basic rights" and instructed the group to develop recommendations for "services which will enable women to continue their role as wives and mothers while making a maximum contribution to the world around them."[3]

The nitty-gritty work of the commission was carried out by specialists appointed to seven separate committees, each assigned to investigate a specific subject and report back to the full commission. In October 1963 the commission's final report, entitled *American Women,* was submitted to the president. Its point of view was supportive of women's needs, but it was by no means a militant document. In fact, the commission often seemed at pains to point out that its recommendations would also benefit men and the country as a whole—as if benefit to women alone were not a sufficiently compelling reason for action. Nor did the report endorse an Equal Rights Amendment to the Constitution, a disappointment to some, but by no means all, advocates for women. (Labor unions and Women's Bureau personnel, along with some women's organizations, feared that the amendment might make illegal the gender-based protective labor laws put in place by an earlier generation to safeguard poor female workers.)

The underlying assumption of *American Women* was that the fundamental responsibility of women is to be wives, mothers, and homemakers. Although the report acknowledged the growing participation of women in the paid workforce, its implicit acceptance of the primacy of women's domestic role colored its approach to all aspects of women's lives.

Despite its limitations, *American Women* was an innovative study, and it remains an important document in the history of modern feminism. It was aptly described decades after its publication as "a coda to forty years of weakened feminist consciousness as well as the opening salvo of a reborn women's movement."[4]

[3]Executive Order 10980, December 14, 1961, in *American Women* (Washington, DC: U.S. Government Printing Office, 1963), p. 76.

[4]Lois Scharf, *Eleanor Roosevelt, First Lady of American Liberalism* (Boston: Twayne, 1987), p. 173.

The following excerpts deal with the need for more child-care facilities (from the section "Home and Community"), the existence of gender discrimination in the job market (from "Women in Employment"), and the paucity of women in public office (from "Women as Citizens")—all problems that, despite much progress, still are a long way from being adequately addressed.

Home and Community

NOT SO LONG AGO, and not only in rural areas, family tasks were shared by members of two or more generations—by grandmothers, mothers or mothers-in-law, and maiden aunts, as well as by women with young children. Sisters and sisters-in-law often lived under the same roof or close by.

Now, though fathers often take a larger share in the performance of household tasks than they used to and the older children help in many ways, in most families the mother is the only grown person present to assume day-to-day responsibility in the home. And the family is more than likely to be an anonymous newcomer among strange neighbors in an urban or suburban setting. These simultaneous changes in the composition of families and communities have altered the very nature of family life.

Child-care services are needed in all communities, for children of all kinds of families who may require day care, after-school care, or intermittent care. In putting major emphasis on this need, the Commission affirms that child-care facilities are essential for women in many different circumstances, whether they work outside the home or not. It is regrettable when women with children are forced by economic necessity or by the regulations of welfare agencies to seek employment while their children are young. On the other hand, those who decide to work should have child-care services available.

The gross inadequacy of present child-care facilities is apparent. Across the country, licensed day care is available to some

185,000 children only. In nearly half a million families with children under six years, the mother is frequently the sole support. There are 117,000 families with children under six with only a father in the home. Almost 3 million mothers of children under six work outside the home although there is a husband present. Other mothers, though not at work, may be ill, living in overcrowded slum conditions with no play opportunities for children, responsible for mentally retarded or emotionally handicapped children, or confronting family crises. Migrant families have no fixed income.

In the absence of adequate child-care facilities, many of these mothers are forced to resort to makeshift arrangements or to leave their children without care. A 1958 survey disclosed no less than 400,000 children under twelve whose mothers worked full time and for whose supervision no arrangements whatsoever had been made. Suitable afterschool supervision is especially crucial for children whom discrimination in housing forces into crowded neighborhoods.

Plans for housing developments, community centers, urban renewal projects, and migratory labor camps should provide space for child-care centers under licensing procedures insuring adequate standards.

Localities should institute afterschool and vacation activities, in properly supervised places, for school-age children whose mothers must be away from home during hours when children are not in school.

Failure to assure such services reflects primarily a lack of community awareness of the realities of modern life. Recent federal legislation offering assistance to communities establishing day care is a first step in raising its provision to the level of national policy. As a number of localities have discovered, child care can be provided in many ways as long as proper standards are assured: cooperatively by groups of parents; by public or private agencies with fees on a sliding scale according to ability to pay; or as a public undertaking.

Where group programs serve children from a cross section of a city, they provide training grounds for democratic social development. Their educational possibilities range from preparing underprivileged children for school, to providing constructive activities for normal youngsters, to offering especially gifted children additional means of development.

For the benefit of children, mothers, and society, child-care services should be available for children of families at all economic levels. Proper standards of child care must be maintained, whether services are in homes or in centers. Costs should be met by fees scaled to parents' ability to pay, contributions from voluntary agencies, and public appropriations.

Women in Employment

AMERICAN WOMEN WORK both in their homes, unpaid, and outside their homes, on a wage or salary basis. Among the great majority of women, as among the great majority of men, the motive for paid employment is to earn money. For some, work has additional—or even primary—value as self-fulfillment.

When America was an agricultural country, most of both man's and woman's work was an unpaid contribution to family subsistence. As production developed in factory and city centers, many women began to do outside, for pay, what they had formerly done, unpaid, in their homes—making textiles or garments, processing food, nursing the sick, teaching children. Women's participation in paid employment importantly increases the nation's labor force: one worker in three is a woman.

In any average month in 1962, there were some 23 million women at work; the forecast is for 30 million in 1970. Approximately three out of five women workers are married. Among married women, one in three is working; among nonwhites, almost one in two. Many of these women, nearly a third, work part time; three-fifths of all part-time work is done by married women. Some 17 million women, in an average month, are full-time workers.

Their occupations range widely: the 1960 census recorded

431 geologists and geophysicists and 18,632 bus drivers. The largest concentration—7 million—is in the clerical field. Three other main groupings—service workers (waitresses, beauticians, hospital attendants), factory operatives, and professional and technical employees (teachers, nurses, accountants, librarians)— number between 3 and 3¾ million each.

Though women are represented in the highly paid professions, in industry, in business, and in government, most jobs that women hold are in low-paid categories. Some occupations—nursing and household work, for instance—are almost entirely staffed by women. The difference in occupational distribution of men and women is largely responsible for the fact that in 1961, the earnings of women working full time averaged only about 60 percent of those of men working full time. But in various occupations where both sexes were employed, the levels of women's earnings were likewise demonstrably lower than those of men.

The existence of differentials in pay between men and women for the same kind of work has been substantiated by studies from numerous sources: an analysis of 1,900 companies, for example, showed that one out of three had dual pay scales in effect for similar office jobs.

The Commission attempted to gather informed views as to the extent to which access to jobs, rates of pay, and opportunities for training and advancement are based on the qualifications of the women who apply for or hold them, and the extent to which discriminations are made against them in these regards solely because they are women.

The reasons given by employers for differential treatment cover a considerable range. Frequently, they say they prefer male employees because the nonwage costs of employing women are higher. They say that the employment pattern of younger women is in and out of the labor force, working for a time before marriage and thereafter putting family obligations first until their children are grown. They say that women's rates of sickness, absenteeism, and turnover are higher than men's; that the hiring of married women introduces one more element into the turnover rate because the residence of a married couple is normally determined by the occupation of the man. They say that though attendance rates of older women are often better than those of men, insurance and pensions for older workers are expensive, and that compliance with protective labor legislation applying to women is sometimes disruptive of schedules. They say that men object to working under women supervisors.

Because many personnel officers believe that women are less likely than men to want to make a career in industry, equally well-prepared young women are passed over in favor of men for posts that lead into management training programs and subsequent exercise of major executive responsibility.

Actually, situations vary far too much to make generalizations applicable, and more information is needed on rates of quits, layoffs, absenteeism, and illness among women workers and on the qualifications of women for responsible supervisory or executive positions. However, already available statistics on absenteeism and turnover indicate that the level of skill of the job, the worker's age, length of service with the employer, and record of job stability all are much more relevant than the fact that the worker is a man or a woman.

Reluctance to consider women applicants on their merits results in underutilization of capacities that the economy needs and stunts the development of higher skills.

Women as Citizens

FOR OVER FORTY YEARS, since the Nineteenth Amendment to the U.S. Constitution gave American women the right to vote in national elections in 1920, political participation by women has grown in many directions. But full participation in all of the functions of a citizen is not yet a fact. . . .

In the federal Congress, only 2 of 100 Senators and 11 of 435 Representatives are women. Only two women have held cabinet rank in the federal government; only six have served as ambassadors or ministers. In federal judicial office, no women are on the Supreme Court or the courts of appeals. One woman judge serves on the U.S. Customs Court and one on the Tax Court of the United States. Of 307 federal district judges, only two are women.

Among appointive posts in the upper levels of the federal executive branch, a study of occupants of the key offices listed in the *U.S. Government Organization Manual* shows that under the past three administrations women have comprised a constant percent—2.4—of a rising number: 79 of 3,273 in 1951–52; 84 of 3,491 in 1958–59; 93 of 3,807 in 1961–62.

In the states, as of 1962, of approximately 7,700 seats in state legislatures, 234 were held by women.

Few women have been elected or appointed to state executive offices of cabinet rank; secretary of state, treasurer, and auditor are the posts most commonly held. In some states, appointments of women to public office have clustered in certain fields regarded as "women's areas": those dealing with juveniles, school affairs, health, welfare, libraries. At all levels of government, efforts should be made to widen the range of positions to which women are normally appointed.

The low proportion of women in public office reflects the low proportion of women prominent in the private occupations that normally lead to political activity and advancement. Few women possess the practical experience obtained at middle and upper levels of administrative and executive responsibility, and they therefore lack the public visibility that goes with such posts and in turn becomes a basis for appointment to public office. . . .

As more and more women plan ahead for a career after their children are grown, and apply themselves in earlier years to a grassroots apprenticeship, the scale of their political activity is likely to broaden. Even those with active home responsibilities can undertake municipal or county contests for the school board or the town council or accept appointment on local advisory bodies, and more and more of them are doing so. For women whose families are grown, the presence at the state capital required by membership in the state legislature—normally for two to three months every other year—is not insuperable; it is frequently easier for them to get away than for men other than those who are self-employed.

Women should be encouraged to seek elective and appointive posts at local, state, and national levels and in all three branches of government.

BETTY FRIEDAN

The Feminine Mystique

When the call was sounded that reawakened millions of women to their lot *as women* and set in motion the second wave of American feminism, it came not from students and others who joined together in the early sixties to combat racism, poverty, and war but from a vaguely dissatisfied suburban mother of three who had graduated from college over twenty years before. Her name was Betty Friedan (b. 1921).

For some years Friedan had pursued a career as an occasional contributor of articles to popular magazines. Then, in 1963, *The Feminine Mystique* was published—a virtually unknown writer's first book. Its effect was immediate and stunning. In retrospect, we can see that part of the reason for the book's tremendous impact was that it connected with the important shift in women's behavior that had been developing, nearly unnoticed, for a decade and a half: the movement of women, especially older married women, into the labor force.

The book grew out of an intensive questionnaire Friedan circulated among her former Smith College classmates, in 1957, on the fifteenth anniversary of their graduation, in which she asked intimate questions about the problems and satisfactions of their present lives. The women's answers set Friedan to thinking: Many of her classmates' "personal" problems were very similar. Might they have common roots?

Friedan's approach was more practical, more here and now, than de Beauvoir's. She saw herself as "a reporter on the trail of a story" as she analyzed the results of her often ingenious research. What she detected was a concerted campaign waged since the end of World War II to convince American women they could achieve happiness in life only through marriage and motherhood—an ideology she labeled "the feminine mystique." She identified women's magazines, educators, and advertising experts as the chief perpetrators of this sophisticated brainwashing; the intellectual underpinnings were provided by Freudian psychology and the popular writings about "natural" women in "primitive" societies by anthropologist Margaret Mead.

Friedan pointed out that the feminine mystique served several important social needs. First, it was aimed at retiring the wartime female wage earner back to the kitchen, thus freeing jobs for returning servicemen. Second, it was intended to instill in women a passionate desire for new consumer goods—a new washing machine and toaster and baby carriage—in order to boost the nation's peacetime economy. "The really important role that women serve as housewives is *to buy more things for the house,*" Friedan observed wryly.

The author saw that trying to conform to the image of the happy homemaker was causing women a great deal of pain. "The core of the problem for women today," she wrote, "is . . . a problem of identity—a stunting or evasion of growth that is perpetuated by the feminine mystique. It is my thesis that as the Victorian culture did not permit women to accept or gratify their basic sexual needs, our culture does not permit women to accept or gratify their basic need to grow and fulfill their potentialities as human beings."

The Feminine Mystique was not without shortcomings, as no pioneering work can be. First, for the homebound wife and mother who wished to get out in the world, it offered few specific remedies. Second, it neglected the subject of men's self-interest in sustaining their privileged position, which resulted in underestimation of what it would take to free women. Finally, it was narrowly directed to the educated American housewife who found herself some years down the road, bored and depressed, wielding broom and dustpan in a well-appointed surburban home. It did not deal with the dissatisfactions of poor and often immigrant or minority women, who worked out of necessity rather than for personal fulfillment.

But despite these deficiencies, for women to whom it spoke, *The Feminine Mystique* was a compelling and ultimately transforming experience. It stands alongside those few books in our century that have changed the thinking of vast numbers of people. Two of Friedan's subsequent books—*It Changed My Life* (1976) and *The Second Stage* (1981)—dealt with feminism and the women's movement. In 1993 the author tackled a new topic, aging, in *The Fountain of Age*.

The following selection is the first chapter of *The Feminine Mystique,* "The Problem That Has No Name."

THE PROBLEM LAY BURIED, UNSPOKEN, for many years in the minds of American women. It was a strange stirring, a sense of dissatisfaction, a yearning that women suffered in the middle of the twentieth century in the United States. Each suburban wife struggled with it alone. As she made the beds, shopped for groceries, matched slipcover material, ate peanut butter sandwiches with her children, chauffeured Cub Scouts and Brownies, lay beside her husband at night—she was afraid to ask even of herself the silent question—"Is this all?"

For over fifteen years there was no word of this yearning in the millions of words written about women, for women, in all the columns, books and articles by experts telling women their role was to seek fulfillment as wives and mothers. Over and over women heard in voices of tradition and of Freudian sophistication that they could desire no greater destiny than to glory in their own femininity. Experts told them how to catch a man and keep him, how to breastfeed children and handle their toilet training, how to cope with sibling rivalry and adolescent rebellion; how to buy a dishwasher, bake bread, cook gourmet snails, and build a swimming pool with their own hands; how to dress, look, and act more feminine and make marriage more exciting; how to keep their husbands from dying young and their sons from growing into delinquents. They were taught to pity the neurotic, unfeminine, unhappy women who wanted to be poets or physicists or presidents. They learned that truly feminine women do not want careers, higher education, political rights—the independence and the opportunities that the old-fashioned feminists fought for. Some women, in their forties and fifties, still remembered painfully giving up those dreams, but most of the younger women no longer even thought about them. A thousand expert voices applauded their femininity, their adjustment, their new maturity. All they had to do was devote their lives from earliest girlhood to finding a husband and bearing children.

By the end of the nineteen-fifties, the average marriage age of women in America dropped to twenty, and was still dropping, into the teens. Fourteen million girls were engaged by seventeen. The proportion of women attending college in comparison with men dropped from 47 percent in 1920 to 35 percent in 1958. A century earlier, women had fought for higher education; now girls went to college to get a husband. By the mid-fifties, 60 percent dropped out of college to marry, or because they were afraid too much education would be a marriage bar. Colleges built dormitories for "married students," but the students were almost always the husbands. A new degree was instituted for the wives—"Ph.T." (Putting Husband Through).

Then American girls began getting married in high school. And the women's magazines, deploring the unhappy statistics about these young marriages, urged that courses on marriage, and marriage counselors, be installed in the high schools. Girls started going steady at twelve and thirteen, in junior high. Manufacturers put out brassieres with false bosoms of foam rubber for little girls of ten. And an advertisement for a child's dress, sizes 3–6x, in the *New York Times* in the fall of 1960, said: "She Too Can Join the Man-Trap Set."

By the end of the fifties, the United States birthrate was overtaking India's. The birth-control movement, renamed Planned Parenthood, was asked to find a method whereby women who had been advised that a third or fourth baby would be born dead or defective might have it anyhow. Statisticians were especially astounded at the fantastic increase in the number of babies among college women. Where once they had two children, now they had four, five, six. Women who had once wanted careers were now making careers out of having babies. So rejoiced

Life magazine in a 1956 paean to the movement of American women back to the home.

In a New York hospital, a woman had a nervous breakdown when she found she could not breastfeed her baby. In other hospitals, women dying of cancer refused a drug which research had proved might save their lives: its side effects were said to be unfeminine. "If I have only one life, let me live it as a blonde," a larger-than-life-sized picture of a pretty, vacuous woman proclaimed from newspaper, magazine, and drugstore ads. And across America, three out of every ten women dyed their hair blonde. They ate a chalk called Metrecal, instead of food, to shrink to the size of the thin young models. Department-store buyers reported that American women, since 1939, had become three and four sizes smaller. "Women are out to fit the clothes, insead of vice-versa," one buyer said.

Interior decorators were designing kitchens with mosaic murals and original paintings, for kitchens were once again the center of women's lives. Home sewing became a million-dollar industry. Many women no longer left their homes, except to shop, chauffeur their children, or attend a social engagement with their husbands. Girls were growing up in America without ever having jobs outside the home. In the late fifties, a sociological phenomenon was suddenly remarked: a third of American women now worked, but most were no longer young and very few were pursuing careers. They were married women who held part-time jobs, selling or secretarial, to put their husbands through school, their sons through college, or to help pay the mortgage. Or they were widows supporting families. Fewer and fewer women were entering professional work. The shortages in the nursing, social work, and teaching professions caused crises in almost every American city. Concerned over the Soviet Union's lead in the space race, scientists noted that America's greatest source of unused brainpower was women. But girls would not study physics: it was "unfeminine." A girl refused a science fellowship at Johns Hopkins to take a job in a real-estate office. All she wanted, she said, was what every other American girl wanted—to get married, have four children and live in a nice house in a nice suburb.

The suburban housewife—she was the dream image of the young American women and the envy, it was said, of women all over the world. The American housewife—freed by science and labor-saving appliances from the drudgery, the dangers of child-birth and the illnesses of her grandmother. She was healthy, beautiful, educated, concerned only about her husband, her children, her home. She had found true feminine fulfillment. As a housewife and mother, she was respected as a full and equal partner to man in his world. She was free to choose automobiles, clothes, appliances, supermarkets; she had everything that women ever dreamed of.

In the fifteen years after World War II, this mystique of feminine fulfillment became the cherished and self-perpetuating core of contemporary American culture. Millions of women lived their lives in the image of those pretty pictures of the American suburban housewife, kissing their husbands goodbye in front of the picture window, depositing their stationwagonsful of children at school, and smiling as they ran the new electric waxer over the spotless kitchen floor. They baked their own bread, sewed their own and their children's clothes, kept their new washing machines and dryers running all day. They changed the sheets on the beds twice a week instead of once, took the rug-hooking class in adult education, and pitied their poor frustrated mothers, who had dreamed of having a career. Their only dream was to be perfect wives and mothers; their highest ambition to have five children and a beautiful house, their only fight to get and keep their husbands. They had no thought for the unfeminine problems of the world outside the home; they wanted the men to make the major decisions. They gloried in their role as women, and wrote proudly on the census blank: "Occupation: housewife."

For over fifteen years, the words written for women, and the words women used when they talked to each other, while their husbands sat on the other side of the room and talked shop or politics or septic tanks, were about problems with their children, or how to keep their husbands happy, or improve their children's school, or cook chicken or make slipcovers. Nobody argued whether women were inferior or superior to men; they were simply different. Words like "emancipation" and "career" sounded strange and embarrassing; no one had used them for years. When a Frenchwoman named Simone de Beauvoir wrote a book called *The Second Sex,* an American critic commented that she obviously "didn't know what life was all about," and besides, she was talking about French women. The "woman problem" in America no longer existed.

If a woman had a problem in the 1950s and 1960s, she knew that something must be wrong with her marriage, or with herself. Other women were satisfied with their lives, she thought. What kind of a woman was she if she did not feel this mysterious fulfillment waxing the kitchen floor? She was so ashamed to admit her dissatisfaction that she never knew how many other women shared it. If she tried to tell her husband, he didn't understand what she was talking about. She did not really understand it herself. For over fifteen years women in America found it harder to talk about this problem than about sex. Even the psychoanalysts had no name for it. When a woman went to a psychiatrist for help, as many women did, she would say, "I'm so ashamed," or "I must be hopelessly neurotic." "I don't know what's wrong with women today," a suburban psychiatrist said uneasily. "I only know something is wrong because most of my patients happen to be women. And their problem isn't sexual." Most women with this problem did not go to see a psychoanalyst, however. "There's nothing wrong really," they kept telling themselves. "There isn't any problem."

But on an April morning in 1959, I heard a mother of four, having coffee with four other mothers in a suburban development fifteen miles from New York, say in a tone of quiet desperation, "the problem." And the others knew, without words, that she was not talking about a problem with her husband, or her children, or her home. Suddenly they realized they all shared the same problem, the problem that has no name. They began, hesitantly, to talk about it. Later, after they had picked up their children at nursery school and taken them home to nap, two of the women cried, in sheer relief, just to know they were not alone.

· · ·

Gradually I came to realize that the problem that has no name was shared by countless women in America. As a magazine writer I often interviewed women about problems with their children, or their marriages, or their houses, or their communities. But after a while I began to recognize the telltale signs of this other problem. I saw the same signs in suburban ranch houses and split-levels on Long Island and in New Jersey and Westchester County; in colonial houses in a small Massachusetts town; on patios in Memphis; in suburban and city apartments; in living rooms in the Midwest. Sometimes I sensed the problem, not as a reporter, but as a suburban housewife, for during this time I was also bringing up my own three children in Rockland County, New York. I heard echoes of the problem in college dormitories and semiprivate maternity wards, at PTA meetings and luncheons of the League of Women Voters, at suburban cocktail parties, in stationwagons waiting for trains, and in snatches of conversation overheard at Schrafft's. The groping words I heard from other women, on quiet afternoons when children were at school or on quiet evenings when husbands worked late, I think I understood first as a woman long before I understood their larger social and psychological implications.

Just what was this problem that has no name? What were the words women used when they tried to express it? Sometimes a woman would say, "I feel empty somehow . . . incomplete." Or she would say, "I feel as if I don't exist." Sometimes she blotted out the feeling with a tranquilizer. Sometimes she thought the problem was with her husband, or her children, or that what she really needed was to redecorate her house, or move to a better neighborhood, or have an affair, or another baby. Sometimes, she went to a doctor with symptoms she could hardly describe: "A tired feeling . . . I get so angry with the children it scares me . . . I feel like crying without any reason." (A Cleveland doctor called it "the housewife's syndrome.") A number of women told me about great bleeding blisters that break out on their hands and arms. "I call it the housewife's blight," said a family doctor in Pennsylvania. "I see it so often lately in these young women with four, five and six children who bury themselves in their dishpans. But it isn't caused by detergent and it isn't cured by cortisone."

Sometimes a woman would tell me that the feeling gets so strong she runs out of the house and walks through the streets. Or she stays inside her house and cries. Or her children tell her a joke, and she doesn't laugh because she doesn't hear it. I talked to women who had spent years on the analyst's couch, working out their "adjustment to the feminine role," their blocks to "fulfillment as a wife and mother." But the desperate tone in these women's voices, and the look in their eyes, was the same as the tone and the look of other women, who were sure they had no problem, even though they did have a strange feeling of desperation.

A mother of four who left college at nineteen to get married told me:

I've tried everything women are supposed to do—hobbies, gardening, pickling, canning, being very social with my neighbors, joining committees, running PTA teas. I can do it all, and I like it, but it doesn't leave you anything to think about—any feeling of who you are. I never had any career ambitions. All I wanted was to get married and have four children. I love the kids and Bob and my home. There's no problem you can even put a name to. But I'm desperate. I begin to feel I have no personality. I'm a server of food and a putter-on of pants and a bedmaker, somebody who can be called on when you want something. But who am I?

A twenty-three-year-old mother in blue jeans said:

I ask myself why I'm so dissatisfied. I've got my health, fine children, a lovely new home, enough money. My husband has a real future as an electronics engineer. He doesn't have any of these feelings. He says maybe I need a vacation, let's go to New York for a weekend. But that isn't it. I always had this idea we should do everything together. I can't sit down and read a book alone. If the children are napping and I have one hour to myself I just walk through the house waiting for them to wake up. I don't make a move until I know where the rest of the crowd is going.

It's as if ever since you were a little girl, there's always been some-body or something that will take care of your life: your parents, or college, or falling in love, or having a child, or moving to a new house. Then you wake up one morning and there's nothing to look forward to.

A young wife in a Long Island development said:

I seem to sleep so much. I don't know why I should be so tired. This house isn't nearly so hard to clean as the cold-water flat we had when I was working. The children are at school all day. It's not the work. I just don't feel alive.

In 1960, the problem that has no name burst like a boil through the image of the happy American housewife. In the tele-vision commercials the pretty housewives still beamed over their foaming dishpans and *Time*'s cover story on "The Suburban Wife, an American Phenomenon" protested: "Having too good a time . . . to believe that they should be unhappy." But the ac-tual unhappiness of the American housewife was suddenly being reported—from the *New York Times* and *Newsweek* to *Good Housekeeping* and CBS Television ("The Trapped Housewife"), although almost everybody who talked about it found some su-perficial reason to dismiss it. It was attributed to incompetent appliance repairmen (*New York Times*), or the distances chil-dren must be chauffeured in the suburbs (*Time*), or too much PTA (*Redbook*). Some said it was the old problem—education: more and more women had education, which naturally made them unhappy in their role as housewives. "The road from Freud to Frigidaire, from Sophocles to Spock, has turned out to be a bumpy one," reported the *New York Times* (June 28, 1960). "Many young women—certainly not all—whose edu-cation plunged them into a world of ideas feel stifled in their homes. They find their routine lives out of joint with their train-ing. Like shut-ins, they feel left out. In the last year, the problem of the educated housewife has provided the meat of dozens of speeches made by troubled presidents of women's colleges who maintain, in the face of complaints, that sixteen years of academic training is realistic preparation for wifehood and motherhood."

There was much sympathy for the educated housewife. ("Like a two-headed schizophrenic . . . once she wrote a paper on the Graveyard poets; now she writes notes to the milkman. Once she determined the boiling point of sulphuric acid; now she determines her boiling point with the overdue repairman. . . . The housewife often is reduced to screams and tears. . . . No one, it seems, is appreciative, least of all herself, of the kind of person she becomes in the process of turning from poetess into shrew.")

Home economists suggested more realistic preparation for housewives, such as high-school workshops in home appliances. College educators suggested more discussion groups on home management and the family, to prepare women for the adjustment to domestic life. A spate of articles appeared in the mass magazines offering "Fifty-eight Ways to Make Your Marriage More Exciting." No month went by without a new book by a psychiatrist or sexologist offering technical advice on finding greater fulfillment through sex.

A male humorist joked in *Harper's Bazaar* (July 1960) that the problem could be solved by taking away woman's right to vote. ("In the pre–19th Amendment era, the American woman was placid, sheltered and sure of her role in American society. She left all the political decisions to her husband and he, in turn, left all the family decisions to her. Today a woman has to make both the family *and* the political decisions, and it's too much for her.")

A number of educators suggested seriously that women no longer be admitted to the four-year colleges and universities: in the growing college crisis, the education which girls could not use as housewives was more urgently needed than ever by boys to do the work of the atomic age.

The problem was also dismissed with drastic solutions no one could take seriously. (A woman writer proposed in *Harper's* that women be drafted for compulsory service as nurses' aides and baby-sitters.) And it was smoothed over with the age-old panaceas: "love is their answer," "the only answer is inner help," "the secret of completeness—children," "a private means of intellectual fulfillment," "to cure this toothache of the spirit— the simple formula of handing one's self and one's will over to God."

The problem was dismissed by telling the housewife she doesn't realize how lucky she is—her own boss, no time clock, no junior executive gunning for her job. What if she isn't happy—does she think men are happy in this world? Does she really, secretly, still want to be a man? Doesn't she know yet how lucky she is to be a woman?

The problem was also, and finally, dismissed by shrugging that there are no solutions: this is what being a woman means, and what is wrong with American women that they can't accept their role gracefully? As *Newsweek* put it (March 7, 1960):

> She is dissatisfied with a lot that women of other lands can only dream of. Her discontent is deep, pervasive, and impervious to the superficial remedies which are offered at every hand. . . . An army of professional explorers have already charted the major sources of trouble. . . . From the beginning of time, the female cycle has defined and confined woman's role. As Freud was credited with saying: "Anatomy is destiny." Though no group of women has ever pushed these natural restrictions as far as the American wife, it seems that she still cannot accept them with good grace. . . . A young mother with a beautiful family, charm, talent and brains is apt to dismiss her role apologetically. "What do I do?" you hear her say. "Why nothing. I'm just a housewife." A good education, it seems, has given this paragon among women an understanding of the value of everything except her own worth.

And so she must accept the fact that "American women's unhappiness is merely the most recently won of women's rights," and adjust and say with the happy housewife found by *Newsweek:* "We ought to salute the wonderful freedom we all have and be proud of our lives today. I have had college and I've worked, but being a housewife is the most rewarding and satisfying role. . . . My mother was never included in my father's business affairs . . . she couldn't get out of the house and away from us children. But I am an equal to my husband; I can go along with him on business trips and to social business affairs."

The alternative offered was a choice that few women would contemplate. In the sympathetic words of the *New York Times:* "All admit to being deeply frustrated at times by the lack of privacy, the physical burden, the routine of family life, the confinement of it. However, none would give up her home and family if she had the choice to make again." *Redbook* commented: "Few women would want to thumb their noses at husbands, children and community and go off on their own. Those who do may be talented individuals, but they rarely are successful women."

The year American women's discontent boiled over, it was also reported (*Look*) that the more than 21 million American women who are single, widowed, or divorced do not cease even after fifty their frenzied, desperate search for a man. And the search begins early—for 70 percent of all American women now marry before they are twenty-four. A pretty twenty-five-year-old secretary took thirty-five different jobs in six months in the futile hope of finding a husband. Women were moving from one political club to another, taking evening courses in accounting or sailing, learning to play golf or ski, joining a number of churches in succession, going to bars alone, in their ceaseless search for a man.

Of the growing thousands of women currently getting private psychiatric help in the United States, the married ones were reported dissatisfied with their marriages, the unmarried ones suffering from anxiety and, finally, depression. Strangely, a number of psychiatrists stated that, in their experience, unmarried women patients were happier than married ones. So the door of all those pretty suburban houses opened a crack to permit a glimpse of uncounted thousands of American housewives who suffered alone from a problem that suddenly everyone was talking about, and beginning to take for granted, as one of those unreal problems in American life that can never be solved—like the hydrogen bomb. By 1962 the plight of the trapped American housewife had become a national parlor game. Whole issues of magazines, newspaper columns, books learned and frivolous, educational conferences and television panels were devoted to the problem.

Even so, most men, and some women, still did not know that this problem was real. But those who had faced it honestly knew that all the superficial remedies, the sympathetic advice, the scolding words and the cheering words were somehow drowning the problem in unreality. A bitter laugh was beginning to be heard from American women. They were admired, envied, pitied, theorized over until they were sick of it, offered drastic solutions or silly choices that no one could take seriously. They got all kinds of advice from the growing armies of marriage and child-guidance counselors, psychotherapists, and armchair psychologists, on how to adjust to their role as housewives. No other road to fulfillment was offered to American women in the middle of the twentieth century. Most adjusted to their role and suffered or ignored the problem that has no name. It can be less painful, for a woman, not to hear the strange, dissatisfied voice stirring within her.

It is no longer possible to ignore that voice, to dismiss the desperation of so many American women. This is not what being a woman means, no matter what the experts say. For human suffering there is a reason; perhaps the reason has not been found because the right questions have not been asked, or pressed far enough. I do not accept the answer that there is no problem because American women have luxuries that women in other times and lands never dreamed of; part of the strange newness of the problem is that it cannot be understood in terms of the age-old material problems of man: poverty, sickness, hunger, cold. The women who suffer this problem have a hunger that food cannot fill. It persists in women whose husbands are struggling interns and law clerks, or prosperous doctors and lawyers; in wives of workers and executives who make $5,000 a year or $50,000. It is not caused by lack of material advantages; it may not even be felt by women preoccupied with desperate problems of hunger, poverty or illness. And women who think it will be solved by more money, a bigger house, a second car, moving to a better suburb, often discover it gets worse.

It is no longer possible today to blame the problem on loss of femininity: to say that education and independence and equality with men have made American women unfeminine. I have heard so many women try to deny this dissatisfied voice within themselves because it does not fit the pretty picture of femininity the experts have given them. I think, in fact, that this is the first clue to the mystery: The problem cannot be understood in the generally accepted terms by which scientists have studied women, doctors have treated them, counselors have advised them, and writers have written about them. Women who suffer this problem, in whom this voice is stirring, have lived their whole lives in the pursuit of feminine fulfillment. They are not career women (although career women may have other problems); they are women whose greatest ambition has been marriage and children. For the oldest of these women, these daughters of the American middle class, no other dream was possible. The ones in their forties and fifties who once had other dreams gave them up and threw themselves joyously into life as housewives. For the youngest, the new wives and mothers, this was the only dream. They are the ones who quit high school and college to marry, or marked time in some job in which they had no real interest, until they married. These women are very "feminine" in the usual sense, and yet they still suffer the problem.

Are the women who finished college, the women who once had dreams beyond housewifery, the ones who suffer the most? According to the experts they are, but listen to these four women:

> My days are all busy, and dull, too. All I ever do is mess around. I get up at eight—I make breakfast, so I do the dishes, have lunch, do some more dishes and some laundry and cleaning in the afternoon. Then it's supper dishes and I get to sit down a few minutes before the children have to be sent to bed. . . . That's all there is to my day. It's just like any other wife's day. Humdrum. The biggest time, I am chasing kids.

Ye Gods, what do I do with my time? Well, I get up at six. I get my son dressed and then give him breakfast. After that I wash dishes and bathe and feed the baby. Then I get lunch and, while the children nap, I sew or mend or iron and do all the other things I can't get done before noon. Then I cook supper for the family and my husband watches TV while I do the dishes. After I get the children to bed, I set my hair and then I go to bed.

The problem is always being the children's mommy, or the minister's wife and never being myself.

A film made of any typical morning in my house would look like an old Marx Brothers' comedy. I wash the dishes, rush the older children off to school, dash out in the yard to cultivate the chrysanthemums, run back in to make a phone call about a committee meeting, help the youngest child build a blockhouse, spend fifteen minutes skimming the newspapers so I can be well-informed, then scamper down to the washing machines where my thrice-weekly laundry includes enough clothes to keep a primitive village going for an entire year. By noon I'm ready for a padded cell. Very little of what I've done has been really necessary or important. Outside pressures lash me through the day. Yet I look upon myself as one of the more relaxed housewives in the neighborhood. Many of my friends are even more frantic. In the past sixty years we have come full circle and the American housewife is once again trapped in a squirrel cage. If the cage is now a modern plate-glass-and-broadloom ranch house or a convenient modern apartment, the situation is no less painful than when her grandmother sat over an embroidery hoop in her gilt-and-plush parlor and muttered angrily about women's rights.

The first two women never went to college. They live in developments in Levittown, New Jersey, and Tacoma, Washington, and were interviewed by a team of sociologists studying workingmen's wives. The third, a minister's wife, wrote on the fifteenth reunion questionnaire of her college that she never had any career ambitions, but wishes now she had. The fourth, who has a Ph.D. in anthropology, is today a Nebraska housewife with three children. Their words seem to indicate that house-

wives of all educational levels suffer the same feeling of desperation.

The fact is that no one today is muttering angrily about
"women's rights," even though more and more women have
gone to college. In a recent study of all the classes that have
graduated from Barnard College, a significant minority of earlier graduates blamed their education for making them want
"rights," later classes blamed their education for giving them career dreams, but recent graduates blamed the college for making
them feel it was not enough simply to be a housewife and
mother; they did not want to feel guilty if they did not read
books or take part in community activities. But if education is
not the cause of the problem, the fact that education somehow
festers in these women may be a clue.

If the secret of feminine fulfillment is having children, never
have so many women, with the freedom to choose, had so many
children, in so few years, so willingly. If the answer is love, never
have women searched for love with such determination. And yet
there is a growing suspicion that the problem may not be sexual,
though it must somehow be related to sex. I have heard from
many doctors evidence of new sexual problems between man
and wife—sexual hunger in wives so great their husbands cannot satisfy it. "We have made woman a sex creature," said a
psychiatrist at the Margaret Sanger marriage counseling clinic.
"She has no identity except as a wife and mother. She does not
know who she is herself. She waits all day for her husband to
come home at night to make her feel alive. And now it is the
husband who is not interested. It is terrible for the women, to lie
there, night after night, waiting for her husband to make her feel
alive." Why is there such a market for books and articles offering sexual advice? The kind of sexual orgasm which Kinsey
found in statistical plenitude in the recent generations of
American women does not seem to make this problem go away.

On the contrary, new neuroses are being seen among
women—and problems as yet unnamed as neuroses—which
Freud and his followers did not predict, with physical symptoms, anxieties, and defense mechanisms equal to those caused
by sexual repression. And strange new problems are being re-

ported in the growing generations of children whose mothers were always there, driving them around, helping them with their homework—an inability to endure pain or discipline or pursue any self-sustained goal of any sort, a devastating boredom with life. Educators are increasingly uneasy about the dependence, the lack of self-reliance, of the boys and girls who are entering college today. "We fight a continual battle to make our students assume manhood," said a Columbia dean.

A White House conference was held on the physical and muscular deterioration of American children: were they being over-nurtured? Sociologists noted the astounding organization of suburban children's lives: the lessons, parties, entertainments, play and study groups organized for them. A suburban housewife in Portland, Oregon, wondered why the children "need" Brownies and Boy Scouts out here. "This is not the slums. The kids out here have the great outdoors. I think people are so bored, they organize the children, and then try to hook everyone else on it. And the poor kids have no time left just to lie on their beds and daydream."

Can the problem that has no name be somehow related to the domestic routine of the housewife? When a woman tries to put the problem into words, she often merely describes the daily life she leads. What is there in this recital of comfortable domestic detail that could possibly cause such a feeling of desperation? Is she trapped simply by the enormous demands of her role as modern housewife: wife, mistress, mother, nurse, consumer, cook, chauffeur; expert on interior decoration, child care, appliance repair, furniture refinishing, nutrition, and education? Her day is fragmented as she rushes from dishwasher to washing machine to telephone to dryer to stationwagon to supermarket, and delivers Johnny to the Little League field, takes Janey to dancing class, gets the lawnmower fixed and meets the 6:45. She can never spend more than fifteen minutes on any one thing; she has no time to read books, only magazines; even if she had time, she has lost the power to concentrate. At the end of the day, she is so terribly tired that sometimes her husband has to take over and put the children to bed.

This terrible tiredness took so many women to doctors in the

1950s that one decided to investigate it. He found, surprisingly, that his patients suffering from "housewife's fatigue" slept more than an adult needed to sleep—as much as ten hours a day—and that the actual energy they expended on housework did not tax their capacity. The real problem must be something else, he decided—perhaps boredom. Some doctors told their women patients they must get out of the house for a day, treat themselves to a movie in town. Others prescribed tranquilizers. Many suburban housewives were taking tranquilizers like cough drops. "You wake up in the morning, and you feel as if there's no point in going on another day like this. So you take a tranquilizer because it makes you not care so much that it's pointless."

It is easy to see the concrete details that trap the suburban housewife, the continual demands on her time. But the chains that bind her in her trap are chains in her own mind and spirit. They are chains made up of mistaken ideas and misinterpreted facts, of incomplete truths and unreal choices. They are not easily seen and not easily shaken off.

How can any woman see the whole truth within the bounds of her own life? How can she believe that voice inside herself, when it denies the conventional, accepted truths by which she has been living? And yet the women I have talked to, who are finally listening to that inner voice, seem in some incredible way to be groping through to a truth that has defied the experts.

I think the experts in a great many fields have been holding pieces of that truth under their microscopes for a long time without realizing it. I found pieces of it in certain new research and theoretical developments in psychological, social, and biological science whose implications for women seem never to have been examined. I found many clues by talking to suburban doctors, gynecologists, obstetricians, child-guidance clinicians, pediatricians, high-school guidance counselors, college professors, marriage counselors, psychiatrists, and ministers—questioning them not on their theories, but on their actual experience in treating American women. I became aware of a growing body of evidence, much of which has not been reported publicly because it does not fit current modes of thought about women—evidence which throws into question the standards of feminine normality, feminine adjustment, feminine fulfillment, and feminine maturity by which most women are still trying to live.

I began to see in a strange new light the American return to early marriage and the large families that are causing the population explosion; the recent movement to natural childbirth and breastfeeding; suburban conformity, and the new neuroses, character pathologies, and sexual problems being reported by the doctors. I began to see new dimensions to old problems that have long been taken for granted among women: menstrual difficulties, sexual frigidity, promiscuity, pregnancy fears, childbirth depression, the high incidence of emotional breakdown and suicide among women in their twenties and thirties, the menopause crises, the so-called passivity and immaturity of American men, the discrepancy between women's tested intellectual abilities in childhood and their adult achievement, the changing incidence of adult sexual orgasm in American women, and persistent problems in psychotherapy and in women's education.

If I am right, the problem that has no name stirring in the minds of so many American women today is not a matter of loss of femininity or too much education, or the demands of domesticity. It is far more important than anyone recognizes. It is the key to these other new and old problems which have been torturing women and their husbands and children, puzzling their doctors and educators for years. It may well be the key to our future as a nation and a culture. We can no longer ignore that voice within women that says: "I want something more than my husband and my children and my home."

An Early Victory

CIVIL RIGHTS ACT OF 1964,
TITLE VII

The 1960s saw the first major legislative advances for American women since the suffrage amendment. President Kennedy set the process in motion by establishing the Commission on the Status of Women and, in 1962, issuing a directive prohibiting federal agencies from discriminating against female employees in appointments or promotions. The following year Congress enacted the Equal Pay Act, authored by Representative Edith Green, Democrat of Oregon—a severely limited but precedent-setting measure requiring employers to offer equal pay for equal work, without regard to gender. But far and away the most important step forward for women came unexpectedly from Title VII of the landmark 1964 Civil Rights Act. When Title VII was voted into law, equal employment opportunity for women was made the official national policy of the United States for the first time. But before the historic promise embodied in this measure could be realized, the efforts of many people over many years would be necessary.

The Civil Rights Act, a response by the Johnson administration to the black freedom movement, was intended primarily to alleviate injustices suffered on account of race. Women came into it by the back door, more or less uninvited. What happened was that during congressional debate on the proposed legislation, Representative Howard W. Smith, Democrat of Virginia, an old-line southern conservative who vehemently opposed it, submitted a surprise amendment. To Title VII of the bill—which barred discrimination in employment on the basis of race, color, religion, or national origin—Smith proposed an additional basis: sex. By saddling the cause of black civil rights with the unpopular cause of women's rights, he hoped to deter legislators from passing the entire bill.

Ironically, the idea of amending the bill so that its protections would also apply to women had previously been discussed within small networks of women's-rights advocates in Washington. These groups included elderly suffragists from the fifty-year-old National Woman's Party; participants in the President's Commission; lawyers and other professionals interested in wider career opportunities for women; government employees clustered especially in the Women's Bureau of the Department of Labor; and a congresswoman, Representative Martha Griffiths, Democrat of Michigan. Griffiths had wanted to introduce such an amendment in Congress herself but had delayed because she felt she could not muster enough support to assure its passage.

However, Representative Smith's cynical maneuver backfired. With the support of many fellow southerners and right-wingers, his sex amendment was adopted—but he lost the war anyway when the civil rights bill passed the House. Though opposition to the Smith amendment developed in the Senate, Congresswoman Griffiths—with help from Senator Margaret Chase Smith, Republican of Maine, and an impromptu women's lobby—seized the moment and fought tenaciously to prevent the amendment's last-minute withdrawal. In July 1964 Congress enacted the Civil Rights Act—with *sex* still firmly embedded in Title VII.

The new law provided for establishment of a federal agency, the Equal Employment Opportunity Commission (EEOC), to hear complaints of bias in the workplace. That women needed and welcomed such relief was proved in the EEOC's initial year of operation, when about a third of the grievances brought to it—some 1,600—involved discrimination based on sex.

But, unfortunately, Title VII had no real teeth. On finding that a violation had taken place, the EEOC could only "endeavor to eliminate any . . . alleged unlawful employment practice by informal methods of conference, conciliation, and persuasion." Moreover, many workingwomen were not covered under Title VII, and, even worse, the EEOC itself displayed little interest in pursuing gender-based grievances. Month after month, such complaints were shuffled aside. It seemed women were to be disappointed in obtaining the help they sought.

The marvel is that, despite everything, women managed to change the face of the American workplace over the next decade. The EEOC was pushed and prodded to carry out its mandate, and several new measures helpful to women were enacted. In 1972 the agency was empowered to enforce its decisions in the courts, and that same year the coverage of Title VII was broadened to encompass educational institutions, which had formerly been excluded. Eventually female airline "hostesses" won reversal of policies calling for mandatory dismissal at marriage or on reaching the age of thirty-five; the telephone company was forced to hire men as telephone operators and women as telephone-repair personnel; separate newspaper help-wanted listings under "Male" or "Female" headings were abolished; craft unions were opened to women who wished to work as carpenters, plumbers, and the like; women with the necessary skills were for the first time employed at the highest-paying industrial jobs; and charges of discrimination in hiring, pay, and promotion brought by corporate employees, university teachers, bank personnel, and other white-collar workers were favorably resolved.

Reprinted here are excerpts from three key sections of Title VII.

Sec. 703. (a) It shall be an unlawful employment practice for an employer—

(1) to fail or refuse to hire or to discharge any individual, or otherwise discriminate against any individual with respect to his compensation, terms, conditions, or privileges of employment, because of such individual's race, color, religion, sex, or national origin; or

(2) to limit, segregate, or classify his employees in any way which would deprive or tend to deprive any individual of em-

ployment opportunities or otherwise adversely affect his status as an employee, because of such individual's race, color, religion, sex, or national origin.

(b) It shall be an unlawful employment practice for an employment agency to fail or refuse to refer for employment, or otherwise to discriminate against, any individual because of his race, color, religion, sex, or national origin, or to classify or refer for employment any individual on the basis of his race, color, religion, sex, or national origin.

(c) It shall be an unlawful employment practice for a labor organization—

(1) to exclude or to expel from its membership, or otherwise to discriminate against, any individual because of his race, color, religion, sex, or national origin;

(2) to limit, segregate, or classify its membership, or to classify or fail or refuse to refer for employment any individual, in any way which would deprive or tend to deprive any individual of employment opportunities, or would limit such employment opportunities or otherwise adversely affect his status as an employee or as an applicant for employment, because of such individual's race, color, religion, sex, or national origin; or

(3) to cause or attempt to cause an employer to discriminate against an individual in violation of this section.

(d) It shall be an unlawful employment practice for any employer, labor organization, or joint labor-management committee controlling apprenticeship or other training or retraining, including on-the-job training programs, to discriminate against any individual because of his race, color, religion, sex, or national origin in admission to, or employment in, any program established to provide apprenticeship or other training.

(e) Notwithstanding any other provision of this title . . . it shall not be an unlawful employment practice for an employer to hire and employ employees . . . on the basis of . . . religion, sex, or national origin in those certain instances where religion, sex, or national origin is a bona fide occupational qualification reasonably necessary to the normal operation of that particular business or enterprise. . . .

Sec. 704. (b) It shall be an unlawful employment practice for an employer, labor organization, or employment agency to print or publish or cause to be printed or published any notice or advertisement relating to employment by such an employer or membership in or any classification or referral for employment by such a labor organization, or relating to any classification or referral for employment by such an employment agency, indicating any preference, limitation, specification, or discrimination, based on race, color, religion, sex, or national origin, except that such a notice or advertisement may indicate a preference, limitation, specification, or discrimination based on religion, sex, or national origin when religion, sex, or national origin is a bona fide occupational qualification for employment.

Sec. 705. (a) There is hereby created a Commission to be known as the Equal Employment Opportunity Commission, which shall be composed of five members, not more than three of whom shall be members of the same political party. Members of the Commission shall be appointed by the President by and with the advice and consent of the Senate.

Jane Crow and the Law:
Sex Discrimination and Title VII

To fulfill the potential of Title VII in the face of widespread resistance required the devoted labors of resolute women like the attorney Pauli Murray (1910–1985) and her younger colleague Mary O. Eastwood. Murray and Eastwood were active in the circle of early women's-rights advocates. Both participated in the President's Commission on the Status of Women, where, as Murray later remarked, "like-minded women found one another, bonds developed through working together, and an informal feminist network emerged to act as leaven in the broader movement that followed."[1] As a member of the President's Commission, Murray was able to formulate a compromise by which the commission could support the principle of gender equality while evading a clear-cut stand on the then controversial and potentially divisive issue of an Equal Rights Amendment to the Constitution.

Murray and Eastwood were involved in the fight for passage of Title VII in the Senate and the subsequent ongoing effort to compel the Equal Employment Opportunity Commission (EEOC) to implement the statute. In addition, they were among the twenty-eight honored "founding mothers" of the National Organization for Women (NOW).

Pauli Murray received her law degree from Howard University and a doctorate from Yale Law School. A black woman who was a lifelong supporter of civil rights, Murray took part in a sit-in during World War II that successfully desegregated a

---

[1]Pauli Murray, *Song in a Weary Throat* (New York: Harper & Row, 1987), p. 348. Other commission participants who afterward worked loyally on behalf of women's issues were Marguerite Rawalt and Catherine East.

Washington, D.C., cafeteria. Eleanor Roosevelt was a longtime friend, and Murray is said to have "moved her further along the road in the civil-rights struggle than she might otherwise have traveled."[2] Murray wrote several books, including a volume of poetry; taught in universities in the African republic of Ghana and in the United States; and was ordained a priest in the Episcopal Church.

Mary Eastwood was employed by the federal government in the Office of Legal Counsel. After helping to found NOW, she donated time during evenings and weekends to NOW's legal committee, which consisted of four volunteer women lawyers—three of whom, including Eastwood, held down full-time jobs. This overworked team strove to keep up with a deluge of requests from women about how to use Title VII.

The following selection, "Jane Crow and the Law," is excerpted from *The George Washington Law Review,* December 1965. The authors later identified it as the first article on Title VII written by feminist lawyers. They commented, "In 1965, most lawyers and government officials charged with enforcing the equal employment opportunity provisions of Title VII regarded the sex discrimination prohibition as unimportant and openly asserted that this aspect of the law need not be enforced with the same seriousness as discrimination by reason of race."[3]

Analyzing Title VII from a feminist viewpoint, Murray and Eastwood brought to their discussion the frequently overlooked interests of black workingwomen. In addition they argued that the "bona fide occupational qualification" (bfoq) exemption in the new law—which permitted an employer to hire on the basis of sex in certain instances—could open the door to its virtual repeal and should be interpreted extremely narrowly. They discussed how newspapers could assist advertisers in complying with the law's ban on sex-segregated help-wanted ads. Finally, they outlined potential conflicts between Title VII and various

[2]Blanche Wiesen Cook, *Eleanor Roosevelt, Volume One 1884–1933* (New York: Viking, 1992), p. 7.

[3]From a "1971 Note" by Murray and Eastwood, in *Radical Feminism,* ed. Anne Koedt, Ellen Levine, and Anita Rapone (New York: Quadrangle, 1973), p. 165.

state laws passed decades earlier to protect the health and safety of women workers.

The EEOC's first guidelines on sex discrimination, issued in December 1965, did interpret the bfoq exemption narrowly. However, regarding state protective labor laws that applied to women, the EEOC was indecisive, and women workers were forced to test the validity of many such laws one by one in the courts. As for newspapers' hallowed custom of listing help-wanted ads by sex, it took a U.S. Supreme Court decision in 1973 to finally end it.

THE COMMITTEE ON PRIVATE EMPLOYMENT of the President's Commission on the Status of Women noted in its report that "increased employment of women and the need for their services has brought forcefully to public attention the necessity for equal employment opportunities for that one-third of the Nation's work force composed of women. . . . "

The United States Department of Labor reports that 24 million women were in the work force as of April 1962. . . . One-eighth, or approximately 3 million, of these women are non-white, of which 2,455,000 are Negro. It is estimated that eight or nine of every ten women will be gainfully employed during some portion of their lives. Since women have a longer life span than men, many older women will be returning to the job market for longer periods of time than formerly. About three out of five women workers are married; among married women, one in three is working; among non-white married women, almost one in two. These figures show that women constitute a permanent sector of the labor force that will increase, not diminish.

Women are the responsible heads of 4,643,000, or one-tenth of all families in the United States, which constitutes a minority comparable in size to the Negro minority. Among non-white families, more than 23 percent are headed by women. Nearly half the families headed by women have incomes of less than

$3,000. Nearly three-fourths of non-white families headed by women live in poverty.

Since a substantial number of women are the responsible heads of families, the nature of their employment opportunities is crucial to the welfare of one-tenth of the families in the United States; it is, of course, also important to many other families not headed by women, but in which women contribute to family support.

If "sex" had not been added to the equal employment opportunity provisions of the Civil Rights Act of 1964, Negro women would have shared with white women the common fate of discrimination since it is exceedingly difficult to determine whether a Negro woman is being discriminated against because of race or sex. Without the addition of "sex," Title VII would have protected only half the potential Negro work force.

The Bona Fide Occupational Qualification Exception

THE MOST IMPORTANT ISSUE in administering the sex discrimination provisions of Title VII is the interpretation of the bona fide occupational qualification exception. . . .

A loose definition of bona fide occupational qualification as to sex could subvert the purpose of Title VII, which is to provide equal employment opportunity. The language of this exception in section 703(e), providing that it shall apply "in those certain instances" where it is reasonably necessary "to the normal operation of that particular business or enterprise," does not permit exclusion of women (or men) in any broad or general category of jobs.

The House Judiciary Committee report which preceded the addition of sex to the civil rights bill states that the section

provides for a very limited exception to the provisions of the title. Notwithstanding any other provisions, it shall not be an unlawful employment practice for an employer to employ persons of a particular religion or national origin in those rare situations where religion or national origin is a bona fide occupational qualification.

The application of this exception to sex discrimination should also be extremely limited. . . .

Excuses for Sex Discrimination

SEVERAL TYPES OF EXCUSES are likely to be claimed as bona fide occupational qualifications that have no relationship to ability to perform a job. One might be based on assumptions of the life patterns of women in general: for example, the assumption that women are only temporary workers because they leave to marry and raise children, or the assumption that turnover among women is high because they must leave the job if the family moves. Such assumptions are often mythical. However, even if it could be proved that women are likely to leave the job earlier, this should not justify pre-judging a particular individual.

A second excuse an employer might use for refusing to hire a woman is sex prejudice on the part of the public, customers, other employees, or some other group. Similarly, this assumption may be false; even if the assumption could be proved true, the prejudice may not affect the particular woman's performance of the job; she may even be able to overcome the prejudice and perhaps change the discriminatory attitudes. . . .

A third excuse employers might offer as a bona fide occupational qualification is based on the assumption that certain attributes are peculiar to one sex. For example, women express emotions differently than men; men may be considered less capable of operating intricate equipment; men are stronger than women; women have more endurance than men, and so forth. Individual variations are, of course, more significant than any generality as to characteristics, even if the generality can be shown to be valid and the characteristic be relevant to performance of the job. . . .

Employment Advertisements

UNDER SECTION 704(b) of the Civil Rights Act, employment advertisements may not indicate a preference, limitation, specification, or discrimination based on sex except where sex is a bona fide occupational qualification for employment. . . .

The continued use of sex-segregated newspaper advertisements indicates that compliance with section 704(b) of the Civil Rights Act is very slow. Newspapers could assist employers and employment agencies in complying with this provision . . . by discontinuing separate help-wanted columns for men and women. A few newspapers—for example *The Blade* (Toledo, Ohio), *Toledo Times, The Phoenix Gazette,* the *Honolulu Star Bulletin*—have done this. *The Blade* and *Toledo Times* also print the following notice:

> Attention: Help Wanted Advertisers. Effective July 2, 1965, it will be unlawful to discriminate among employment applicants because of sex unless this is a bona fide occupation requirement. This is one of the provisions of the new Civil Rights Act and is covered in Title VII, section 704(b) of the Act. No reference to sex should be made in your ad unless necessary for the performance of the job. The Blade and Toledo Times suggest you consult your legal counsel if you have questions regarding the new Act.

Where sex is a bona fide occupational qualification, it could be specified in the individual advertisements. Sex-segregated columns encourage employers to place sex labels on jobs, thereby unnecessarily restricting employment opportunities of both men and women.

Women are likely to be discouraged from applying for a job listed under a newspaper column heading that specifies men, even if the advertisement is accompanied by some form of disclaimer and disavowal of intent to violate federal or state law. The better paying jobs are often listed in the male column. Even for those women who would have the courage to apply for positions listed under the male column, the necessity of reading both male and female columns instead of one column would be, at best, an inconvenience. . . .

Effect of Title VII on State Laws
Regulating the Employment of Women

THE MAJOR TYPES OF STATE LAWS regulating the employment of women are: laws prohibiting the employment of women in certain occupations, such as employment in bars and mines; maximum hour laws for women; minimum wage laws for women; laws prohibiting the employment of women during certain hours of the night in certain industries; weight lifting limitations for women; and laws requiring special facilities for women employees, such as seats and restrooms.

The debate in the House of Representatives when "sex" was added to Title VII of the civil rights bill indicates that both proponents and opponents of the amendment thought it might remove the "restriction" or "protection," depending on the point of view, of these state labor laws. . . .[4]

A law prohibiting the employment of women in certain occupations might require an employer to do an act that would be an unlawful employment practice under the Civil Rights Act; such a state law would require an employer to refuse to hire a woman because of her sex even though she were otherwise qualified.

On the other hand, a minimum wage law for women does not require an employer to discriminate in payment of compensation. Such a law merely prescribes a standard for women; the lack of a legal standard for men does not affirmatively permit discrimination against men. Under this reasoning, the employer

[4]Speaking in favor of the amendment, Rep. Griffiths stated, "Some people have suggested to me that labor opposes 'no discrimination on account of sex' because they feel that through the years protective legislation has been built up to safeguard the health of women. Some protective legislation was to safeguard the health of women, but it should have safeguarded the health of men, also. Most of the so-called protective legislation has really been to protect men's rights in better paying jobs. . . ."

would not be relieved from complying with state minimum wage laws for women. To comply with Title VII, however, he would have to pay male employees the same wage he pays female employees doing the same work. As a practical matter, there are relatively few cases where men are paid less than women at the minimum wage level.

Similarly, state laws requiring rest periods and special facilities, such as seats, dressing rooms, or restrooms, for women would not necessarily permit discrimination in the conditions of employment merely because the requirements are imposed only for women employees. Nor do they affirmatively permit an employer to refuse to hire a woman. To comply with Title VII, the employer could provide for male employees what the state law requires him to provide for female employees.

More difficult problems are presented by state laws prohibiting the employment of women in excess of a specified maximum hours per day or week, laws prohibiting the employment of women between certain hours at night, and laws imposing weight lifting limitations. These laws would be consistent with Title VII only if the employer could readjust the manner of operating his business so that the treatment of all his employees, male or female, met the standards prescribed for females under state law. This would mean, however, that an employer might have to discontinue overtime employment entirely, close his business during certain hours of the night, or reduce the weight of his equipment or product. This result, of course, would be unrealistic and far removed from the purpose of the Civil Rights Act to prohibit class discrimination.

It could be argued that, since compliance with these state laws would impose unreasonable requirements on employers, compliance may be tantamount to requiring employers to refuse to hire women at all for certain jobs; such a requirement would be unlawful under Title VII except in cases where being a male is a bona fide occupational qualification.

State maximum hour laws for women are the most controversial of the state protective laws as well as the most common. Forty-three states and the District of Columbia have laws that regulate the number of hours, daily or weekly or both, of work for women in one or more industries. The President's Commission on the Status of Women stated that "the best way to discourage excessive hours for all workers is by broad and effective minimum wage coverage, both federal and state, providing overtime of at least time and a half the regular rate for all hours in excess of eight a day or forty a week." . . . The Commission further recommended that executive, administrative, and professional women be exempt from existing maximum hour laws and noted that such women "frequently find that limitations on hours adversely affect their opportunities for employment and advancement." . . .

The recommendations of the state commissions on the status of women show that the states will be moving toward elimination of sex distinctions in labor legislation if the recommendations of the commissions are implemented. For example, the Washington Governor's Commission recommended repeal of the state laws regulating hours of work for women only. The New York Governor's Committee recommended re-examination of the state's laws regulating hours of work and conditions of labor for women. The Tennessee Governor's Commission also recommended study of the question of maximum hour laws "to enhance further employment opportunities for women." The North Carolina Governor's Commission recommended legislation to prohibit wage, salary, or hours discrimination on the basis of sex and to provide uniformity for men and women in hours legislation.

Twenty-one states and Puerto Rico prohibit or regulate night work by women in certain occupations or industries. The Report of the President's Commission on the Status of Women states:

> Night work, especially on the graveyard shift, is undesirable for most people, and should be discouraged for both men and women. Overly rigid prohibitions, however, may work to the disadvantage of women in some circumstances. Strict regulations to prevent abuse are therefore normally preferable to prohibitions.

Twelve states restrict the amount of weight women employees may lift, carry, or lift and carry. In those states where the restriction may be applicable to any occupation the highest maximums established are as follows: Utah—fifteen pounds; Alaska and Ohio—twenty-five pounds; Georgia—thirty pounds; Michigan—thirty-five pounds. The President's Commission pointed out:

> Restrictions that set fixed maximum limits upon weights women are allowed to lift do not take account of individual differences, are sometimes unrealistic and always rigid. They should be replaced by flexible regulations, applicable to both men and women and set by appropriate regulatory bodies.

In view of the waning utility of these state protective laws that make compliance with Title VII difficult, relatively little harm would result if employers were relieved of complying with the state laws. . . . Furthermore, attempts to preserve all state protective laws under the bona fide occupational qualification exception could virtually read "sex" out of the Civil Rights Act.

The problem of possible conflict between Title VII and a state law regulating the employment of women is likely to be short lived. Although the effect of state protective laws for women in elevating labor standards for all workers should not be underrated, the trend is away from sex distinctions in labor standards legislation and towards recognition of governmental responsibility in providing equality of opportunity. . . .

Conclusion

ACCORDING WOMEN . . . EQUAL EMPLOYMENT OPPORTUNITY, through positive implementation of Title VII of the Civil Rights Act of 1964, would not likely result in any immediate, drastic change in the pattern of women's employment. But great scientific and social changes have already taken place, such as longer life span, smaller families, and lower infant death rate, with the result that motherhood consumes smaller proportions of women's lives. Thus, the effects of sex discrimination are felt by more women today.

The recent increase in activity concerning the status of women indicates that we are gradually coming to recognize that the proper role of the law is not to protect women by restrictions and confinement, but to protect both sexes from discrimination.

We are entering the age of human rights. In the United States, perhaps our most important concerns are with the rights to vote and to representative government and with equal rights to education and employment. Hopefully, our economy will outgrow concepts of class competition, such as Negro v. white, youth v. age, or male v. female, and, at least in matters of employment, standards of merit and individual quality will control rather than prejudice.

Sisterhood

A Kind of Memo
from Casey Hayden and Mary King to a Number of Other Women in the Peace and Freedom Movements

From the outset of the civil rights movement, women played a prominent part. Rosa Parks, a black woman from Montgomery, Alabama, set off a boycott of public transportation when she refused to give up her seat in a bus to a white passenger. Ella Baker, a seasoned NAACP leader who helped found the Student Nonviolent Coordinating Committee (SNCC), inspired many of the younger generation of civil rights activists. And Fannie Lou Hamer, a former Mississippi sharecropper, challenged the regular delegates from her state at the 1964 Democratic National Convention. Among the thousands of brave, idealistic young people, both black and white, who enlisted in the fight for racial justice, many were female.

In 1963 a young white college graduate named Mary King joined the staff of SNCC in Atlanta. She worked there through the 1964 Mississippi Freedom Summer, which brought 800 student volunteers from all over the United States to Mississippi for a few months to teach in "freedom schools" and assist in voter registration. Afterward, SNCC called a meeting at Waveland, Mississippi, to plan the future of the organization. King decided to write a position paper for Waveland, raising the question "of how my growing perception of myself as a woman might affect the structure and program of SNCC." But, as she recalled in her memoir, *Freedom Song,* "When it came time to sit down at the typewriter, I was shaken with doubt." King was convinced the reaction of her co-workers would be ridicule, since within the civil rights movement at that time "women's rights had no meaning and indeed did not exist."

King's "growing perception" of herself as a woman had come about as a result of her observation of the unequal treatment of women in SNCC, as well as through her reading. She and a former roommate, Casey Hayden, another female staff member at SNCC, had spent many evenings after work discussing both *The Second Sex* and the fiction of Doris Lessing. Now King approached her friend with her plan, and Hayden said she would join in the statement.

"We decided not to venture into the profound implications of the worldwide second-class status of women which Simone de Beauvoir had sharpened for us, but to limit the paper to behavior in the movement," King recounted. The resulting statement pointed out that assumptions of male superiority are as widespread and deep-rooted as assumptions of white supremacy—and just as crippling to the victim: "Consider why it is in SNCC that women who are competent, qualified, and experienced are automatically assigned to the 'female' kinds of jobs"—typing, desk work, cooking—"yet they are not given equal say-so when it comes to day-to-day decision making." When the paper was presented at Waveland, in November 1964, the response, as feared, was "crushing criticism."[1]

A year later Hayden and King coauthored a second document on the same topic and mailed it to forty women who were active in movements for social change; it was subsequently published in *Liberation* magazine, a pacifist periodical. This memo, reprinted here in full, was composed as American women were on the brink of the largest and most powerful feminist movement ever known. But its authors—isolated from feminist circles forming in the North among older, more established women—

[1]Mary King, *Freedom Song: A Personal Story of the 1960s Civil Rights Movement* (New York: Morrow, 1987), pp. 443–467. The position paper is reprinted in an appendix, pp. 567–569.

clearly had no idea of what lay just ahead. Their touching appeal to female comrades—"Perhaps we can start to talk with each other more openly"—was uttered in the lonely certainty that no united effort in behalf of women was imaginable at that time.

November 18, 1965

WE'VE TALKED A LOT, to each other and to some of you, about our own and other women's problems in trying to live in our personal lives and in our work as independent and creative people. In these conversations we've found what seem to be recurrent ideas or themes. Maybe we can look at these things many of us perceive, often as a result of insights learned from the movement:

· Sex and caste: There seem to be many parallels that can be drawn between treatment of Negroes and treatment of women in our society as a whole. But in particular, women we've talked to who work in the movement seem to be caught up in a common-law caste system that operates, sometimes subtly, forcing them to work around or outside hierarchical structures of power which may exclude them. Women seem to be placed in the same position of assumed subordination in personal situations too. It is a caste system which, at its worst, uses and exploits women.

This is complicated by several facts, among them: (1) The caste system is not institutionalized by law (women have the right to vote, to sue for divorce, etc.); (2) Women can't withdraw from the situation (à la nationalism) or overthrow it; (3) There are biological differences (even though those biological differences are usually discussed or accepted without taking present and future technology into account so we probably can't be sure what these differences mean). Many people who are very hip to the implications of the racial caste system, even people in the movement, don't seem to be able to see the sexual-caste system, and if the question is raised they respond with: "That's the way it's supposed to be. There are biological differences." Or with other statements which recall a white segregationist confronted with integration.

• Women and problems of work: The caste-system perspective dictates the roles assigned to women in the movement, and certainly even more to women outside the movement. Within the movement, questions arise in situations ranging from relationships of women organizers to men in the community, to who cleans the freedom house, to who holds leadership positions, to who does secretarial work, and to who acts as spokesman for groups. Other problems arise between women with varying degrees of awareness of themselves as being as capable as men but held back from full participation, or between women who see themselves as needing more control of their work than other women demand. And there are problems with relationships between white women and black women.

• Women and personal relations with men: Having learned from the movement to think radically about the personal worth and abilities of people whose role in society had gone unchallenged before, a lot of women in the movement have begun trying to apply those lessons to their own relations with men. Each of us probably has her own story of the various results, and of the internal struggle occasioned by trying to break out of very deeply learned fears, needs, and self-perceptions, and of what happens when we try to replace them with concepts of people and freedom learned from the movement and organizing.

• Institutions: Nearly everyone has real questions about those institutions which shape perspectives on men and women: marriage, childrearing patterns, women's (and men's) magazines, etc. People are beginning to think about and even to experiment with new forms in these areas.

• Men's reactions to the questions raised here: A very few men seem to feel, when they hear conversations involving these problems, that they have a right to be present and participate in them, since they are so deeply involved. At the same time, very few men can respond nondefensively, since the whole idea is either beyond their comprehension or threatens and exposes them. The usual response is laughter. That inability to see the whole issue as serious, as the straitjacketing of both sexes, and as societally determined often shapes our own response so that we learn to think in their terms about ourselves and to feel silly rather than to trust our inner feelings. The problems we're listing here, and what others have said about them, are therefore largely drawn from conversations among women only—and that difficulty in establishing dialogue with men is a recurring theme among people we've talked to.

• Lack of community for discussion: Nobody is writing, or organizing, or talking publicly about women in any way that reflects the problems that various women in the movement come across and which we've tried to touch above. Consider this quote from an article in the centennial issue of *The Nation*:[2]

> However equally we consider men and women, the work plans for husbands and wives cannot be given equal weight. A woman should not aim for "a second-level career" because she is a *woman;* from girlhood on she should recognize that, if she is also going to be a wife and mother, she will not be able to give as much to her work as she would if single. That is, she should not feel that she cannot aspire to directing the laboratory simply because she is a woman, but rather because she is also a wife and mother; as such, her work as a lab technician (or the equivalent in another field) should bring both satisfaction and the knowledge that, through it, she is fulfilling an additional role, making an additional contribution.

And that's about as deep as the analysis goes publicly, which is not nearly so deep as we've heard many of you go in chance conversations.

The reason we want to try to open up dialogue is mostly subjective. Working in the movement often intensifies personal problems, especially if we start trying to apply things we're learning there to our personal lives. Perhaps we can start to talk with each other more openly than in the past and create a com-

[2]In 1965.—*Ed.*

munity of support for each other so we can deal with ourselves and others with integrity and can therefore keep working.

Objectively, the chances seem nil that we could start a movement based on anything as distant to general American thought as a sex-caste system. Therefore, most of us will probably want to work full time on problems such as war, poverty, race. The very fact that the country can't face, much less deal with, the questions we're raising means that the movement is one place to look for some relief. Real efforts at dialogue within the movement and with whatever liberal groups, community women, or students might listen are justified. That is, all the problems between men and women and all the problems of women functioning in society as equal human beings are among the most basic that people face. We've talked in the movement about trying to build a society which would see basic human problems (which are now seen as private troubles), as public problems and would try to shape institutions to meet human needs rather than shaping people to meet the needs of those with power. To raise questions like those above illustrates very directly that society hasn't dealt with some of its deepest problems and opens discussion of why that is so. (In one sense, it is a radicalizing question that can take people beyond legalistic solutions into areas of personal and institutional change.) The second objective reason we'd like to see discussion begin is that we've learned a great deal in the movement and perhaps this is one area where a determined attempt to apply ideas we've learned there can produce some new alternatives.

THE NATIONAL ORGANIZATION FOR WOMEN
STATEMENT OF PURPOSE

When the President's Commission on the Status of Women was disbanded in 1963, state commissions on the status of women were set up all around the country—yet another legacy of that influential enterprise. In 1966 Betty Friedan came to Washington, DC, to attend the annual national conference of representatives of the state commissions. "That's where it actually began," she later said.[1]

For months before the conference, women's-rights advocates in Washington had warned Friedan that the survival of the sex provision of Title VII was at risk, and briefed her on the foot-dragging of the Equal Employment Opportunity Commission (EEOC). They urged the formation of a feminist pressure group—what they dubbed an NAACP for women. Friedan agreed, and one evening during the conference she made the proposal to a group of about fifteen women whom she had invited to her hotel room. Following heated debate, the majority of those present rejected the idea of an independent women's advocacy organization, in favor of working within existing governmental avenues. The next morning a few conference delegates who had attended the Friedan meeting tried to introduce a resolution recommending that the EEOC enforce its mandate to end sex discrimination in employment. However, conference officials informed them that they did not have the power to take any action whatsoever, not even to pass a resolution! The women were furious—and convinced, without another word being spoken, that a new organization was essential.

[1]Betty Friedan, *It Changed My Life: Writings on the Women's Movement* (New York: Random House, 1976), p. 81.

At the closing luncheon of the status-of-women conference, while Women's Bureau officials and cabinet members delivered addresses, the rebels scribbled notes to one another and held whispered conversations as they founded the National Organization for Women (NOW). Kathryn Clarenbach, head of the Wisconsin Commission on the Status of Women, was named temporary coordinator.

On October 29, 1966, the first organizing conference of NOW was held in Washington, and Betty Friedan was elected president. The NOW Statement of Purpose, adopted at that time, is reprinted here. Friedan has said that it was accepted basically as she wrote it, with one exception: "As I wrote it, it also spelled out the right of the woman to choose, and to control her own childbearing, which meant access to birth control and abortion—the others said that was too controversial."[2]

In one year, NOW's membership quadrupled, going from 300 to 1,200. At its national convention in 1967, NOW endorsed reproductive rights.

WE, MEN AND WOMEN who hereby constitute ourselves as the National Organization for Women, believe that the time has come for a new movement toward true equality for all women in America, and toward a fully equal partnership of the sexes, as part of the world-wide revolution of human rights now taking place within and beyond our national borders.

The purpose of NOW is to take action to bring women into full participation in the mainstream of American society now, exercising all the privileges and responsibilities thereof in truly equal partnership with men.

We believe the time has come to move beyond the abstract argument, discussion, and symposia over the status and special nature of women which has raged in America in recent years;

[2]Ibid., pp. 83–84.

the time has come to confront, with concrete action, the conditions that now prevent women from enjoying the equality of opportunity and freedom of choice which is their right, as individual Americans, and as human beings.

NOW is dedicated to the proposition that women, first and foremost, are human beings, who, like all other people in our society, must have the chance to develop their fullest human potential. We believe that women can achieve such equality only by accepting to the full the challenges and responsibilities they share with all other people in our society, as part of the decision-making mainstream of American political, economic, and social life.

We organize to initiate or support action, nationally, or in any part of this nation, by individuals or organizations, to break through the silken curtain of prejudice and discrimination against women in government, industry, the professions, the churches, the political parties, the judiciary, the labor unions, in education, science, medicine, law, religion, and every other field of importance in American society.

Enormous changes taking place in our society make it both possible and urgently necessary to advance the unfinished revolution of women toward true equality, now. With life span lengthened to nearly seventy-five years it is no longer either necessary or possible for women to devote the greater part of their lives to child-rearing; yet childbearing and rearing—which continues to be a most important part of most women's lives—still is used to justify barring women from equal professional and economic participation and advance.

Today's technology has reduced most of the productive chores which women once performed in the home and in mass-production industries based upon routine unskilled labor. This same technology has virtually eliminated the quality of muscular strength as a criterion for filling most jobs, while intensifying American industry's need for creative intelligence. In view of this new industrial revolution created by automation in the mid-twentieth century, women can and must participate in old and new fields of society in full equality—or become permanent outsiders.

Despite all the talk about the status of American women in recent years, the actual position of women in the United States has declined, and is declining, to an alarming degree throughout the 1950s and '60s. Although 46.4 percent of all American women between the ages of eighteen and sixty-five now work outside the home, the overwhelming majority—75 percent—are in routine clerical, sales, or factory jobs, or they are household workers, cleaning women, hospital attendants. About two-thirds of Negro women workers are in the lowest paid service occupations. Working women are becoming increasingly—not less—concentrated on the bottom of the job ladder. As a consequence full-time women workers today earn on the average only 60 percent of what men earn, and that wage gap has been increasing over the past twenty-five years in every major industry group. . . .

Further, with higher education increasingly essential in today's society, too few women are entering and finishing college or going on to graduate or professional school. Today, women earn only one in three of the B.A.'s and M.A.'s granted, and one in ten of the Ph.D.'s.

In all the professions considered of importance to society, and in the executive ranks of industry and government, women are losing ground. Where they are present it is only a token handful. Women comprise less than 1 percent of federal judges; less than 4 percent of all lawyers; 7 percent of doctors. Yet women represent 51 percent of the U.S. population. And, increasingly, men are replacing women in the top positions in secondary and elementary schools, in social work, and in libraries—once thought to be women's fields.

Official pronouncements of the advance in the status of women hide not only the reality of this dangerous decline, but the fact that nothing is being done to stop [it]. The excellent reports of the President's Commission on the Status of Women and of the state commissions have not been fully implemented. Such commissions have power only to advise. They have no power to enforce their recommendations; nor have they the freedom to organize American women and men to press for action on them. The reports of these commissions have, however, created a basis upon which it is now possible to build.

Discrimination in employment on the basis of sex is now prohibited by federal law, in Title VII of the Civil Rights Act of 1964. But although nearly one-third of the cases brought before the Equal Employment Opportunity Commission during the first year dealt with sex discrimination and the proportion is increasing dramatically, the Commission has not made clear its intention to enforce the law with the same seriousness on behalf of women as of other victims of discrimination. Many of these cases were Negro women, who are the victims of the double discrimination of race and sex. Until now, too few women's organizations and official spokesmen have been willing to speak out against these dangers facing women. Too many women have been restrained by the fear of being called "feminist."

There is no civil rights movement to speak for women, as there has been for Negroes and other victims of discrimination. The National Organization for Women must therefore begin to speak.

WE BELIEVE that the power of American law, and the protection guaranteed by the U.S. Constitution to the civil rights of all individuals, must be effectively applied and enforced to isolate and remove patterns of sex discrimination, to ensure equality of opportunity in employment and education, and equality of civil and political rights and responsibilities on behalf of women, as well as for Negroes and other deprived groups.

We realize that women's problems are linked to many broader questions of social justice; their solution will require concerted action by many groups. Therefore, convinced that human rights for all are indivisible, we expect to give active support to the common cause of equal rights for all those who suffer discrimination and deprivation, and we call upon other organizations committed to such goals to support our efforts toward equality for women.

WE DO NOT ACCEPT the token appointment of a few women to high-level positions in government and industry as a substitute for a serious continuing effort to recruit and advance women according to their individual abilities. To this end, we urge American government and industry to mobilize the same resources of ingenuity and command with which they have

solved problems of far greater difficulty than those now imped-
ing the progress of women.

WE BELIEVE that this nation has a capacity at least as great
as other nations, to innovate new social institutions which will
enable women to enjoy true equality of opportunity and responsibility in society, without conflict with their responsibilities as
mothers and homemakers. In such innovations, America does
not lead the Western world, but lags by decades behind many
European countries. We do not accept the traditional assumption that a woman has to choose between marriage and motherhood, on the one hand, and serious participation in industry or
the professions on the other. We question the present expectation that all normal women will retire from job or profession for
ten or fifteen years, to devote their full time to raising children,
only to reenter the job market at a relatively minor level. This,
in itself, is a deterrent to the aspirations of women, to their acceptance into management or professional training courses, and
to the very possibility of equality of opportunity or real choice,
for all but a few women. Above all, we reject the assumption
that these problems are the unique responsibility of each individual woman, rather than a basic social dilemma which society
must solve. True equality of opportunity and freedom of choice
for women requires such practical and possible innovations as a
nationwide network of child-care centers, which will make it
unnecessary for women to retire completely from society until
their children are grown, and national programs to provide retraining for women who have chosen to care for their own children full-time.

WE BELIEVE that it is as essential for every girl to be educated to her full potential of human ability as it is for every
boy—with the knowledge that such education is the key to effective participation in today's economy and that, for a girl as
for a boy, education can only be serious when there is expectation that it will be used in society. We believe that American educators are capable of devising means of imparting such
expectations to girl students. Moreover, we consider the decline
in the proportion of women receiving higher and professional
education to be evidence of discrimination. This discrimination

may take the form of quotas against the admission of women to colleges and professional schools; lack of encouragement by parents, counselors, and educators; denial of loans or fellowships; or the traditional or arbitrary procedures in graduate and professional training geared in terms of men, which inadvertently discriminate against women. We believe that the same serious attention must be given to high school dropouts who are girls as to boys.

WE REJECT the current assumptions that a man must carry the sole burden of supporting himself, his wife, and family, and that a woman is automatically entitled to lifelong support by a man upon her marriage, or that marriage, home, and family are primarily woman's world and responsibility—hers, to dominate, his to support. We believe that a true partnership between the sexes demands a different concept of marriage, an equitable sharing of the responsibilities of home and children and of the economic burdens of their support. We believe that proper recognition should be given to the economic and social value of homemaking and child-care. To these ends, we will seek to open a reexamination of laws and mores governing marriage and divorce, for we believe that the current state of "half-equality" between the sexes discriminates against both men and women, and is the cause of much unnecessary hostility between the sexes.

WE BELIEVE that women must now exercise their political rights and responsibilities as American citizens. They must refuse to be segregated on the basis of sex into separate-and-not-equal ladies' auxiliaries in the political parties, and they must demand representation according to their numbers in the regularly constituted party committees—at local, state, and national levels—and in the informal power structure, participating fully in the selection of candidates and political decision-making, and running for office themselves.

IN THE INTERESTS OF THE HUMAN DIGNITY OF WOMEN, we will protest, and endeavor to change, the false image of women now prevalent in the mass media, and in the texts, ceremonies, laws, and practices of our major social institutions. Such images perpetuate contempt for women by society and by women for themselves. We are similarly opposed to all policies and practices—in church, state, college, factory, or office—which, in the guise of protectiveness, not only deny opportunities but also foster in women self-denigration, dependence, and evasion of responsibility, undermine their confidence in their own abilities, and foster contempt for women.

NOW WILL HOLD ITSELF INDEPENDENT OF ANY POLITICAL PARTY in order to mobilize the political power of all women and men intent on our goals. We will strive to ensure that no party, candidate, president, senator, governor, congressman, or any public official who betrays or ignores the principle of full equality between the sexes is elected or appointed to office. If it is necessary to mobilize the votes of men and women who believe in our cause, in order to win for women the final right to be fully free and equal human beings, we so commit ourselves.

WE BELIEVE THAT women will do most to create a new image of women by acting now, and by speaking out in behalf of their own equality, freedom, and human dignity—not in pleas for special privilege, nor in enmity toward men, who are also victims of the current half-equality between the sexes—but in an active, self-respecting partnership with men. By so doing, women will develop confidence in their own ability to determine actively, in partnership with men, the conditions of their life, their choices, their future, and their society.

AN SDS STATEMENT
ON THE LIBERATION OF WOMEN

The large and vigorous left-wing youth movement that shook the United States and other Western democracies in the 1960s had no feminist component for several years. However, halfway through the decade this situation changed suddenly, dramatically, and radically, which was the way most things happened then.

The biggest and most influential New Left organization in the United States in the mid-sixties was Students for a Democratic Society (SDS). The goals of SDS at that time included the eradication of racism and poverty, more student control in colleges and universities, and withdrawal of U.S. forces from Vietnam—but they did *not* include any recognition of the oppression of women. Then, in December 1965, a group of women attending an SDS conference conducted a workshop titled "Women in the Movement," which produced a statement calling for increased "initiative and participation by women" in SDS.[1] The intrepid few who brought this fairly innocuous statement to the floor were reportedly greeted with "storms of ridicule and verbal abuse," such as "She just needs a good screw" or "She's a castrating female."[2]

Taunts and hostility, however, did not dampen female protest within SDS. On the contrary, in the following months women's caucuses and workshops became familiar features of SDS gatherings, and complaints from women became more forceful. A year and a half later the organization was still

[1]Kirkpatrick Sale, *SDS* (New York: Random House, 1973), p. 252.
[2]Marlene Dixon, "On Women's Liberation," *Radical America,* vol. 4, no. 2, February 1970, p. 27.

racked with discord over the woman question. At a convention in Ann Arbor, Michigan, in June 1967, a statement drafted in the Women's Liberation Workshop challenged "brothers" in SDS to root out "male chauvinism" within *themselves* as well as within the organization, and it offered a program for achieving this objective.[3] The assembled delegates approved the program—a gesture that probably reflected recognition of the groundswell of feminist sentiment among SDS women more than it did any true enthusiasm for self-improvement among the "brothers." For when the women's statement was reprinted in *New Left Notes,* the official SDS organ, it was accompanied by a derisive drawing of a young woman wearing a short, polka-dot, baby-doll dress with puffed sleeves and matching panties, and holding a placard that read: "We want our rights and we want them now!"

The 1967 Ann Arbor statement is reprinted here just as it appeared in *New Left Notes.* It is one of the earliest documents to use the term *women's liberation.*

———————————————————————

THE SDS NATIONAL CONVENTION adopts the following statement and program as written by the Women's Liberation Workshop.

We call for all programs which will free women from their traditional roles in order that we may participate with all of our resources and energies in meaningful and creative activity. The family unit perpetuates the traditional role of women and the autocratic and paternalistic role of men. Therefore we must seek new forms that will allow children to develop in an environment which is democratic and where the relationships between people are those of equal human beings. These new forms will allow men to benefit from the experience of and responsibility for the

[3]Sale, *SDS,* p. 362 n, credits Jane Adams, Susan Cloke, Jean Peak, and Elizabeth Sutherland with authorship of this document.

protection and continuation of life. The following suggestions are programs which point in the direction of the new relationships which we are creating:

1. The creation of communal child care centers which would be staffed by the men and women and controlled by the staff and children involved in each center.

2. In order to help women in their struggle for independence we call for the right of women to choose when they will have children. This means (a) the dissemination of birth control information and devices to all women regardless of age and marital status, and (b) the availability of a competent medical abortion for all women who so desire.

3. Ultimately technology and automation will eliminate work which is now necessary for the maintenance of the home. Until this occurs every adult person living in the household will have to assume an equal share of the work.

People who identify with the movement and feel that their own lives are part of the base to bring about radical social change must recognize the necessity for the liberation of women. Our brothers must recognize that because they were brought up in the United States they cannot be free of the burden of male chauvinism.

1. Therefore we demand that our brothers recognize that they must deal with their own problems of male chauvinism in their personal, social, and political relationships.

2. It is obvious from this convention that full advantage is not taken of the abilities and potential contributions of movement women. We call upon women to demand full participation in all aspects of movement work, from licking stamps to assuming leadership positions.

3. People in leadership positions must be aware of the dynamic of creating leadership and are responsible for cultivating all of the resources available to the movement.

4. All SDS chapters must recognize that campus regulations discriminate against women in particular and any program must include in its demands a call for women's rights. The above is also true of all programs conceived and initiated by SDS.

Educating people and generating discussion about the liberation of women shall be the responsibility of the internal education arm of SDS:

1. The editor of NLN [*New Left Notes*] shall solicit articles on the subject.

2. Bibliography and pamphlets on the subject shall be part of the program.

3. A committee shall be set up by the National Council to develop an analysis of the exploitation of women as producers and consumers in the American capitalist economy, and to present a report to the December NC upon which concrete proposals of a programmatic nature can be based.

We seek the liberation of all human beings. The struggle for liberation of women must be part of the larger fight for human freedom. We recognize the difficulty our brothers will have in dealing with male chauvinism and we will assume our full responsibility in helping to resolve the contradiction.

freedom now! we love you!

The basis for discussion was laid with a presentation by the women in the Women's Liberation Workshop of the following analysis. "The following analysis of women's role came out of the Women's Liberation Workshop; as such it cannot be changed and is therefore not open to debate.

"What is open to this body is the acceptance or refusal of programs designed to (1) free women to participate in other meaningful activities and (2) relieve our brothers of the burden of male chauvinism.

"Analysis: In the world today there are three main divisions among people: Those of the capitalist world, the socialist world and the Third World. The crisis of our time is the transformation from capitalism to socialism. The role of the Third World in this transformation is revolutionary, but an integral part of their fight is the necessity of their own independence.

"As we analyze the position of women in capitalist society and especially in the United States we find that women are in a colonial relationship to men and we recognize ourselves as part of the Third World. Although we realize that our sisters in the socialist world have problems with male supremacy, we feel that an analysis of their position would be different than ours and is not necessary for the purposes of this statement.

"Women, because of their colonial relationship to men, have to fight for their own independence. This fight for our own independence will lead to the growth and development of the revolutionary movement in this country. Only the independent woman can be truly effective in the larger revolutionary struggle."

With a woman in the chair, debate opened over the question of male participation and voting on the analysis. This was handled by having a general discussion of the position presented in the resolution in a Committee of the Whole and then the Women's Liberation committee withdrew the analysis section as something to be voted on.

Discussion focused around the analogy used to relate American women to the Third World. A number of critiques were raised over the lack of material dealing with the role of women in the economy, etc., however, it was generally agreed upon that the importance in the analogy was its placing of the problem of male chauvinism within a clear social and political context [and] that there is a vital need for much study and discussion in order to begin to develop a solid analysis from which we can begin to seriously attack the problem of male chauvinism.

BEVERLY JONES

Toward a Female
Liberation Movement

During 1967 and 1968 leftist women in several cities around the country banded together in small, independent groups to discuss gender discrimination and how to combat it. Most were former movement activists: either refugees from SNCC—which, with adoption of "black power" tactics, had become inhospitable to whites—or New Left dropouts disillusioned by the sexism of male comrades.

What was probably the first of these discussion groups—which evolved into the Chicago Westside Group—was founded in fall 1967 by Jo Freeman, Naomi Weisstein, Shulamith Firestone, and a few other women.[1] As described by Weisstein decades later, their motivation was unfocused—composed of anger, inchoate need, confusion, and frustration—and their purpose was equally unclear. The women started to talk, she wrote, "and we found that we couldn't stop talking. We talked about the contempt and hostility we felt from men. . . . We were afraid to call ourselves feminists, since in the New Left that was hopelessly 'bourgeois.' We finally came up with 'women's liberation,' an analogy with Third World struggles (since we couldn't yet imagine the legitimacy of our own)." Their talk at first centered on socialist theory and women, "but after we had kicked around capitalist disaccumulation for a while, we zoomed right back and talked about monogamy and . . . community and . . . children."[2]

---

[1]Other founders of the Chicago group were Heather Booth, Amy Kesselman, Fran Rominski, and Laya Firestone.

[2]Naomi Weisstein, "Chicago '60s: Ecstasy as Our Guide," *Ms.*, September–October 1990, p. 65. Based on an earlier article published in *Phoebe*, a feminist journal, and prepared with the assistance of several friends.

Jo Freeman founded and edited a newsletter in Chicago that circulated nationally among the scattered knots of left-wing feminists. It was called *Voice of the Women's Liberation Movement*—a title that was somewhat expansive, since nothing that could rightfully be called a movement existed yet.

As they talked to one another, participants in the small groups became aware of striking similarities in their "personal" experiences and attitudes; they concluded that these resemblances stemmed from the similar limitations and expectations society imposes on all women. "The first step" in female liberation, advised Beverly Jones in the selection that follows, "is to accept our plight as a common plight, to see other women as reflections of ourselves." It was a thrilling insight, one that freed the individual woman from the crippling burdens of self-blame and self-contempt.

Another belief that took hold in some groups was that men enjoy special privileges in life as a direct result of the oppression of the opposite sex. No matter how progressive a man might be in theory, he was not likely to give up his privileged status easily. Thus, men could not be counted on as allies in the fight against sexism—they were, in fact, not part of the solution but part of the problem. The next step was to realize how deep and tenacious the roots of sexism were, and to shed the facile notion that socialism would automatically solve everything.

Ultimately, radical women split into two camps. On one side were the "radical feminists," who believed that the subordinate status of women was caused by a system of sex-role stereotypes that could be dislodged only by a *separate* movement dedicated solely to women's liberation. On the other side were the "politicos," those women who saw capitalism as the root of the problem and who continued to work against sexism from within various New Left organizations.

The following reading is excerpted from an early radical-feminist position paper that became known as the Florida Paper because both authors participated in a women's group in Gainesville, Florida. First published in the fall of 1968 by the New England Free Press, and widely read and discussed by like-minded women, the Florida Paper was extremely influential.

The excerpt here is from Part I, by Beverly Jones (b. 1927); Part II (not reprinted here) was written by Judith Brown, a younger associate. The essay begins by sharply criticizing the 1967 statement by SDS women, and goes on to outline what must be done to found an effective movement for the liberation of women.

The Manifesto

FOR A MIDDLE-AGED FEMALE accustomed to looking to militant youth for radical leadership, it was a shock to read the Women's Manifesto which issued from the female caucus of the national SDS convention last summer (1967). . . . Here were a group of "radical women" demanding respect and leadership in a radical organization and coming on with soft-minded NAACP logic and an Urban League list of grievances and demands.[3] One need only substitute the words "white" and "black" for "male" and "female" respectively, replace references to "SDS" with "the city council," and remember all the fruitless approaches black groups made and are still making to local white power groups to realize how ludicrous this manifesto is. . . .

There is also a rather pathetic attempt on the part of the caucus to prove its credentials by mimicking the dominant group's rhetoric on power politics. Thus there ensues some verbiage about the capitalist world, the socialist world, and the Third World in which it is implied that women are somehow better off under socialism.

It must have been disappointing indeed to the women who drew up the "analysis of women's role" and insisted it be printed verbatim in *New Left Notes* to find Castro quoted the following month in the *National Guardian*[4] to the effect that he

[3]The NAACP and Urban League were disparaged by sixties radicals, who favored SNCC, the Black Panther Party, and similar groups.—*Ed.*
[4]A far left weekly newspaper.—*Ed.*

is assuredly grateful to the women of Cuba for having fought in the hills and otherwise aided the revolution, but now all that is past and women's place is once again servant to husband and children, in the home. . . .

What lessons are to be learned from this fantastic document [the Women's Manifesto], the discrimination which preceded it, and the unchanging scene which followed? I think the lessons are several and serious. I'd like to list them first and discuss each one separately.

1. People don't get radicalized (engaged with basic truths) fighting other people's battles.

2. The females in SDS (at least those who wrote the Manifesto) essentially reject an identification with their own sex and are using the language of female power in an attempt to advance themselves personally in the male power structure they are presently concerned with.

3. That for at least two reasons radical females do not understand the desperate condition of women in general. In the first place, as students they occupy some sexy, sexless, limbo area where they are treated by males in general with less discrimination than they will ever again face. And in the second place, few of them are married or if married have children.

4. For their own salvation and for the good of the movement, women must form their own group and work primarily for female liberation.

People Don't Get Radicalized Fighting Other People's Battles

No one can say that women in the movement lack courage. As a matter of fact they have been used, aside from their clerical role, primarily as bodies on the line. Many have been thrown out of school, disowned by their families, clubbed by the cops, raped by the nuts, and gone to jail with everyone else.

What happened to them throughout the movement is very much what happened to all whites in the early civil rights days. Whites acted out of moral principles, many acted courageously, and they became liberalized but never radicalized. Which is to say, they never quite came to grips with the reality of anybody's situation. It is interesting to speculate on why this should be the case. At least one reason, it seems to me, is that people who set about to help other people generally manage to maintain important illusions about our society, how it operates, and what is required to change it. It is not just that they somehow manage to maintain these illusions, they are compelled to maintain them by their refusal to recognize the full measure of their own individual oppression, the means by which it is brought about, and what it would take to alter their condition.

Any honest appraisal of their own condition in this society would presumably lead people out of logic, impulse, and desire for self-preservation, to shoot at the guys who are shooting at them. Namely, first of all, to fight their own battles. . . .

The best thing that ever happened to potential white radicals in civil rights happened when they got thrown out by SNCC and were forced to face their own oppression in their own world, when they started fighting for control of the universities, against the draft, the war, and the business order. And the best thing that may yet happen to potentially radical young women is that they will be driven out of both of these groups. That they will be forced to stop fighting for the "movement" and start fighting primarily for the liberation and independence of women.

Only when they seriously undertake this struggle will they begin to understand that they aren't just ignored or exploited—they are feared, despised, and enslaved.

If the females in SDS ever really join the battle they will quickly realize that no sweet-talking list of grievances and demands, no appeal to male conscience, no behind-the-scenes or in-the-home maneuvering is going to get power for women. If they want freedom, equality, and respect, they are going to have to organize and fight for them realistically and radically.

Radical Females Essentially Reject an Identification
with Their Sex and Use the Languge of Female

Liberation in an Attempt to Advance Themselves in the
Male Power Structure of the Movement.

. . . If the women in SDS want study committees on the problems of women, why don't they form them? If they want bibli-
ographies, why don't they gather them? If they want to protest
university discrimination against women, why don't they do
so? No one in SDS is going to stop them. They can even use
SDS auspices and publish in *New Left Notes,* for a while anyway.

But that isn't what they want. They want to be treated like
"white people" and work on the problems important to "white
people" like planning, zoning, and attracting industry, or in this
case the war, the draft, and university reform.

The trouble with using the language of black or female liberation for *this* purpose . . . is twofold. In the first place it is immoral—a Tom betrayal of a whole people. In the second place it
won't work. There is an almost exact parallel between the role
of women and the role of black people in this society. Together
they constitute the great maintenance force sustaining the white
American male. They wipe his ass and breast-feed him when he
is little, they school him in his youthful years, do his clerical
work and raise his replacements later, and all through his life in
the factories, on the migrant farms, in the restaurants, hospitals,
offices, and homes, they sew for him, stoop for him, cook for
him, clean for him, sweep, run errands, haul away his garbage,
and nurse him when his frail body falters.

Together they send him out into his own society, shining and
healthy, his mind freed from all concern with the grimy details
of living. And there in that unreal world of light and leisure he
becomes bemused and confused with ideas of glory and omnipotence. He spends his time saving the world from dragons,
or fighting evil knights, proscribing and enforcing laws and social systems, or just playing with the erector sets of manhood—
building better bridges, computers, and bombs.

Win or lose on that playground, he likes the games and wants
to continue playing—unimpeded. That means that the rest of

the population, the blacks and females who maintain this elite playboy force, must be kept at their jobs.

Oh, occasionally it occurs to one or another of the most self-conscious, self-confident, and generous white men that the system could be changed. That it might be based on something other than race or sex. But what? Who would decide? Might not the change affect the rules of the game or even the games themselves? And where would his place be in it all? It becomes too frightening to think about. It is less threatening and certainly less distracting simply to close ranks, hold fast, and keep things the way they are.

This is done by various techniques, some of which are: sprinkling the barest pinch of blacks and women over the playground to obscure the fact that it is an all white male facility; making a sacred cow out of home and family; supporting a racist and antifeminist church to befuddle the minds of the support force and to divert what little excess energy is available to it; and most importantly, developing among white men a consensus with regard to blacks and females and a loyalty to each other which supersedes that to either of the other groups or to individual members of them, thus turning each white man into an incorruptible guard of the common white male domain.

The gist of that consensus which is relevant to the point at issue here is,

1. Women and blacks are of inherently inferior and alien mentality. Their minds are vague, almost inchoate, and bound by their personal experiences (scatterbrained, or just dumb). They are incapable of truly abstract, incisive, logical, or tactical thinking.

2. Despite or perhaps because of this inferior mentality women and blacks are happy people. All they ask out of life is a little attention, somebody to screw them regularly, second-hand Cadillacs, new hats, dresses, refrigerators, and other baubles.

3. They do not join mixed groups for the stated purposes of the groups but to be with whites or to find a man.

Radical Women Do Not Really Understand the
Desperate Conditions of Women in General—As

students, they occupy some sexy, sexless limbo where
they are treated by males with less discrimination than
they will ever again face.

It may seem strange, but one of the main advantages of a female
student, married or unmarried, with or without children, is that
she is still public. She has in her classes, in her contacts on campus, the opportunity to express her ideas publicly to males and
females of all ranks. Indeed, she is expected to do so—at least in
good schools, or in good seminars. Anyway, she has this opportunity on an equal basis with men.

Moreover, her competition with men, at least scholastically,
is condoned—built into the system. This creates in the girl an illusion of equality and harmony between the sexes very much as
a good integrated school (where students visit each other's
homes even for weekends and are always polite) creates in the
black the illusion of change and the faith in continued good relations upon graduation.

These female illusions are further nurtured by the social life
of students. Since many live in dorms or other places where they
cannot entertain members of the opposite sex,[5] most social intercourse of necessity takes place in public. I mean that people
congregate in coffee houses, pubs, movies, or at parties of the
privileged few with off-campus apartments or houses. And since
most students are unmarried, unsure of themselves, and lonely,
they are constantly on the make. Thus they dance with each
other and talk with each other. The conversation between the
sexes is not necessarily serious or profound but it takes place,
and, as we have said, takes place, in the great main, publicly.
Each tries to find out more about the other, attempts to discover
what future relations might be possible between them, tries to
impress the other in some way.

So that the female student feels like a citizen, like an individual among others in the body politic, in the civil society, in the
world of the intellect. What she doesn't understand is that upon

[5]Single-sex college dormitories that were off limits to members of the opposite sex were the rule during the sixties.—*Ed.*

graduation she is stripped of her public life and relegated to the level of private property. Enslavement is her farewell present. As things stand now, she is doomed to become someone's secretary, or someone's nurse, or someone's wife, or someone's mistress. From now on if she has some contribution to make to society she is expected to make it privately through the man who owns some part of her. . . .

But slavery is an intricate system. As an institution it cannot be maintained by force alone. Somehow or other slaves must be made to conceive of themselves as inferior beings and slave holders must not be permitted to falter in the confidence of their superiority. . . .

Almost all men are involved in the male mystique. No matter how unnecessary it may be, particularly for the bright and most able among them, each rests his ego in some measure on the basic common denominator, being a man. In the same way white people, consciously or unconsciously, derive ego support from being white, and Americans from being American.

Allowing females to participate in some group on the basis of full equality presents a direct threat to each man in that group. And though an individual male leader may be able to rise above this personal threat, he cannot deviate from the rules of the game without jeopardizing his own leadership and the group itself. If he permits the public disclosure in an irrefutable manner of the basic superiority of half of the women to half the men, he breaks the covenant and the men will not follow him. Since they are not obliged to, they will not suffer this emasculation, and the group will fall apart.

To think that women, by asserting themselves individually in SDS, can democratize it, can remove the factor of sex, is equally silly. In the first place the men will not permit it and in the second place, as things stand now, the women are simply incapable of that kind of aggressive individual assertion. The socialization process has gone too far, they are already scrambled. Meeting after meeting their silence bears witness to their feelings of inferiority. Who knows what they get out of it? Are they listening, do they understand what is being said, do they accept it, do they have reservations? Would urging them to speak out have any effect other than to cut down their numbers at the next meeting?

Though female students objectively have more freedom than most older married women, their life is already a nightmare. Totally unaware, they long ago accepted the miserable role male society assigned to them: help-mate and maintenance worker. Upon coming to college they eagerly and "voluntarily" flood the great service schools—the college of education, the college of nursing, the departments of social work, physical therapy, counseling, and clinical psychology. In some places they even major in home economics. . . .

They are also in a panic, an absolute frenzy, to fulfill their destiny: to find a man and get married. It is not that they have all been brainwashed by the media to want a husband, split-level house, three children, a dog, a cat, and a station wagon. Many just want out from under their parents. They just can't take the slow slaughter anymore but they don't have the courage to break away. They fear the wrath of the explosion but even more they fear the ensuing loneliness and isolation.

Generally, a single girl's best friend is still her family. They are the only people she can rely upon for conversation, for attention, for concern with her welfare, no matter how misdirected. And everyone needs some personal attention or they begin to experience a lack of identity. Thus the big push to find the prince charming who will replace the chains with a golden ring. . . .

Radical Women Do Not Really Understand the
Desperate Conditions of Women in General—because
so few are married or, if married, have no children.

No one would think to judge a marriage by its first hundred days. To be sure there are cases of sexual trauma, or sudden and violent misunderstandings, but in general all is happiness; the girl has finally made it, the past is but a bad dream. All good things are about to come to her. And then reality sets in. It can be held off a little as long as they are both students and particularly if they have money, but sooner or later it becomes entrenched. The man moves to insure his position of power and dominance.

There are several more or less standard pieces of armament used in this assault upon wives, but the biggest gun is generally the threat of divorce or abandonment. With a plucky woman a man may actually feel it necessary to openly and repeatedly toy with this weapon, but usually it is sufficient simply to keep it in the house undercover somewhere. We all know the bit—we have heard it and all the others I am about to mention on television marital comedies and in night club jokes; it is supposed to be funny.

The husband says to the wife who is about to go somewhere that doesn't meet with his approval, "If you do, you need never come back." Or . . . he slams his way out of the house, claiming that she is trying to destroy him, that he can no longer take these endless, senseless scenes; that "this isn't a marriage, it's a meat grinder." Or he may simply lay down the law that, God damn it, her first responsibility is to her family and he will not permit or tolerate something or other. Or if she wants to maintain the marriage she is simply going to have to accommodate herself.

There are thousands of variations on this theme and it is really very clever the way male society creates for women this premarital hell so that some man can save her from it and control her ever after by the threat of throwing her back. Degrading her further, the final crisis is usually averted or postponed by a tearful reconciliation in which the wife apologizes for her shortcomings, namely the sparks of initiative still left to her. . . .

Or, playing the part of both cops in the jailhouse interrogation scene, he may, after the first explosion, switch roles. In this double-take he becomes the calm and considerate husband, remorseful, apologizing. . . . Predictably, done in by the tender tone, she falls in with the plot and confesses. She confesses her loneliness, her dependence, her mental agony, and they discuss *her* problem. Her problem, as though it were some genetic defect, some personal shortcoming, some inscrutable psychosis. Now he can comfort her, avowing how he understands how she must feel, he only wished there were something he could do to help. . . .

Sooner or later, if she can, she has children. Assuming the husband has agreed to the event, the wife's pregnancy does abate or deflect the drift of their marriage, for a while anyway.

The pregnancy presents to the world visible proof of the husband's masculinity, potency. This visible proof shores up the basic substructure of his ego, the floor beyond which he cannot now fall. Pathetically his stock goes up in society, in his own eyes. He is a man. He is grateful to his wife and treats her, at least during the first pregnancy, with increased tenderness and respect. He pats her tummy and makes noises about mystic occurrences. And since pregnancy is not a male thing and he is a man, since this is cooperation, not competition, he can even make out that he feels her role is pretty special.

The wife is grateful. Her husband loves her. She is suffused with happiness and pride. There is at last something on her side of the division of labor which her husband views with respect, and, delight of delights, with perhaps a twinge of jealousy.

Of course, it can't last. After nine months the child is bound to be born. And there we are back at the starting gate. Generally speaking, giving birth must be like a bad trip with the added feature of prolonged physical exhaustion. . . .

The Return from the Never-Never Land

WOMEN WHO WOULD AVOID or extricate themselves from the common plight I've described, and would begin new lives, new movements, and new worlds, must first learn to acknowledge the reality of their present condition. They have got to reject the blind and faulty categories of thought foisted on them by a male order for its own benefit. They must stop thinking in terms of "the grand affair," of the love which overcomes or substitutes for everything else, of the perfect moment, the perfect relationship, the perfect marriage. In other words, they must reject romanticism. Romance, like the rabbit of the dog track, is the illusive, fake, and never-attained reward which for the benefit and amusement of our masters keeps us running and thinking in safe circles.

A relationship between a man and a woman is no more or less personal a relationship than is the relationship between a woman and her maid, a master and his slave, a teacher and his student. Of course, there are personal, individual qualities to a particular relationship in any of these categories but they are so overshadowed by the class nature of the relationship, by the volume of class response as to be almost insignificant.

There is something horribly repugnant in the picture of women performing the same menial chores all day, having almost interchangeable conversations with their children, engaging in standard television arguments with their husbands, and then, in the late hours of the night, each agonizing over what is considered her personal lot, her personal relationship, her personal problem. If women lack self-confidence, there seems no limit to their egotism. And unmarried women cannot in all honesty say their lives are in much greater measure distinct from each other's. We are a class, we are oppressed as a class, and we each respond within the limits allowed us as members of that oppressed class. Purposely divided from each other, each of us is ruled by one or more men for the benefit of all men. There is no personal escape, no personal salvation, no personal solution.

The first step, then, is to accept our plight as a common plight, to see other women as reflections of ourselves, without obscuring, of course, the very real differences intelligence, temperament, age, education, and background create. I'm not saying let's now create new castes or classes among our own. I just don't want women to feel that the movement requires them to identify totally with and moreover love every other woman. For the general relationship, understanding and compassion should suffice.

We who have been raised on pap must develop a passion for honest appraisal. The real differences between women and between men and women are the guideposts within and round which we must dream and work.

Having accepted our common identity the next thing we must do is to get in touch with each other. I mean that absolutely literally. Women see each other all the time, open their mouths and make noises, but communicate on only the most superficial level. We don't talk to each other about what we consider our real problems because we are afraid to look insecure, because we don't trust or respect each other, and because we are afraid to look or be disloyal to our husbands and benefactors. . . .

I cannot make it too clear that I am not talking about group therapy or individual catharsis (we aren't sick, we are oppressed). I'm talking about movement. Let's get together to decide in groups of women how to get out of this bind, to discover and fight the techniques of domination in and out of the home. To change our physical and social surroundings to free our time, our energy, and our minds—to start to build for ourselves, for all mankind, a world without horrors.

Women involved in this struggle together will come to respect, love, and develop deep and abiding friendships with each other. If these do not thoroughly compensate for losses that may be ours, they will carry us through. For different ages and different stages there are different projects. Young married or unmarried women without children are sympathetic to the problems of mothers but do not pretend to fully understand them. In all honesty, as a middle-aged mother I cannot really grasp the special quality of life of an unmarried young woman in this generation. Her circumstance is too distinct from mine, and my memories of youth are by this time too faded to bridge the gap. Youth has available to it perspectives and paths not destined to be shared by many in the older generation. We must work together but not presuppose for each other. . . . Before this part of the paper is ended, however, I would like to mention briefly projects I think women my age must undertake as part of the overall movement. If they have any relevancy for young women, so much the better.

1. Women must resist pressure to enter into movement activities other than their own. There cannot be real restructuring of this society until the relationships between the sexes are restruc-

tured. The inequalitarian relationship in the home is perhaps the basis of all evil. Men can commit any horror, or cowardly suffer any mutilation of their souls and retire to the home to be treated there with awe, respect, and perhaps love. Men will never face their true identity or their real problems under these circumstances, nor will we.

If movement men were not attempting to preserve their prerogative as men while fighting "the system," they would welcome an attack launched upon that system from another front. That they do not, shows how trapped they are in the meshes of the very system they oppose. Our vision must not be limited by theirs. We must urge in speech and in print that women go their own way.

2. Since women in great measure are ruled by the fear of physical force, they must learn to protect themselves. Women who are able ought to take jujitsu or karate until they are proficient in the art. Certainly they ought to organize and enroll their daughters in such courses. . . .

3. We must force the media to a position of realism. Ninety percent of the women in this country have an inferiority complex because they do not have turned-up noses, wear a size ten or under dress, have "good legs," flat stomachs, and fall within a certain age bracket. According to television no man is hot for a middle-aged woman. If she is his wife he may screw her but only because he is stuck with her. More important than that, women are constantly portrayed as stupid. . . .

4. Women must share their experiences with each other until they understand, identify, and explicitly state the many psychological techniques of domination in and out of the home. These should be published and distributed widely until they are common knowledge. No woman should feel befuddled and helpless in an argument with her husband. She ought to be able to identify his stratagems and to protect herself against them. . . .

5. Somebody has got to start designing communities in which women can be freed from their burdens long enough for them to experience humanity. Houses might be built around schools to be rented only to people with children enrolled in the particular school, and only as long as they were enrolled. This geographi-

cally confined community could contain cheap or cooperative cafeterias and a restaurant so that mothers would not have to cook. This not only would free the woman's time but would put her in more of a position of equality with Daddy when he comes home from work. The parents could both sit down and eat at the same time in front of and with the children, a far different scene from that of a conversing family being served by a harassed mother who rarely gets to sit down and is usually two courses behind. These geographic school complexes could also contain full-time nurseries. They could offer space for instrument, dance, and self-defense lessons. In other words, a woman could live in them and be relieved of cooking, childcare for the greater part of the day, and chauffeuring. The center might even have nighttime or overnight babysitting quarters. Many women will be totally lost to us and to themselves if projects like this are not begun. And the projects themselves, by freeing a woman's time and placing her in innumerable little ways into more of a position of equality, will go a long way toward restructuring the basic marital and parental relationships.

6. Women must learn their own history because they have a history to be proud of and a history which will give pride to their daughters. . . . To keep us from our history is to keep us from each other. To keep us from our history is to deny to us the group pride from which individual pride is born—to deny to us the possibility of revolt. Our rulers, consciously, unconsciously, perhaps intuitively, know these truths. That's why there is no black or female history in high school texts. . . . Courageous women brought us out of total bondage to our present improved position. We must not forsake them but learn from them and allow them to join the cause once more. The market is ripe for feminist literature, historic and otherwise. We must provide it.

7. Women who have any scientific competency at all ought to begin to investigate the real temperamental and cognitive differences between the sexes. This area has been hexed with a sort of liberal taboo like the study of race differences. Presumably, we and blacks were being saved from humiliation by a liberal establishment which was at least in pretense willing to grant that,

aside from color and sexual anatomy, we differed from white men in no significant aspect. But suppose we do? Are we to be kept ignorant of those differences? Who is being saved from what?

8. Equal pay for equal work has been a project poo-pooed by the radicals but it should not be. . . . If women, particularly women with children, cannot leave their husbands and support themselves decently, they are bound to remain under all sorts of degrading circumstances. In this same line, college entrance discrimination against females, and job discrimination in general, must be fought, no matter what we think about the striving to become professional. A guaranteed annual income would also be of direct relevance to women.

9. In what is hardly an exhaustive list, I must mention abortion laws. All laws relating to abortion must be stricken from the books. Abortion, like contraceptives, must be legal and available if women are to have control of their bodies, their lives, and their destiny.

REDSTOCKINGS MANIFESTO

In fall 1968, some 200 demonstrators suddenly appeared at the annual Miss America beauty pageant in Atlantic City, New Jersey. The demonstrators—young women carrying picket signs with such messages as "Women are people, not livestock" and "Can makeup cover the wounds of our oppression?"—had come to Atlantic City to denounce beauty contests as harmful to women's self-image. They set up a "freedom trash can," into which women were invited to toss "objects of female torture," like hair curlers, girdles, bras, and high heels.[1] The novelty of this event attracted tremendous media notice. The protesters were inaccurately branded "bra-burners," an epithet that afterward was widely applied to feminists. But all the publicity at least had the effect of alerting the nation to the fact that a new wave of feminism was forming and gathering force among the unpredictable younger generation.

The Miss America protest was organized by members of New York Radical Women, one of the earliest women's liberation groups.[2] As political differences gradually developed among its members, they split up and joined a number of new groups— Redstockings, WITCH, The Feminists, and New York Radical Feminists.[3] From this nucleus of creative, intensely committed radical feminists in New York City came not only many of the key concepts of second-wave feminism but also a vocabulary

[1]Kathie Sarachild, "Consciousness-Raising as a Radical Weapon," in *Feminist Revolution,* by Redstockings of the Women's Liberation Movement (New York: Random House, 1975, 1978), p. 147.

[2]The organization, founded in 1967 by Pam Allen and Shulamith Firestone, was originally known as Radical Women.

[3]The Feminists was founded by Ti-Grace Atkinson; New York Radical Feminists by Anne Koedt and Shulamith Firestone.

with which to discuss them ("sisterhood is powerful," "the personal is political," and "consciousness raising" all were their contributions). They communicated with other activist women around the country through the journals *Notes from the First Year* (June 1968) and *Notes from the Second Year* (1970).

Redstockings was founded in New York City in 1969.[4] Its name was a play on *bluestockings,* a put-down designation for brainy women. The Redstockings women were radical feminists who saw male supremacy as the oldest, most basic oppression of one human being by another. They declared in their manifesto: "We cannot rely on existing ideologies as they are all products of male supremacist culture." Convinced that women's own experiences and feelings were the only valid starting point for feminist analysis, Redstockings was dedicated to consciousness raising. But its members were also strongly action-oriented.

The Redstockings collective celebrated its formation by disrupting a New York State legislative committee hearing on abortion reform: "Why are fourteen men and only one woman on your list of speakers—and she a nun?" one of the demonstrators burst out. Redstockings then organized a follow-up abortion speak-out, held in the basement of a New York City church, at which women publicly described their often harrowing experiences with illegal abortions. One of those listening, a woman who was reminded of her own secret abortion, was a reporter from *New York* magazine named Gloria Steinem. She later referred to this meeting as a key experience in her evolution as a feminist.

The Redstockings Manifesto is reprinted here in full.

————————————————————————

[4]The founders of Redstockings were Shulamith Firestone (who coined the group's name) and Ellen Willis.

I. AFTER CENTURIES OF INDIVIDUAL and preliminary political struggle, women are uniting to achieve their final liberation from male supremacy. Redstockings is dedicated to building this unity and winning our freedom.

II. Women are an oppressed class. Our oppression is total, affecting every facet of our lives. We are exploited as sex objects, breeders, domestic servants, and cheap labor. We are considered inferior beings, whose only purpose is to enhance men's lives. Our humanity is denied. Our prescribed behavior is enforced by the threat of physical violence.

Because we have lived so intimately with our oppressors, in isolation from each other, we have been kept from seeing our personal suffering as a political condition. This creates the illusion that a woman's relationship with her man is a matter of interplay between two unique personalities, and can be worked out individually. In reality, every such relationship is a *class* relationship, and the conflicts between individual men and women are *political* conflicts that can only be solved collectively.

III. We identify the agents of our oppression as men. Male supremacy is the oldest, most basic form of domination. All other forms of exploitation and oppression (racism, capitalism, imperialism, etc.) are extensions of male supremacy; men dominate women, a few men dominate the rest. All power structures throughout history have been male-dominated and male-oriented. Men have controlled all political, economic, and cultural institutions and backed up this control with physical force. They have used their power to keep women in an inferior position. *All men* receive economic, sexual, and psychological benefits from male supremacy. *All men* have oppressed women.

IV. Attempts have been made to shift the burden of responsibility from men to institutions or to women themselves. We condemn these arguments as evasions. Institutions alone do not oppress; they are merely tools of the oppressor. To blame institutions implies that men and women are equally victimized, obscures the fact that men benefit from the subordination of women, and gives men the excuse that they are forced to be oppressors. On the contrary, any man is free to renounce his superior position provided that he is willing to be treated like a woman by other men.

We also reject the idea that women consent to or are to blame for their own oppression. Women's submission is not the result of brainwashing, stupidity, or mental illness but of continual, daily pressure from men. We do not need to change ourselves, but to change men.

The most slanderous evasion of all is that women can oppress men. The basis for this illusion is the isolation of individual relationships from their political context and the tendency of men to see any legitimate challenge to their privileges as persecution.

V. We regard our personal experience, and our feelings about that experience, as the basis for an analysis of our common situation. We cannot rely on existing ideologies as they are all products of male supremacist culture. We question every generalization and accept none that are not confirmed by our experience.

Our chief task at present is to develop female class consciousness through sharing experience and publicly exposing the sexist foundation of all our institutions. Consciousness-raising is not "therapy," which implies the existence of individual solutions and falsely assumes that the male-female relationship is purely personal, but the only method by which we can ensure that our program for liberation is based on the concrete realities of our lives.

The first requirement for raising class consciousness is honesty, in private and in public, with ourselves and other women.

VI. We identify with all women. We define our best interest as that of the poorest, most brutally exploited woman.

We repudiate all economic, racial, educational, or status privileges that divide us from other women. We are determined to recognize and eliminate any prejudices we may hold against other women.

We are committed to achieving internal democracy. We will do whatever is necessary to ensure that every woman in our movement has an equal chance to participate, assume responsibility, and develop her political potential.

VII. We call on all our sisters to unite with us in struggle.

We call on all men to give up their male privileges and support women's liberation in the interest of our humanity and their own.

In fighting for our liberation, we will always take the side of women against their oppressors. We will not ask what is "revolutionary" or "reformist," only what is good for women.

The time for individual skirmishes has passed. This time we are going all the way.

Bread and Roses

Through the late sixties and early seventies countless new women's groups emerged around the country; most of them were organized locally and lasted only a year or two. A number of such groups—composed mainly of young, radical women—named themselves. There were Seattle's Radical Women; San Francisco's Sisters of Lilith, SALT (Sisters All Learning Together), and Sudsofloppen (a nonsense term, to indicate the group's openness to new ideas); Boston's Cell 16, and Bread and Roses (from a slogan used by Lawrence, Massachusetts, textile workers, many of them women, during a strike in 1912); New York City's The Feminists (which began as a dissenting faction from the New York chapter of NOW), and several spinoffs from New York Radical Women, including Redstockings and the first "coven" of WITCH (Women's International Terrorist Conspiracy from Hell, or, in other permutations of the acronym, Women Inspired to Commit Herstory or Women Intent on Toppling Consumer Holidays). WITCH, with branches soon in a few cities, livened the political scene with "hexings" of bridal fairs, the stock exchange, and United Fruit Company.

On the national scene, NOW continued to dominate, with a membership that had multiplied tenfold—from 300 at its founding in 1966 to approximately 3,000 in 1970. A number of other moderate nationwide associations of older, established women also existed, including Women's Equity Action League, which focused on economic inequality; Federally Employed Women; Business and Professional Women; and women's caucuses formed by academics in several disciplines.

By early 1971 more than a hundred journals and newspapers

devoted to women's issues were being published,[1] such as *It Ain't Me, Babe* (Berkeley, California), *off our backs* (Washington, DC), *No More Fun and Games* (Somerville, Massachusetts), *Women: A Journal of Liberation* (Baltimore, Maryland), *Ain't I a Woman?* (Iowa City, Iowa), *Lilith* (Seattle, Washington), *The Pedestal* (Vancouver, Canada), and *Up from Under* (New York City). In July 1972 the preview issue of *Ms.* magazine appeared, edited by Gloria Steinem, Joanne Edgar, Letty Cottin Pogrebin, Mary Peacock, and others. This monthly was the first nationally distributed commercial feminist publication.

Less visible than the "name" women's groups, but just as influential in their own way, were the countless anonymous small groups of unaffiliated women who met weekly in suburban living rooms, college dormitories, and city apartments from coast to coast to talk intimately about their lives as women. These consciousness-raising groups, as they were by then widely known, arose spontaneously and functioned independently, yet they were remarkably effective—if unconventional—agents of movement building. For in such groups, participants confronted the effects of sexism in personal terms and became firmly committed to the women's movement. It is not an exaggeration to say that within these gatherings of neighbors and friends, genuine conversion experiences often took place, and it was a common observation that women who engaged in consciousness raising never viewed the world in quite the same way again.

However, despite the impressive growth of the women's movement in numbers and celebrity, it must also be said that the movement cut a narrow swath: Overwhelmingly, women who identified with feminism were white and middle class. NOW elected a black woman, Aileen Hernandez, as president in 1970; but the organization failed to attract a significant black constituency. The radical student groups were also unsuccessful in achieving meaningful race or class diversity.

The essay excerpted here, "Bread and Roses," argues that the women's movement could be made more relevant to poor

[1]Judith Hole and Ellen Levine, *Rebirth of Feminism* (New York: Quadrangle, 1971), p. 271.

women if it stressed *simultaneously* economic oppression (issues of "bread") and the psychological effects of sexism ("roses"). The authors wrote from a socialist perspective. Kathy McAfee was an SDS alumna who became an editor of the underground paper *Leviathan,* where this piece first appeared in June 1969; Myrna Wood had been affiliated with the Student Union for Peace Action, a Canadian counterpart of SDS. But though connected to the "politico" camp, McAfee and Wood clearly were moving toward acceptance of many radical feminist ideas—a turn more and more women who started out in the New Left were taking.

Later McAfee worked as a staff writer for Oxfam America. She is the author of the book *Storm Signals: Structural Adjustment and Development Alternatives in the Caribbean* (1991).

One

A GREAT DEAL OF CONFUSION EXISTS TODAY about the role of women's liberation in a revolutionary movement. Hundreds of women's groups have sprung up within the past year or two, but among them, a number of very different and often conflicting ideologies have developed. The growth of these movements has demonstrated the desperate need that many women feel to escape their own oppression, but it has also shown that organization around women's issues need not lead to revolutionary consciousness, or even to an identification with the left. (Some groups mobilize middle class women to fight for equal privileges as businesswomen and academics; others maintain that the overthrow of capitalism is irrelevant for women.)

Many movement women have experienced the initial exhilaration of discovering women's liberation as an issue, of realizing that the frustration, anger, and fear we feel are not a result of individual failure but are shared by all our sisters, and of sensing—if not fully understanding—that these feelings stem from the same oppressive conditions that give rise to racism, chauvinism and the barbarity of American culture. But many movement women, too, have become disillusioned after a time by their experiences with women's liberation groups. More often than not these groups never get beyond the level of therapy sessions; rather than aiding the political development of women and building a revolutionary women's movement, they often encourage escape from political struggle.

The existence of this tendency among women's liberation groups is one reason why many movement activists (including some women) have come out against a women's liberation movement that distinguishes itself from the general movement, even if it considers itself part of the left. A movement organized by women around the oppression of women, they say, is bound to emphasize the bourgeois and personal aspects of oppression and to obscure the material oppression of working class women *and men.* . . .

This attitude toward women's liberation is mistaken and dangerous. By discouraging the development of a revolutionary women's liberation movement, it avoids a serious challenge to what, along with racism, is the deepest source of division and false consciousness among workers. By setting up (in the name of Marxist class analysis) a dichotomy between the "bourgeois," personal and psychological forms of oppression, on the one hand, and the "real" material forms on the other, it substitutes a mechanistic model of class relations for a more profound understanding of how these two aspects of oppression depend upon and reinforce each other. Finally, this anti–women's liberationist attitude makes it easier for us to by-pass a confrontation of male chauvinism and the closely related values of elitism and authoritarianism which are weakening our movement.

Before we can discuss the potential of a women's liberation movement, we need a more precise description of the way the oppression of women functions in a capitalist society. This will also help us understand the relation of psychological to material oppression.

1. Male chauvinism—the attitude that women are the
passive and inferior servants of society and of men—
sets women apart from the rest of the working class.

Even when they do the same work as men, women are not considered workers in the same sense, with the need and right to
work to provide for their families or to support themselves independently. They are expected to accept work at lower wages and
without job security. Thus they can be used as a marginal or re-
serve labor force when profits depend on extra low costs or
when men are needed for war.

Women are not supposed to be independent, so they are not
supposed to have any "right to work." This means, in effect,
that although they do work, they are denied the right to organize and fight for better wages and conditions. Thus the role of
women in the labor force undermines the struggles of male
workers as well. The boss can break a union drive by threatening to hire lower paid women or blacks. In many cases, where
women are organized, the union contract reinforces their inferior position, making women the least loyal and militant union
members. . . .

In general, because women are defined as docile, helpless,
and inferior they are forced into the most demeaning and mind-
rotting jobs—from scrubbing floors to filing cards—under the
most oppressive conditions, where they are treated like children
or slaves. Their very position reinforces the idea, even among
the women themselves, that they are fit for and should be satisfied with this kind of work.

2. Apart from the direct, material exploitation of
women, male supremacy acts in more subtle ways to
undermine class consciousness.

The tendency of male workers to think of themselves primarily
as men (i.e., powerful) rather than as workers (i.e., members of
an oppressed group) promotes a false sense of privilege and
power, and an identification with the world of men, including
the boss. The petty dictatorship which most men exercise over

their wives and families enables them to vent their anger and frustration in a way which poses no challenge to the system. The role of the man in the family reinforces aggressive individualism, authoritarianism, and a hierarchical view of social relations— values which are fundamental to the perpetuation of capitalism. In this system we are taught to relieve our fears and frustrations by brutalizing those weaker than we are: a man in uniform turns into a pig; the foreman intimidates the man on the line; the husband beats his wife, child, and dog.

3. Women are further exploited in their roles as housewives and mothers, through which they reduce the costs (social and economic) of maintaining the labor force.

All of us will admit that inadequate as it may be, American workers have a relatively decent standard of living, in a strictly material sense, when compared to workers of other countries or periods of history. But American workers are exploited and ha-rassed in other ways than through the size of the weekly pay-check. They are made into robots on the job; they are denied security; they are forced to pay for expensive insurance and can rarely save enough to protect them from sudden loss of job or emergency. They are denied decent medical care and a livable en-vironment. They are cheated by inflation. They are "given" a regimented education that prepares them for a narrow slot or for nothing. And they are taxed heavily to pay for these "benefits."

In all these areas, it is a woman's responsibility to make up for the failures of the system. In countless working class families, it is mother's job that bridges the gap between week to week subsis-tence and relative security. It is her wages that enable the family to eat better food, to escape their oppressive surroundings through a trip, an occasional movie, or new clothes. It is her re-sponsibility to keep her family healthy despite the cost of decent medical care; to make a comfortable home in an unsafe and un-livable neighborhood; to provide a refuge from the alienation of work and to keep the male ego in good repair. It is she who must struggle daily to make ends meet despite inflation. She must make up for the fact that her children do not receive a decent education and she must salvage their damaged personalities.

A woman is judged as a wife and mother—the only role she is allowed—according to her ability to maintain stability in her family and to help her family "adjust" to harsh realities. She therefore transmits the values of hard work and conformity to each generation of workers. It is she who forces her children to stay in school and "behave" or who urges her husband not to risk his job by standing up to the boss or going on strike.

Thus the role of wife and mother is one of social mediator and pacifier. She shields her family from the direct impact of class oppression. She is the true opiate of the masses.

4. Working class women and other women as well are exploited as consumers.

They are forced to buy products which are necessities, but which have waste built into them, like the soap powder, the price of which includes fancy packaging and advertising. They also buy products which are wasteful in themselves because they are told that a new car or TV will add to their families' status and satisfaction, or that cosmetics will increase their desirability as sex objects. Among "middle class" women, of course, the second type of wasteful consumption is more important than it is among working class women, but all women are victims of both types to a greater or lesser extent, and the values which support wasteful consumption are part of our general culture.

5. All women, too, are oppressed and exploited sexually.

For working class women this oppression is more direct and brutal. They are denied control of their own bodies, when as girls they are refused information about sex and birth control, and when as women they are denied any right to decide whether and when to have children. Their confinement to the role of sex partner and mother, and their passive submission to a single man are often maintained by physical force. The relative sexual freedom of "middle class" or college educated women, however, does not bring *them* real independence. Their sexual role is still primarily a passive one; their value as individuals still determined by their ability to attract, please, and hold on to a man. The definition of women as docile and dependent, inferior in intellect and weak in character cuts across class lines.

A woman of any class is expected to sell herself—not just her body but her entire life, her talents, interests, and dreams—to a man. She is expected to give up friendships, ambitions, pleasures, and moments of time to herself in order to serve his career or his family. In return, she receives not only her livelihood but her identity, her very right to existence, for unless she is the wife of someone or the mother of someone, a woman is nothing.

In this summary of the forms of oppression of women in this society, the rigid dichotomy between material oppression and psychological oppression fails to hold, for it can be seen that these two aspects of oppression reinforce each other at every level. A woman may seek a job out of absolute necessity, or in order to escape repression and dependence at home. In either case, on the job she will be persuaded or forced to accept low pay, indignity and a prison-like atmosphere because a woman isn't supposed to need money or respect. Then, after working all week turning tiny wires, or typing endless forms, she finds that cooking and cleaning, dressing up and making up, becoming submissive and childlike in order to please a man is her only relief, so she gladly falls back into her "proper" role.

All women, even including those of the ruling class, are oppressed as women in the sense that their real fulfillment is linked to their role as girlfriend, wife or mother. This definition of women is part of bourgeois culture—the whole superstructure of ideas that serves to explain and reinforce the social relations of capitalism. It is applied to all women, but it has very different consequences for women of different classes. For a ruling class woman, it means she is denied real independence, dignity, and sexual freedom. For a working class woman it means this too, but it also justifies her material super-exploitation and physical coercion. Her oppression is a total one.

Two

IT IS TRUE, AS THE MOVEMENT CRITICS ASSERT, that the present women's liberation groups are almost entirely based among "middle class" women, that is, college and career women; and the issues of psychological and sexual exploitation and, to a lesser extent, exploitation through consumption, have been the most prominent ones.

It is not surprising that the women's liberation movement should begin among bourgeois women, and should be dominated in the beginning by their consciousness and their particular concerns. Radical women are generally the postwar middle class generation that grew up with the right to vote, the chance at higher education, and training for supportive roles in the professions and business. Most of them are young and sophisticated enough to have not yet had children and do not have to marry to support themselves. In comparison with most women, they are capable of a certain amount of control over their lives.

The higher development of bourgeois democratic society allows the women who benefit from education and relative equality to see the contradictions between its rhetoric (every boy can become president) and their actual place in that society. The working class woman might believe that education could have made her financially independent but the educated career woman finds that money has not made her independent. In fact, because she has been allowed to progress halfway on the upward-mobility ladder she can see the rest of the distance that is denied her only because she is a woman. She can see the similarity between her oppression and that of other sections of the population. Thus, from their own experience, radical women in the movement are aware of more faults in the society than racism and imperialism. Because they have pushed the democratic myth to its limits, they know concretely how it limits them.

At the same time that radical women were learning about American society they were also becoming aware of the male chauvinism in the movement. In fact, that is usually the cause of their first conscious verbalization of the prejudice they feel; it is more disillusioning to know that the same contradiction exists between the movement's rhetoric of equality and its reality, for we expect more of our comrades.

This realization of the deep-seated prejudice against themselves in the movement produces two common reactions among its women: (1) a preoccupation with this immediate barrier (and perhaps a resultant hopelessness), and (2) a tendency to retreat inward, to buy the fool's gold of creating a personally liberated life style.

However, our concept of liberation represents a consciousness that conditions have forced on us while most of our sisters are chained by other conditions, biological and economic, that overwhelm their humanity and desires for self-fulfillment. Our background accounts for our ignorance about the stark oppression of women's daily lives.

Few radical women really know the worst of women's condition. They do not understand the anxious struggle of an uneducated girl to find the best available man for financial security and escape from a crowded and repressive home. They have not suffered years of fear from ignorance and helplessness about pregnancies. Few have experienced constant violence and drunkenness of a brutalized husband or father. They do not know the day to day reality of being chained to a house and family, with little money and lots of bills, and no diversions but TV.

Not many radical women have experienced nine to eleven hours a day of hard labor, carrying trays on aching legs for rude customers who may leave no tip, but leave a feeling of degradation from their sexual or racist remarks—and all of this for eighty to ninety dollars a week. Most movement women have not learned to blank out their thoughts for seven hours in order to type faster or file endless numbers. They have not felt their own creativity deadened by this work, while watching men who

were not trained to be typists move on to higher level jobs requiring "brain-work."

In summary: because male supremacy (assumption of female
inferiority, regulation of women to service roles, and sexual objectification) crosses class lines, radical women are conscious of
women's oppression, but because of their background, they lack
consciousness of most women's class oppression.

Three

THE DEVELOPMENT OF THE MOVEMENT has produced different
trends within the broad women's liberation movement. Most
existing women's groups fall into one of the four following categories:

1. Personal Liberation Groups

This type of group has been the first manifestation of consciousness of their own oppression among movement women. By talking about their frustrations with their role in the movement,
they have moved from feelings of personal inadequacy to the realization that male supremacy is one of the foundations of the
society that must be destroyed. Because it is at the level of the
direct oppression in our daily lives that most people become
conscious, it is not surprising that this is true of women in the
movement. Lenin once complained about this phenomenon to
Clara Zetkin, leader of the German women's socialist movement: "I have been told that at the evening meetings arranged
for reading and discussion with working women, sex and marriage problems come first."

But once women have discovered the full extent of the prejudice against them they cannot ignore it, whether Lenin approves
or not, and they have found women's discussions helpful in
dealing with their problems. These groups have continued to
grow and split into smaller, more viable groups, showing just
how widespread is women's dissatisfaction.

However, the level of politicization of these groups has been kept low by the very conditions that keep women underdeveloped in this society; and alienation from the male dominated movement has prolonged the politicization process. These groups still see the source of their oppression in "chauvinist attitudes," rather than in the social relations of capitalism that produce those attitudes. Therefore, they don't confront male chauvinism collectively or politically. They become involved solely in "personal liberation"—attempts to create free life styles and define new criteria for personal relations in the hoped for system of the future. Bernadine Dohrn's criticism of these groups was a just one: "Their program is only a cycle that produces more women's groups, mostly devoted to a personal liberation/therapy function and promises of study which are an evasion of practice" (*New Left Notes,* v. 4, no. 9).

2. Anti-Left Groups

Many women have separated from the movement out of bitterness and disillusionment with the left's ability to alter its built-in chauvinism. Some are now vociferously anti-left; others simply see the movement as irrelevant. In view of the fate of the ideal of women's equality in most socialist countries, their skepticism is not surprising. Nor is it surprising that individuals with leadership abilities who are constantly thwarted in the movement turn to new avenues.

These women advocate a radical feminist movement totally separate from any other political movement. Their program involves female counter-institutions, such as communes and political parties, and attacks upon those aspects of women's oppression that affect all classes (abortion laws, marriage, lack of child care facilities, job discrimination, images of women in the media).

The first premise of the theory with which these radical feminists justify their movement is that women have always been exploited. They admit that women's oppression has a social basis—*men as a group oppress women as a group*—therefore, women must organize to confront male supremacy collectively. But they say that since women were exploited before capitalism,

as well as in capitalist and "socialist" societies, the overthrow
of capitalism is irrelevant to the equality of women. Male
supremacy is a phenomenon outside the left-right political spec-
trum and must be fought separately.

But if one admits that female oppression has a social basis, it
is necessary to specify the social relations on which this condition is based, and then to change those relations. (We maintain
that the oppression of women is based on class divisions; these
in turn are derived from the division of labor which developed
between the stronger and weaker, the owner and the owned;
e.g., women, under conditions of scarcity in primitive society.)
Defining those relations as "men as a group *vs.* women as a
group," as the anti-left groups seem to do, is ultimately reducible only to some form of biological determinism (women
are inherently oppress-able) and leads to no solution in practice
other than the elimination of one group or the other.

3. Movement Activists

Many radical women who have become full time activists accept
the attitude of most men in the movement that women's liberation is bourgeois and "personalist." They look at most of the
present women's liberation groups and conclude that a movement based on women's issues is bound to emphasize the relatively mild forms of oppression experienced by students and
"middle class" women while obscuring the fundamental importance of class oppression. "Sure middle class women are oppressed," they say, "but how can we concentrate on making our
own lives more comfortable when working class women and
men are so much more oppressed." Others point out that
"women cannot be free in an unfree society; their liberation will
come with that of the rest of us." These people maintain that organizing around women's issues is reformist because it is an attempt to ameliorate conditions within bourgeois society. Most
movement activists agree that we should talk about women's
oppression, but say we should do so only in terms of the super-
exploitation of working women, especially black and brown

working women, and not in terms of personal, psychological, and sexual oppression, which they see as a very different (and bourgeois) thing. They also say we should organize around women's oppression, but only as an aspect of our struggles against racism and imperialism. In other words, there should not be a separate revolutionary women's organization.

Yet strangely enough, demands for the liberation of women seldom find their way into movement programs, and very little organizing of women, within or apart from other struggles, is actually going on:

• In student organizing, no agitation for birth control for high school and college girls; no recognition of the other special restrictions that keep them from controlling their own lives; no propaganda about how women are still barred from many courses, especially those that would enable them to demand equality in employment.

• In open admission fights, no propaganda about the channeling of girls into low-paying, dead-end service occupations.

• In struggles against racism, talk about the black man's loss of manhood, but none about the sexual objectification and astounding exploitation of black women.

• In anti-repression campaigns, no fights against abortion laws; no defense of those "guilty" of abortion.

• In analysis of unions, no realization that women make less than black men and that most women aren't even organized yet. The demands for equal wages were recently raised in the Women's Resolution (at the December SDS, NC [National Council]), but there are as yet no demands for free child care and equal work by husbands that would make the demand for equal wages more than an empty gesture.

It is clear that radical women activists have not been able to educate the movement about its own chauvinism or bring the issue of male supremacy to an active presence in the movement's program any more than have the personal liberation groups. . . .

At the same time, most [movement] women are becoming acutely aware, along with the rest of the movement, of their own comfortable and privileged backgrounds compared with those of workers (and feel guilty about them). It is this situation that causes them to regard women's liberation as a sort of counter-revolutionary self-indulgence.

There is a further reason for this; in the movement we have all become aware of the central importance of working people in a revolutionary movement and of the gap between their lives and most of our own. But at this point our understanding is largely an abstract one; we remain distant from and grossly ignorant of the real conditions working people face day to day. Thus our concept of working class oppression tends to be a one-sided and mechanistic one, contrasting "real" economic oppression to our "bourgeois hang-ups" with cultural and psychological oppression. We don't understand that the oppression of working people is a total one, in which the "psychological" aspects—the humiliation of being poor, uneducated, and powerless, the alienation of work, and the brutalization of family life—are not only real forms of oppression in themselves, but reinforce material oppression by draining people of their energy and will to fight. Similarly, the "psychological" forms of oppression that affect all women—sexual objectification and the definition of women as docile and serving—work to keep working class women in a position where they are super-exploited as workers and as housewives.

But because of our one-sided view of class oppression, most movement women do not see the relationship of their own oppression to that of working class women. This is why they conclude that a women's liberation movement cannot lead to class consciousness and does not have revolutionary potential.

4. Advocates of a Women's
Liberation Movement

A growing number of radical women see the need for an organized women's movement because: (1) they see revolutionary potential in women organizing against their direct oppression, that is, against male supremacy as well as their exploitation as workers; and (2) they believe that a significant movement for women's equality will develop within any socialist movement only through the conscious efforts of organized women, and they have seen that such consciousness does not develop in a male chauvinist movement born of a male supremacist society.

These women believe that radical women must agitate among young working class girls, rank and file women workers, and workers' wives, around a double front; against their direct oppression by male supremacist institutions, and against their exploitation as workers. They maintain that the cultural conditions of people's lives is as important as the economic basis of their oppression in determining consciousness. If the movement cannot incorporate such a program, these women say, then an organized women's liberation movement distinguished from the general movement must be formed, for only through such a movement will radical women gain the consciousness to develop and carry through this program. . . .

Four

IN ORDER TO FORM A WOMEN'S LIBERATION MOVEMENT based on the oppression of working class women we must begin to agitate on issues of "equal rights" and specific rights. Equal rights means all those "rights" that men are supposed to have: the right to work, to organize for equal pay, promotions, better conditions, equal (and *not* separate) education. Specific rights means those rights women must have if they are to be equal in the other areas: free adequate child care, abortions, birth control for young women from puberty, self-defense, desegregation of all institutions (schools, unions, jobs). It is not so much an academic question of what is correct theory as an inescapable empirical fact; women must fight their conditions just to participate in the movement.

The first reason why we need to fight on these issues is that we must serve the people. That slogan is not just rhetoric with the Black Panthers but reflects their determination to end the exploitation of their people. Similarly, the women's liberation movement will grow and be effective only to the extent that it abominates and fights the conditions of misery that so many women suffer every day. It will gain support only if it speaks to the immediate needs of women. For instance:

1. We must begin to disseminate birth control information in high schools and fight the tracking of girls into inferior education. . . .

2. We must raise demands for maternity leave and child care facilities provided (paid for, but not controlled) by management as a rightful side benefit of women workers. . . .

3. We must agitate for rank and file revolt against the male supremacist hierarchy of the unions and for demands for equal wages. Only through winning such struggles for equality can the rank and file *be* united and see their common enemies—management and union hierarchy. Wives of workers must fight the chauvinist attitudes of their husbands simply to be able to attend meetings.

4. We must organize among store clerks, waitresses, office workers, and hospitals, where vast numbers of women have no bargaining rights or security. . . .

5. We must insist at all times on the right of every woman to control her own body.

6. We must demand the right of women to protect themselves. Because . . . the violence created by the brutalization of many men in our society is often directed at women, and because not all women are willing or able to sell themselves (or to limit their lives) for the protection of a male, women have a right to self-protection.

This is where the struggle must begin, although it cannot end here. In the course of the fight we will have to raise the issues of the human relationships in which the special oppression of women is rooted: sexual objectification, the division of labor in the home, and the institutions of marriage and the nuclear family. But organizing "against the family" cannot be the basis of a program. An uneducated working class wife with five kids is perfectly capable of understanding that marriage has destroyed most of her potential as a human being—probably she already understands this—but she is hardly in a position to repudiate her source of livelihood and free herself of those children. If we expect that of her, we will never build a movement.

As the women's liberation movement gains strength, the development of cooperative child care centers and living arrangements, and the provision of birth control may allow more working class women to free themselves from slavery as sex objects and housewives. But at the present time, the insistence by some women's liberation groups that we must "organize against sexual objectification," and that only women who repudiate the family can really be part of the movement, reflects the class chauvinism and lack of seriousness of women who were privileged enough to avoid economic dependence and sexual slavery in the first place.

In no socialist country have women yet achieved equality or full liberation, but in the most recent revolutions (Vietnam, Cuba, and China's cultural revolution) the women's struggle has intensified. It may be that in an advanced society such as our own, where women have had relatively more freedom, a revolutionary movement may not be able to avoid a militant women's movement developing within it. But the examples of previous attempts at socialist revolutions prove that the struggles must be instigated *by* militant women; liberation is not handed down from above.

ROBIN MORGAN

Goodbye to All That

Robin Morgan (b. 1941), describing her personal political journey, said that she was active in the male-dominated left for about six years, then in 1969 began "inching my way toward a more feminist position."[1] She had done freelance writing for a leading New Left, alternative-culture newspaper in New York City called *Rat* but in late 1969 refused to contribute to it any longer because of its "blatant sexism." In January 1970 she received a telephone call from Jane Alpert, a *Rat* staffer, informing her that women had seized the paper and inviting her to join them. Morgan accepted and was associated with the women's collective that put out *Rat* for the next year. Her article for the first edition of the liberated *Rat* was the farewell to the New Left reprinted here in full, which, she later said, "had been boiling inside me for some time."[2] When she wrote it, she was active with the New York City coven of WITCH.

Morgan has worked in the women's liberation movement as a writer, editor, and activist ever since. Her spirited 1970 anthology of feminist writings, *Sisterhood Is Powerful,* came to define the early movement for hundreds of thousands of people. Her international feminist anthology *Sisterhood Is Global* appeared in 1984. In addition to her nonfiction, she has published five volumes of poetry and a novel, *Dry Your Smile* (1987). In 1990, Morgan became editor in chief of a revivified, advertisement-free *Ms.* magazine, from which position she retired in 1993. A collation of her essays spanning twenty-five years—*The Word of a Woman: Feminist Dispatches 1968–1992*—shows her to be

[1]Robin Morgan, *Going Too Far: The Personal Chronicle of a Feminist* (New York: Random House, 1977), p. 116.

[2]Ibid., p. 121.

still passionately concerned with the lives of women everywhere.

"Goodbye to All That," which appeared in *Rat* in February 1970, has an unmistakable flavor of the period, with many contemporary allusions that need explaining today—thus, the editor's annotations included here. Morgan herself interpreted the list of women's names at the end of the piece as follows: "All the women on this list were at that time captives of a male-supremacist Leftist man and/or of patriarchal Leftist political beliefs—with two exceptions."[3] The exceptions were Kim Agnew, daughter of Vice President Spiro Agnew, and Valerie Solanas, convicted of shooting Andy Warhol.

(WITCH—Women Inspired to Commit Herstory)

So, *Rat* has been liberated, for this week, at least. Next week? If the men return to reinstate the porny photos, the sexist comic strips, the "nude-chickie" covers (along with their patronizing rhetoric about being in favor of Women's Liberation)—if this happens, our alternatives are clear. *Rat* must be taken over permanently by women—or *Rat* must be destroyed.

Why *Rat*? Why not *EVO*[4] or even the obvious new pornizines (Mafia-distributed alongside the human pornography of prostitution)? First, they'll get theirs, but it won't be a takeover, which is reserved for something at least *worth* taking over. Nor should they be censored. They should just be helped not to exist—by any means necessary. But *Rat*, which has always tried to be a really radical *cum* life-style paper—that's another matter. It's the liberal co-optative masks on the face of sexist hate and fear, worn by real nice guys we all know and like, right? We have met the enemy and he's our friend. And dangerous. "What

[3] Ibid., p. 130.
[4] *East Village Other*, a counterculture newspaper.

the hell, let the chicks do an issue; maybe it'll satisfy 'em for a while, it's a good controversy, and it'll maybe sell papers"—runs an unheard conversation that I'm sure took place at some point last week.

And that's what I wanted to write about—the friends, brothers, lovers in the counterfeit male-dominated Left. The good guys who think they know what "Women's Lib," as they so chummily call it, is all about—and who then proceed to degrade and destroy women by almost everything they say and do: The cover on the last issue of *Rat* (front *and* back). The token "pussy power" or "clit militancy" articles. The snide descriptions of women staffers on the masthead. The little jokes, the personal ads, the smile, the snarl. No more, brothers. No more well-meaning ignorance, no more co-optation, no more assuming that this thing we're all fighting for is the same; one revolution under *man,* with liberty and justice for all. No more.

Let's run it on down. White males are most responsible for the destruction of human life and environment on the planet today. Yet who is controlling the supposed revolution to change all that? White males (yes, yes, even with their pasty fingers back in black and brown pies again). It just could make one a bit uneasy. It seems obvious that a legitimate revolution must be led by, *made* by those who have been most oppressed: black, brown, and white *women*—with men relating to that the best they can. A genuine Left doesn't consider anyone's suffering irrelevant or titillating; nor does it function as a microcosm of capitalist economy, with men competing for power and status at the top, and women doing all the work at the bottom (and functioning as objectified prizes or "coin" as well). Goodbye to all that.

Run it all the way down.

Goodbye to the male-dominated peace movement, where sweet old Uncle Dave[5] can say with impunity to a woman on the staff of *Liberation,* "The trouble with you is you're an aggressive woman."

---

[5]David Dellinger, leader in the peace movement, editor of *Liberation* magazine, defendant in the Chicago Eight conspiracy trial.

Goodbye to the "straight" male-dominated Left—to PL,[6] who will allow that some workers are women, but won't see all women (say, housewives) as workers (just like the System itself); to all the old Leftover parties who offer these "Women's Liberation caucuses" to us as if that were not a contradiction in terms; to the individual anti-leadership leaders who hand-pick certain women to be leaders and then relate only to them, either in the male Left or in Women's Liberation—bringing their hangups about power-dominance and manipulation to everything they touch.

Goodbye to the WeatherVain,[7] with the Stanley Kowalski image and theory of free sexuality but practice of sex on demand for males. "Left Out!"—not Right On to the Weather Sisters who, and they know better—they know, reject their own radical feminism for that last desperate grab at male approval that we all know so well, for claiming that the *machismo* style and the gratuitous violence is their own style by "free choice" and for believing that this is the way for a woman to make her revolution . . . all the while, oh my sister, not meeting my eyes because WeatherMen chose Manson as their—and your—Hero. (Honest, at least . . . since Manson is only the logical extreme of the normal American male's fantasy, whether he is Dick Nixon or Mark Rudd: master of a harem, women to do all the shitwork, from raising babies and cooking and hustling to killing people on order.) Goodbye to all that shit that sets women apart from women; shit that covers the face of any WeatherWoman which is the face of any Manson Slave which is the face of Sharon Tate which is the face of Mary Jo Kopechne which is the face of Beulah Saunders which is the face of me which is the face of Pat Nixon which is the face of Pat Swinton. *In the dark we are all the same*—and you better believe it: we're in the dark, baby. (Remember the old joke: Know what they call a black man with a Ph.D.? A nigger. Variation: Know what they call a

[6]Progressive Labor, a Maoist political party.

[7]A play on "Weatherman," a political group believing in militant actions; a faction of SDS. Mark Rudd, mentioned below, was a leading Weather spokesperson.

WeatherWoman? A heavy cunt. Know what they call a Hip Revolutionary Woman? A groovy cunt. Know what they call a radical militant feminist? A crazy cunt.) Amerika is a land of free choice—take your pick of titles. Left Out, my Sister—don't you see? Goodbye to the illusion of strength when you run hand in hand with your oppressors; goodbye to the dream that being in the leadership collective will get you anything but gonorrhea.

Goodbye to RYM II,[8] as well, and all the other RYMs—not that the Sisters there didn't pull a cool number by seizing control, but because they let the men back in after only *a day or so* of self-criticism on male chauvinism. (And goodbye to the inaccurate blanket use of that phrase, for that matter: male chauvinism is an *attitude*—male supremacy is the *objective reality, the fact*.) Goodbye to the Conspiracy[9] who, when lunching with fellow sexist bastards Norman Mailer and Terry Southern in a bunny-type club in Chicago, found Judge Hoffman at the neighboring table—no surprise: *in the light they are all the same*.

Goodbye to Hip Culture and the so-called Sexual Revolution, which has functioned toward women's freedom as did the Reconstruction toward former slaves—reinstituted oppression by another name. Goodbye to the assumption that Hugh Romney[10] is safe in his "cultural revolution," safe enough to refer to "our women, who make all our clothes" without somebody not forgiving that. Goodbye to the arrogance of power indeed that lets Czar Stan Freeman of the Electric Circus[11] sleep without fear at night, or permits Tomi Ungerer to walk unafraid in the street after executing the drawings for the Circus advertising campaign against women. Goodbye to the idea that Hugh Hefner is groovy 'cause he lets Conspirators come to parties at the Mansion—goodbye to Hefner's dream of a ripe old age. Goodbye to Tuli and the Fugs and all the boys in the front room—who always knew they hated the women they loved.

[8] A group that emphasized working-class organizing.

[9] The Chicago Eight, tried for organizing demonstrations at the 1968 Democratic National Convention, in Chicago.

[10] Counterculture figure, leader of commune The Hog Farm.

[11] A New York City discotheque.

Goodbye to the notion that good ol' Abbie[12] is any different from any other up and coming movie star (like, say Cliff Robertson) who ditches the first wife and kids, good enough for the old days but awkward once you're Making It. Goodbye to his hypocritical double standard that reeks through all the tattered charm. Goodbye to lovely pro–Women's-Liberation Paul Krassner,[13] with all his astonished anger that women have lost their sense of humor "on this issue" and don't laugh anymore at little funnies that degrade and hurt them; farewell to the memory of his "Instant Pussy" aerosol-can poster, to his column for *Cavalier,* to his dream of a Rape-In against legislators' wives, to his Scapegoats and Realist Nuns and cute anecdotes about the little daughter he sees as often as any proper divorced Scarsdale middle-aged (thirty-eight) father; goodbye forever to the notion that he is my brother who, like Paul, buys a prostitute for the night as a birthday gift for a male friend, or who, like Paul, reels off the names in alphabetical order of people in the Women's Movement he has fucked, reels off names in the best locker-room tradition—as proof that *he's* no sexist oppressor.

Let it all hang out. Let it seem bitchy, catty, dykey, frustrated, crazy, Solanasesque,[14] nutty, frigid, ridiculous, bitter, embarrassing, man-hating, libelous, pure, unfair, envious, intuitive, low-down, stupid, petty, liberating. We are the women that men have warned us about.

And let's put one lie to rest for all time: the lie that men are oppressed, too, by sexism—the lie that there can be such a thing as "men's liberation groups." Oppression is something that one group of people commits against another group specifically because of a "threatening" characteristic shared by the latter group—skin color or sex or age, etc. The oppressors are indeed *fucked up* by being masters (racism hurts whites, sexual stereotypes are harmful to men) but those masters are not *oppressed.* Any master has the alternative of divesting himself of sexism or

[12]Abbie Hoffman, writer and leader of the radical-anarchist Yippie movement; Chicago Eight conspiracy trial defendant.

[13]Editor of *The Realist.*

[14]Refers to Valerie Solanas, convicted of shooting Andy Warhol.

racism—the oppressed have no alternative—for they have no power—but to fight. In the long run, Women's Liberation will of course free men—but in the short run it's going to *cost* men a lot of privilege, which no one gives up willingly or easily. Sexism is *not* the fault of women—kill your fathers, not your mothers.

Run it on down. Goodbye to a beautiful new ecology movement that could fight to save us all if it would stop tripping off women as earth-mother types or frontier chicks, if it would *right now* cede leadership to those who have *not* polluted the planet because that action implies power and women haven't had any power in about 5,000 years, cede leadership to those whose brains are as tough and clear as any man's but whose bodies are also unavoidably aware of the locked-in relationship between humans and their biosphere—the earth, the tides, the atmosphere, the moon. Ecology is no big *shtick* if you're a woman—it's always been there.

Goodbye to the complicity inherent in the Berkeley Tribesmen being part publishers of Trashman Comics; goodbye, for that matter, to the reasoning that finds whoremaster Trashman a fitting model, however comic-strip far out, for a revolutionary man—somehow related to the same Supermale reasoning that permits the first statement on Women's Liberation and male chauvinism that came out of the Black Panther Party[15] to be made *by a man,* talkin' a whole lot 'bout how the Sisters should speak up for themselves. Such ignorance and arrogance ill befits a revolutionary.

We know how racism is worked deep into the unconscious by our System—the same way sexism is, as it appears in the very name of The Young Lords.[16] What are you if you're a "macho woman"—a female Lord? Or, god forbid, a Young Lady? Change it, change it to The Young Gentry if you must, or never assume that the name itself is innocent of pain, of oppression.

Theory and practice—and the light-years between them. "Do it!" says Jerry Rubin[17] in *Rat*'s last issue—but he doesn't, or

[15]African-American radical group.
[16]Puerto Rican radical organization.
[17]Counterculture leader; defendant in the Chicago Eight conspiracy trial.

every *Rat* reader would have known the pictured face next to his article as well as they know his own much-photographed face: it was Nancy Kurshan, the power behind the clown.

Goodbye to the New Nation and Earth People's Park, for that matter, conceived by men, announced by men, led by men—doomed before its birth by the rotting seeds of male supremacy which are to be transplanted in fresh soil. Was it my brother who listed human beings among the *objects* which would be easily available after the Revolution: "Free grass, free food, free women, free acid, free clothes, etc."? Was it my brother who wrote, "Fuck your women till they can't stand up" and said that groupies were liberated chicks 'cause they dug a tit-shake instead of a handshake? The epitome of female exclusionism—"men will make the Revolution—and their chicks." Not my brother, no. Not my revolution. Not one breath of my support for the new counterfeit Christ—John Sinclair.[18] Just one less to worry about for ten years. I do not choose my enemy for my brother.

Goodbye, goodbye. The hell with the simplistic notion that automatic freedom for women—or non-white peoples—will come about ZAP! with the advent of a socialist revolution. Bullshit. Two evils pre-date capitalism and have been clearly able to survive and post-date socialism: sexism and racism. Women were the first property when the Primary Contradiction occurred: when one half of the human species decided to subjugate the other half, because it was "different," alien, the Other. From there it was an easy enough step to extend the Other to someone of different skin shade, different height or weight or language—or strength to resist. Goodbye to those simple-minded optimistic dreams of socialist equality all our good socialist brothers want us to believe. How liberal a politics that is! How much further we will have to go to create those profound changes that would give birth to a genderless society. *Profound*, Sister. Beyond what is male or female. Beyond standards we all adhere to now without daring to examine them as male-created, male-dominated, male–fucked-up, and in male self-interest.

[18]Then in jail on drug charges.

Beyond all known standards, especially those easily articulated revolutionary ones we all rhetorically invoke. Beyond, to a species with a new name, that would not dare define itself as Man.

I once said, "I'm a revolutionary, not just a woman," and knew my own lie even as I said the words. The pity of that statement's eagerness to be acceptable to those whose revolutionary zeal no one would question, i.e., any male supremacist in the counterleft. But to become a true revolutionary one must first become one of the oppressed (not organize or educate or manipulate them, but become one of them)—or realize that you *are* one of them already. No woman wants that. Because that realization is humiliating, it hurts. It hurts to understand that at Woodstock or Altamont[19] a woman could be declared uptight or a poor sport if she didn't want to be raped. It hurts to learn that the Sisters still in male-Left captivity are putting down the crazy feminists to make themselves look okay and unthreatening to our mutual oppressors. It hurts to be pawns in those games. It hurts to try and change *each day of your life right now*—not in talk, not "in your head," and not only conveniently "out there" in the Third World (half of which is women) or the black and brown communities (half of which are women) but in your own home, kitchen, bed. No getting away, no matter how else you are oppressed, from the primary oppression of being female in a patriarchal world. It hurts to hear that the Sisters in the Gay Liberation Front, too, have to struggle continually against the male chauvinism of their gay brothers. It hurts that Jane Alpert[20] was cheered when rapping about imperialism, racism, the Third World, and All Those Safe Topics but hissed and booed by a Movement crowd of men who wanted none of it when she began to talk about Women's Liberation. The backlash is upon us.

They tell us the alternative is to hang in there and "struggle," to confront male domination in the counterleft, to fight beside or

[19]Rock-music festivals.
[20]Leftist activist.

behind or beneath our brothers—to show 'em we're just as tough, just as revolushunerry, just as whatever-image-they-now-want-of-us-as-once-they-wanted-us-to-be-feminine-and-keep-the-home-fire-burning. They will bestow titular leadership on our grateful shoulders, whether it's being a token woman on the Movement Speakers Bureau Advisory Board, or being a Conspiracy groupie or one of the "respectable" chain-swinging Motor City Nine.[21] Sisters all, with only one real alternative: to seize our own power into our own hands, all women, separate and together, and make the Revolution the way it must be made—no priorities this time, no suffering group told to wait until after.

It is the job of revolutionary feminists to build an ever stronger independent Women's Liberation Movement, so that the Sisters in counterleft captivity will have somewhere to turn, to use their power and rage and beauty and coolness in their own behalf for once, on their own terms, on their own issues, in their own style—whatever that may be. Not for us in Women's Liberation to hassle them and confront them the way their men do, nor to blame them—or ourselves—for what any of us are: an oppressed people, but a people raising our consciousness toward something that is the other side of anger, something bright and smooth and cool, like action unlike anything yet contemplated or carried out. It is for us to survive (something the white male radical has the luxury of never really worrying about, what with all his options), to talk, to plan, to be patient, to welcome new fugitives from the counterfeit Left with no arrogance but only humility and delight, to plan, to push—to strike.

There's something every woman wears around her neck on a thin chain of fear—an amulet of madness. For each of us, there exists somewhere a moment of insult so intense that she will reach up and rip the amulet off, even if the chain tears at the flesh of her neck. And the last protection from seeing the truth will be gone. Do you think, tugging furtively every day at the chain and going nicely insane as I am, that I can be concerned

---

[21]A group of nonfeminist leftist women.

with the puerile squabbles of a counterfeit Left that laughs at my pain? Do you think such a concern is noticeable when set alongside the suffering of more than half the human species for the past 5,000 years—due to a whim of the other half? No, no, no, goodbye to all that.

Women are Something Else. This time, we're going to kick out all the jams, and the boys will just have to hustle to keep up, or else drop out and openly join the power structure of which they are already the illegitimate sons. Any man who claims he is serious about wanting to divest himself of cock privilege should trip on this: all male leadership out of the Left is the only way; and it's going to happen, whether through men stepping down, or through women seizing the helm. It's up to the "brothers"— after all, sexism is their concern, not ours; we're too busy getting ourselves together to have to deal with their bigotry. So they'll have to make up their own minds as to whether they will be divested of just cock privilege or—what the hell, why not say it, *say* it?—divested of cocks. How deep the fear of that loss must be, that it can be suppressed only by the building of empires and the waging of genocidal wars!

Goodbye, goodbye forever, counterfeit Left, counterleft, male-dominated cracked-glass-mirror reflection of the Amerikan Nightmare. Women are the real Left. We are rising; powerful in our unclean bodies; bright glowing mad in our inferior brains; wild hair flying, wild eyes staring, wild voices keening; undaunted by blood we who hemorrhage every twenty-eight days; laughing at our own beauty we who have lost our sense of humor; mourning for all each precious one of us might have been in this one living time-place had she not been born a woman; stuffing fingers into our mouths to stop the screams of fear and hate and pity for men we have loved and love still; tears in our eyes and bitterness in our mouths for children we couldn't have, or couldn't *not* have, or didn't want, or didn't want *yet*, or wanted and had in this place and this time of horror. We are rising with a fury older and potentially greater than any force in history, and this time we will be free or no one will survive. Power to all the people or to none. All the way down, this time.

Free Kathleen Cleaver!   Free Kim Agnew!
Free Anita Hoffman!   Free Holly Krassner!
Free Bernadine Dohrn!   Free Lois Hart!
Free Donna Malone!   Free Alice Embree!
Free Ruth Ann Miller!   Free Nancy Kurshan!
Free Leni Sinclair!   Free Lynn Phillips!
Free Jane Alpert!   Free Dinky Forman!
Free Gumbo!   Free Sharon Krebs!
Free Bonnie Cohen!   Free Iris Luciano!
Free Judy Lampe!   Free Robin Morgan!
Free Valerie Solanas!

FREE OUR SISTERS! FREE OURSELVES!

RADICALESBIANS

The Woman-Identified Woman

At the Second Congress to Unite Women, convened in New York City in May 1970, an unscheduled event interrupted the first evening's program. As some 400 feminist activists listened to the final moments of a presentation by the drama group Burning City, the auditorium suddenly went dark. When the lights came up again, twenty women wearing T-shirts imprinted "Lavender Menace" stood at the front of the room.

Lavender Menace was a recently formed collective of lesbian feminists. Its name derived from a remark attributed to Betty Friedan—that lesbians in the women's movement were a "lavender menace" that could ultimately hurt the cause.[1] Actually, lesbians had been involved in the women's movement from its inception, most often without identifying themselves as homosexual. But since the birth of the gay liberation movement in 1969, many lesbians had wished to end what seemed to them a demeaning charade. A few had revealed their sexual orientation—only to encounter antagonism where they least expected it: in the feminist family.

The Lavender Menace, arrayed at the front of the auditorium, spoke to those attending the congress about discrimination against lesbians in the women's movement. When they called for sympathetic members of the audience to come forward, about thirty women responded. The next day, conference participants crowded into impromptu workshops on lesbianism conducted by the Menaces. Similar events occurred at a congress on the West

---

[1]In some versions of the anecdote, Friedan is said to have called the charge of lesbianism in the movement a "lavender herring"—a play on "red herring," a term from the 1950s.

Coast. The issue of gays in the women's movement—long hidden in the shadows—had emerged into the light.

One of the first projects of Lavender Menace, who renamed themselves Radicalesbians, was to produce a position paper titled "The Woman-Identified Woman." Lesbians began to pressure NOW to publicly support their struggle for basic human rights, and many bitter feuds erupted. By 1971, however, NOW passed a resolution affirming a woman's right "to define and express her own sexuality" and stating that "NOW acknowledges the oppression of lesbians as a legitimate concern of feminism." Two years later NOW incorporated lesbian rights into its legislative agenda.

But this was by no means the end of the matter. The lesbian issue continued to generate personal and ideological splits among feminists—including among radical feminists—that sisterhood could not always surmount. Lesbians and straights both played a part in this unfortunate turn of events: Some straight feminists were afraid of being labeled dykes and wished to dissociate both the movement and themselves from lesbianism, while some lesbians claimed that lesbianism was an example of feminism in action and preached that the only true feminists were those who renounced relations with the opposite sex entirely. Such proselytizing apparently influenced a number of feminists to become lesbians by choice; but others, like longtime activist Anne Koedt, found the claims "outrageous." Koedt wrote, "It seems to me to show a disrespect for another woman to presume that it is any group's (or individual's) prerogative to pass revolutionary judgment on the progress of her life. . . . Feminism is an offering, not a directive."[2]

The Radicalesbian position paper, "The Woman-Identified Woman," originally appeared in *Rat* and *Come Out!* and was published in pamphlet form in 1972 by Gay Flames, a group of male homosexuals active in New York's Gay Liberation Front. It is reprinted here in full.

---

[2] Anne Koedt, "Lesbianism and Feminism," in *Radical Feminism*, ed. Anne Koedt, Ellen Levine, and Anita Rapone (New York: Quadrangle, 1973), pp. 255–256. Reprinted from *Notes from the Third Year* (1971).

WHAT IS A LESBIAN? A lesbian is the rage of all women condensed to the point of explosion. She is the woman who, often beginning at an extremely early age, acts in accordance with her inner compulsion to be a more complete and freer human being than her society—perhaps then, but certainly later—cares to allow her. These needs and actions, over a period of years, bring her into painful conflict with people, situations, the accepted ways of thinking, feeling and behaving, until she is in a state of continual war with everything around her, and usually with herself. She may not be fully conscious of the political implications of what for her began as personal necessity, but on some level she has not been able to accept the limitations and oppression laid on her by the most basic role of her society—the female role. The turmoil she experiences tends to induce guilt proportional to the degree to which she feels she is not meeting social expectations, and/or eventually drives her to question and analyze what the rest of her society more or less accepts. She is forced to evolve her own life pattern, often living much of her life alone, learning usually much earlier than her "straight" (heterosexual) sisters about the essential aloneness of life (which the myth of marriage obscures) and about the reality of illusions. To the extent that she cannot expel the heavy socialization that goes with being female, she can never truly find peace with herself. For she is caught somewhere between accepting society's view of her—in which case she cannot accept herself—and coming to understand what this sexist society has done to her and why it is functional and necessary for it to do so. Those of us who work that through find ourselves on the other side of a tortuous journey through a night that may have been decades long. The perspective gained from that journey, the liberation of self, the inner peace, the real love of self and of all women, is something to be shared with all women—because we are all women.

It should first be understood that lesbianism, like male homosexuality, is a category of behavior possible only in a sexist society characterized by rigid sex roles and dominated by male supremacy. Those sex roles dehumanize women by defining us as a supportive/serving caste *in relation to* the master caste of men, and emotionally cripple men by demanding that they be alienated from their own bodies and emotions in order to perform their economic/political/military functions effectively. Homosexuality is a by-product of a particular way of setting up roles (or approved patterns of behavior) on the basis of sex; as such it is an inauthentic (not consonant with "reality") category. In a society in which men do not oppress women, and sexual expression is allowed to follow feelings, the categories of homosexuality and heterosexuality would disappear.

But lesbianism is also different from male homosexuality, and serves a different function in the society. "Dyke" is a different kind of put-down from "faggot," although both imply you are not playing your socially assigned sex role . . . are not therefore a "real woman" or a "real man." The grudging admiration felt for the tomboy, and the queasiness felt around a sissy boy point to the same thing: the contempt in which women—or those who play a female role—are held. And the investment in keeping women in that contemptuous role is very great. Lesbian is the word, the label, the condition that holds women in line. When a woman hears this word tossed her way, she knows she is stepping out of line. She knows that she has crossed the terrible boundary of her sex role. She recoils, she protests, she reshapes her actions to gain approval. Lesbian is a label invented by the Man to throw at any woman who dares to be his equal, who dares to challenge his prerogatives (including that of all women as part of the exchange medium among men), who dares to assert the primacy of her own needs. To have the label applied to people active in women's liberation is just the most recent instance of a long history; older women will recall that not so long ago, any woman who was successful, independent, not orienting her whole life about a man, would hear this word. For in this sexist society, for a woman to be independent means she *can't* be a *woman*—she *must* be a *dyke*. That in itself should tell us where women are at. It says as clearly as can be said: women and person are contradictory terms. For a lesbian is not considered a "real woman." And yet, in popular thinking, there is really only one essential difference between a lesbian and other women: that of sexual orientation—which is to say, when you strip off all the packaging, you must finally realize that the essence of being a "woman" is to get fucked by men.

"Lesbian" is one of the sexual categories by which men have divided up humanity. While all women are dehumanized as sex objects, as the objects of men they are given certain compensations: identification with his power, his ego, his status, his protection (from other males), feeling like a "real woman," finding social acceptance by adhering to her role, etc. Should a woman confront herself by confronting another woman, there are fewer rationalizations, fewer buffers by which to avoid the stark horror of her dehumanized condition. Herein we find the overriding fear of many women towards exploring intimate relationships with other women: the fear of being used as a sexual object by a woman, which not only will bring her no male-connected compensations, but also will reveal the void which is woman's real situation. This dehumanization is expressed when a straight woman learns that a sister is a lesbian; she begins to relate to her lesbian sister as her potential sex object, laying a surrogate male role on the lesbian. This reveals her heterosexual conditioning to make herself into an object when sex is potentially involved in a relationship, and it denies the lesbian her full humanity. For women, especially those in the movement, to perceive their lesbian sisters through this male grid of role definitions is to accept this male cultural conditioning and to oppress their sisters much as they themselves have been oppressed by men. Are we going to continue the male classification system of defining all females in *sexual relation* to some *other* category of people? Affixing the label "lesbian" not only to a woman who aspires to be a person, but also to any situation of real love, real solidarity, real primacy among women is a primary form of divisiveness among women: it is the condition which keeps women within the confines of the feminine role, and it is the debunking/scare term that keeps women from forming any primary attachments, groups, or associations among ourselves.

Women in the movement have in most cases gone to great lengths to avoid discussion and confrontation with the issue of lesbianism. It puts people up-tight. They are hostile, evasive, or try to incorporate it into some "broader issue." They would rather not talk about it. If they have to, they try to dismiss it as a "lavender herring." But it is no side issue. It is absolutely essential to the success and fulfillment of the women's liberation movement that this issue be dealt with. As long as the label "dyke" can be used to frighten a woman into a less militant stand, keep her separate from her sisters, keep her from giving primacy to anything other than men and family—then to that extent she is controlled by the male culture. Until women see in each other the possibility of a primal commitment which includes sexual love, they will be denying themselves the love and value they readily accord to men, thus affirming their second-class status. As long as male acceptability is primary—both to individual women and to the movement as a whole—the term "lesbian" will be used effectively against women. Insofar as women want only more privileges within the system, they do not want to antagonize male power. They instead seek acceptability for women's liberation, and the most crucial aspect of the acceptability is to deny lesbianism—i.e., deny any fundamental challenge to the basis of the female role.

It should also be said that some younger, more radical women have honestly begun to discuss lesbianism, but so far it has been primarily as a sexual "alternative" to men. This, however, is still giving primacy to men, both because the idea of relating more completely to women occurs as a *negative reaction to men,* and because the lesbian relationship is being characterized simply by sex, which is divisive and sexist. On one level, which is both personal and political, women may withdraw emotional and sexual energies from men, and work out various alternatives for those energies in their own lives. On a different political/psychological level, it must be understood that what is crucial is that women begin disengaging from male-defined response patterns. In the privacy of our own psyches, we must cut those cords to the core. For irrespective of where our love and sexual energies flow, if we are male-identified in our heads, we cannot realize our autonomy as human beings.

But why is it that women have related to and through men? By virtue of having been brought up in a male society, we have

internalized the male culture's definition of ourselves. That definition views us as relative beings who exist not for ourselves, but
for the servicing, maintenance and comfort of men. That definition consigns us to sexual and family functions, and excludes us
from defining and shaping the terms of our lives. In exchange
for our psychic servicing and for performing society's non–
profit-making functions, the man confers on us just one thing:
the slave status which makes us legitimate in the eyes of the society in which we live. This is called "femininity" or "being a real
woman" in our cultural lingo. We are authentic, legitimate, real
to the extent that we are the property of some man whose name
we bear. To be a woman who belongs to no man is to be invisible, pathetic, inauthentic, unreal. He confirms his image of us—
of what we have to be in order to be acceptable by him—but not
our real selves; he confirms our womanhood—as he defines it, in
relation to him—but cannot confirm our personhood, our own
selves as absolutes. As long as we are dependent on the male
culture for this definition, for this approval, we cannot be free.

The consequence of internalizing this role is an enormous
reservoir of self-hate. This is not to say the self-hate is recognized or accepted as such; indeed most women would deny it. It
may be experienced as discomfort with her role, as feeling
empty, as numbness, as restlessness, a paralyzing anxiety at the
center. Alternatively, it may be expressed in shrill defensiveness
of the glory and destiny of her role. But it does exist, often beneath the edge of her consciousness, poisoning her existence,
keeping her alienated from herself, her own needs, and rendering her a stranger to other women. They try to escape by identifying with the oppressor, living through him, gaining status and
identity from his ego, his power, his accomplishments. And by
not identifying with other "empty vessels" like themselves.
Women resist relating on all levels to other women who will reflect their own oppression, their own secondary status, their
own self-hate. For to confront another woman is finally to confront one's self—the self we have gone to such lengths to avoid.
And in that mirror we know we cannot really respect and love
that which we have been made to be.

As the source of self-hate and the lack of real self are rooted in our male-given identity, we must create a new sense of self. As long as we cling to the idea of "being a woman," we will sense some conflict with that incipient self, that sense of I, that sense of a whole person. It is very difficult to realize and accept that being "feminine" and being a whole person are irreconcilable. Only women can give each other a new sense of self. That identity we have to develop with reference to ourselves, and not in relation to men. This consciousness is the revolutionary force from which all else will follow, for ours is an organic revolution. For this we must be available and supportive to one another, give our commitment and our love, give the emotional support necessary to sustain this movement. Our energies must flow toward our sisters, not backwards toward our oppressors. As long as women's liberation tries to free women without facing the basic heterosexual structure that binds us in one-to-one relationship with our own oppressors, tremendous energies will continue to flow into trying to straighten up each particular relationship with a man, how to get better sex, how to turn his head around—into trying to make the "new man" out of him, in the delusion that this will allow us to be the "new woman." This obviously splits our energies and commitments, leaving us unable to be committed to the construction of the new patterns which will liberate us.

It is the primacy of women relating to women, of women creating a new consciousness of and with each other which is at the heart of women's liberation, and the basis for the cultural revolution. Together we must find, reinforce and validate our authentic selves. As we do this, we confirm in each other that struggling, incipient sense of pride and strength, the divisive barriers begin to melt, we feel this growing solidarity with our sisters. We see ourselves as prime, find our centers inside of ourselves. We find receding the sense of alienation, of being cut off, of being behind a locked window, of being unable to get out what we know is inside. We feel a realness, feel at last we are coinciding with ourselves. With that real self, with that consciousness, we begin a revolution to end the imposition of all coercive identifications, and to achieve maximum autonomy in human expression.

AUDRE LORDE

Who Said It Was Simple

Audre Lorde (1934–1992) was born in Harlem of West Indian
parents. After battling cancer for fourteen years, she died at
her home in St. Croix, the Virgin Islands.

Lorde was the author of nine collections of poetry and five
of prose. Among her works are *Cables to Rage* (1970), *Coal*
(1976), *The Black Unicorn* (1978), *The Cancer Journals* (1980),
a fictionalized memoir called *Zami—A New Spelling of My
Name* (1982), and *Sister Outsider: Essays and Speeches* (1984).
A collection of her essays, *A Burst of Light,* won an American
Book Award in 1989. A posthumously published collection of
her last poems, *The Marvelous Arithmetics of Distance,* appeared in 1993.

Lorde's poetry is firmly rooted in time and place, yet it is
timeless and without boundary. A 1969 work, "Equinox," is
one of many that illustrate the scope of her poetic vision:

> . . . dark mangled children
> came streaming out of the atlas
> Hanoi Angola Guinea-Bissau Mozambique Phnom Penh
> merging into Bedford-Stuyvesant and Hazelhurst Mississippi
> haunting my New York tenement that terribly bright summer
> while Detroit and Watts and San Francisco were burning

African history and African matriarchal myths also supplied
Lorde with rich stores of imagery and ideas for her work—as in
the poem "The Women of Dan Dance with Swords in Their
Hands to Mark the Time When They Were Warriors."[1]

---

[1]According to a glossary in *The Black Unicorn,* Dan was "an ancient name
for the kingdom of Dahomey," now Benin, in West Africa.—*Ed.*

Lorde insisted upon being fully herself. "It's easier to deal with a poet, certainly a Black woman poet," she once said, "when you categorize her, narrow her so she can fulfill your expectations. . . . I am not one piece of myself. I cannot be simply a Black person, and not be a woman, too, nor can I be a woman without being a lesbian."[2]

The following poem was written in 1970. Originally published in the volume *From a Land Where Other People Live* (1973), it is reprinted here from *Undersong: Chosen Poems, Old and New, Revised* (1992). In "Who Said It Was Simple," the poet speaks candidly of the complications of interracial sisterhood. She sketches deftly a group of affluent white women with whom she has stopped at a lunch counter before going to march in a feminist demonstration. With perplexity tinged with rueful humor, Lorde considers her particular burden of multiple oppressions as a black and a lesbian, no less than as a woman.

There are so many roots to the tree of anger
that sometimes the branches shatter
before they bear.

Sitting in Nedicks
the women rally before they march
discussing the problematic girls
they hire to make them free.
An almost white counterman passes
a waiting brother to serve them first

[2]Audre Lorde, "My Words Will Be There," from *Black Women Writers (1950–1980): A Critical Evaluation,* ed. Mari Evans (New York: Doubleday, 1984); quoted in *The Norton Anthology of Modern Poetry, 2d Edition,* ed. Richard Ellmann and Robert O'Clair (New York: Norton, 1988), p. 1429.

and the ladies neither notice nor reject
the slighter pleasures of their slavery.

But I who am bound by my mirror
as well as my bed
see cause in color
as well as sex.

and sit here wondering
which me will survive
all these liberations.

NATIONAL BLACK FEMINIST ORGANIZATION
STATEMENT OF PURPOSE

Many differences in outlook divided white middle-class feminists and black women, even when they basically agreed about gender equality. For example, white feminists tended to see paid employment as a route to independence and self-realization; most black women regarded jobs as an unpleasant part of life, just something one had to do if one wanted to eat. White feminists insisted that all restrictions on abortion should be lifted; black women feared the overuse of abortion (and sterilization) in the black community for "population control." Condemnation of men, a key motif of radical feminism, made black women uneasy because of their bond with black men as partners in the struggle against racism. (The novelist Alice Walker once commented sadly that "many black women are more loyal to black men than they are to themselves.")[1] Finally, social issues of vital importance to black women were not being dealt with by existing feminist organizations.

The result was an underrepresentation of blacks in the organized women's movement. But as early as 1970 writer Toni Cade (Bambara) observed that within the black community women were drawing together in "work-study groups, discussion clubs, cooperative nurseries, cooperative businesses, consumer education groups, women's workshops on the campuses, women's caucuses within existing organizations, Afro-American women's magazines."[2] In the next few years this trend devel-

---

[1] Walker reported this comment in "Other Voices, Other Moods," *Ms.*, February 1979, p. 70.
[2] Toni Cade, ed., *The Black Woman* (New York: Signet, 1970), p. 9.

oped further, as awareness of sexism was sharpened among all American women.

Starting in 1973, black feminists began to join forces. Black Women Organized for Action was formed by fifteen women in the San Francisco Bay area in January 1973; it had over 300 members a few years later. In May 1973, a meeting of black women in New York City became the impetus for the formation of the National Black Feminist Organization (NBFO).

Margaret Sloan, a contributing editor at *Ms.* magazine and first chair of NBFO, recalled the occasion: "About thirty of us sat in closeness because the room was not big enough. . . . All the things that have divided black women from each other in the past, kept us from getting to that room sooner, seemed not to be important."[3] The organization was launched in August 1973; over 400 women showed up for its first conference, in November. Among the issues that NBFO was concerned with were welfare, domestic workers, reproductive freedom, unwed mothers, the media, drug addiction, prisons, the arts, the black lesbian, and rape.

Branches of NBFO sprang up in more than ten cities, but membership peaked at about 2,000, and by the end of the seventies the organization had died. Michele Wallace, a founding member who quickly became disillusioned, wrote in 1975, "It is very possible that NBFO was not meant to happen when it did. Most of the prime movers in the organization were representing some other organization and whatever commitment they might have had to black women's issues took a backseat. . . . Despite a sizable number of black feminists who have contributed much to the leadership of the Women's Movement, there is no Black Women's Movement and it appears there won't be for some time to come."[4]

The National Black Feminist Organization's Statement of Purpose, issued in 1973, is reprinted here in full.

---

[3]Margaret Sloan, "Black Feminism: A New Mandate," *Ms.*, May 1974, p. 98.
[4]Michele Wallace, "On the National Black Feminist Organization," in Redstockings, *Feminist Revolution* (New York: Random House, 1975, 1978), p. 174.

THE DISTORTED MALE-DOMINATED MEDIA IMAGE of the Women's Liberation Movement has clouded the vital and revolutionary importance of this movement to Third World women, especially black women. The Movement has been characterized as the exclusive property of so-called white middle-class women and any black women seen involved in this Movement have been seen as "selling out," "dividing the race," and an assortment of nonsensical epithets. Black feminists resent these charges and have therefore established The National Black Feminist Organization, in order to address ourselves to the particular and specific needs of the larger, but almost cast-aside half of the black race in Amerikkka, the black woman.

Black women have suffered cruelly in this society from living the phenomenon of being black and female, in a country that is *both* racist and sexist. There has been very little real examination of the damage it has caused on the lives and on the minds of black women. Because we live in a patriarchy, we have allowed a premium to be put on black male suffering. No one of us would minimize the pain or hardship or the cruel and inhumane treatment experienced by the black man. But history, past or present, rarely deals with the malicious abuse put upon the black woman. We were seen as breeders by the master; despised and historically polarized from/by the master's wife; and looked upon as castrators by our lovers and husbands. The black woman has had to be strong, yet we are persecuted for having survived. We have been called "matriarchs" by white racists and black nationalists; we have virtually no positive self-images to validate our existence. Black women want to be proud, dignified, and free from all those false definitions of beauty and womanhood that are unrealistic and unnatural. *We,* not white men or black men, must define our own self-image as black women and not fall into the mistake of being placed upon the pedestal which is even being rejected by white women. It has been hard for black women to emerge from the myriad of distorted images that have portrayed us as grinning Beulahs, castrating Sapphires, and pancake-box Jemimas. As black feminists we realized the need to establish ourselves as an independent black feminist organization. Our aboveground presence will lend enormous credibility to the current Women's Liberation Movement, which unfortunately is not seen as the serious political and economic revolutionary force that it is. We will strengthen the current efforts of the Black Liberation struggle in this country by encouraging *all* of the talents and creativities of black women to emerge, strong and beautiful, not to feel guilty or divisive, and assume positions of leadership and honor in the black community. We will encourage the black community to stop falling into the trap of the white male Left, utilizing women only in terms of domestic or servile needs. We will continue to remind the Black Liberation Movement that there can't be liberation for half the race. We must, together, as a people, work to eliminate racism, from without the black community, which is trying to destroy us as an entire people; but we must remember that sexism is destroying and crippling us from within.

THE COMBAHEE RIVER COLLECTIVE
STATEMENT

The Combahee River Collective was a black feminist group founded in Boston in 1974. It took its name from a guerrilla action planned and led by Harriet Tubman during the Civil War. This military operation, which occurred in the Port Royal region of South Carolina, resulted in the freeing of more than 750 slaves.[1]

The statement excerpted here, composed in 1977 by three members of the collective—Barbara Smith, Beverly Smith, and Demita Frazier—tells the story of the first three years of the group's existence. The hundreds of women who enlisted in one phase or another of the collective's activities were battle-scarred veterans of the New Left, civil rights, and early women's movements. Most of them were drawn to Combahee because they had never felt fully at home in any of the organizations in which they had worked. "Every Black woman who came," the statement explains, "came out of a strongly-felt need for some level of possibility that did not previously exist in her life." Among the critical issues for African-American women that the statement details are the effects of racism and sexism on personal development, obstacles to organizing black women, and the prevalence of sexism in the black community. Adrienne Rich has described the statement as "a major document of the U.S. women's movement, which gives a clear and uncompromising Black-feminist naming to the experience of simultaneity of oppressions."[2]

[1]*Home Girls: A Black Feminist Anthology,* ed. Barbara Smith (Latham, NY: Kitchen Table: Women of Color Press, 1983), p. 272 n.

[2]Adrienne Rich, "Notes Toward a Politics of Location," in *Blood, Bread, and Poetry, Selected Prose, 1979–1985* (New York: Norton, 1986), p. 218.

Many of those associated with the collective later had the opportunity to share their insights widely with other women, thus enlarging the network of those exposed to its analysis. The collective sponsored a series of seven black feminist retreats in the seventies that forged links among scores of activist women from cities along the East Coast. Coauthor of the Combahee River Statement, Barbara Smith (b. 1946), wrote numerous essays that appeared in black and feminist periodicals, and she coedited with Gloria T. Hull and Patricia Bell Scott the collection *All the Women Are White, All the Blacks Are Men, but Some of Us Are Brave*, published by the Feminist Press in 1981. In addition, she was a cofounder with Audre Lorde, in the early 1980s, of Kitchen Table: Women of Color Press.

After nearly a decade of feminist organizing among black women, Barbara Smith wrote in her introduction to *Home Girls: A Black Feminist Anthology*, which she edited for Kitchen Table, "It is safe to say in 1982 that we have a movement of our own. . . . I feel we are still in just the beginning of developing a workable politics and practice. Yet the feminism of women of color, particularly of Afro-American women, has wrought many changes during these years, has had both obvious and unrecognized impact upon the development of other political groupings and upon the lives and hopes of countless women."[3]

WE ARE A COLLECTIVE OF BLACK FEMINISTS who have been meeting together since 1974. During that time we have been involved in the process of defining and clarifying our politics, while at the same time doing political work within our own group and in coalition with other progressive organizations and move-

---

[3]*Home Girls,* "Introduction," p. xxxi. Smith defined "women of color" as Afro-American, Native-American, and Asian-American women, and Latinas.

ments. The most general statement of our politics at the present time would be that we are actively committed to struggling against racial, sexual, heterosexual, and class oppression, and see as our particular task the development of integrated analysis and practice based upon the fact that the major systems of oppression are interlocking. The synthesis of these oppressions creates the conditions of our lives. As Black women we see Black feminism as the logical political movement to combat the manifold and simultaneous oppressions that all women of color face. . . .

1. The Genesis of Contemporary Black Feminism

Before looking at the recent development of Black feminism, we would like to affirm that we find our origins in the historical reality of Afro-American women's continuous life-and-death struggle for survival and liberation. Black women's extremely negative relationship to the American political system (a system of white male rule) has always been determined by our membership in two oppressed racial and sexual castes. As Angela Davis points out in "Reflections on the Black Woman's Role in the Community of Slaves," Black women have always embodied, if only in their physical manifestation, an adversary stance to white male rule and have actively resisted its inroads upon them and their communities in both dramatic and subtle ways. There have always been Black women activists—some known, like Sojourner Truth, Harriet Tubman, Frances E. W. Harper, Ida B. Wells Barnett, and Mary Church Terrell, and thousands upon thousands unknown—who have had a shared awareness of how their sexual identity combined with their racial identity to make their whole life situation and the focus of their political struggles unique. Contemporary Black feminism is the outgrowth of countless generations of personal sacrifice, militancy, and work by our mothers and sisters.

A Black feminist presence has evolved most obviously in connection with the second wave of the American women's movement beginning in the late 1960s. Black, other Third World, and working women have been involved in the feminist movement from its start, but both outside reactionary forces and racism and elitism within the movement itself have served to obscure our participation. In 1973, Black feminists, primarily located in New York, felt the necessity of forming a separate Black feminist group. This became the National Black Feminist Organization (NBFO).

Black feminist politics also have an obvious connection to movements for Black liberation, particularly those of the 1960s and 1970s. Many of us were active in those movements (Civil Rights, Black nationalism, the Black Panthers), and all of our lives were greatly affected and changed by their ideologies, their goals, and the tactics used to achieve their goals. It was our experience and disillusionment within these liberation movements, as well as experience on the periphery of the white male left, that led to the need to develop a politics that was anti-racist, unlike those of white women, and anti-sexist, unlike those of Black and white men.

There is also undeniably a personal genesis for Black feminism, that is, the political realization that comes from the seemingly personal experiences of individual Black women's lives. Black feminists and many more Black women who do not define themselves as feminists have all experienced sexual oppression as a constant factor in our day-to-day existence. As children we realized that we were different from boys and that we were treated differently. For example, we were told in the same breath to be quiet both for the sake of being "ladylike" and to make us less objectionable in the eyes of white people. As we grew older we became aware of the threat of physical and sexual abuse by men. However, we had no way of conceptualizing what was so apparent to us, what we *knew* was really happening.

Black feminists often talk about their feelings of craziness before becoming conscious of the concepts of sexual politics, patriarchal rule, and most importantly, feminism, the political analysis and practice that we women use to struggle against our oppression. The fact that racial politics and indeed racism are pervasive factors in our lives did not allow us, and still does not allow most Black women, to look more deeply into our own experiences and, from that sharing and growing consciousness, to build a politics that will change our lives and inevitably end our oppression. Our development must also be tied to the contemporary economic and political position of Black people. The post–World War II generation of Black youth was the first to be able to minimally partake of certain educational and employment options, previously closed completely to Black people. Although our economic position is still at the very bottom of the American capitalistic economy, a handful of us have been able to gain certain tools as a result of tokenism in education and employment which potentially enable us to more effectively fight our oppression.

A combined anti-racist and anti-sexist position drew us together initially, and as we developed politically we addressed ourselves to heterosexism and economic oppression under capitalism.

2. What We Believe

Above all else, our politics initially sprang from the shared belief that Black women are inherently valuable, that our liberation is a necessity not as an adjunct to somebody else's but because of our need as human persons for autonomy. This may seem so obvious as to sound simplistic, but it is apparent that no other ostensibly progressive movement has ever considered our specific oppression as a priority or worked seriously for the ending of that oppression. Merely naming the pejorative stereotypes attributed to Black women (e.g., mammy, matriarch, Sapphire, whore, bulldagger), let alone cataloguing the cruel, often murderous, treatment we receive, indicates how little value has been placed upon our lives during four centuries of bondage in the Western hemisphere. We realize that the only people who care enough about us to work consistently for our liberation are us. Our politics evolve from a healthy love for ourselves, our sisters and our community, which allows us to continue our struggle and work.

This focusing upon our own oppression is embodied in the concept of identity politics. We believe that the most profound and potentially most radical politics come directly out of our own identity, as opposed to working to end somebody else's oppression. In the case of Black women this is a particularly repugnant, dangerous, threatening, and therefore revolutionary concept because it is obvious from looking at all the political movements that have preceded us that anyone is more worthy of liberation than ourselves. We reject pedestals, queenhood, and walking ten paces behind. To be recognized as human, levelly human, is enough.

We believe that sexual politics under patriarchy is as pervasive in Black women's lives as are the politics of class and race. We also often find it difficult to separate race from class from sex oppression because in our lives they are most often experienced simultaneously. We know that there is such a thing as racial-sexual oppression which is neither solely racial nor solely sexual, e.g., the history of rape of Black women by white men as a weapon of political repression.

Although we are feminists and Lesbians, we feel solidarity with progressive Black men and do not advocate the fractionalization that white women who are separatists demand. Our situation as Black people necessitates that we have solidarity around the fact of race, which white women of course do not need to have with white men, unless it is their negative solidarity as racial oppressors. We struggle together with Black men against racism, while we also struggle with Black men about sexism.

We realize that the liberation of all oppressed peoples necessitates the destruction of the political-economic systems of capitalism and imperialism as well as patriarchy. We are socialists because we believe that work must be organized for the collective benefit of those who do the work and create the products, and not for the profit of the bosses. Material resources must be equally distributed among those who create these resources. We are not convinced, however, that a socialist revolution that is not also a feminist and anti-racist revolution will guarantee our liberation. We have arrived at the necessity for developing an understanding of class relationships that takes into account the specific class position of Black women who are generally marginal in the labor force, while at this particular time some of us are temporarily viewed as doubly desirable tokens at white-collar and professional levels. We need to articulate the real class situation of persons who are not merely raceless, sex- less workers, but for whom racial and sexual oppression are significant determinants in their working/economic lives. Although we are in essential agreement with Marx's theory as it applied to the very specific economic relationships he analyzed, we know that his analysis must be extended further in order for us to understand our specific economic situation as Black women.

A political contribution which we feel we have already made is the expansion of the feminist principle that the personal is po- litical. In our consciousness-raising sessions, for example, we have in many ways gone beyond white women's revelations be- cause we are dealing with the implications of race and class as well as sex. Even our Black women's style of talking/testifying in Black language about what we have experienced has a reso- nance that is both cultural and political. We have spent a great deal of energy delving into the cultural and experiential nature of our oppression out of necessity because none of these matters has ever been looked at before. No one before has ever exam- ined the multilayered texture of Black women's lives. An exam- ple of this kind of revelation/conceptualization occurred at a meeting as we discussed the ways in which our early intellectual interests had been attacked by our peers, particularly Black males. We discovered that all of us, because we were "smart" had also been considered "ugly," i.e., "smart-ugly." "Smart- ugly" crystallized the way in which most of us had been forced to develop our intellects at great cost to our "social" lives. The sanctions in the Black and white communities against Black women thinkers is comparatively much higher than for white women, particularly ones from the educated middle and upper classes.

As we have already stated, we reject the stance of Lesbian separatism because it is not a viable political analysis or strategy for us. It leaves out far too much and far too many people, particularly Black men, women, and children. We have a great deal of criticism and loathing for what men have been socialized to be in this society: what they support, how they act, and how they oppress. But we do not have the misguided notion that it is their maleness, per se—i.e., their biological maleness—that makes them what they are. As Black women we find any type of biological determinism a particularly dangerous and reactionary basis upon which to build a politic. We must also question whether Lesbian separatism is an adequate and progressive political analysis and strategy, even for those who practice it, since it so completely denies any but the sexual sources of women's oppression, negating the facts of class and race.

3. Problems in Organizing Black Feminists

During our years together as a Black feminist collective, we have experienced success and defeat, joy and pain, victory and failure. We have found that it is very difficult to organize around Black feminist issues, difficult even to announce in certain contexts that we *are* Black feminists. We have tried to think about the reasons for our difficulties, particularly since the white women's movement continues to be strong and to grow in many directions. In this section we will discuss some of the general reasons for the organizing problems we face and also talk specifically about the stages in organizing our own collective.

The major source of difficulty in our political work is that we are not just trying to fight oppression on one front, or even two, but instead to address a whole range of oppressions. We do not have racial, sexual, heterosexual, or class privilege to rely upon, nor do we have even the minimal access to resources and power that groups who possess any one of these types of privilege have.

The psychological toll of being a Black woman and the difficulties this presents in reaching political consciousness and doing political work can never be underestimated. There is very low value placed upon Black women's psyches in this society, which is both racist and sexist. As an early group member once said, "We are all damaged people merely by virtue of being Black women." We are dispossessed psychologically and on every other level, and yet we feel the necessity to struggle to change the condition of all Black women. In "A Black Feminist's Search for Sisterhood," Michele Wallace arrives at this conclusion:

> We exist as women who are Black who are feminists, each stranded for the moment, working independently because there is not yet an environment in this society remotely congenial to our struggle—because, being on the bottom, we would have to do what no one else has done: we would have to fight the world.[4]

Wallace is pessimistic but realistic in her assessment of Black feminists' position, particularly in her allusion to the nearly classic isolation most of us face. We might use our position at the bottom, however, to make a clear leap into revolutionary action. If Black women were free, it would mean that everyone else would have to be free, since our freedom would necessitate the destruction of all the systems of oppression.

Feminism is, nevertheless, very threatening to the majority of Black people because it calls into question some of the most basic assumptions about our existence, i.e., that sex should be a determinant of power relationships. Here is the way male and female roles were defined in a Black nationalist pamphlet from the early 1970s:

> . . . The man is the head of the house. He is the leader of the house/nation because his knowledge of the world is broader, his awareness is greater, his understanding is fuller and his application of this information is wiser. . . . Women cannot do the same things as men—they are made by nature to function differently. Equality of men and women is something that cannot happen even in the abstract world. . . .[5]

[4]Michele Wallace, "A Black Feminist's Search for Sisterhood," *Village Voice*, July 28, 1975, pp. 6–7.
[5]Mumininas of Committee for Unified Newark, Mwanamke Mwananchi (The Nationalist Woman), Newark, NJ, 1971, pp. 4–5.

The material conditions of most Black women would hardly lead them to upset both economic and sexual arrangements that seem to represent some stability in their lives. Many Black women have a good understanding of both sexism and racism, but because of the everyday constrictions of their lives, cannot risk struggling against them both.

The reaction of Black men to feminism has been notoriously negative. They are, of course, even more threatened than Black women by the possibility that Black feminists might organize around our own needs. They realize that they might not only lose valuable and hardworking allies in their struggles but that they might also be forced to change their habitually sexist ways of interacting with and oppressing Black women. Accusations that Black feminism divides the Black struggle are powerful deterrents to the growth of an autonomous Black women's movement.

Still, hundreds of women have been active at different times during the three-year existence of our group. And every Black woman who came, came out of a strongly-felt need for some level of possibility that did not previously exist in her life.

When we first started meeting early in 1974 after the NBFO first eastern regional conference, we did not have a strategy for organizing, or even a focus. We just wanted to see what we had. After a period of months of not meeting, we began to meet again late in the year and started doing an intense variety of consciousness-raising. The overwhelming feeling that we had is that after years and years we had finally found each other. Although we were not doing political work as a group, individuals continued their involvement in Lesbian politics, sterilization abuse and abortion rights work, Third World Women's International Women's Day activities, and support activity for the trials of Dr. Kenneth Edelin, Joan Little, and Inéz García. During our first summer, when membership had dropped off considerably, those of us remaining devoted serious discussion to the possibility of opening a refuge for battered women in a Black community. (There was no refuge in Boston at that time.) We also decided around that time to become an independent collective since we had serious disagreements with NBFO's bourgeois-feminist stance and their lack of a clear political focus.

We also were contacted at that time by socialist feminists with whom we had worked on abortion rights activities, who wanted to encourage us to attend the National Socialist Feminist Conference in Yellow Springs. One of our members did attend and, despite the narrowness of the ideology that was promoted at that particular conference, we became more aware of the need for us to understand our own economic situation and to make our own economic analysis.

In the fall, when some members returned, we experienced several months of comparative inactivity and internal disagreements which were first conceptualized as a Lesbian-straight split but which were also the result of class and political differences. During the summer those of us who were still meeting had determined the need to do political work and to move beyond consciousness-raising and serving exclusively as an emotional support group. At the beginning of 1976, when some of the women who had not wanted to do political work and who also had voiced disagreements stopped attending of their own accord, we again looked for a focus. We decided at that time, with the addition of new members, to become a study group. We had always shared our reading with each other, and some of us had written papers on Black feminism for group discussion a few months before this decision was made. We began functioning as a study group and also began discussing the possibility of starting a Black feminist publication. We had a retreat in the late spring which provided a time for both political discussion and working out interpersonal issues. Currently we are planning to gather together a collection of Black feminist writing. We feel that it is absolutely essential to demonstrate the reality of our politics to other Black women and believe that we can do this through writing and distributing our work. The fact that individual Black feminists are living in isolation all over the country, that our own numbers are small, and that we have some skills in writing, printing, and publishing makes us want to carry out these kinds of projects as a means of organizing Black feminists as we continue to do political work in coalition with other groups.

4. Black Feminist Issues and Projects

During our time together we have identified and worked on many issues of particular relevance to Black women. The inclusiveness of our politics makes us concerned with any situation that impinges upon the lives of women, Third World and working people. We are of course particularly committed to working on those struggles in which race, sex, and class are simultaneous factors in oppression. We might, for example, become involved in workplace organizing at a factory that employs Third World women or picket a hospital that is cutting back on already inadequate health care to a Third World community, or set up a rape crisis center in a Black neighborhood. Organizing around welfare and daycare concerns might also be a focus. The work to be done and the countless issues that this work represents merely reflect the pervasiveness of our oppression.

Issues and projects that collective members have actually worked on are sterilization abuse, abortion rights, battered women, rape, and health care. We have also done many workshops and educationals on Black feminism on college campuses, at women's conferences, and most recently for high school women.

One issue that is of major concern to us and that we have begun to publicly address is racism in the white women's movement. As Black feminists we are made constantly and painfully aware of how little effort white women have made to understand and combat their racism, which requires among other things that they have a more than superficial comprehension of race, color, and Black history and culture. Eliminating racism in the white women's movement is by definition work for white women to do, but we will continue to speak to and demand accountability on this issue.

In the practice of our politics we do not believe that the end always justifies the means. Many reactionary and destructive acts have been done in the name of achieving "correct" political goals. As feminists we do not want to mess over people in the name of politics. We believe in collective process and a nonhierarchical distribution of power within our own group and in our vision of a revolutionary society. We are committed to a continual examination of our politics as they develop through criticism and self-criticism as an essential aspect of our practice. In her introduction to *Sisterhood Is Powerful* Robin Morgan writes:

> I haven't the faintest notion what possible revolutionary role white heterosexual men could fulfill, since they are the very embodiment of reactionary-vested-interest-power.[6]

As Black feminists and Lesbians we know that we have a very definite revolutionary task to perform and we are ready for the lifetime of work and struggle before us.

[6] Robin Morgan, *Sisterhood Is Powerful* (New York: Vintage, 1970), p. xxxv.

IV

"We Cannot Rely
on Existing Ideologies"

CYNTHIA OZICK

The Demise of the Dancing Dog

It was while teaching at a leading American university that novelist and essayist Cynthia Ozick (b. 1928) first encountered what she wryly termed "the Ovarian Theory of Literature." This "theory," espoused by students and professors alike, held that the human mind has gender and that the products of human intelligence (especially literature) can be identified as having emanated from a male or female person. Despite nearly unanimous acceptance of this concept on the university campus, Ozick firmly rejected it in her essay "The Demise of the Dancing Dog," written in 1965.

When Ozick included the piece in the 1983 collection of her nonfiction writings, *Art and Ardor,* she expanded the title[1] and added an introductory note, in which she remarked that the language of the essay now seemed to her stiff. "I was writing from a briar patch on a desert island in the middle of a bog—an uncomfortable and lonely place to be," she explained. "Feminism was, in those years, a private tenet one held alone, in an archaic voice."[2]

The author broached the topic of the relationship between mind and gender again in a 1977 *Ms.* magazine article. By then, the women's movement was in high gear and some feminists had themselves embraced a doctrine of female specialness. Ozick deplored their emphasis on gender diffrences, singling out for particular criticism the term *woman writer.* This phrase, she argued, hinges on the false idea that "there are 'male' and 'female' states

---

[1] The new title was "Previsions of the Demise of the Dancing Dog."
[2] *Art and Ardor* (New York: Knopf, 1983), p. 262.

of intellect and feeling, hence of prose." Not only is the idea of a separate female sensibility contrary to the basic principles of feminism, she insisted, but it ultimately can be used to put women down.[3]

Ozick's works in fiction include *Trust* (1966), *The Cannibal Galaxy* (1983), *The Messiah of Stockholm* (1987), and *The Shawl* (1989). A second volume of her collected essays is entitled *Metaphor and Memory* (1989).

The following selection is excerpted from *Art and Ardor*.

SEVERAL YEARS AGO I DEVOTED A YEAR to Examining the Minds of the Young. It was a curious experience, like going into theater after theater in a single night, and catching bits of first acts only. How will the heroine's character develop? Will the hero turn out to be captain of his fate or only of some minor industry? I never arrived at the second act, and undoubtedly I will never be witness to the denouement. But what I saw of all those beginnings was extraordinary: they were all so similar. All the characters were exactly the same age, and most had equal limitations of imagination and aspiration. Is "the individual," I wondered, a sacred certainty, and the human mind infinitely diversified, as we are always being told? Examine for yourself the Minds of the Young and it is possible you will begin to think the opposite. Democratic theory is depressingly correct in declaring all men equal. Just as every human hand is limited at birth by its five fingers, so is every human mind stamped from a single, equally obvious pattern. "I have never in all my various travels seen but two sorts of people, and those very like one another; I mean men and women, who always have been, and ever will be, the same," wrote Lady Mary Wortley Montagu in the middle of the eighteenth century. Human nature is one.

[3]Ibid., pp. 284–290; originally published in *Ms.*, December 1977.

The vantage point from which I came to these not unusual conclusions was not from reading the great philosophers, or even from reading Lady Mary—it was from a job. I was hired by a large urban university to teach English to freshmen: three classes of nearly a hundred young men and women, all seventeen, some city-born, some suburban, some well-off, some only scraping by, of every ethnic group and of every majority religion but Hindu. Almost all were equipped with B high-school averages; almost all were more illiterate than not; almost all possessed similar prejudices expressed in identical platitudes. Almost all were tall, healthy, strong-toothed, obedient, and ignorant beyond their years. They had, of course, very few ideas—at seventeen this can hardly be called a failing; but the ideas they had were plainly derived not from speculation but from indoctrination. They had identical minuscule vocabularies, made identical errors of grammar and punctuation, and were identically illogical. They were identically uneducated, and the minds of the uneducated young women were identical with the minds of the uneducated young men.

Now this last observation was the least surprising of all. Though unacquainted with the darkest underbrush of the human mind (and here it must be emphatically averred that deep scrutiny, at indecently short intervals, of one hundred freshman themes is the quickest and most scarifying method of achieving intimacy with the human mind in its rawest state), I had never doubted that the human mind was a democratic whole, that it was androgynous, epicene, asexual, call it what you will; it had always seemed axiomatic to me that the minds of men and women were indistinguishable.

My students confirmed this axiom to the last degree. You could not tell the young men's papers from the young women's papers. They thought alike (badly), they wrote alike (gracelessly), and they believed alike (docilely). And what they all believed was this: that the minds of men and women were spectacularly unlike.

They believed that men write like men, and women like women; that men think like men, and women like women; that men believe like men, and women like women. And they were all identical in this belief.

But I have said, after all, that they were alike in illiteracy, undereducation, ignorance, and prejudice.

Still, to teach at a university is not simply to teach; the teacher is a teacher among students, but he is also a teacher among teachers. He has colleagues, and to have colleagues is to have high exchanges, fruitful discourses, enlightening quarrels. Colleagues, unlike students, are not merely literate but breathtakingly literary; not merely educated but bent under the weight of multitudinous higher degrees; not merely informed but dazzlingly knowledgeable; not merely unprejudiced but brilliantly questing. And my colleagues believed exactly what my students believed.

My colleagues were, let it be noted, members of the Department of English in the prestige college of an important university. I was, let it be revealed, the only woman instructor in that department. Some years before, the college had been all male. Then the coeds were invited in, and now and then in their wake a woman was admitted, often reluctantly, to the faculty. Before my own admittance, I had been living the isolated life of a writer—my occupation for some years had consisted in reading great quantities and in writing embarrassingly tiny quantities. I was, I suppose, not in that condition generally known as "being in touch with the world." I was in touch with novels, poetry, essays, enlarging meditations; but of "the world," as it turned out, I apparently knew little.

I came to the university in search of the world. I had just finished an enormous novel, the writing of which had taken many more years than any novel ought to take, and after so long a retreat my lust for the world was prodigious. I wanted Experience, I wanted to sleep under bridges—but finding that all the bridges had thickly trafficked cloverleaves under them, I came instead to the university. I came innocently. I had believed, through all those dark and hope-sickened years of writing, that it was myself ("myself"—whatever that means for each of us) who was doing the writing. In the university, among my colleagues, I discovered two essential points: (1) that it was a "woman" who had done the writing—not a mind—and that I was a "woman writer"; and (2) that I was now not a teacher, but a "woman teacher."

I was suspect from the beginning—more so among my colleagues than among my students. My students, after all, were accustomed to the idea of a "woman teacher," having recently been taught by several in high school. But my colleagues were long out of high school, and they distrusted me. I learned that I had no genuinely valid opinions, since every view I might hold was colored by my sex. If I said I didn't like Hemingway, I could have no *critical* justification, no *literary* reason; it was only because, being a woman, I obviously could not be sympathetic toward Hemingway's "masculine" subject matter—the hunting, the fishing, the bullfighting, which no woman could adequately digest. It goes without saying that among my colleagues there were other Hemingway dissenters; but their reasons for disliking Hemingway, unlike mine, were not taken to be simply ovarian.

In fact, both my students and my colleagues were equal adherents of the Ovarian Theory of Literature, or, rather, its complement, the Testicular Theory. A recent camp follower (I cannot call him a pioneer) of this explicit theory is, of course, Norman Mailer, who has attributed his own gift, and the literary gift in general, solely and directly to the possession of a specific pair of organs. One writes with these organs, Mailer has said in *Advertisements for Myself;* and I have always wondered with what shade of ink he manages to do it.

I recall my first encounter with the Ovarian Theory. My students had been assigned the reading of *Wise Blood,* the novel by Flannery O'Connor. Somewhere in the discussion I referred to the author as "she." The class stirred in astonishment; they had not imagined that "Flannery" could connote a woman, and this somehow put a different cast upon the narrative and their response to it. Now among my students there was a fine young woman, intelligent and experimental rather than conforming, one of my rare literates, herself an anomaly because she was enrolled in the overwhelmingly male College of Engineering. I knew that her mind usually sought beyond the commonplace—she wrote with the askew glance of the really inquisitive. Up went her hand. "But I could *tell* she was a woman," she insisted. "Her sentences are a woman's sentences." I asked her what she meant and how she could tell. "Because they're sentimental," she said, "they're not concrete like a man's." I pointed out whole paragraphs, pages even, of unsentimental, so-called tough prose. "But she *sounds* like a woman—she has to sound that way because she is," said the future engineer, while I speculated whether her bridges and buildings would loom plainly as woman's work. Moreover, it rapidly developed that the whole class now declared that it too, even while ignorant of the author's sex, had nevertheless intuited all along that this was a woman's prose; it had to be, since Flannery was a she.

My second encounter with the idea of literature-as-physiology was odder yet. This time my interlocutor was a wonderfully gentle, deeply intellectual young fellow teacher; he was going to *prove* what my freshmen had merely maintained. "But of course style is influenced by physical make-up," he began in his judicious graduate-assistant way. Here was his incontrovertible evidence: "Take Keats, right? Keats fighting tuberculosis at the end of his life. You don't suppose Keats's poetry was totally unaffected by his having had tuberculosis?" And he smiled with the flourish of a young man who has made an unanswerable point. "Ah, but *you* don't suppose," I put it to him cheerfully enough, "that being a woman is a *disease*?"

But comparing literary women with having a debilitating disease is the least of it. My colleague, after all, was a kindly sort, and stuck to human matters; he did not mention dogs. On the other hand, almost everyone remembers Dr. Johnson's remark upon hearing a woman preacher—she reminded him, he said, of a dog dancing on its hind legs; one marvels not at how well it is done, but that it is done at all. That was two centuries ago; wise Lady Mary was Johnson's contemporary. Two centuries, and the world of letters has not been altered by a syllable, unless you regard the switch from dogs to disease as a rudimentary advance. Perhaps it is. We have advanced so far that the dullest as well as the best of freshmen can scarcely be distinguished from Dr. Johnson, except by a bark.

And our own Dr. Johnson—I leave you to guess his name—

hoping to insult a rival writer, announces that the rival "reminds me of nothing so much as a woman writer."

Consider, in this vein, the habits of reviewers. I think I can say in good conscience that I have never—repeat, *never*—read a review of a novel or, especially, of a collection of poetry by a woman that did not include somewhere in its columns a gratuitous allusion to the writer's sex and its supposed effects. The Ovarian Theory of Literature is the property of all society, not merely of freshmen and poor Ph.D. lackeys: you will find it in all the best periodicals, even the most highbrow. . . .

With respect to woman and with respect to literature . . . ours is among the most backward areas on earth. It is true that woman has . . . the vote . . . and has begun to enter most professions, though often without an invitation. We are far past the grievances Virginia Woolf grappled with in *A Room of One's Own* and *Three Guineas*—books still sneered at as "feminist." In 1929, when Virginia Woolf visited Oxford (or was it Cambridge? she is too sly to say which), she was chased off a lawn forbidden to the feet of women. By then, of course, our colleges were already full of coeds, though not so full as now. And yet the question of justification remains. Only a few months ago, in my own college, a startling debate was held— "Should a Woman Receive a College Education?" The audience was immense, but the debaters were only three: an instructor in anthropology (female), a professor of history (male), and a fiercely bearded professor of psychology (ostentatiously male). According to the unironic conventions of chivalry, the anthropologist spoke first. She spoke of opportunities and of problems. She spoke of living wholly and well. She did not ignore the necessities and difficulties of housekeeping and childrearing; she spoke of the relations of parents, children, and work-in-the-world; she talked extensively about nursery schools. She took as her premise not merely that woman ought to be fully educated, but that her education should be fully used in society. She was reasoned and reasonable; she had a point of view. Perhaps it was a controversial point of view, perhaps not—her listeners never had the chance of a serious evaluation. Her point of view was never assailed or refuted. It was overlooked. She spoke—against mysterious whispered cackles in the audience—and sat. Then up rose the laughing psychologist, and cracked jokes through his beard. Then up rose the laughing historian, and cracked jokes through his field—I especially remember one about the despotism of Catherine the Great. "That's what happens when a woman gets emancipated." Laughter from all sides. Were the historian and the psychologist laughing at the absurdity of the topic the callow students' committee had selected for debate? An absurd topic—it deserves to be laughed out of court, and surely that is exactly what is happening, since here in the audience are all these coeds, censuring and contradicting by their very presence the outrageous question. Yet look again: the coeds are laughing too. Everyone is laughing the laughter of mockery. They are not laughing at the absurdly callow topic. They are laughing at the buffoonery of the historian and the psychologist, who are themselves laughing at the subject of the topic: the whole huge room, packed to the very doors and beyond with mocking boys and girls, is laughing at the futility of an educated woman. *She* is the absurdity.

The idea of an educated woman is not yet taken seriously in American universities. She is not chased off the campus, she is even welcomed there—but she is not taken seriously as a student, and she will not be welcomed if she hopes to return as a serious lifelong scholar. Nor will she be welcomed afterward in the "world." A law firm may hire her, but it will hide her in its rear research offices, away from the eyes of clients. The lower schools will receive her, as they always have, since she is their bulwark; their bulwark, but not their principal, who is a man. We have seen her crawling like Griselda through the long ordeal of medicine: she is almost always bound to be a pediatrician, since it is in her nature to "work with children."

I will not forget the appalling laughter of the two mocking debaters. But it was not so appalling as the laughter of the young men and the young women in the audience. In the laughter of the historian and the psychologist I heard the fussy cry—a cry of violated venerable decorum, no doubt—of the beadle who chased Virginia Woolf off the grass in 1929. But what of that youthful mockery? Their laughter was hideous; it showed something ugly and self-shaming about the nature of our society and the nature of our education—and by "our education" I do not mean the colleges, I mean the kindergartens, I mean the living rooms at home, I mean the fathers and the mothers, the men and the women. . . .

My students—let us come back to *them*, since they are our societal prototypes . . . could not write intelligibly—no one had ever mentioned the relevance of writing to thinking, and thinking had never been encouraged or induced in them. By "thinking" I mean, of course, not the simple ability to make equations come out right, but the devotion to speculation on that frail but obsessive distraction known as the human condition. My students—male and female—did not need to speculate on what goals are proper to the full life; male and female, they already knew their goals. And their goals were identical. They all wanted to settle down into a perpetual and phantom coziness. They were all at heart sentimentalists—and sentimentalists, Yeats said, are persons "who believe in money, in position, in a marriage bell, and whose understanding of happiness is to be so busy whether at work or play, that all is forgotten but the momentary aim." Accordingly, they had all determined, long ago, to pursue the steady domestic life, the enclosed life, the restricted life—the life, in brief, of the daydream, into which the obvious must not be permitted to thrust its scary beams.

By the "obvious" I mean . . . the gifts and teachings and life-illuminations of art. The methods of art are variegated, flexible, abstruse, and often enough mysterious. But the burden of art is obvious: here is the world, here are human beings, here is childhood, here is struggle, here is hate, here is old age, here is death. None of these is a fantasy, a romance, or a sentiment, none is an imagining; all are obvious. A culture that does not allow itself to look clearly at the obvious through the universal accessibility of art is a culture of tragic delusion, hardly living. . . . It will turn out role-playing stereotypes (the hideousness of the phrase is appropriate to the concept) instead of human beings. It will shut the children away from half the population. It will shut aspiration away from half the population. It will glut its colleges with young people enduringly maimed by illusions learned early and kept late. It will sup on make-believe. But a humanist society— you and I do not live in one—is one in which a voice is heard: "Come," it says, "here is a world requiring architects, painters, playwrights, sailors, bridge-builders, jurists, captains, composers, discoverers, and a thousand things besides, all real and all obvious. Partake," it says; "live."

Is it a man's voice or a woman's voice? Students, colleagues, listen again; it is two voices. "How obvious," you will one day reply, and if you laugh, it will be at the quaint folly of obsolete custom, which once failed to harness the obvious; it will not be at a dancing dog.

JULIET MITCHELL

Women: The Longest Revolution

Juliet Mitchell (b. 1940), a British socialist feminist, surveyed the classics of socialist literature—writings by Fourier, Bebel, Marx, Engels—for explanations of the subordination of the female sex. What she discovered were ideas that seemed to her, despite her own ideological commitment to socialism, superficial, and almost incidental to the authors' main arguments. "The liberation of women," she concluded, "remains . . . an adjunct to socialist theory, not structurally integrated into it."

Mitchell's article "Women: The Longest Revolution" was the first important theoretical work on the condition of women to be produced by a member of her generation. It was published in England in 1966 by *New Left Review,* a Marxist journal of which she was an editor. When her paper appeared, British feminism was still dormant; not until the late sixties were there initial "stirrings of consciousness" in England, and the first women's liberation conference did not occur until 1970.[1]

Mitchell proposed a new analytic framework for studying women. The condition of women in any society, she suggested, is composed of four elements, or "structures": production, reproduction, sexuality, and the socialization of children. These structures are continually in flux; throughout history they have changed in nature and in relative importance, according to the material and social conditions of the time. A successful revolutionary movement in behalf of women, Mitchell said, could begin by attacking the most vulnerable structure—sexuality,

---

[1]Sheila Rowbotham, *The Past Is Before Us* (Boston: Beacon Press, 1989), p. xii.

which was already undergoing rapid change. With the transformation of all four of the structures, "authentic liberation of women" was a possibility in the developed Western nations.

The selection here is excerpted from the opening section and the conclusion of Mitchell's *New Left Review* essay. She is the author, too, of the books *Woman's Estate* (1971) and *Psychoanalysis and Feminism* (1974).

Women in Socialist Theory

THE PROBLEM OF THE SUBORDINATION OF WOMEN and the need for their liberation was recognized by all the great socialist thinkers in the nineteenth century. It is part of the classical heritage of the revolutionary movement. Yet today, in the West, the problem has become a subsidiary, if not an invisible, element in the preoccupations of socialists. Perhaps no other major issue has been so forgotten. . . .

Why has the problem of woman's condition become an area of silence within contemporary socialism? August Bebel, whose book *Woman in the Past, Present and Future* was one of the standard texts of the German Social-Democratic Party in the early years of this century, wrote: "Every Socialist recognizes the dependence of the workman on the capitalist, and cannot understand that others, and especially the capitalists themselves, should fail to recognize it also; but the same Socialist often does not recognize the dependence of women on men because the question touches his own dear self more or less nearly." But this genre of explanation—psychologistic and moralistic—is clearly inadequate. Much deeper and more structural causes have clearly been at work. To consider these would require a major historical study, impossible here. But it can be said with some certainty that part of the explanation for the decline in socialist debate on the subject lies not only in the real historical processes, but in the original weaknesses in the traditional discussion of the subject in the classics. For while the great studies of the last century all stressed the importance of the problem, they did not *solve* it theoretically. The limitations of their approach have never been subsequently transcended. . . . The liberation of women remains a normative ideal, an adjunct to socialist theory, not structurally integrated into it.

The contrary is true of de Beauvoir's massive work *The Second Sex*—to this day the greatest single contribution on the subject. Here the focus is the status of women through the ages. But socialism as such emerges as a curiously contingent solution at the end of the work, in a muffled epilogue. De Beauvoir's main theoretical innovation was to fuse the "economic" and "reproductive" explanations of women's subordination by a psychological interpretation of both. . . . [But] the framework of discussion is an evolutionist one which nevertheless fails noticeably to project a convincing image of the future, beyond asserting that socialism will involve the liberation of women as one of its constituent "moments."

What is the solution to this impasse? It must lie in differentiating woman's condition, much more radically than in the past, into its separate structures, which together form a complex—not a simple—unity. This will mean rejecting the idea that woman's condition can be deduced derivatively from the economy or equated symbolically with society. Rather, it must be seen as a *specific* structure, which is a unity of different elements. The variations of woman's condition throughout history will be the result of different combinations of these elements. . . . The key structures can be listed as follows: Production, Reproduction, Sex and Socialization of children. The concrete combination of these produces the "complex unity" of her position; but each separate structure may have reached a different "moment" at any given historical time. Each then must be examined separately in order to see what the present unity is and how it might be changed. . . .

Conclusion

THE LIBERATION OF WOMEN can only be achieved if *all four* structures in which they are integrated are transformed. A modification of any one of them can be offset by a reinforcement of another, so that mere permutation of the form of exploitation is achieved. . . .

It is only in the highly developed societies of the West that an authentic liberation of women can be envisaged today. But for this to occur, there must be a transformation of all the structures into which they are integrated. . . . A revolutionary movement must base its analysis on the uneven development of each, and attack the weakest link in the combination. This may then become the point of departure for a general transformation. What is the situation of the different structures today?

1. Production

The long-term development of the forces of production must command any socialist perspective. The hopes which the advent of machine technology raised as early as the nineteenth century . . . proved illusory. Today, automation promises the *technical* possibility of abolishing completely the physical differential between man and woman in production, but under capitalist relations of production, the *social* possibility of this abolition is permanently threatened, and can easily be turned into its opposite, the actual diminution of woman's role in production as the labor force contracts.

This concerns the future; for the present the main fact to register is that woman's role in production is virtually stationary, and has been so for a long time now. In England in 1911, 30 percent of the work-force were women; in the 1960s, 34 percent. The composition of these jobs has not changed decisively either. The jobs are very rarely "careers." When they are not in the lowest positions on the factory-floor they are normally white-collar auxiliary positions (such as secretaries)—supportive to masculine roles. They are often ... "service" tasks. Parsons says bluntly: "Within the occupational organization they are analogous to the wife-mother role in the family."[2] The educational system underpins this role-structure. Seventy-five percent of eighteen-year-old girls in England are receiving neither training nor education today. The pattern [of the father's and mother's role in the family] ... is not substantially changed when the woman is gainfully employed, as her job tends to be inferior to that of the man's, to which the family then adapts.

Thus, in all essentials, work as such—of the amount and type effectively available today—has not proved a salvation for women.

2. Reproduction

Scientific advance in contraception could ... make involuntary reproduction—which accounts for the vast majority of births in the world today, and for a major proportion even in the West— a phenomenon of the past. But oral contraception—which has so far been developed in a form which exactly repeats the sexual inequality of Western society—is only at its beginnings. It is inadequately distributed across classes and countries and awaits further technical improvements. Its main initial impact is, in the advanced countries, likely to be psychological—it will certainly free women's sexual experience from many of the anxieties and inhibitions which have always afflicted it. It will definitely divorce sexuality from procreation, as necessary complements.

The demographic pattern of reproduction in the West may or may not be widely affected by oral contraception. One of the most striking phenomena of very recent years in the United States has been the sudden increase in the birth-rate. In the last decade it has been higher than that of under-developed countries such as India, Pakistan, and Burma. In fact, this reflects simply the lesser economic burden of a large family in conditions of

[2] Talcott Parsons and Robert F. Bales, eds., *Family Socialization and Interaction Process* (Glencoe, IL: Free Press, 1955), p. 15 n.

economic boom in the richest country in the world. But it also reflects the magnification of familial ideology as a social force. This leads to the next structure.

3. Socialization

The changes in the composition of the work-force, the size of the family, the structure of education, etc.—however limited from an ideal standpoint—have undoubtedly diminished the societal function and importance of the family. As an organization it is not a significant unit in the political power system, it plays little part in economic production, and it is rarely the sole agency of integration into the larger society; thus at the macroscopic level it serves very little purpose.

The result has been a major displacement of emphasis on to the family's psycho-social function, for the infant and for the couple. Parsons writes: "The trend of the evidence points to the beginning of the relative stabilization of a *new* type of family structure in a new relation to a general social structure, one in which the family is more specialized than before, but not in any general sense less important, because the society is dependent *more* exclusively on it for the performance of *certain* of its vital functions."[3] [There is a] vital nucleus of truth in the emphasis on socialization of the child. . . . It is essential that socialists should acknowledge it and integrate it entirely into any program for the liberation of women. . . . However, there is no doubt that the need for permanent, intelligent care of children in the initial three or four years of their lives can (and has been) exploited ideologically to perpetuate the family as a total unit, when its other functions have been visibly declining. Indeed, the attempt to focus women's existence exclusively on bringing up children, is manifestly harmful to children. Socialization as an exceptionally delicate process requires a serene and mature socializer—a type which the frustrations of a *purely* familial role are not liable to produce. Exclusive maternity is often in this sense "counter-productive." The mother discharges her own frustra-

[3]Ibid., pp. 9–10.

tions and anxieties in a fixation on the child. An increased awareness of the critical importance of socialization, far from leading to a restitution of classical maternal roles, should lead to a reconsideration of them—of what makes a good socializing agent, who can genuinely provide security and stability for the child.

The same arguments apply, *a fortiori,* to the psycho-social role of the family for the couple. The beliefs that the family provides an impregnable enclave of intimacy and security in an atomized and chaotic cosmos assumes the absurd—that the family can be isolated from the community, and that its internal relationships will not reproduce in their own terms the external relationships which dominate the society. The family as refuge in a bourgeois society inevitably becomes a reflection of it.

4. Sexuality

It is difficult not to conclude that the major structure which at present is in rapid evolution is sexuality. Production, reproduction, and socialization are all more or less stationary in the West today, in the sense that they have not changed for three or more decades. There is moreover, no widespread *demand* for changes in them on the part of women themselves—the governing ideology has effectively prevented critical consciousness. By contrast, the dominant sexual ideology is proving less and less successful in regulating spontaneous behavior. Marriage in its classical form is increasingly threatened by the liberalization of relationships before and after it which affects all classes today. In this sense, it is evidently the weak link in the chain—the particular structure that is the site of the most contradictions. The progressive potential of these contradictions [is clear]. In a context of juridical equality, the liberation of sexual experience from relations which are extraneous to it—whether procreation or property—could lead to true inter-sexual freedom. But it could also lead simply to new forms of neocapitalist ideology and practice. For one of the forces behind the current acceleration of sexual freedom has undoubtedly been the conversion of contemporary capitalism from a production-and-work ethos to a consumption-

and-fun ethos. . . . Bourgeois society at present can well afford a play area of premarital *non*-procreative sexuality. Even marriage can save itself by increasing divorce and remarriage rates, signifying the importance of the institution itself. These considerations make it clear that sexuality, while it presently may contain the greatest potential for liberation—can equally well be organized against any increase of its human possibilities. New forms of reification are emerging which may void sexual freedom of any meaning. This is a reminder that while one structure may be the *weak link* in a unity like that of woman's condition, there can never be a solution through it alone. . . . This means a rejection of two beliefs prevalent on the left:

> **Reformism:** This now takes the form of limited ameliorative demands: equal pay for women, more nursery-schools, better retraining facilities, etc. In its contemporary version it is wholly divorced from any fundamental critique of women's condition or any vision of the real liberation (it was not always so). Insofar as it represents a tepid embellishment of the *status quo,* it has very little progressive content left.

> **Voluntarism:** This takes the form of maximalist demands—the abolition of the family, abrogation of all sexual restrictions, forceful separation of parents from children—which have no chance of winning any wide support at present, and which merely serve as a substitute for the job of theoretical analysis or practical persuasion. By pitching the whole subject in totally intransigent terms, voluntarism objectively helps to maintain it outside the framework of normal political discussion.

What, then, is the responsible revolutionary attitude? It must include both immediate and fundamental demands, in a single critique of the *whole* of women's situation, that does not fetishize any dimension of it. Modern industrial development, as has been seen, tends towards the separating out of the originally unified function of the family—procreation, socialization, sexuality, economic subsistence, etc.—even if this "structural differentiation" (to use a term of Parsons') has been checked and disguised by the maintenance of a powerful family ideology.

This differentiation provides the real historical basis for the ideal demands which should be posed: structural differentiation is precisely what distinguishes an advanced from a primitive society (in which all social functions are fused *en bloc*).

In practical terms this means a coherent system of demands. The four elements of women's condition cannot merely be considered each in isolation; they form a structure of specific interrelations. The contemporary bourgeois family can be seen as a triptych of sexual, reproductive, and socializatory functions (the woman's world) embraced by production (the man's world)—precisely a structure which in the final instance is determined by the economy. The exclusion of women from production—social human activity—and their confinement to a monolithic condensation of functions in a unity—the family—which is precisely unified in the *natural part* of each function, is the root cause of the contemporary *social* definition of women as *natural* beings. Hence the main thrust of any emancipation movement must still concentrate on the economic element—the entry of women fully into public industry. The error of the old socialists was to see the other elements as reducible to the economic; hence the call for the entry of women into production was accompanied by the purely abstract slogan of the abolition of the family. Economic demands are still primary, but must be accompanied by coherent policies for the other three elements, policies which at particular junctures may take over the primary role in immediate action.

Economically, the most elementary demand is not the right to work or receive equal pay for work—the two traditional reformist demands—but *the right to equal work itself*. At present, women perform unskilled, uncreative, service jobs that can be regarded as "extensions" of their expressive familial role. They are overwhelmingly waitresses, office-cleaners, hair-dressers, clerks, typists. In the working class occupational mobility is thus sometimes easier for girls than boys—they can enter the white-collar sector at a lower level. But only two in a hundred women are in administrative or managerial jobs, and less than five in a thousand are in the professions. Women are poorly unionized . . . and receive less money than men for the manual work they do perform. . . .

Education

THE WHOLE PYRAMID OF DISCRIMINATION rests on a solid extra-economic foundation—education. The demand for equal work, in Britain, should above all take the form of a demand for an *equal educational system,* since this is at present the main single filter selecting women for inferior work-roles. . . . Education is probably the key area for immediate economic advance at present.

Only if it is founded on equality can production be truly differentiated from reproduction and the family. But this in turn requires a whole set of non-economic demands as a complement. Reproduction, sexuality, and socialization also need to be free from coercive forms of unification. Traditionally, the socialist movement has called for the "abolition of the bourgeois family." This slogan must be rejected as incorrect today. It is maximalist in the bad sense, posing a demand which is merely a negation without any coherent construction subsequent to it. . . . The reasons for the historic weakness of the notion is that the family was never analyzed structurally—in terms of its different functions. It was a hypostasized entity; the abstraction of its abolition corresponds to the abstraction of its conception. The strategic concern for socialists should be for the equality of the sexes, not the abolition of the family. The consequences of this demand are no less radical, but they are concrete and positive, and can be integrated into the real course of history. The family as it exists at present is, in fact, incompatible with the equality of the sexes. But this equality will not come from its administrative abolition, but from the historical differentiation of its functions. The revolutionary demand should be for the liberation of these functions from a monolithic fusion which oppresses each. Thus dissociation of reproduction from sexuality frees sexuality from alienation in unwanted reproduction (and fear of it), and reproduction from subjugation to chance and uncontrollable causality. It is thus an elementary demand to press for free State provision of oral contraception. The legalization of homosexuality—which is one of the forms of non-reproductive sexuality—should be supported for just the same reason, and regressive campaigns against it in Cuba or elsewhere should be unhesitatingly criticized. The straightforward abolition of illegitimacy as a legal notion as in Sweden and Russia has a similar implication; it would separate marriage civically from parenthood.

From Nature to Culture

THE PROBLEM OF SOCIALIZATION poses more difficult questions, as has been seen. But the need for intensive maternal care in the early years of a child's life does not mean that the present single sanctioned form of socialization—marriage and family—is inevitable. Far from it. The fundamental characteristic of the present system of marriage and family is in our society its *monolithism*: there is only one institutionalized form of inter-sexual or inter-generational relationship possible. It is that or nothing. That is why it is essentially a denial of life. For all human experience shows that inter-sexual and inter-generational relationships are infinitely various—indeed, much of our creative literature is a celebration of the fact—while the institutionalized expression of them in our capitalist society is utterly simple and rigid. It is the poverty and simplicity of the institutions in this area of life which are such an oppression. Any society will require some institutionalized and social recognition of personal relationships. But there is absolutely no reason why there should be only one legitimized form—and a multitude of unlegitimized experience. Socialism should properly mean not the abolition of the family, but the diversification of the socially acknowledged relationships which are today forcibly and rigidly compressed into it. This would mean a plural range of institutions—where the family is only one, and its abolition implies none. Couples living together or not living together, long-term unions with children, single parents bringing up children, children socialized by conventional rather than biological parents, extended kin groups, etc.—all these could be encompassed in a range of institutions which matched the free invention and variety of men and women.

It would be illusory to try and specify these institutions.

Circumstantial accounts of the future are idealist and, worse, static. Socialism will be a process of change, of becoming. A fixed image of the future is in the worst sense ahistorical. . . . The liberation of women under socialism will not be "rational" but a human achievement, in the long passage from Nature to Culture which is the definition of history and society.

NAOMI WEISSTEIN

Kinder, Küche, Kirche as Scientific Law: Psychology Constructs the Female

"**K**inder, Küche, Kirche as Scientific Law" is a witty and wise debunking of traditional psychology's "scientific" studies of the nature of women. At the time of its composition, Naomi Weisstein (b. 1939) was a psychologist with a Ph.D. from Harvard—awarded after only two and a half years of study—and had also completed postdoctoral work in mathematical biology at the University of Chicago. Her credentials as a feminist were equally impressive: she was a founding member of the first women's liberation collective in the country.

The article's central argument, as described by the author, is that "psychology has nothing to say about what women are really like . . . because psychology does not know." Weisstein ridiculed specialists in human personality—including Freud—who presented unsupported theories about women as if they were fact. They "essentially made up myths without any evidence to support these myths," she commented.

"Kinder, Küche, Kirche" was originally written for feminist activists rather than psychologists. It was first printed in 1968 by the New England Free Press, then reprinted in a special women's liberation issue of *Motive* magazine the following year.[1] The selection here is from the article as it appeared in *Motive,* with the addition of a section titled "Biologically-Based Theories"

[1]*Motive* [a publication of the United Methodist Church], vol. 29, nos. 6 and 7, March–April 1969. Guest editors for this special issue were Joanne Cooke, Charlotte Bunch Weeks, and Robin Morgan (poetry editor).

from a revised and expanded version of the paper Weisstein prepared for the journal *Social Education*.[2]

During the seventies, Weisstein became associate professor of psychology at Loyola University in Chicago, then professor of psychology at the State University of New York in Buffalo; she did research in the areas of vision and cognition. Since she was stricken with acute chronic fatigue syndrome, in 1980, her ability to work has been limited.

In June 1993, the British journal *Feminism & Psychology* marked the twenty-fifth anniversary of her landmark article with a symposium to which Weisstein contributed a response. She noted that "an understanding of how important the social context is in determining behavior seems now to have faded from consciousness," and she suggested that feminist psychologists "begin to focus on questions of social change," especially "how people resist power."[3]

PSYCHOLOGISTS HAVE SET ABOUT DESCRIBING the true nature of women with an enthusiasm and absolute certainty which is rather disquieting. Bruno Bettelheim, of the University of Chicago, tells us (1965) that "we must start with the realization that, as much as women want to be good scientists or engineers, they want first and foremost to be womanly companions of men and to be mothers."[4]

Erik Erikson of Harvard University (1964), upon noting that young women often ask whether they can "have an identity be-

---

[2] Naomi Weisstein, "Psychology Constructs the Female," a revised and expanded version of "Kinder, Küche, Kirche as Scientific Law," in *Social Education*, April 1971, pp. 363–373.

[3] " 'Psychology Constructs the Female': A Reappraisal," *Feminism & Psychology*, vol. 3, no. 2, 1993, pp. 184–245.

[4] "The Commitment Required of a Woman Entering a Scientific Profession in Present Day American Society," *Woman and the Scientific Professions*, MIT Symposium on American Women in Science and Engineering.

fore they know whom they will marry, and for whom they will make a home," explains somewhat elegiacally that "much of a young woman's identity is already defined in her kind of attractiveness and in the selectivity of her search for the man (or men) by whom she wishes to be sought. . . ." Mature womanly fulfillment, for Erikson, rests on the fact that a woman's ". . . somatic design harbors an 'inner space' destined to bear the offspring of chosen men, and with it, a biological, psychological, and ethical commitment to take care of human infancy."[5]

Some psychiatrists even see the acceptance of woman's role by women as a solution to societal problems. "Woman is nurturance . . . ," writes Joseph Rheingold (1964), a psychiatrist at Harvard Medical School, ". . . anatomy decrees the life of a woman . . . when women grow up without dread of their biological functions and without subversion by feminist doctrine, and therefore enter upon motherhood with a sense of fulfillment and altruistic sentiment, we shall attain the goal of a good life and a secure world in which to live it."[6]

These views from men of high prestige reflect a fairly general consensus: liberation for women will consist first in their attractiveness, so that second, they may obtain the kinds of homes (and men) which will allow joyful altruism and nurturance.

Business does not disagree. If views such as Bettelheim's and Erikson's do indeed have something to do with real liberation for women, then seldom in human history has so much money and effort been spent on helping a group of people realize their true potential. Clothing, cosmetics and home furnishings are multi-million dollar businesses: if you don't like investing in firms that make weaponry and flaming gasoline, there's a lot of cash in "inner space."

It is an interesting but limited exercise to show that psychologists' ideas of women's nature fit so remarkably the common prejudice and serve industry and commerce so well. Just because it's good for business doesn't mean it's wrong. *It is wrong,* and there isn't the tiniest shred of evidence that these fantasies of

[5]"Inner and Outer Space: Reflections on Womanhood," *Daedalus* 93.
[6]*The Fear of Being a Woman* (New York: Grune and Stratton).

servitude and childish dependence have anything to do with women's true potential. The idea of the nature of human possibility which rests on the accidents of individual development or genitalia, on what is possible today because of what happened yesterday, on the fundamentalist myth of sex organ causality, has strangled and deflected psychology so that it is relatively useless in describing, explaining, or predicting humans and their behavior. Present psychology is less than worthless in contributing to a vision which could truly liberate—men as well as women.

Psychology has nothing to say about what women are really like, what they need and what they want, essentially, because psychology does not know. This failure is not limited to women; rather, the kind of psychology which has addressed itself to how people act and who they are has failed to understand, in the first place, why people act the way they do, and has certainly failed to understand what might make them act differently.

The kind of psychology which has addressed itself to these questions is in large part clinical psychology and psychiatry, which in America means endless commentary and refinement of Freudian theory. Here, the causes of failure are obvious and appalling: Freudians and neo-Freudians, and clinicians and psychiatrists in general, have simply refused to look at the evidence against their theory and their practice, and have used as evidence for their theory and their practice stuff so flimsy and transparently biased as to have absolutely no standing as empirical evidence. But even psychology that conforms to rigorous methodology has gone about looking at people in such a way as to have limited usefulness. This is because it has been a central assumption for most psychologists of human personality that human behavior rests primarily on an individual and inner dynamic, perhaps fixed in infancy, perhaps fixed by genitalia, perhaps simply arranged in a rather immovable cognitive network.

This assumption is rapidly losing ground as personality psychologists fail again and again to get consistency in the assumed personalities of their subjects (Block, 1968)[7] and as the evidence

[7]J. Block, "Some Reasons for the Apparent Inconsistency of Personality," *Psychological Bulletin* 70.

collects that what a person does and who he believes himself to be, will in general be a function of what people around him expect him to be, and what the overall situation in which he is acting implies that he is. Compared to the influence of the social context within which a person lives, his or her history and "traits," as well as biological makeup, may simply be random variations, "noise" superimposed on the true signal which can predict behavior.

To summarize: the first reason for psychology's failure to understand what people are and how they act, is that clinicians and psychiatrists, who are generally the theoreticians on these matters, have essentially made up myths without any evidence to support these myths. The second reason for psychology's failure is that personality theory has looked for inner traits when it should have been looking at social context.

The first cause of failure is the acceptance by psychiatrists and clinical psychologists of theory without evidence. If we inspect the literature of personality, it is immediately obvious that the bulk of it is written by clinicians and psychiatrists, and that the major support for their theories is "years of intensive clinical experience." This is a tradition started by Freud. His "insights" occurred during the course of his work with his patients. There is nothing wrong with such an approach to theory *formulation;* a person is free to make up theories with any inspiration which works: divine revelation, intensive clinical practice, a random numbers table. But he is not free to claim any validity for his theory until it has been tested and confirmed.

Theories are treated in no such tentative way in ordinary clinical practice. Consider Freud. What he thought constituted evidence violated the most minimal conditions of scientific rigor. In *The Sexual Enlightenment of Children,* the classic document which is supposed to demonstrate empirically the existence of a castration complex and its connection to a phobia, Freud based his analysis on the reports of the father of the little boy, himself in therapy, and a devotee of Freudian theory. I really don't have to comment further on the contamination in this kind of evidence. It is remarkable that only recently Freud's classic theory on the sexuality of women—the notion of the double orgasm—has been tested physiologically and found plain wrong.

Those who claim that fifty years of psychoanalytic experience constitute evidence enough of the essential truths of Freud's theory should ponder the robust health of the double orgasm. Did women, until Masters and Johnson (1966)[8] believe they were having two different kinds of orgasm? Did their psychiatrists cow them into reporting something that was not true? If so, were there other things they reported that were also not true? Did psychiatrists ever learn anything different from what their theories had led them to believe? If clinical experience means anything at all, surely we should have been done with the double orgasm myth long before the Masters and Johnson studies.

But certainly, you may object, "years of intensive clinical experience" is the only reliable measure in a discipline which rests for its findings on insight, sensitivity, and intuition. The problem with insight, sensitivity, and intuition, is that these can confirm for all time the biases that one started out with. People used to be absolutely convinced of their ability to tell which of their number were engaging in witchcraft.

Years of intensive clinical experience is not the same thing as empirical evidence. The first thing an experimenter learns in any kind of experiment which involves humans is the concept of the "double blind." The term is taken from medical experiments, where one group is given a drug which is presumably supposed to change behavior in a certain way, and a control group is given a placebo. If the observers or the subjects know which group took which drug, the result invariably comes out on the positive side for the new drug. Only when it is not known which subject took which pill, is validity remotely approximated.

In judgments of human behavior, it is so difficult to precisely tie down just what behavior is going on, let alone what behavior should be expected, that one must test again and again the reliability of judgments. How many judges, blind, will agree in their observations? Can they replicate their own judgments at some

---

[8]W. H. Masters and V. E. Johnson, *Human Sexual Response* (Boston: Little, Brown).

later time? When, in actual practice, these judgment criteria are tested for clinical judgments, then we find that the judges cannot judge reliably nor can they judge consistently: they do no better than chance in identifying which of a certain set of stories were written by men and which by women; which of a whole battery of clinical test results are the products of homosexuals and which are the products of heterosexuals (Hooker, 1957)[9]; and which, of a battery of clinical test results *and* interviews (where questions are asked such as "do you have delusions?") ... (Little and Schneidman, 1959)[10] are products of psychotics, neurotics, psychosomatics, or normals.

Lest this summary escape your notice, let me stress the implications of these findings. The ability of judges, chosen for their clinical expertise, to distinguish male heterosexuals from male homosexuals on the basis of three widely used clinical projective tests—the Rorschach, the TAT, and the MAP—was *no better than chance*. The reason this is such devastating news, of course, is that sexuality is considered by personality theorists to be of fundamental importance in the deep dynamic of personality; if what is considered gross sexual deviance cannot be caught, then what are psychologists talking about when they claim, for instance, that at the basis of paranoid psychosis is "latent homosexual panic"? They can't even identify what homosexual anything is, let alone "latent homosexual panic"!

More frightening, expert clinicians cannot be consistent on what diagnostic category to assign to a person, again on the basis of both tests and interviews; a number of normals in the Little and Schneidman study were described as psychotic, in such categories as "schizophrenic with homosexual tendencies," or "schizoid character with depressive trends." But most disheartening, when the judges were asked to rejudge the test protocols some weeks later, their diagnoses of the same subjects on the basis of the same protocol differed markedly from their initial judgments. It is obvious that even simple descriptive conven-

[9]E. Hooker, "Male Homosexuality in the Rorschach," *Journal of Projective Techniques* 21.

[10]K. B. Little and E. S. Schneidman, "Congruences Among Interpretations of Psychological Test and Anamestic Data," *Psychological Monographs* 73.

tions in clinical psychology cannot be consistently applied; that these descriptive conventions have any explanatory significance is therefore, of course, out of the question.

As a student in a graduate class at Harvard, some years ago, I was a member of a seminar which was asked to identify which of two piles of a clinical test, the TAT, had been written by males, and which of the two piles had been written by females. Only four students out of twenty identified the piles correctly, and this was after one and a half months of intensively studying the differences between men and women. Since this result is below chance, that is, this result would occur by chance about four out of a thousand times, we may conclude that there *is* finally a consistency here; students are judging knowledgeably within the context of psychological teaching about the differences between men and women; the teachings themselves are erroneous.

Ah, you may argue, the theory may be scientifically "unsound" but at least it cures people. There is no evidence that it does. In 1952, Eysenck[11] reported the results of what is called an "outcome of therapy" study of neurotics which showed that, of the patients who received psychoanalysis, the improvement rate was 44 percent; of the patients who received psychotherapy, the improvement rate was 64 percent; and the patients who received no treatment at all, the improvement rate was 72 percent. These findings have never been refuted; subsequent later studies have confirmed the negative results of the Eysenck study. (Barron and Leary, 1955; Bergin, 1963; Cartwright and Vogel, 1960; Truax, 1963.)[12]

How can clinicians and psychiatrists, then, in all good conscience, continue to practice? Largely by ignoring these results

[11]H. J. Eysenck, "The Effects of Psychotherapy: An Evaluation," *Journal of Consulting Psychology* 16.

[12]F. Barron and T. Leary, "Changes in Psychoneurotic Patients with and without Therapy," *Journal of Consulting Psychology* 19; A. E. Bergin, "The Effects of Psychotherapy: Negative Results Revisited," *Journal of Consulting Psychology* 10; R. D. Cartwright and J. L. Vogel, "A Comparison of Changes in Psychoneurotic Patients During Matched Periods of Therapy and No-Therapy," *Journal of Consulting Psychology* 24; and C. B. Truax, "Effective Ingredients in Psychotherapy: An Approach to Unraveling the Patient-Therapist Interaction," *Journal of Counseling Psychology* 10.

and being careful not to do outcome-of-therapy studies. The attitude is nicely summarized by Rotter (1960, quoted in Astin, 1961): "Research studies in psychotherapy tend to be concerned more with some aspects of the psychotherapeutic procedure and less with outcome . . . to some extent, it reflects an interest in the psychotherapy situation as a kind of personality laboratory."[13] Some laboratory.

Thus, . . . since clinical experience and tools can be shown to be worse than useless when tested for consistency, efficacy, agreement, and reliability, we can safely conclude that theories of a clinical nature advanced about women are also worse than useless. It has become increasingly clear that in order to understand why people do what they do, and certainly in order to change what people do, psychologists must turn away from the theory of the causal nature of the inner dynamic and look to the social context within which individuals live.

Block's work (1968) established that personality tests never yield consistent predictions; a rigid authoritarian on one measure will be unauthoritarian on the next. But the reason for this inconsistency is only now becoming clear, and it seems overwhelmingly to have much more to do with the social situation in which the subject finds himself than with the subject himself.

In a series of brilliant experiments, Rosenthal and his coworkers . . . have shown that if one group of experimenters has one hypothesis about what they expect to find, and another group of experimenters has the opposite hypothesis, both groups will obtain results in accord with their hypotheses. Thus, in a success rating task, where subjects were required to rate faces cut out from magazines on a twenty point scale from -10, very unsuccessful, to +10, highly successful, the group of subjects whose experimenters had been told would rate the faces high, had mean ratings, in every case, above the highest mean rating for the group of subjects whose experimenters expected the subjects to rate the faces low. In all, about 375 subjects were tested; the results would have happened by chance about one in

[13]J. B. Rotter, "Psychotherapy," quoted in A. W. Astin, "The Functional Autonomy of Psychotherapy," *American Psychologist* 16.

one thousand times. The experimenters were instructed to read the same set of instructions, and to say no more than was in the instructions; obviously, the cues which influenced the subjects were nonverbal. . . .[14]

Rosenthal and Jacobson (1968)[15] extended their analysis to the natural classroom situation. Here, they found that when teachers expected randomly selected students to "show great promise," these students' I.Q.'s increased significantly from control group students, with the most dramatic increments in the area of reasoning ability.

Thus, even in carefully controlled experiments, and with no outward or conscious difference in behavior, the hypotheses we start with will influence enormously the behavior of another organism. These studies are extremely important when assessing the validity of psychological studies of women. Since it is fairly safe to say that most of us start with hypotheses as to the nature of men and women, the validity of a number of observations of sex differences is questionable, even when these observations have been taken under carefully controlled conditions.

Second, and more important, the Rosenthal experiments point quite clearly to the influence of social expectation. In some extremely important ways, people are what you expect them to be or at least they behave as you expect them to behave. Thus, if women, according to Bruno Bettelheim, want first and foremost to be good wives and mothers, it is extremely likely that that is what Bettelheim, and the rest of society, want them to be.

There is another series of social psychological experiments which points to the inescapable overwhelming effect of social context in an extremely vivid way. These are the obedience experiments of Stanley Milgram (1965),[16] concerned with the extent to which subjects in psychological experiments will obey the orders

[14]R. Rosenthal, *Experimenter Effects in Behavioral Research* (New York: Appleton-Century-Crofts).

[15]R. Rosenthal and L. Jacobson, *Pygmalion in the Classroom: Teacher Expectation and Pupil's Intellectual Development* (New York: Holt, Rinehart & Winston).

[16]S. Milgram, "Some Conditions of Obedience and Disobedience to Authority," *Human Relations* 18.

of unknown experimenters, even when these orders carry them to the distinct possibility that the subject is killing somebody.

Briefly, a subject is made to administer electric shocks in ascending 15 volt increments to another person whom the subject believes to be another subject, but who is in fact a stooge. The voltages range from 15 to 450 volts; for each four consecutive voltages there are verbal descriptions such as "mild shock," "danger, severe shock," and finally, for the 435 and 450 volt switches, simply a red XXX marked over the switches. The stooge, as the voltage increases, begins to cry out against the pain; he then screams that he has a heart condition, begging the subject to stop, and finally, he goes limp and stops responding altogether at a certain voltage. Since even at this point, the subject is instructed to keep increasing the voltage, it is possible for the subjects to continue all the way up to the end switch—450 volts.

The percentage of subjects who do so is quite high; all in all about 1,000 subjects were run, and about 65 percent would go to the end switch in an average experiment. No tested individual differences between subjects predicted which of the subjects would continue to obey and which would break off the experiment. Predictions were far below actual percentages, with an average prediction that 3 percent of the subjects would obey to the end. But, even though psychiatrists have no idea of how people are going to behave in this situation . . . , and even though individual differences do not predict which subjects are going to obey and which are not, it is very easy to predict when subjects will be obedient and when they will be defiant. All the experimenter has to do is change the social situation. In a variant of the experiment (Milgram, 1965),[17] when two other stooges who were also administering electric shocks refused to continue, only 10 percent of the subjects continued to the end switch. This is critical for personality theory; for it indicates that the lawful behavior is the behavior that can be predicted from the social situation, not from the individual history.

Finally, an ingenious experiment by Schachter and Singer

---

[17]S. Milgram, "Liberating Effects of Group Pressure," *Journal of Personality and Social Psychology* 1.

(1962)[18] showed that subjects injected with adrenaline, which produces a state of physiological arousal in all but minor respects identical to that which occurs when subjects are extremely afraid, became euphoric when they were in a room with a stooge who was acting euphoric, and became extremely angry when they were placed in a room with a stooge who was acting extremely angry.

To summarize: if subjects under quite innocuous and noncoercive social conditions can be made to kill other subjects and under other types of social conditions will positively refuse to do so; if subjects can react to a state of physiological fear by becoming euphoric because there is somebody else euphoric, if students become intelligent because teachers expect them to be intelligent, and rats run mazes better because experimenters are told that the rats are bright, then it is obvious that a study of human behavior requires, first and foremost, a study of the social contexts within which people move, the expectations as to how they will behave, and the authority which tells them who they are and what they are supposed to do.

Biologically-Based Theories[19]

Biologists also have at times assumed they could describe the limits of human potential from their observations of animal rather than human behavior. Here, as in psychology, there has been no end of theorizing about the sexes, again with a sense of absolute certainty. These theories fall into two major categories.

One biological theory of differences in nature argues that since females and males differ in their sex hormones, and sex hormones enter the brain (Hamburg and Lunde in Maccoby, 1966),[20] there must be innate behavioral differences. But the

---

[18]S. Schachter and J. E. Singer, "Cognitive, Social, and Physiological Determinants of Emotional State," *Psychological Review* 69.

[19]This section is reprinted from *Social Education*, April 1971. —*Ed.*

[20]D. A. Hamburg and D. T. Lunde, "Sex Hormones in the Development of Sex Differences in Human Behavior," in Eleanor E. Maccoby, ed., *The Development of Sex Differences* (Stanford University Press).

only thing this argument tells us is that there are differences in physiological state. The problem is whether these differences are at all relevant to behavior.

Consider, for example, differences in testosterone levels. A man who calls himself Tiger[21] has recently argued (1970) that the greater quantities of testosterone found in human males as compared with human females (of a certain age group) determine innate differences in aggressiveness, competitiveness, dominance, ability to hunt, ability to hold public office, and so forth. But Tiger demonstrates in this argument the same manly and courageous refusal to be intimidated by evidence which we have already seen in our consideration of the clinical and psychiatric tradition. The evidence does not support his argument and, in some cases, directly contradicts it. Testosterone level co-varies neither with hunting ability, nor with dominance, nor with aggression, nor with competitiveness. As Storch has pointed out (1970),[22] all normal male mammals in the reproductive age group produce much greater quantities of testosterone than females; yet many of these males are neither hunters nor are they aggressive. Among some hunting mammals, such as the large cats, it turns out that more hunting is done by the female than the male. And there exist primate species where the female is clearly more aggressive, competitive, and dominant than the male. . . . Thus, for some species, being female, and therefore, having less testosterone than the male of that species means hunting more, or being more aggressive, or being more dominant. Nor does having *more* testosterone preclude behavior commonly thought of as "female": there exist primate species where females do not touch infants except to feed them; the males care for the infants. . . . So it is not clear what testosterone or any other sex-hormonal difference means for differences in nature of sex-role behavior. . . .

There is a second category of theory based on biology, a reductionist theory. It goes like this. Sex-role behavior in some pri-

[21]L. Tiger, "Male Dominance? Yes. Alas. A Sexist Plot? No," *New York Times Magazine*, October 25, 1970.

[22]M. Storch, "Reply to Tiger," 1970, unpublished manuscript.

mate species is described, and it is concluded that this is the "natural" behavior for humans. Putting aside the not insignificant problem of observer bias . . . there are a number of problems with this approach.

The most general and serious problem is that there are no grounds to assume that anything primates do is necessary, natural, or desirable in humans, for the simple reason that humans are not non-humans. For instance, it is found that male chimpanzees placed alone with infants will not "mother" them. Jumping from hard data to ideological speculation researchers conclude from this information that *human* females are necessary for the safe growth of human infants. It would be as reasonable to conclude, following this logic, that it is quite useless to teach human infants to speak, since it has been tried with chimpanzees and it does not work. . . .

Is there then any value at all in primate observations as they relate to human females and males? There is a value but it is limited: its function can be no more than to show some extant examples of diverse sex-role behavior. It must be stressed, however, that this is an extremely limited function. The extant behavior does not begin to suggest all the possibilities, either for non-human primates or for humans. Bearing these caveats in mind, it is nonetheless interesting that if one inspects the limited set of existing non-human primate sex-role behaviors, one finds, in fact, a much larger range of sex-role behavior than is commonly believed to exist. "Biology" appears to limit very little; the fact that a female gives birth does not mean, even in non-humans, that she necessarily cares for the infant (in marmosets, for instance, the male carries the infant at all times except when the infant is feeding [Mitchell, 1969]);[23] "natural" female and male behavior varies all the way from females who are much more aggressive and competitive than males (e.g., Tamarins, see Mitchell, 1969) and male "mothers" (e.g., Titi monkeys, night monkeys, and marmosets, see Mitchell, 1969) to submissive and passive females and male antagonists (e.g., rhesus monkeys).

But even for the limited function that primate arguments

[23]G. D. Mitchell, "Paternalistic Behavior in Primates," *Psychological Bulletin* 71.

serve, the evidence has been misused. Invariably, only those primates have been cited which exhibit exactly the kind of behavior that the proponents of the biological basis of human female behavior wish were true for humans. Thus, baboons and rhesus monkeys are generally cited: males in these groups exhibit some of the most irritable and aggressive behavior found in primates, and if one wishes to argue that females are naturally passive and submissive, these groups provide vivid examples. There are abundant counter examples, such as those mentioned above (Mitchell, 1969); in fact, in general, a counter example can be found for every sex-role behavior cited, including, as mentioned in the case of marmosets, male "mothers."

But the presence of counter examples has not stopped florid and overarching theories of the natural or biological basis of male privilege from proliferating. For instance, there have been a number of theories dealing with the innate incapacity in human males for monogamy. Here, as in most of this type of theorizing, baboons are a favorite example, probably because of their fantasy value: the family unit of the hamadryas baboon, for instance, consists of a highly constant pattern of one male and a number of females and their young. And again, the counter examples, such as in the invariably monogamous gibbon, are ignored. . . .

In brief, the uselessness of present psychology with regard to women is simply a special case of the general conclusion: one must understand social expectations about women if one is going to characterize the behavior of women.

How are women characterized in our culture, and in psychology? They are inconsistent, emotionally unstable, lacking a strong conscience or superego, weaker, "nurturant" rather than productive, "intuitive" rather than intelligent, and, if they are at all "normal," suited to the home and the family. In short, the list adds up to a typical minority group stereotype of inferiority (Hacker, 1951):[24] if they know their place, which is in the home, they are really quite lovable, happy, childlike, loving creatures.

[24]H. M. Hacker, "Women as a Minority Group," *Social Forces* 30.

In a review of the intellectual differences between little boys and little girls, Eleanor Maccoby (1966)[25] has shown that there are no intellectual differences until about high school, or, if there are, girls are slightly ahead of boys. At high school, girls begin to do worse on a few intellectual tasks, such as arithmetical reasoning, and beyond high school, the achievement of women now measured in terms of accomplishment drops off even more rapidly.

There are a number of other, non-intellectual tests which show sex differences: I chose the intellectual differences since it is seen clearly that women start becoming inferior. It is no use to talk about women being different but equal; all of the tests I can think of have a "good" outcome and a "bad" outcome. Women usually end up at the "bad" outcome. In light of social expectations about women, what is surprising is not that women end up where society expects they will; what is surprising is that little girls don't get the message that they are supposed to be stupid until high school; and what is even more remarkable is that some women resist this message even after high school, college, and graduate school.

I began with remarks on the task of discovering the limits of human potential. Until psychologists realize that it is they who are limiting discovery of human potential by their refusal to accept evidence, if they are clinical psychologists, or, if they are rigorous, by their assumption that people move in a context-free ether with only their innate dispositions and their individual traits determining what they will do, then psychology will have nothing of substance to offer in this task. I don't know what immutable differences exist between men and women apart from differences in their genitals; perhaps there are some other unchangeable differences; probably there are a number of irrelevant differences. But it is clear that until social expectations for men and women are equal, until we provide equal respect for both men and women, our answers to this question will simply reflect our prejudices.

[25]E. Maccoby, "Sex Differences in Intellectual Functioning," in Maccoby, ed., *Development of Sex Differences*.

KATE MILLETT

Sexual Politics

*S*exual Politics, published in 1970, applied a feminist perspective to thinking about sexual relations between men and women. The main thesis of author Kate Millett (b. 1934), as she explained in her preface, was that "sex has a frequently neglected political aspect." That is, in the patriarchal state—and all modern states are patriarchal—men dominate women in sex, as they do in other aspects of life. Looking at literature through feminist glasses is commonplace today, but back in 1970 it was unusual. Millett described her mixture of literary and cultural criticism as "something of an anomaly, a hybrid, possibly a new mutation altogether."

To illustrate her thesis, Millett analyzed the role of power and domination in fictional scenes of sexual encounters depicted by Henry Miller, Norman Mailer, D. H. Lawrence, and Jean Genet. The encounters she presented take place between domineering, even brutal, men and passive, submissive women—or, in the case of Genet, between "masculine" and "feminine" homosexual men. Millett intended for the reader to view these scenes as emblematic of sexual politics in society in general. "Coitus," she asserted, "can scarcely be said to take place in a vacuum; although of itself it appears a biological and physical activity, it is set so deeply within the larger context of human affairs that it serves as a charged microcosm of the variety of attitudes and values to which culture subscribes."

Sexual Politics was that rare phenomenon, a doctoral dissertation that becomes a best-selling book and makes its author famous. Time magazine did a cover story about scholar-artist-writer-activist Millett, and The New York Times called her the "principal theoretician" of the women's movement. Millett herself, as she later disclosed, was acutely embarrassed by the celebrity status conferred upon her.[1]

Over the years Millett has proved a versatile writer with wide-ranging interests. Her books include *Sita* (1977), *The Basement* (1980), *Going to Iran* (1982), *The Loony-Bin Trip* (1990), and *Politics of Cruelty* (1993).

The selection here—excerpted from Chapter 1 of *Sexual Politics*, "Instances of Sexual Politics"—examines passages from books by the American novelist Henry Miller (1891–1980) and the Frenchman Jean Genet (1910–1986).

One

I would ask her to prepare the bath for me. She would pretend to demur but she would do it just the same. One day, while I was seated in the tub soaping myself, I noticed that she had forgotten the towels. "Ida," I called, "bring me some towels!" She walked into the bathroom and handed me them. She had on a silk bathrobe and a pair of silk hose. As she stooped over the tub to put the towels on the rack her bathrobe slid open. I slid to my knees and buried my head in her muff. It happened so quickly that she didn't have time to rebel or even to pretend to rebel. In a moment I had her in the tub, stockings and all. I slipped the bathrobe off and threw it on the floor. I left the stockings on—it made her more lascivious looking, more the Cranach type. I lay back and pulled her on top of me. She was just like a bitch in heat, biting me all over, panting, gasping, wriggling like a worm on the hook. As we were drying ourselves, she bent over and began nibbling at my prick. I sat on the edge of the tub and she kneeled at my feet gobbling it. After a while I made her stand up, bend over; then I let her have it from the rear. She had a small juicy cunt, which fitted me like a glove. I bit the nape of her neck, the lobes of her ears, the sensitive spot on her shoulder, and as I pulled away I

[1]Kate Millett, *Flying* (New York: Knopf, 1974), pp. 12–13.

left the mark of my teeth on her beautiful white ass. Not a word spoken.[2]

This colorful descriptive prose is taken from Henry Miller's celebrated *Sexus,* first published in Paris in the forties but outlawed from the sanitary shores of his native America until the Grove Press edition of 1965. Miller, alias Val, is recounting his seduction of Ida Verlaine, the wife of his friend Bill Woodruff. As an account of sexual passage, the excerpt has much in it of note beyond that merely biological activity which the narrator would call "fucking." Indeed, it is just this other content which gives the representation of the incident its value and character.

First, one must consider the circumstances and the context of the scene. Val has just met Bill Woodruff outside a burlesque theater where Ida Verlaine is performing. In the rambling fashion of Miller's narrative, this meeting calls up the memory of the hero's sexual bouts with Ida ten years before, whereupon follow eleven pages of vivid re-enactment. First, there is Ida herself:

> She was just exactly the way her name sounded—pretty, vain, theatrical, faithless, spoiled, pampered, petted. Beautiful as a Dresden doll, only she had raven tresses and a Javanese slant to her soul. If she had a soul at all! Lived entirely in the body, in her senses, her desires—and she directed the show, the body show, with her tyrannical little will which poor Woodruff translated as some monumental force of character. . . . Ida swallowed everything like a pythoness. She was heartless and insatiable.

Woodruff himself is given out as a uxorious fool: "The more he did for her the less she cared for him. She was a monster from head to toe." The narrator claims to be utterly immune to Ida's power but is nonetheless subject to coldly speculative curiosity:

> I just didn't give a fuck for her, as a person, though I often wondered what she might be like as a piece of fuck, so to speak. I

[2]Henry Miller, *Sexus* (New York: Grove Press, 1965).

wondered about it in a detached way, but somehow it got across to her, got under her skin.

As a friend of the family, Val is entitled to spend the night at the Woodruff house, followed by breakfast in bed while husband Bill goes off to work. Val's initial tactic of extracting service from Ida is important to the events which follow:

> She hated the thought of waiting on me in bed. She didn't do it for her husband and she couldn't see why she should do it for me. To take breakfast in bed was something I never did except at Woodruff's place. I did it expressly to annoy and humiliate her.

In accord with one of the myths at the very heart of a Miller novel, the protagonist, who is always some version of the author himself, is sexually irresistible and potent to an almost mystical degree. It is therefore no very great surprise to the reader that Ida falls into his hands. To return to the plucking then, and the passage quoted at length above. The whole scene reads very much like a series of stratagems, aggressive on the part of the hero and acquiescent on the part of what custom forces us to designate as the heroine of the episode. His first maneuver, for example, is to coerce further service in the form of a demand for towels, which reduces Ida to the appropriate roles of a hostess and a domestic. That Ida has dressed herself in a collapsible bathrobe and silk stockings is not only accommodating but almost romancelike. The female reader may realize that one rarely wears stockings without the assistance of other paraphernalia, girdle or garters, but classic masculine fantasy dictates that nudity's most appropriate exception is some gauzelike material, be it hosiery or underwear.

Val makes the first move: "I slid to my knees and buried my head in her muff." The locution "muff" is significant because it is a clue to the reader that the putative humility of the action and the stance of petition it implies are not to be taken at face value. "Muff" carries the tone, implicit in the whole passage, of one male relating an exploit to another male in the masculine vocabulary and with its point of view. Considerably more revealing as to the actual character of the action is the comment which follows: "It happened so quickly she didn't have time to rebel or even to pretend to rebel." Since the entire scene is a description not so much of sexual intercourse, but rather of intercourse in the service of power, "rebel" is a highly charged word. Val had already informed the reader that "she wanted to bring me under her spell, make me walk the tight-rope, as she had done with Woodruff and her other suitors." The issue, of course, is which of the two is to walk a tight-rope, who shall be master?

Having immediately placed Ida under his domination, Val acts fast to forestall insubordination. This prompts the next re-markable event—Val brings her into his element, as it were, and places her in the distinctly ridiculous position of being in a bath-tub with her clothes on. Again the language indicates the under-lying issue of power: "I had her in the bathtub." The reader is also advised that credit should be given the narrator for his speed and agility; Ida is swooshed into the tub in a trice. Having assumed all initiative, Val then proceeds to divest his prey of her redundant bathrobe and throw it on the floor.

The display of stockings and nudity is brought forward for aes-thetic delectation; it contributes to make Ida "more lascivious looking, more the Cranach type." The frail perfection of a Cranach nude had been mentioned earlier as Ida's comparable body type. Juxtaposing the innocence and rarity of this image with the traditional "girlie" figure in silk stockings is an eminent bit of strategy. The word "lascivious" implies a deliberate sensuality and is dependent upon a relish for the prurient, and particularly for the degrading in sexual activity, which, in its turn, relies on the distinctly puritanical conviction that sexuality is indeed dirty and faintly ridiculous. Webster defines "lascivious" as "wanton; lewd; lustful" or a "tendency to produce lewd emotions." The Cranach in question is most likely to be the delicate and rather morbid Eve of the Genesis Panel, now depreciated to a calendar girl.

Val proceeds—his manner coolly self-assured and redolent of comfort: "I lay back and pulled her on top of me." What fol-lows is purely subjective description. Ceasing to admire himself, the hero is now lost in wonder at his effects. For the fireworks which ensue are Ida's, though produced by a Pavlovian mecha-nism. Like the famous programmed dog, in fact "just like a bitch in heat," Ida responds to the protagonist's skillful manipulation: ". . . biting me all over, panting, gasping, wriggling like a worm on the hook." No evidence is ever offered to the reader of any such animal-like failure of self-restraint in the response of our hero. It is he who is the hook, and she who is the worm: the implication is clearly one of steely self-composure contrasted to loverlike servility and larval vulnerability. Ida has—in the double, but related, meaning of the phrase—been had.

In the conventional order of this genre of sexual narrative, one position of intercourse must rapidly be followed by another less orthodox and therefore of greater interest. Miller obliges the reader with a quick instance of dorsal intercourse, preceded by a flitting interlude of fellatio. But more pertinent to the larger issues under investigation is the information that Ida is now so "hooked" that it is she who makes the first move: ". . . she bent over and began nibbling at my prick." The hero's "prick," now very center stage, is still a hook and Ida metamorphosed into a very gullible fish. (Perhaps all of this aquatic imagery was inspired by the bathtub.)

Furthermore, positions are significantly reversed: "I sat on the edge of the tub and she kneeled at my feet gobbling it." The power nexus is clearly outlined. It remains only for the hero to assert his victory by the arrogance of his final gesture: "After a while I made her stand up, bend over; then I let her have it from the rear."

What the reader is vicariously experiencing at this juncture is a nearly supernatural sense of power—should the reader be a male. For the passage is not only a vivacious and imaginative use of circumstance, detail, and context to evoke the excitations of sexual intercourse, it is also a male assertion of dominance over a weak, compliant, and rather unintelligent female. It is a case of sexual politics at the fundamental level of copulation. Several satisfactions for the hero and reader alike undoubtedly accrue upon this triumph of the male ego, the most tangible one being communicated in the following: "She had a small juicy cunt, which fitted me like a glove."

The hero then caters to the reader's appetite in telling how he fed upon his object, biting ". . . the nape of her neck, the lobes of her ears, the sensitive spot on her shoulder, and as I pulled

away I left the mark of my teeth on her beautiful white ass."
The last bite is almost a mark of patent to denote possession
and use, but further still, to indicate attitude. Val had previously
informed us that Bill Woodruff was so absurd and doting a
groveler that he had demeaned himself to kiss this part of his
wife's anatomy. Our hero readjusts the relation of the sexes by
what he believes is a more normative gesture.

Without question the most telling statement in the narrative is
its last sentence: "Not a word spoken." Like the folk hero who
never condescended to take off his hat, Val has accomplished the
entire campaign, including its *coup de grace,* without stooping to
one word of human communication. The recollection of the affair continues for several more pages of diversified stimulation by
which the hero now moves to consolidate his position of power
through a series of physical and emotional gestures of contempt.
In answer to her question: " 'You don't really like me, do you?' "
he replies with studied insolence, " 'I like *this,*' said I, giving her a
stiff jab." His penis is now an instrument of chastisement,
whereas Ida's genitalia are but the means of her humiliation: "I
like your cunt, Ida . . . it's the best thing about you."

All further representations conspire to convince the reader of
Val's superior intelligence and control, while demonstrating the
female's moronic complaisance and helpless carnality; each moment exalts him further and degrades her lower: a dazzling instance of the sexual double standard:

> "You never wear any undies do you? You're a slut, do you
> know it?"
> I pulled her dress up and made her sit that way while I fin-
> ished my coffee.
> "Play with it a bit while I finish this."
> "You're filthy," she said, but she did as I told her.
> "Take your two fingers and open it up. I like the color of it." . . .
> "You can make me do anything, you dirty devil."
> "You like it, don't you?"

Val's imperious aptitude sets the tone for the dramatic events
which follow, and the writing soars off into that species of fantasy
which Steven Marcus calls "pornotopic," a shower of orgasms:

I laid her on a small table and when she was on the verge of exploding I picked her up and walked around the room with her; then I took it out and made her walk on her hands holding her by the thighs, letting it slip out now and then to excite her still more.

In both the foregoing selections the most operative verbal phrases are: "I laid her on a small table" (itself a pun), "made her walk on her hands," "she did as I told her," and "I pulled her dress up and made her sit that way." Ida is putty, even less substantial than common clay, and like a bullied child, is continually taking orders for activity which in the hero's view degrades her while it aggrandizes him.

Meanwhile, the hero's potency is so superb and overwhelming that he is lost in admiration: "It went on like this until I had such an erection that even after I shot a wad into her it stayed up like a hammer. That excited her terribly." And emerging from his efforts covered with so much credit and satisfaction, he takes account of his assets: "My cock looked like a bruised rubber hose; it hung between my legs, extended an inch or two beyond its normal length and swollen beyond recognition."

Ida, who has never demanded much of his attention, nor of ours, is quickly forgotten as the hero goes off to feast in his inimitable fashion: "I went to the drug store and swallowed a couple of malted milks." His final pronouncement on his adventure also redounds to his credit: "A royal bit of fucking, thought I to myself, wondering how I'd act when I met Woodruff again." Royal indeed.

During the course of the episode, Val obliges the reader with intelligence of the Woodruffs' marital incompatibility, a misalliance of a curiously physical character. Mr. Woodruff possesses a genital organ of extraordinary proportions, "a veritable horse cock." "I remember the first time I saw it—I could scarcely believe my eyes," whereas Mrs. Woodruff's dimensions have already been referred to under the rubric "small juicy cunt." But lest this irreconcilable misfortune in any way excuse her in seeking out other satisfaction, it is repeatedly underlined, throughout the section of the novel where she figures that she is an uppity woman. Therefore the hero's exemplary behavior in reducing her to the status of a mere female. Moreover, we are given to understand that she is an insatiable nymphomaniac—thus his wit and prosperity in discovering and exploiting her. . . .

Three[3]

A few days later, when I met him near the docks, Armand ordered me to follow him. Almost without speaking, he took me to his room. With the same apparent scorn he subjected me to his pleasure.

Dominated by his strength and age, I gave the work my utmost care. Crushed by that mass of flesh, which was devoid of the slightest spirituality, I experienced the giddiness of finally meeting the perfect brute, indifferent to my happiness. I discovered the sweetness that could be contained in a thick fleece on torso, belly and thighs and what force it could transmit. I finally let myself be buried in that stormy night. Out of gratitude or fear I placed a kiss on Armand's hairy arm.

"What's eating you? Are you nuts or something?"

"I didn't do any harm."

I remained at his side in order to serve his nocturnal pleasure. When we went to bed, Armand whipped his leather belt from the loops of his trousers and made it snap. It was flogging an invisible victim, a shape of transparent flesh. The air bled. If he frightened me then, it was because of his powerlessness to be the Armand I see, who is heavy and mean. The snapping accompanied and supported him. His rage and despair at not being *him* made him tremble like a horse subdued by darkness, made him tremble more and more. He would not, however, have tolerated my living idly. He advised me to prowl around the station or the zoo and pick up customers. Knowing the terror inspired in me by his person, he didn't deign to keep any eye on me. The money I earned I brought back intact.[4]

This quotation from Jean Genet's autobiographical novel *The Thief's Journal* is the first passage in which the author's identifi-

---

[3]Part Two, dealing with Norman Mailer, is omitted here.

[4]Jean Genet, *The Thief's Journal,* translated from the French by Bernard Frechtman (New York: Grove Press, 1964).

cation is with the "female figure." Jean Genet is both male and female. Young, poor, a criminal and a beggar, he was also initially the despised drag queen, the *maricone* (faggot), contemptible because he was the female partner in homosexual acts. Older, distinguished by fame, wealthy and secure, he became a male; though never ascending to the full elevation of the pimp (or supermale).

Sexual role is not a matter of biological identity but of class or caste in the hierocratic homosexual society projected in Genet's novels. Because of the perfection with which they ape and exaggerate the "masculine" and "feminine" of heterosexual society, his homosexual characters represent the best contemporary insight into its constitution and beliefs. Granted that their caricature is grotesque, and Genet himself is fully aware of the morbidity of this pastiche, his homosexuals nonetheless have unerringly penetrated to the essence of what heterosexual society imagines to be the character of "masculine" and "feminine," and which it mistakes for the nature of male and female, thereby preserving the traditional relation of the sexes. Sartre's brilliant psychoanalytic biography of Genet describes the sexual life of the pimps and queens, male and female figures, in terms that bear out these distinctions of character and prestige:

> This is murder: submissive to a corpse, neglected, unnoticed, gazed at unmindfully and manipulated from behind, the girl queen is metamorphosed into a contemptible female object. She does not even have for the pimp the importance that the sadist attributes to his victim. The latter, though tortured and humiliated, at least remains the focal point of her tormentor's concern. It is indeed she whom he wishes to reach, in her particularity, in the depths of her consciousness. But the fairy is only a receptacle, a vase, a spittoon, which one uses and thinks no more of and which one discards by the very use one makes of it. The pimp masturbates in her. At the very instant when an irresistible force knocks her down, turns her over and punctures her, a dizzying word swoops down upon her, a power hammer that strikes her as if she were a medal: "Encule!" [Faggot][5]

[5] Jean-Paul Sartre, *Saint Genet, Actor and Martyr*, translated from the French by Bernard Frechtman (New York: Braziller, 1963), p. 125.

This is mainly a description of what it is to be female as reflected in the mirror society of homosexuality. But the passage also implies what it is to be male. It is to be master, hero, brute, and pimp. Which is also to be irremediably stupid and cowardly. In this feudal relationship of male and female, pimp and queen, one might expect exchange of servitude for protection. But the typical pimp never protects his slave, and allows him/her to be beaten, betrayed, or even killed, responding only with ambiguous amusement. One is naturally curious to discover just what the queen does receive in return. The answer appears to be an intensity of humiliation which constitutes identity for those who despise themselves. . . .

Genet's two great novels, *Our Lady of the Flowers* and *The Thief's Journal* . . . together with the rest of his prose fiction . . . constitute a painstaking exegesis of the barbarian vassalage of the sexual orders, the power structure of "masculine" and "feminine" as revealed by a homosexual, criminal world that mimics with brutal frankness the bourgeois heterosexual society. In this way the explication of the homosexual code becomes a satire on the heterosexual one. By virtue of their earnestness, Genet's community of pimps and fairies call into ridicule the behavior they so fervently imitate:

> As for slang Divine did not use it, any more than did her cronies the other Nellys . . .
>
> Slang was for men. It was the male tongue. Like the language of men among the Caribees, it became a secondary sexual attribute. It was like the colored plumage of male birds, like the multi-colored silk garments which are the prerogatives of the warriors of the tribe. It was a crest and spurs. Everyone could understand it, but the only ones who could speak it were the men who at birth received as a gift the gestures, the carriage of the hips, legs and arms, the eyes, the chest, with which one can speak it. One day at one of our bars, when Mimosa ventured the following words in the source of a sentence ". . . his screwy stories . . ." the men frowned. Someone said with a threat in his voice: "Broad acting tough."[6]

[6]Jean Genet, *Our Lady of the Flowers*, translated by Bernard Frechtman (New York: Grove Press, 1963).

The virility of the pimp is a transparent egotism posing as strength. His "masculinity" is in fact the most specious of petty self-inflations and is systematically undermined by the true heroes of these adventures, the queens. Though Genet is a great romantic and has created in Divine what is perhaps the last and possibly the most illustrious of those archetypal great-hearted whores so dear to the French tradition, Genet is just as certainly a cold-blooded rationalist whose formidable analytic mind has fastened upon the most fundamental of society's arbitrary follies, its view of sex as a caste structure ratified by nature.

Beginning with the dissection of sexual attitudes in his prose fiction, Genet has gone on in his plays to survey the parent world of the parasitic homosexual community—that larger society where most of us imagine we are at home. Emerging from the little world of homosexual crime which still concerned him in *Deathwatch* and *The Maids,* he brought the truths he had learned there to bear on the complacencies of the "normal" world which for so long had banished and condemned him. His most scathing critique of sexual politics is found in his most recent works for the theater, *The Blacks, The Balcony,* and *The Screens.*

What he has to tell this snug and pious enclave will hardly furnish it with the reassuring bromides they have begun to feel the need of and take as a balm from old retainers like Norman Mailer and Henry Miller. Genet submits the entire social code of "masculine" and "feminine" to a disinterested scrutiny and concludes that it is odious.

If Armand is but a brute and a fool, there is really, as Genet demonstrates, no cause for surprise. He was schooled to be such through every element of his education and was clearly given to understand that these traits were no less than the fulfillment of his very nature as a male. All he has learned has taught him to identify "masculine" with force, cruelty, indifference, egotism, and property. It is no wonder that he regards his penis as a talisman: both an instrument to oppress and the very symbol, in fact the reality, of his status: "My cock," he once said, "is worth its weight in gold. . . ." At other times he boasts that he can lift a heavy man on the end of it. Armand automatically associated sexuality with power, with his solitary pleasure, and with the pain and humiliation of his partner, who is nothing but an object to him in the most literal sense. Intercourse is an assertion of mastery, one that announces his own higher caste and proves it upon a victim who is expected to surrender, serve, and be satisfied.

Armand, for all his turpitude, is at once both more primitive and more logical than a "gentleman," and more honest and direct than the respectable bourgeois whose real convictions he has simply put into practice, and who, by no accident, enjoys reading such passages for the vicarious illusion of mastery which he fancies is offered therein.

The Balcony is Genet's theory of revolution and counterrevolution. The play is set in a brothel and concerns a revolution which ends in failure, as the patrons and proprietors of a whorehouse are persuaded to assume the roles of the former government. Having studied human relationships in the world of pimp and faggot, Genet has come to understand how sexual caste supersedes all other forms of inegalitarianism: racial, political, or economic. *The Balcony* demonstrates the futility of all forms of revolution which preserve intact the basic unit of exploitation and oppression, that between the sexes, male and female, *or* any of the substitutes for them. Taking the fundamental human connection, that of sexuality, to be the nuclear model of all the more elaborate social constructs growing out of it, Genet perceives that it is in itself not only hopelessly tainted but the very prototype of institutionalized inequality. He is convinced that by dividing humanity into two groups and appointing one to rule over the other by virtue of birthright, the social order has already established and ratified a system of oppression which will underlie and corrupt all other human relationships as well as every area of thought and experience.

The first scene, which takes place between a prostitute and a bishop, epitomizes the play much as it does the society it describes. The cleric holds power only through the myth of religion, itself dependent on the fallacy of sin, in turn conditional on the lie that the female is sexuality itself and therefore an evil worthy of the bishop's condign punishment. By such devious routes does power circle round and round the hopeless mess we have made of sexuality. Partly through money: for it is with money that the woman is purchased, and economic dependency is but another sign of her bondage to a system whose coercive agents are actual as well as mythical. Delusions about sex foster delusions of power, and both depend on the reification of woman.

That the Bishop is actually a gasman visiting the bordello's "chambers of illusions" so that he can vicariously share in the power of the church only clarifies the satire on the sexual class system. Those males relegated to reading gas meters may still participate in the joys of mastery through the one human being any male can buy—a female as whore. And the whore, one wonders, what profits her? Nothing. Her "role" in the ritual theater where sexual, political, and social institutions are so felicitously combined is merely to accommodate the ruling passion of each of her rentiers.

In the second scene, the whore is a thief and a criminal (versions of Genet himself) so that a bank clerk may play at justice and morality. Her judge may order her whipped by a muscular executioner or grant her mercy in a transcendent imitation of the powers-that-be, powers reserved to other more fortunate males. The General of Scene III, following his own notions of masculine majesty, converts his whore into his mount and plays at hero while her mouth bleeds from the hit. No matter with which of the three leading roles of sinner, malefactor, or animal the male client may choose to mime his delusions of grandeur, the presence of the woman is utterly essential. To each masquerading male the female is a mirror in which he beholds himself. And the penultimate moment in his illusory but purchasable power fantasy is the moment when whether as Bishop, Judge, or General, he "fucks" her as woman, as subject, as chattel.

The political wisdom implicit in Genet's statement in the play is that unless the ideology of real or fantasized virility is abandoned, unless the clinging to male supremacy as a birthright is finally foregone, all systems of oppression will continue to function simply by virtue of their logical and emotional mandate in the primary human situation.

But what of the madame herself? Irma, *The Balcony*'s able and dedicated administrator, makes money by selling other women, wherein it may be observed how no institution holds sway without collaborators and overseers. Chosen as queen under the counterrevolution, Irma does nothing at all, for queens do not rule. In fact, they do not even exist in themselves; they die as persons once they assume their function, as the Envoy graciously explains. Their function is to serve as figureheads and abstractions to males, just as Chantal, a talented former whore who moves for a moment toward human realization by means of her hope in the revolution, wavers, and then is sold anew and converted into the sexual figurehead for the rising when it becomes corrupt and betrays its radical ideals under the usual excuse of expediency. "In order to win" it adopts the demented consciousness of its opponent and establishes a rotten new version of all it had once stood against. In no time it turns the rebellion into a suicidal carnival, an orgy of blood connected to the old phallic fantasy of "shoot and screw." Its totem is the ritual scapegoat provided by every army's beauty queen since Troy. Once Chantal enters upon the mythical territory of a primitive standard and prize over whom males will tear each other apart, the revolution passes irrevocably into counterrevolution.

Throughout *The Balcony* Genet explores the pathology of virility, the chimera of sexual congress as a paradigm of power over other human beings. He appears to be the only living male writer of first-class literary gifts to have transcended the sexual myths of our era. His critique of the heterosexual politic points the way toward a true sexual revolution, a path which must be explored if any radical social change is to come about. In Genet's analysis, it is fundamentally impossible to change society without changing personality, and sexual personality as it has generally existed must undergo the most drastic overhaul.

If we are to be free at last, Genet proposes in the last scenes of the play, we must first break those chains of our own making through our blind acceptance of common ideas. The three great cages in which we are immured must be dismantled. The first is the potential power of the "Great Figures"—the cleric, the judge, and the warrior—elements of myth which have enslaved consciousness in a coil of self-imposed absurdity. The second is the omnipotence of the police state, the only virtual power in a corrupt society, all other forms of coercion being largely psychological. Last, and most insidious of all, is the cage of sex, the cage in which all others are enclosed: for is not the totem of Police Chief George a six-foot rubber phallus, a "prick of great stature"? And the old myth of sin and virtue, the myth of guilt and innocence, the myth of heroism and cowardice on which the Great Figures repose, the old pillars of an old and decadent structure, are also built on the sexual fallacy. (Or as one is tempted to pun, phallacy.) By attempting to replace this corrupt and tottering edifice while preserving its foundations, the revolution's own bid for social transformation inevitably fails and turns into the counterrevolution where the Grand Balcony, a first-class whorehouse, furnishes both costumes and actors for the new pseudo-government.

Genet's play ends as it had begun. Irma turning out the lights informs us we may go home, where all is falser than the theater's rites. The brothel will open again tomorrow for an identical ritual. The sounds of revolution begin again offstage, but unless the Police Chief is permanently imprisoned in his tomb and unless the new rebels have truly forsworn the customary idiocy of the old sexual politics, there will be no revolution. Sex is deep at the heart of our troubles, Genet is urging, and unless we eliminate the most pernicious of our systems of oppression, unless we go to the very center of the sexual politic and its sick delirium of power and violence, all our efforts at liberation will only land us again in the same primordial stews.

SHULAMITH FIRESTONE

The Dialectic of Sex: The Case for Feminist Revolution

Shulamith Firestone was born in Canada to an orthodox Jewish family and was educated at a yeshiva and at the Art Institute of Chicago, where she earned a degree in fine arts. *The Dialectic of Sex: The Case for Feminist Revolution,* dedicated to Simone de Beauvoir, was published in 1970, when she was twenty-five years old. It was the culmination of several whirlwind years.

In 1967, Firestone was a founding member of the earliest women's liberation collective, which became the Chicago Westside Group. Afterward, she moved to New York City; there, she and others started the highly influential New York Radical Women, Redstockings, and New York Radical Feminists—each new group representing a shift in ideology and tactics. About half of New York Radical Women's lively twenty-eight-page mimeographed journal, *Notes from the First Year* ("$.50 to Women, $1.00 to Men"), consisted of articles by Firestone. In 1968, she helped stage a mock burial of "traditional womanhood" at Arlington National Cemetery, conducted in the midst of a women's anti–Vietnam War peace march, and she took part in the Miss America Pageant protest.

Firestone's book indicates that through all this furious activity she had also thought deeply about feminist theory. *The Dialectic of Sex* was a powerful force in shaping the ideas of radicals in the women's movement—Robin Morgan considered it "a basic building block" of feminism that had been crucial to the development of her thinking.[1]

---

[1] Robin Morgan, *Going Too Far: The Personal Chronicle of a Feminist* (New York: Random House, 1977), p. 119.

Firestone devoted a chapter each to feminist analysis of Marxism and Freudianism. Regarding Marxism, she said that the biological division of the sexes for the purpose of reproduction lies at the origins of class. As to Freudianism, she suggested that power relationships within the patriarchal nuclear family account for the Oedipus and Electra complexes and penis envy: "In a family-based society, repressions due to the incest taboo make a totally fulfilled sexuality impossible for anyone."

The genesis of the family—which Firestone saw as the key institution of oppression of both women and children—lay in the female's need for food and protection during pregnancy and when nursing her young. However, Firestone foresaw a time when women could be freed from the tyranny of their biology by technological advances, such as extrauterine gestation. And further automation of work would make it easier for women to be economically independent of men.

In the final chapter, portions of which are reprinted here, Firestone allowed herself to engage in "utopian speculation" and envisioned "the ultimate revolution."

I. Structural Imperatives

NATURE PRODUCED THE FUNDAMENTAL INEQUALITY—half the human race must bear and rear the children of all of them—which was later consolidated, institutionalized, in the interests of men. Reproduction of the species cost women dearly, not only emotionally, psychologically, culturally but even in strictly material (physical) terms: before recent methods of contraception, continuous childbirth led to constant "female trouble," early aging, and death. Women were the slave class that maintained the species in order to free the other half for the business of the world—admittedly often its drudge aspects, but certainly all its creative aspects as well.

This natural division of labor was continued only at great cultural sacrifice: men and women developed only half of themselves, at the expense of the other half. The division of the psyche into male and female to better reinforce the reproductive division was tragic: the hypertrophy in men of rationalism, aggressive drive, the atrophy of their emotional sensitivity was a physical (war) as well as a cultural disaster. The emotionalism and passivity of women increased their suffering (we cannot speak of them in a symmetrical way, since they were victimized as a class by the division). Sexually men and women were channeled into a highly ordered—time, place, procedure, even dialogue—heterosexuality restricted to the genitals, rather than diffused over the entire physical being.

I submit, then, that the first demand for any alternative system must be:

1. The freeing of women from the tyranny of their reproductive biology by every means available, and the diffusion of the childbearing and childrearing role to the society as a whole, men as well as women.

There are many degrees of this. Already we have a (hard-won) acceptance of "family planning," if not contraception for its own sake. Proposals are imminent for day-care centers, perhaps even twenty-four-hour child-care centers staffed by men as well as women. But this, in my opinion, is timid if not entirely worthless as a transition. We're talking about *radical* change. And though indeed it cannot come all at once, radical goals must be kept in sight at all times. Day-care centers buy women off. They ease the immediate pressure without asking why that pressure is on *women*.

At the other extreme there are the more distant solutions based on the potentials of modern embryology, that is, artificial reproduction, possibilities still so frightening that they are seldom discussed seriously. . . . The fear is to some extent justified: in the hands of our current society and under the direction of current scientists (few of whom are female or even feminist), any attempted use of technology to "free" anybody is suspect. But we are speculating about post-revolutionary systems, and for the purposes of our discussion we shall assume flexibility and good intentions in those working out the change.

To thus free women from their biology would be to threaten the *social* unit that is organized around biological reproduction and the subjection of women to their biological destiny, the family. Our second demand will come also as a basic contradiction to the family, this time the family as an *economic* unit:

2. The full self-determination, including economic independence, of both women and children.

To achieve this goal would require fundamental changes in our social and economic structure. This is why we must talk about a feminist socialism: in the immediate future, under capitalism, there could be at best a token integration of women into the labor force. For women have been found exceedingly useful and cheap as a transient, often highly skilled labor supply, not to mention the economic value of their traditional function, the reproduction and rearing of the next generation of children, a job for which they are now patronized (literally and thus figuratively) rather than paid. But whether or not officially recognized, these are essential economic functions. Women, in this present capacity, are the very foundation of the economic superstructure, vital to its existence. The paeans to self-sacrificing motherhood have a basis in reality: Mom *is* vital to the American way of life, considerably more than apple pie. She is an institution without which the system really *would* fall apart. In official capitalist terms, the bill for her economic services might run as high as one-fifth of the gross national product. But payment is not the answer. To pay her, as is often discussed seriously in Sweden, is a reform that does not challenge the basic division of labor and thus could never eradicate the disastrous psychological and cultural consequences of that division of labor.

As for the economic independence of children, that is really a pipe dream, realized as yet nowhere in the world. And, in the case of children too, we are talking about more than a fair integration into the labor force; we are talking about the abolition of the labor force itself under a cybernetic socialism, the radical restructuring of the economy to make "work," i.e., wage labor, no longer relevant. In our post-revolutionary society adults as well as children would be provided for independent of their social contributions in the first equal distribution of wealth in history.

We have now attacked the family on a double front, challenging that around which it is organized: reproduction of the species by females and its outgrowth, the physical dependence of women and children. To eliminate these would be enough to destroy the family, which breeds the power psychology. However, we will break it down still further.

3. The total integration of women and children into all aspects of the larger society.

All institutions that segregate the sexes, or bar children from adult society . . . must be destroyed.

These three demands predicate a feminist revolution based on advanced technology. And if the male/female and the adult/child cultural distinctions are destroyed, we will no longer need the sexual repression that maintains these unequal classes, allowing for the first time a "natural" sexual freedom. Thus we arrive at:

4. The freedom of all women and children to do whatever they wish to do sexually.

There will no longer be any reason *not* to. (Past reasons: Full sexuality threatened the continuous reproduction necessary for human survival, and thus, through religion and other cultural institutions, sexuality had to be restricted to reproductive purposes, all nonreproductive sex pleasure considered deviation or worse. The sexual freedom of women would call into question the fatherhood of the child, thus threatening patrimony. Child sexuality had to be repressed because it was a threat to the precarious internal balance of the family. These sexual repressions increased proportionately to the degree of cultural exaggeration of the biological family.) In our new society, humanity could finally revert to its natural "polymorphously perverse" sexuality—all forms of sexuality would be allowed and indulged. . . .

II. Fears and Considerations

THESE BROAD IMPERATIVES must form the basis of any more specific radical feminist program. But our revolutionary demands are likely to meet anything from mild balking ("utopian . . . unrealistic . . . farfetched . . . too far in the future . . . impossible . . . well, it may stink, but you haven't got anything better . . .") to hysteria ("inhuman . . . unnatural . . . sick . . . perverted . . . communistic . . . 1984 . . . what? creative motherhood destroyed for babies in glass tubes, monsters made by scientists? etc."). But . . . such negative reactions paradoxically may signify how close we are hitting: revolutionary feminism is the only radical program that immediately cracks through to the emotional strata underlying "serious" politics, thus reintegrating the personal with the public, the subjective with the objective, the emotional with the rational—the female principle with the male.

What are some of the prime components of this resistance that is keeping people from experimenting with alternatives to the family, and where does it come from? We are all familiar with the details of Brave New World: cold collectives, with individualism abolished, sex reduced to a mechanical act, children become robots, Big Brother intruding into every aspect of private life, rows of babies fed by impersonal machines, eugenics manipulated by the state, genocide of cripples and retards for the sake of a super-race created by white-coated technicians, all emotion considered weakness, love destroyed, and so on. The family (which, despite its oppressiveness, is now the last refuge from the encroaching power of the state, a shelter that provides the little emotional warmth, privacy, and individual comfort now available) would be destroyed, letting this horror penetrate indoors.

Paradoxically, one reason The 1984 Nightmare occurs so frequently is that it grows directly out of, signifying an exaggeration of, the evils of our present male-supremacist culture. . . . The Nightmare is directly the product of the attempt to imagine a society in which women have become like men, crippled in the identical way, thus destroying a delicate balance of interlocking dependencies.

However, we are suggesting the opposite: Rather than concentrating the female principle into a "private" retreat, into which men periodically duck for relief, we want to rediffuse it—for the first time creating society from the bottom up. Man's difficult triumph over Nature has made it possible to restore the truly natural: he could undo Adam's and Eve's curse both, to reestablish the earthly Garden of Eden. But in his long toil his imagination has been stifled: he fears an enlargement of his drudgery, through the incorporation of Eve's curse into his own.

But there is a more concrete reason why this subliminal horror image operates to destroy serious consideration of feminism: the failure of past social experiments. Radical experiments, when they have solved problems at all, have created an entirely new—and not necessarily improved—set of problems in their place. . . .[2]

Because their ideology was not founded on the minimal feminist premises above, these experiments never achieved even the more limited democratic goals their (male) theorists and leaders had predicted. However, their success within narrow spheres shows that the biological family unit is amenable to change. But we would have to control totally its institutions to eliminate the oppression altogether.

However—to be fair—it is only recently, in the most advanced industrial countries, that genuine preconditions for feminist revolution have begun to exist. For the first time it is becoming possible to attack the family not only on moral grounds—in that it reinforces biologically-based sex class, promoting adult males, who are then divided further among them-

---

[2]Firestone discusses here three social experiments: attempts to eliminate the family and end sexual repression during the Russian Revolution; the experimental communal system of the kibbutz in Israel; and A. S. Neill's educational experiment in England, Summerhill.—*Ed.*

selves by race and class privilege, over females of all ages and male children—but also on functional grounds: it is no longer necessary or most effective as the basic social unit of reproduction and production. There is no longer a need for universal reproduction, even if the development of artificial reproduction does not soon place biological reproduction itself in question; cybernation, by changing not only man's relation to work, but his need to work altogether, will eventually strip the division of labor at the root of the family of any remaining practical value.

III. The Slow Death of the Family

THE INCREASING EROSION of the functions of the family by modern technology should, by now, have caused some signs of its weakening. However, this is not absolutely the case. Though the institution is archaic, artificial cultural reinforcements have been imported to bolster it: Sentimental sermons, manuals of guidance, daily columns in newspapers and magazines, special courses, services, and institutions for (professional) couples, parents, and child educators, nostalgia, warnings to individuals who question or evade it, and finally, if the number of dropouts becomes a serious threat, a real backlash, including outright persecution of nonconformists. The last has not happened only because it is not yet necessary.

Marriage is in the same state as the Church: Both are becoming functionally defunct, as their preachers go about heralding a revival, eagerly chalking up converts in a day of dread. And just as God has been pronounced dead quite often but has this sneaky way of resurrecting himself, so everyone debunks marriage, yet ends up married.[3]

What is keeping marriage so alive? [One] of the cultural bulwarks of marriage in the twentieth century, the romantic tradi-

---

[3]Ninety-five percent of all American women still marry and 90 percent bear children, most often more than two. Families with children in the medium range (two to four) are as predominant as ever, no longer attributable to the postwar baby boom.

tion of nonmarital love, the hetairism that was the necessary adjunct to monogamic marriage, has been purposely confused with that most pragmatic of institutions, making it more appealing—thus restraining people from experimenting with other social forms that could satisfy their emotional needs as well or better.

Under increasing pressure, with the pragmatic bases of the marriage institution blurred, sex roles relaxed to a degree that would have disgraced a Victorian. *He* had no crippling doubts about his role, nor about the function and value of marriage. To him it was simply an economic arrangement of some selfish benefit, one that would most easily satisfy his physical needs and reproduce his heirs. His wife, too, was clear about her duties and rewards: ownership of herself and of her full sexual, psychological, and housekeeping services for a lifetime, in return for long-term patronage and protection by a member of the ruling class, and—in her turn—limited control over a household and over her children until they reached a certain age. Today this contract based on divided roles has been so disguised by sentiment that it goes completely unrecognized by millions of newlyweds, and even most older married couples.

But this blurring of the economic contract, and the resulting confusion of sex roles, has not significantly eased woman's oppression. In many cases it has put her in only a more vulnerable position. With the clear-cut arrangement of matches by parents all but abolished, a woman, still part of an underclass, must now, in order to gain the indispensable male patronage and protection, play a desperate game, hunting down bored males while yet appearing cool. And even once she is married, any overlap of roles generally takes place on the wife's side, not on the husband's: the "cherish and protect" clause is the first thing forgotten—while the wife has gained the privilege of going to work to "help out," even of putting her husband through school. More than ever she shoulders the brunt of the marriage, not only emotionally, but now also in its more practical aspects. She has simply added his job to hers.

A second cultural prop to the outmoded institution is the privatization of the marriage experience: each partner enters marriage convinced that what happened to his parents, what happened to his friends can never happen to him. Though Wrecked Marriage has become a national hobby, a universal obsession—as witnessed by the booming business of guidebooks to marriage and divorce, the women's magazine industry, an affluent class of marriage counselors and shrinks, whole repertoires of Ball-and-Chain jokes and gimmicks, and cultural products such as soap opera, the marriage-and-family genre on TV, e.g., *I Love Lucy* or *Father Knows Best,* films and plays like Cassavetes' *Faces* and Albee's *Who's Afraid of Virginia Woolf?*— still one encounters everywhere a defiant "We're different" brand of optimism in which the one good (outwardly exemplary, anyway) marriage in the community is habitually cited to prove that *it* is possible.

The privatization process is typified by comments like, "Well, I know I'd make a great mother." It is useless to point out that *everyone* says that, that the very parents or friends now dismissed as "bad" parents and "poor" marital partners all began marriage and parenthood in exactly the same spirit. After all, does anyone *choose* to have a "bad" marriage? Does anyone *choose* to be a "bad" mother? And even if it were a question of "good" vs. "bad" marital partners or parents, there will always be as many of the latter as the former; under the present system of universal marriage and parenthood just as many spouses and children must pull a bad lot as a good one; in fact any classes of "good" and "bad" are bound to re-create themselves in identical proportion. Thus the privatization process functions to keep people blaming themselves, rather than the institution, for its failure: Though the institution consistently proves itself unsatisfactory, even rotten, it encourages them to believe that somehow their own case will be different.

Warnings can have no effect, because logic has nothing to do with why people get married. Everyone has eyes of his own, parents of his own. If he chooses to block all evidence, it is because he must. In a world out of control, the only institutions that grant him an *illusion* of control, that seem to offer any safety, shelter, or warmth, are the "private" institutions: religion, marriage/family, and, most recently, psychoanalytic therapy. But, as we have seen, the family is neither private nor a refuge, but is directly connected to—is even the cause of—the ills of the larger society which the individual is no longer able to confront.

But the cultural bulwarks we have just discussed—the confusion of romance with marriage, the blurring of its economic functions and its rigid sex roles, the privatization process, the illusion of control and refuge, all of which exploit the fears of the modern person living within an increasingly hostile environment—still are not the whole answer to why the institution of marriage continues to thrive. It is unlikely that such negatives alone could support the family unit as a vital institution. It would be too easy to attribute the continuation of the family structure solely to backlash. We will find, I am afraid, in reviewing marriage in terms of our four minimal feminist demands, that it fulfills (in its own miserable way) at least a portion of the requirements at least as well as or better than did most of the social experiments we have discussed.

1. Freedom of women from the tyranny of reproduction and childrearing is hardly fulfilled. However, women are often relieved of its worst strains by a servant class—and in the modern marriage, by modern gynecology, "family planning," and the increasing takeover, by the school, day-care centers, and the like, of the childrearing functions.

2. Though financial *independence* of women and children is not generally granted, there is a substitute: physical *security*.

3. Women and children, segregated from the larger society, are integrated within the family unit, the only place where this occurs. That the little interplay between men, women, and children is concentrated in one social unit makes that unit all the more difficult to renounce.

4. Though the family is the source of sexual repression, it guarantees the conjugal couple a steady, if not satisfactory, sex supply, and provides the others with "aim-inhibited" relationships, which are, in many cases, the only long-term relationships these individuals will ever have.

Thus there are practical assets of marriage to which people

cling. It is not all a cultural sales job. On a scale of percentages, marriage—at least in its desperate liberalized version—would fare us well as most of the experimental alternatives thus far tried, which . . . also fulfilled some of the stipulations and not others, or only partially fulfilled all of them. And marriage has the added advantage of being a known quantity.

And yet marriage in its very definition will never be able to fulfill the needs of its participants, for it was organized around, and reinforces, a fundamentally oppressive biological condition that we only now have the skill to correct. As long as we have the institution we shall have the oppressive conditions at its base. We need to start talking about new alternatives that will satisfy the emotional and psychological needs that marriage, archaic as it is, still satisfies, but that will satisfy them better.

MURIEL RUKEYSER

The Poem as Mask

Long before the birth of the modern women's movement, the American poet Muriel Rukeyser (1913–1980) rebelled against convention and the expectations of her staid, socially prominent family, and reinvented herself as a free woman—a woman not unlike her contemporary Simone de Beauvoir or Doris Lessing's protagonists in *The Golden Notebook*. Devoting herself to left-wing political activism and to writing, Rukeyser supported herself and reared a child on her own.

Rukeyser's formative years came during the thirties, when she was indelibly stamped with the radicalism of that era. While a student at Vassar College, she covered for a campus publication the infamous Scottsboro, Alabama, trial of nine black youths for rape. And during the Spanish Civil War, she was an ardent supporter of the antifascist Loyalists. In her sixties, she was still passionately engaged with the world: She traveled to South Korea as president of the writers' organization PEN to stand vigil for the poet Kim Chi-Ha, who had been sentenced to death. She was arrested while demonstrating against the Vietnam War. She denounced the execution of Kurdish socialists in Iran.

Rukeyser's poetry resounds with protest against injustice and inhumanity, but her work also deals with more intimate subject matter: sexuality, motherhood, creativity, being Jewish, serious illness. In many of her poems she effected a remarkable fusion of social themes with personal motifs—an achievement that was not appreciated, or even understood, until the advent of feminist criticism. Writer Louise Bernikow has pointed out that critics of Rukeyser in the thirties and forties "lumped her with the 'Proletarian Poets,' ignoring the female-centeredness of her work"; while in the fifties, ironically enough, "she was derided . . . for being 'merely personal.' "[1]

Rukeyser published over a dozen volumes of poetry—a body of work, said her obituary in *The New York Times,* "that seemed to mirror United States history from the Depression and the coming of Fascism to World War II and the Vietnam War," along with "private concerns."[2] She was also the author of several books of nonfiction, including two historical biographies of mathematicians: *Willard Gibbs* (1942) and *The Traces of Thomas Hariot* (1971).

"The Poem as Mask," reprinted here from Rukeyser's collection *The Speed of Darkness* (1968), is about the divided self— the poet's often warring identities as woman and as artist. In it, Rukeyser retells the Greek myth of the musician-god Orpheus, which she first related in a 1949 poem. The earlier work, titled "Orpheus," began with the murder of the god, who was torn to pieces by furious Thracian women—his self fragmented, his song silenced, his body parts scattered. However, in "The Poem as Mask" Rukeyser confesses, "when I wrote of the god . . . it was myself, split open, unable to speak, in exile from myself." The poet then connects the image "myself, split open" with the experience of giving birth, a birth in which she herself is reborn. In the final couplet, the poet is healed, and she can create her own song.

"Poems like 'The Poem as Mask,' " wrote one reviewer the year before Rukeyser's death, "make me wonder if Muriel Rukeyser is not our greatest living American poet."[3]

---

[1] Louise Bernikow, "Muriel Rukeyser at Sixty-five: Still Ahead of Her Time," *Ms.,* January 1979, p. 14.

[2] *New York Times,* February 13, 1980, Section 2, p. 6.

[3] Roy B. Hoffman, reviewing *The Collected Poems of Muriel Rukeyser* in *The Village Voice,* February 26, 1979.

Orpheus

When I wrote of the women in their dances and wildness, it
    was a mask,
on their mountain, god-hunting, singing, in orgy,
it was a mask; when I wrote of the god,
fragmented, exiled from himself, his life, the love gone down
    with song,
it was myself, split open, unable to speak, in exile from
    myself.

There is no mountain, there is no god, there is memory
of my torn life, myself split open in sleep, the rescued child
beside me among the doctors, and a word
of rescue from the great eyes.

No more masks! No more mythologies!

Now, for the first time, the god lifts his hand,
the fragments join in me with their own music.

MARY DALY

After the Death of God the Father: Women's Liberation and the Transformation of Christian Consciousness

Theologian Mary Daly (b. 1928) has said, "I am interested . . . in the spiritual dimension of women's liberation."[1] And if we understand the word *spiritual* in its broadest sense, this has indeed been the central concern of her work for several decades.

A scholar in the fields of religion, philosophy, and theology, Daly has a Ph.D. and Th.D. from the University of Fribourg, Switzerland. At the time of the publication of her first book, *The Church and the Second Sex* (1968), which explores the long history of misogyny and patriarchy in the Catholic Church and the implications of a male God, Daly was teaching theology at Boston College in Massachusetts, a Jesuit institution. After the book appeared, she was summarily fired but was reinstated when students protested her dismissal with marches and a petition campaign.

Five years later, in *Beyond God the Father*, Daly argued that God need not be personified at all. To think of God anthropomorphically, as a noun, implies personality and gender, she wrote; instead, God should be conceived as of a verb, since God is Be-ing. Still later, in her 1978 book, *Gyn/Ecology: The Metaethics of Radical Feminism*, she turned her focus from theology in order to chart "the journey of women becoming," a journey in which every woman "can dis-cover the mystery of her own history, and find how it is interwoven with the lives of other women." The middle section of that book describes vari-

[1]From an interview in *Contemporary Authors*, 25–28 Rev., 1971.

ous crimes against women: *suttee,* the murder of widows in India; foot binding in China; genital mutilation in Africa; burning of witches in Europe from the fifteenth through the seventeenth centuries; and finally abuse of women's bodies by gynecology in modern America.

Over the years, Daly herself has provided her readers with a running commentary on the evolution of her ideas. In 1975 she added "A New Feminist Postchristian Introduction" to a second edition of *The Church and the Second Sex,* announcing that she now regarded the 1968 author of the original edition (herself) as a "reformist foresister . . . whose work I respectfully refute." Then, in *Gyn/Ecology* she informed the reader that though she did still consider herself the author of *Beyond God the Father,* she had decided she could no longer use the word *God,* "because there is no way to remove male/masculine imagery" from it. She was therefore now substituting the term *Goddess,* when speaking anthropomorphically of "ultimate reality."[2]

After *Gyn/Ecology,* Daly's writing became increasingly experimental and difficult, as she wrestled with the English language, trying to reshape it to her unique, complex needs. Her subsequent books were *Pure Lust: Elemental Feminist Philosophy* (1984); *Webster's First New Intergalactic Wickedary of the English Language,* with Jane Caputi (1987); and a memoir, *Outercourse: The Be-Dazzling Voyage: Containing Recollections from My Logbook of a Radical Feminist Philosopher* (1992).

The following article, reprinted here in full from *Commonweal* magazine, March 12, 1971, presents Daly's thinking about the Father God—"the great patriarch in heaven"—at a point midway between her first two books. In 1971 she still felt it was possible to talk about God but believed that the women's revolution should "change our whole vision of reality," including Western religious thought and imagery.

---

[2]Mary Daly, *Gyn/Ecology: The Metaethics of Radical Feminism* (Boston: Beacon Press, 1978), p. xi.

THE WOMEN'S LIBERATION MOVEMENT has produced a deluge of books and articles. Their major task has been exposition and criticism of our male-centered heritage. In order to reveal and drive home to readers the oppressive character of our cultural institutions, it was necessary to do careful research, to trot out passages from leading philosophers, psychologists, statesmen, poets, historians, saints, and theologians which make the reader's hair stand on end by the blatancy of their misogynism. Part of the task also has been the tracing of the subtle psychological mechanisms by which society has held men up and women down. This method of exposition and analysis reached its crescendo within this past year when Kate Millett's *Sexual Politics* rocketed her into the role of American counterpart to Simone de Beauvoir.

As far as the level of creative research is concerned, that phase of the work is finished. The skeletons in our cultural closet have been hauled out for inspection. I do not mean to imply that there are not countless more of the same to be uncovered (just the other day I noticed for the first time that Berdyaev blandly affirms there is "something base and sinister in the female element." Etcetera). Nor do I mean that the task of communicating the message is over. Millions have yet to hear the news, let alone to grasp its import. Certainly it would be a mistake and a betrayal to trivialize the fact that our culture is so diseased. That has always been a major tactic in the fine art of suppressing the rage of women. No, what I am saying is that Phase One of critical research and writing in the movement has opened the way for the logical next step in creative thinking. We now have to ask how the women's revolution can and should change our whole vision of reality. What I intend to do here is to sketch some of the ways in which it can influence Western religious thoughts.

The Judaic-Christian tradition has served to legitimate sexually imbalanced patriarchal society. Thus, for example, the image of the Father God, spawned in the human imagination and sustained as plausible by patriarchy, has in turn rendered service to this type of society by making its mechanisms for the oppression of women appear right and fitting. If God in "his" heaven is a father ruling "his" people, then it is in the "nature" of things and according to divine plan and the order of the universe that society be male-dominated. Theologian Karl Barth found it appropriate to write that woman is "ontologically" subordinate to man. Within this context a mystification of roles takes place: the husband dominating his wife represents God himself. What is happening, of course, is the familiar mechanism by which the images and values of a given society are projected into a realm of beliefs, which in turn justify the social infrastructure. The belief system becomes hardened and objectified, seeming to have an unchangeable independent existence and validity of its own. It resists social change, which would rob it of its plausibility. Nevertheless, despite the vicious circle, change does occur in society, and ideologies die, though they die hard.

As the women's revolution begins to have its effect upon the fabric of society, transforming it from patriarchy into something that never existed before—into a diarchal situation that is radically new—it will, I believe, become the greatest single potential challenge to Christianity to rid itself of its oppressive tendencies or go out of business. Beliefs and values that have held sway for thousands of years will be questioned as never before. It is also very possibly the greatest single hope for survival of religious consciousness in the West.

At this point it is important to consider the objection that the liberation of women will only mean that new characters will assume the same old roles, but that nothing will change essentially in regard to structure, ideology, or values. This objection is often based upon the observation that the very few women in "masculine" occupations seem to behave very much as men do. This is really not to the point for it fails to recognize that the effect of tokenism is not to change stereotypes or social systems but to preserve these. What I am discussing here is an emergence of women such as has never taken place before. It is naive to assume that the coming of women into equal power in society generally and in the church in particular will simply mean uncritical acceptance of values formerly given priority by men.

Rather, I suggest that it will be a catalyst for transformation of our culture.

The roles and structures of patriarchy have been developed and sustained in accordance with an artificial polarization of human qualities into the traditional sexual stereotypes. The image of the person in authority and the accepted understanding of "his" role have corresponded to the eternal masculine stereotype, which implies hyperrationality, "objectivity," aggressivity, the possession of dominating and manipulative attitudes toward persons and environment, and the tendency to construct boundaries between the self (and those identified with the self) and "the other." The caricature of a human being which is represented by this stereotype depends for its existence upon the opposite caricature—the eternal feminine (hyper-emotional, passive, self-abasing, etc.). By becoming whole persons, women can generate a counterforce to the stereotype of the leader as they challenge the artificial polarization of human characteristics. There is no reason to assume that women who have the support of their sisters to criticize the masculine stereotype will simply adopt it as a model for themselves. More likely they will develop a wider range of qualities and skills in themselves and thereby encourage men to engage in a comparably liberating procedure (a phenomenon we are beginning to witness already in men's liberation groups). This becoming of *whole* human beings will affect the values of our society, for it will involve a change in the fabric of human consciousness.

Accordingly, it is reasonable to anticipate that this change will affect the symbols which reflect the values of our society, including religious symbols. Since some of these have functioned to justify oppression, women and men would do well to welcome this change. Religious symbols die when the cultural situation that supported them ceases to give them plausibility. This should pose no problem to authentic faith, which accepts the relativity of all symbols and recognizes that fixation upon any of them as absolute in itself is idolatrous.

The becoming of new symbols is not a matter that can arbitrarily be decided around a conference table. Rather, they grow out of a changing communal situation and experience. This does not mean that theologically we are consigned to the role of passive spectators. We are called upon to be attentive to what the new experience of the becoming of women is revealing to us, and to foster the evolution of consciousness beyond the oppressiveness and imbalance reflected and justified by symbols and doctrines throughout the millennia of patriarchy.

This imbalance is apparent first of all in the biblical and popular image of the great patriarch in heaven who rewards and punishes according to his mysterious and arbitrary will. The fact that the effects of this image have not always been humanizing is evident to any perceptive reader of history. The often cruel behavior of Christians toward unbelievers and even toward dissenters among themselves is shocking evidence of the function of that image in relation to values and behavior.

Sophisticated thinkers, of course, have never intellectually identified God with an elderly parent in heaven. Nevertheless it is important to recognize that, even when very abstract conceptualizations of God are formulated in the mind, images have a way of surviving in the imagination in such a way that a person can function on two different and even apparently contradictory levels at the same time. Thus one can speak of God as spirit and at the same time imagine "him" as belonging to the male sex. Such primitive images can profoundly affect conceptualizations which appear to be very refined and abstract. Even the Yahweh of the future, so cherished by the theology of hope, comes through on an imaginative level as exclusively a He-God, and it is perhaps consistent with this that theologians of hope have attempted to develop a political theology which takes no explicit cognizance of the devastation wrought by sexual politics.

The widespread conception of the "Supreme Being" as an entity distinct from this world but controlling it according to plan and keeping human beings in a state of infantile subjection has been a not too subtle mask for the divine patriarch. The Supreme Being's plausibility, and that of the static worldview which accompanies this projection has, of course, declined. This was a projection grounded in specifically patriarchal infrastructures and sustained as subjectively real by the usual processes of generating plausibility. The sustaining power of the social infrastructures has been eroded by a number of developments in recent history, including the general trend toward democratization of society and the emergence of technology with the accompanying sense of mastery over the world and man's destiny. However, it is the women's movement which appears destined to play the key role in the overthrow of such oppressive elements in traditional theism, precisely because it strikes at the source of the imbalance reflected in traditional beliefs.

The women's movement will present a growing threat to patriarchal religion less by attacking it than by simply leaving it behind. Few of the leaders in the movement evince an interest in institutional religion, having recognized it as an instrument of their betrayal. Those who see their commitment to the movement as consonant with concern for the religious heritage are aware that the Christian tradition is by no means bereft of elements which foster genuine experiences and intimations of transcendence. The problem is that their liberating potential is choked off in the surrounding atmosphere of the images, ideas, values, and structures of patriarchy. What will, I think, become possible through the social change coming from radical feminism is a more acute and widespread perception of qualitative differences between those conceptualizations of God and of the human relationship to God which are oppressive in their implications and those which encourage self-actualization and social commitment.

The various theologies that hypostatize transcendence invariably use this "God" to legitimate oppression, particularly that of women. These are irredeemably antifeminine and therefore antihuman. In contrast to this, a more authentic language of transcendence does not hypostatize or objectify God and consequently does not lend itself to such use. So, for example, [Paul] Tillich's way of speaking about God as ground and power of being would be very difficult to use for the legitimation of any sort of oppression. It grows out of awareness of that reality which is both transcendent and immanent, not reducible to or adequately represented by such expressions as *person, father, supreme being*. Awareness of this reality is not achieved by playing theological games but by existential courage. I am not saying that a liberated consciousness necessarily will use Tillich's languge of transcendence. That of [Alfred North] Whitehead, [William] James, [Karl] Jaspers, to mention a few—or an entirely new language—may do as well or better. But it remains true that the driving revelatory force which will make possible an authenticity of religious consciousness is courage in the face of anxiety.

Since the projections of patriarchal religion have been blocking the dynamics of existential courage by offering the false security of alienation—that is, of self-reduction to stereotyped roles—there is reason to see hope for the emergence of genuine religious consciousness in the massive challenge to patriarchy which is now in its initial stages. The becoming of women may be not only the doorway to deliverance from the omnipotent Father in all of his disguises—a deliverance which secular humanism has passionately fought for—but also a doorway to something; that is, the beginning for many of a more authentic search for transcendence; that is, for God.

The imbalance in Christian ideology resulting from sexual hierarchy is manifested not only in the doctrine of God but also in the notion of Jesus as the unique God-man. A great deal of Christian doctrine concerning Jesus has been docetic; that is, it has not really seriously accepted the fact that Jesus was a human being. An effect of the liberation of women will very likely be the loss of plausibility of Christological formulas which come close to reflecting a kind of idolatry in regard to the person of Jesus. As it becomes better understood that God is transcendent and unobjectifiable—or else not at all—it will become less plausible to speak of Jesus as the Second Person of the Trinity who "assumed" a human nature. Indeed, the prevalent emphasis upon the total uniqueness and supereminence of Jesus will, I think, become less meaningful. To say this is not at all to deny his extraordinary character and mission. The point is to attempt a realistic assessment of certain ways of using his image (which in all likelihood he himself would repudiate). It is still not uncommon for priests and ministers, when confronted with the issue of women's liberation, to assert that God become incarnate uniquely as a male, and then to draw arguments for male supremacy from this. Indeed, the tradition itself tends to justify such assertions. The underlying—and often explicit—assumption in the minds of theologians down through the centuries has been that the divinity could not have deigned to become incarnate in the "inferior" sex, and the "fact" that "he" did not do so reinforces the belief in masculine superiority. The transformation of society by the erosion of male dominance will generate serious challenges to such assumptions of the Christological tradition.

It will, I think, become increasingly evident that exclusively masculine symbols for the ideal of "incarnation" will not do. As a uniquely masculine divinity loses credibility, so also the idea of a unique divine incarnation in a human being of the male sex may give way in the religious consciousness to an increased awareness of the divine presence in all human beings, understood as expressing and in a real sense incarnating—although always inadequately—the power of being. The seeds of this awareness are already present, of course, in the traditional doctrine that all human beings are made to the image of God and, in a less than adequate way, in the doctrine of grace. Now it should become possible to work out with increasing realism the implication in both of these doctrines that human beings are called to self-actualization and to the creation of a community that fosters the becoming of women and men. This means that no completely adequate models can be taken from the past. It may be that we will witness a remythologizing of Western religion. Certainly, if the need for parental symbols for God persists, something like the Father-Mother God proposed by Mary Baker Eddy will be more acceptable to the new woman and the new man than the Father God of the past. A symbolism for incarnation of the divine in human beings may continue to be needed in the future, but it is highly unlikely that women or men will continue to find plausible that symbolism which is epitomized in the image of the Virgin kneeling in adoration before her own son. Perhaps this will be replaced by the emergence of bisexual imagery which is not hierarchical. The experience of the past brought forth a new Adam and a new Eve. Perhaps the future will bring a new Christ and a new Mary. For the present, it would appear that we are being called upon to recognize the poverty of all symbols and the fact of our past idolatry regarding them, and to turn to our own resources for bringing about the radically new in our own lives.

The manifestation of God in Jesus was an eschatological event whose fulfilled reality lies in the future. The Jesus of the Gospels was a free person who challenged ossified beliefs and laws. Since he was remarkably free of prejudice against women and treated them as equals insofar as the limitations of his culture would allow, it is certain that he would be working with them for their liberation today. This awakening of women to their human potentiality by creative action as they assume equal partnership with men in society can bring about a manifestation of God in themselves which will be the Second Coming of God incarnate, fulfilling the latent promise in the original revelation that men and women are made to the image of God.

Behind the Mask

It should be evident, then, that women's liberation is an event that can challenge authoritarian, exclusive, and nonexistential notions of faith and revelation. Since women have been extraenvironmentals, to use a McLuhanish term, that is, since they have not been part of the authority structure which uses "faith" and "revelation" to reinforce the mechanisms of alienation, their emergence can effect a more widespread criticalness of idolatry which is often masked by these ideas. There could result from this a more general understanding of faith as a state of ultimate concern and commitment and a heightened sense of relativity concerning the symbols it uses to express this commitment. An awareness might also emerge—not merely in the minds of a theological elite, but in the general consciousness—that revelation is an ongoing experience.

The becoming of women implies also a transvaluation of values in Christian morality. As the old order is challenged and as men and women become freed to experience a wholeness of personality which the old polarizations impeded, the potentiality will be awakened for a change in moral consciousness which will go far beyond Nietzsche's merely reactionary rejection of Christian values.

Much of the traditional theory of Christian virtue appears to be the product of reactions on the part of men—perhaps guilty reactions—to the behavioral excesses of the stereotypic male. There has been theoretical emphasis upon charity, meekness, obedience, humility, self-abnegation, sacrifice, service. Part of the problem with this moral ideology is that it became generally accepted not by men but by women, who have hardly been helped by an ethic which reinforced their abject situation. This emphasis upon the passive virtues, of course, has not challenged exploitativeness but supported it. Part of the syndrome is the prevailing notion of sin as an offense against those in power, or against "God" (the two are often equated). Within the perspective of such a privatized morality, the structures themselves of oppression are not seen as sinful.

Consistent with all of this is the fact that the traditional Christian moral consciousness has been fixated upon the problems of reproductive activity in a manner totally disproportionate to its feeble political concern. This was summed up several years ago in Archbishop Roberts' remark that "if contraceptives had been dropped over Japan instead of bombs which merely killed, maimed, and shriveled up thousands alive there would have been a squeal of outraged protest from the Vatican to the remotest Mass center in Asia." Pertinent also is Simone de Beauvoir's remark that the church has reserved its uncompromising humanitarianism for man in the fetal condition. Although theologians today acknowledge that this privatized morality has failed to cope with the structures of oppression, few seriously face the possibility that the roots of this distortion are deeply buried in the fundamental and all-pervasive sexual alienation which the women's movement is seeking to overcome.

It is well known that Christians under the spell of the jealous God who represents the collective power of his chosen people can use religion to justify that "us and them" attitude which is disastrous in its consequences for the powerless. It is less widely understood that the projection of "the other"—easily adaptable to national, racial, and class differences—has basically and primordially been directed against women. Even the rhetoric of racism finds its model in sexism.

The consciousness-raising which is beginning among women is evoking a qualitatively new understanding of the subtle mechanisms which produce and destroy "the other," and a consequent empathy with all of the oppressed. This gives grounds for the hope that their emergence can generate a counterforce to the exploitative mentality which is destroying persons and the environment. Since the way men and women are seen in society is a prime determinant in the whole social system and ideology, radical women refuse to see their movement as simply one among others. What I am suggesting is that it might be the only chance for the turning of human beings from a course leading to the deterioration and perhaps the end of life on this planet.

Those who see their concern for women's liberation as consonant with an evolving Christianity would be unrealistic to expect much comprehension from the majority of male ecclesiastics. Such writers as Gordon Rattrey Taylor (*The Biological Time Bomb*), Robert Francoeur (*Utopian Motherhood*), and others keep beeping out the message that we are moving into a world in which human sexuality is no longer merely oriented to reproduction of the species—which means that the masculine and feminine mystiques are doomed to evaporate. Within the theological community, however, the predictable and almost universal response has been what one might call the ostrich syndrome. Whereas the old theology justified sexual oppression, the new theology for the most part simply ignores it and goes on in comfortable compatibility with it, failing to recognize its deep connection with such other major problems as war, racism, and environmental pollution. The work of fostering religious consciousness which is explicitly incompatible with sexism will require an extraordinary degree of creative rage, love and hope.

SUSAN BROWNMILLER

Against Our Will:
Men, Women, and Rape

Using fact and theory gleaned from history, classical mythology, psychology, psychoanalysis, sociology, criminology, personal experience, testimony of individual victims, and anything else that came to hand, Susan Brownmiller (b. 1935) vigorously attacked the societal myths surrounding rape. Her book *Against Our Will: Men, Women, and Rape* is an almost encyclopedic survey of the long-neglected topic, viewed in unwavering feminist perspective.

Brownmiller concluded that rape "is nothing more or less than a conscious process of intimidation by which *all men* keep *all women* in a state of fear." She saw rape as an "exercise in power" that perpetuates male domination of women; she deflated the myth of the glamorous, virile "heroic rapist"; and she refuted certain "deadly male myths of rape"—such as "All women want to be raped," "She was asking for it," and "If you're going to be raped, you might as well relax and enjoy it."

An antirape crusade already existed when *Against Our Will* was published in 1975, and the book provided it with intellectual ammunition and cogent analysis. During the early 1970s, activists led the way in creating hundreds of rape crisis centers where rape victims received emotional support and practical assistance. Rape prevention educational campaigns and rape speak-outs were inaugurated.[1] At "Take Back the Night" antirape marches held in several cities around the country, women proclaimed their right to safety on the public streets.

[1] There were approximately 1,500 individual rape projects in operation at the height of the antirape movement, in 1976. See Susan Schechter, *Women and Male Violence: The Visions and Struggles of the Battered Women's Movement* (Boston: South End Press, 1982), p. 39.

A journalist, Brownmiller had served an apprenticeship in the civil rights and women's movements. She was a member of New York Radical Feminists, which sponsored two speak-outs on rape in 1971 and cosponsored with the National Black Feminist Organization a 1974 speak-out on rape and sexual abuse. In *Against Our Will,* Brownmiller credited the women's movement for making her book possible, "by its courage and imagination, and by its contribution of personal testimony that opened up the subject of rape from a woman's point of view for the first time in history." But some feminists later criticized the book for its failure to understand the racist use of the rape charge.[2]

Brownmiller's other writings include the nonfiction book *Femininity* (1984) and *Waverly Place* (1989), a novel dealing with a battered wife.

The following selection is from Chapter 6 of *Against Our Will,* "The Police-Blotter Rapist." It presents the author's argument that rape is not primarily a sexual crime, but a crime of violence.

EVAN CONNELL, A NOVELIST OF SOME REPUTE, wrote a *tour de force* some years ago entitled *The Diary of a Rapist.* Connell's protagonist, Earl Summerfield, was a timid, white, middle-class civil-service clerk, age twenty-seven, who had an inferiority complex, delusions of intellectual brilliance, a wretched, deprived sex life, and an older, nagging, ambitious, "castrating" wife. Connell's book made gripping reading, but the portrait of Earl Summerfield was far from an accurate picture of an average real-life rapist. In fact, Connell's *Diary* contains almost every myth and misconception about rape and rapists that is held in the popular mind. From the no-nonsense FBI statistics and some intensive sociological studies that are beginning to appear, we can see that the typical American rapist is no weirdo, psycho

[2]Ibid., p. 40.

schizophrenic beset by timidity, sexual deprivation, and a domineering wife or mother. Although the psycho rapist, whatever his family background, certainly does exist, just as the psycho murderer certainly does exist, he is the exception and not the rule. The typical American perpetrator of forcible rape is little more than an aggressive, hostile youth who chooses to do violence to women.

We may thank the legacy of Freudian psychology for fostering a totally inaccurate popular conception of rape. Freud himself, remarkable as this may seem, said nothing about rapists. His confederates were slightly more loquacious, but not by much. [Carl] Jung mentioned rape only in a few of his mythological interpretations. Alfred Adler, a man who understood the power thrust of the male and who was a firm believer in equal rights for women, never mentioned rape in any of his writings. [Helene] Deutsch and [Karen] Horney, two brilliant women, looked at rape only from the psychology of the victim.

In the nineteen fifties a school of criminology arose that was decidedly pro-Freudian in its orientation and it quickly dominated a neglected field. But even among the Freudian criminologists there was a curious reluctance to tackle rape head on. The finest library of Freudian and Freudian-related literature, the A. A. Brill Collection, housed at the New York Psychoanalytic Institute, contains an impressive number of weighty tomes devoted to the study of exhibitionism (public exposure of the penis) yet no Freudian or psychoanalytic authority has ever written a major volume on rape. Articles on rape in psychology journals have been sparse to the point of nonexistence.

Why the Freudians could never come to terms with rape is a puzzling question. It would not be too glib to suggest that the male bias of the discipline, with its insistence on the primacy of the penis, rendered it incapable of seeing the forest for the trees. And then, the use of an intuitive approach based largely on analysis of idiosyncratic case studies allowed for no objective sampling. But perhaps most critically, the serious failure of the Freudians stemmed from their rigid unwillingness to make a moral judgment. The major psychoanalytic thrust was always to "understand" what they preferred to call "deviant sexual behavior," but never to condemn.

"Philosophically," wrote Dr. Manfred Guttmacher in 1951, "a sex offense is an act which offends the sex mores of the society in which the individual lives. And it offends chiefly because it generates anxiety among the members of that society. Moreover, prohibited acts generate the greatest anxiety in those individuals who themselves have strong unconscious desires to commit similar or related acts and who have suppressed or repressed them. These actions of others threaten our ego defenses."

This classic paragraph, I believe, explains most clearly the Freudian dilemma.

When the Freudian-oriented criminologists did attempt to grapple with rape they lumped the crime together with exhibitionism (their hands-down favorite!), homosexuality, prostitution, pyromania, and even oral intercourse, in huge, undigestible volumes that sometimes bore a warning notice on the flyleaf that the material contained herein might advisably be restricted to adults. Guttmacher's *Sex Offenses* and Benjamin Karpman's *The Sexual Offender and His Offenses* were two such products of the fifties. Reading through these and other volumes it is possible to stumble on a nugget of fact or a valuable insight, and we ought to keep in mind, I guess, how brave they must have seemed at the time. After all, they were dealing not only with s-e-x, but with aberrant s-e-x, and in their misguided way they were attemping to forge a new understanding. "Moral opprobrium has no place in medical work," wrote Karpman. A fine sentiment, indeed, yet one hundred pages earlier this same Karpman in this same book defined perversity as "a sexual act that defies the biological goal of procreation."

By and large the Freudian criminologists, who loved to quibble with one another, defined the rapist as a victim of an "uncontrollable urge" that was "infantile" in nature, the result of a thwarted "natural" impulse to have intercourse with his mother. His act of rape was "a neurotic overreaction" that stemmed from his "feelings of inadequacy." To sum up in the Freudian's favorite phrase, he was "a sexual psychopath." Rapists, wrote Karpman, were "victims of a disease from which many of them suffer more than their victims."

This, I should amend, was a picture of the Freudians' favorite rapist, the one they felt they might be able to treat. Dr. Guttmacher, for one, was aware that other types of rapists existed but they frankly bored him. Some, he said, were "sadistic," imbued with an exaggerated concept of masculine sexual activity, and some seemed "like the soldier of a conquering army." "Apparently," he wrote, "sexually well-adjusted youths have in one night committed a series of burglaries and, in the course of one of them, committed rape—apparently just as another act of plunder."

Guttmacher was chief medical officer for the Baltimore criminal courts. His chilling passing observation that rapists might be sexually well-adjusted youths was a reflection of his Freudian belief in the supreme rightness of male dominance and aggression, a common theme that runs through Freudian-oriented criminological literature. But quickly putting the "sexually well-adjusted youths" aside, Guttmacher dove into clinical studies of two rapists put at his disposal who were more to his liking. Both were nail-biters and both had "nagging mothers." One had an undescended testicle. In his dreary record of how frequently they masturbated and wet their beds, he never bothered to write down what they thought of women.

Perhaps the quintessential Freudian approach to rape was a 1954 Rorschach study conducted on the *wives* of eight, count 'em, eight, convicted rapists, which brought forth this sweeping indictment from one of the authors, the eminent psychoanalyst and criminologist Dr. David Abrahamsen:

> The conclusions reached were that the wives of the sex offenders on the surface behaved toward men in a submissive and masochistic way but latently denied their femininity and showed an aggressive masculine orientation; they unconsciously invited sexual aggression, only to respond to it with coolness and rejection. They stimulated their husbands into attempts to prove

themselves, attempts which necessarily ended in frustration and increased their husbands' own doubts about their masculinity. In doing so, the wives unknowingly continued the type of relationship the offender had had with his mother. There can be no doubt that the sexual frustration which the wives caused is one of the factors motivating rape, which might be tentatively described as a displaced attempt to force a seductive but rejecting mother into submission.

In the nineteen sixties, leadership in the field of criminology passed to the sociologists, and a good thing it was. Concerned with measuring the behavior of groups and their social values, instead of relying on extrapolation from individual case studies, the sociologists gave us charts, table, diagrams, theories of social relevance, and, above all, hard, cold statistical facts about crime. (Let us give credit where credit is due. The rise of computer technology greatly facilitated this kind of research.)

In 1971 Menachem Amir, an Israeli sociologist and a student of Marvin E. Wolfgang, America's leading criminologist, published a study of rape in the city of Philadelphia, begun ten years before. *Patterns in Forcible Rape,* a difficult book for those who choke on methodological jargon, was annoyingly obtuse about the culturally conditioned behavior of women in situations involving the threat of force, but despite its shortcomings the Philadelphia study was an eye-opener. It was the first pragmatic, in-depth statistical study of the nature of rape and rapists. Going far beyond the limited vision of the police and the [FBI's] *Uniform Crime Reports,* or the idiosyncratic concerns of the Freudians, Amir fed his computer such variables as *modus operandi,* gang rape versus individual rape, economic class, prior relationships between victim and offender, and both racial and interracial factors. For the first time in history the sharpedged profile of the typical rapist was allowed to emerge. It turned out that he was, for the most part, an unextraordinary, violence-prone fellow.

Marvin Wolfgang, Amir's mentor at the University of Pennsylvania's school of criminology, deserves credit for the theory of "the subculture of violence," which he developed at length in his own work. An understanding of the subculture of violence is critical to an understanding of the forcible rapist. "Social class," wrote Wolfgang, "looms large in all studies of violent crime." Wolfgang's theory, and I must oversimplify, is that within the dominant value system of our culture there exists a subculture formed of those from the lower classes, the poor, the disenfranchised, the black, whose values often run counter to those of the dominant culture, the people in charge. The dominant culture can operate within the laws of civility because it has little need to resort to violence to get what it wants. The subculture, thwarted, inarticulate and angry, is quick to resort to violence; indeed, violence and physical aggression become a common way of life. Particularly for young males.

Wolfgang's theory of crime, and unlike other theories his is soundly based on statistical analysis, may not appear to contain all the answers, particularly the kind of answers desired by liberals who want to excuse crimes of violence strictly on the basis of social inequities in the system, but Wolfgang would be the first to say that social injustice is one of the root causes of the subculture of violence. His theory also would not satisfy radical thinkers who prefer to interpret all violence as the product of the governmental hierarchy and its superstructure of repression.

But there is no getting around the fact that most of those who engage in antisocial, criminal violence (murder, assault, rape and robbery) come from the lower socioeconomic classes; and that because of their historic oppression the majority of black people are contained within the lower socioeconomic classes and contribute to crimes of violence in numbers disproportionate to their population ratio in the census figures *but not disproportionate* to their position on the economic ladder.

We are not talking about Jean Valjean, who stole a loaf of bread in *Les Misérables,* but about physical aggression as "a demonstration of masculinity and toughness"—this phrase is Wolfgang's—the prime tenet of the subculture of violence. Or, to use a current phrase, the *machismo* factor. Allegiance or conformity to *machismo,* particularly in a group or gang, is the *sine qua non* of status, reputation and identity for lower-class male youth. Sexual aggression, of course, is a major part of *machismo.*

The single most important contribution of Amir's Philadelphia study was to place the rapist squarely within the subculture of violence. The rapist, it was revealed, had no separate identifiable pathology aside from the individual quirks and personality disturbances that might characterize any single offender who commits any sort of crime.

The patterns of rape that Amir was able to trace were drawn from the central files of the Philadelphia police department for 1958 and 1960, a total of 646 cases and 1,292 offenders.[3] One important fact that Amir's study revealed right off the bat was that in 43 percent of the Philadelphia cases, the rapists operated in pairs or groups, giving the lie to one of the more commonly held myths that the rapist is a secretive, solitary offender.

The median age of the Philadelphia rapist was twenty-three, but the age group most likely to commit rape was the fifteen-to-nineteen bracket. A preponderant number of the Philadelphia rapists were not married, a status attributable to their youthful age. Ninety percent of the Philadelphia rapists "belonged to the lower part of the occupational scale," in descending order "from skilled workers to the unemployed." Half of the Philadelphia rapists had a prior arrest record, and most of these had the usual run of offenses, such as burglary, robbery, disorderly conduct and assault. Only 9 percent of those with prior records had been previously arrested for rape. In other words, rapists were in the mold of the typical youthful offender. . . .

"Contrary to past impression," Amir wrote, "analysis revealed that 71 percent of the rapes were planned." This observation was another of Amir's most significant contributions to the study of rape. Far from being a spontaneous explosion by an individual with pent-up emotions and uncontrollable lusts, he discovered the act was usually planned in advance and elabo-

---

[3]Amir's data was based on statistical information about all reported rapes that the police felt were "founded." Amir did not include cases of attempted rape, but he did include profiles of "known" offenders who were never apprehended. The sociologist used "known" to mean "undeniably existing," not necessarily "known to the police." Of the 1,292 offenders that form the basis of Amir's study, only 845 men were actually arrested.

rately arranged by a single rapist or a group of buddies. In some cases the lone rapist or the gang had a particular victim in mind and coolly took the necessary steps to lure her into an advantageous position. In other cases the *decision* to rape was made in advance by a gang, a pair of cohorts, or a lone-wolf rapist, but *selection* of the female was left to chance. Whoever happened by and could be seized, coerced or enticed to a favorable place became the victim. As might be expected, almost all group rapes in Philadelphia police files were found to have been planned. As a matter of fact, advance planning and coordination proved absolutely essential to the commission of gang rape. A "secure" place had to be located; precautions had to be taken to guarantee that the rape-in-progress would remain undetected by passers-by, police or neighbors; and selection of the victim had to be agreed upon by the group. . . .

Group rape may be defined as two or more men assaulting one woman. As I have mentioned, Amir found that in 43 percent of his Philadelphia cases the female victim had two or more assailants. A Toronto survey came up with a figure of 50 percent. A Washington, D.C., study reported 30 percent. In Toronto and Philadelphia, rapists who operated in groups accounted for 71 percent of the total number of offenders.

"Whatever may be the causal explanation, these results are amazing," wrote Amir, a man not give to hyperbole. The sociologist expressed this astonishment because psychiatric literature on rape had treated the phenomenon of group rape "with silence." Police departments, as a rule, do not tally group-rape statistics for public consumption and the FBI's *Uniform Crime Reports* do not analyze such information.

When men rape in pairs or in gangs, the sheer physical advantage of their position is clear-cut and unquestionable. No simple conquest of man over woman, group rape is the conquest of men over Woman. It is within the phenomenon of group rape, stripped of the possibility of equal combat, that the male ideology of rape is most strikingly evident. Numerical odds are proof of brutal intention. They are proof, too, of male bonding, to borrow a phrase made popular by Lionel Tiger, and proof of a desire to humiliate the victim *beyond* the act of rape through the process of anonymous mass assault. . . .

Amir deals with what he politely calls "sexual humiliation" in his Philadelphia study. Ignoring such acts as urination, ejaculation into the victim's face and hair, and other defilements—perhaps they did not appear in the Philadelphia police reports—he does deal with the incidence of forced cunnilingus, fellatio and "pederasty" or "sodomy." By these last two imprecise terms I think he was referring to anal penetration. He concludes that "these are not the acts of an 'impotent,' which the psychiatric school so emphatically suggests."

Including repeated intercourse in his definition of "sexual humiliation" Amir found that in more than one-quarter of his cases the victim was subjected to some form of extra insult beyond the simple rape. Sexual humiliation ran higher in group rapes than in individual rapes, and the most common form of extra insult in group rape was repeated intercourse. Amir remarked, "Taking repeated turns is part of what group rape can 'offer' to the participants."

As the act of intercourse itself is deliberately perverted in rape by forcing it on an unwilling participant, so, too, the purpose of any sidebar activity is to further humiliate and degrade, and not to engage in sophisticated erotics. (The purpose is never to satisfy the victim.) At best, fringe defilements can be in the nature of clinical experiments performed by initiates who are convinced that all sex is dirty and demeaning. Not surprisingly in Amir's study, when it came to oral sex, few rapists showed interest in cunnilingus. What they demanded was fellatio done on them. What these rapists were looking for was another avenue or orifice by which to invade and thus humiliate their victim's physical integrity, her private inner space. . . .

As . . . defined by the statistical profiles of the sociologists and the FBI, America's police-blotter rapists are dreary and banal. To those who know them, no magic, no mystery, no Robin Hood bravura, infuses their style. Rape is a dull, blunt, ugly act committed by punk kids, their cousins and older brothers, not by charming, witty, unscrupulous, heroic, sensual rakes, or by timid souls deprived of a "normal" sexual outlet, or by *supermenschen* possessed of uncontrollable lust. And yet, on the shoulders of these unthinking, predictable, insensitive, violence-prone young men there rests an age-old burden that amounts to a historic mission: the perpetuation of male domination over women by force.

The Greek warrior Achilles used a swarm of men descended from ants, the Myrmidons, to do his bidding as hired henchmen in battle. Loyal and unquestioning, the Myrmidons served their master well, functioning in anonymity as effective agents of terror. Police-blotter rapists in a very real sense perform a myrmidon function for all men in our society. Cloaked in myths that obscure their identity, they, too, function as anonymous agents of terror. Although they are the ones who do the dirty work, the actual *attentat*, to other men, their superiors in class and station, the lasting benefits of their simple-minded evil have always accrued.

A world without rapists would be a world in which women moved freely without fear of men. That *some* men rape provides a sufficient threat to keep all women in a constant state of intimidation, forever conscious of the knowledge that the biological tool must be held in awe, for it may turn to weapon with sudden swiftness born of harmful intent. Myrmidons to the cause of male dominance, police-blotter rapists have performed their duty well, so well in fact that the true meaning of their act has largely gone unnoticed. Rather than society's aberrants or "spoilers of purity," men who commit rape have served in effect as front-line masculine shock troops, terrorist guerrillas in the longest sustained battle the world has ever known.

DOROTHY DINNERSTEIN

The Mermaid and the Minotaur: Sexual Arrangements and Human Malaise

Psychologist Dorothy Dinnerstein (1923–1992) worked for a decade on *The Mermaid and the Minotaur: Sexual Arrangements and Human Malaise,* her only book. In developing her ideas, she fused feminist insights, especially those of de Beauvoir, with Freudian theory about the psyche of the human infant. When it was published in 1976, the book was hailed by one reviewer as passionate and intelligent, a volume that "belongs in every permanent library of feminist thought."[1] Another critic, although finding the work "dense, urgent, repetitively argued," added that it would "repay slow, careful reading with a sense of the poetry and paradox of life."[2]

What stirred the imagination of readers was that Dinnerstein offered an all-encompassing explanation for the troubled state of current gender arrangements and, beyond that, for what she called "human malaise." She argued that the underlying cause of much that ails us is our nearly universal practice of assigning care of infants and young children to the female of the species; that if fathers were equal partners with mothers in the responsibilities of parenting, both sexes would be infinitely more human. For when the primal relationship of babies and young children is exclusively with a female parent, certain injurious psychological consequences follow inevitably.

The profound effects of female dominion in the nursery, as described by Dinnerstein, include the sexual double standard, scapegoating of women, woman-hating, lack of joy among

---

[1] Vivian Gornick, *New York Times Book Review,* November 14, 1976, pp. 5, 70.

[2] Quoted from *Kirkus Reviews.*

women, male monopoly of worldly power, violent behaviors, and the existence of political despotism. Moreover, the mother-child bond—with its intense, conflictful feelings of love and hate, dependence and autonomy, shame and pride—produces adults who are trapped in symbiotic relationship with the opposite sex. Thus, women "deep down" acquiesce in the present inequitable gender arrangements.

Negative assessments of the book have centered on its attribution of a wide variety of problems to a single cause. Sociologist Barbara Katz Rothman, for example, wrote, "I do not believe that mothers rearing children is the source of male dominance any more than I think that black women rearing white children is the source of racism."[3] And Adrienne Rich criticized the book as "ahistorical" and noted its "obsession with psychology to the neglect of economic and other material realities."[4]

Dinnerstein's book was not a practical, how-to tract. She said little about how men were to be persuaded to enter the nursery, or about the economic adjustments that such an alteration, if carried out on a large scale, would require. But she emphasized that the task was an imperative one if human life was to prosper—or perhaps, in an age of nuclear weapons, even to survive. And she acknowledged that change in this intimate sphere of our lives would be difficult and painful, and would require courage.

The following excerpt from *The Mermaid and the Minotaur* is from Chapter 8, "The Ruling of the World."[5]

---

[3]Barbara Katz Rothman, *Reinventing Motherhood: Ideology and Technology in a Patriarchal Society* (New York: Norton, 1989), p. 213.

[4]Adrienne Rich, "Compulsory Heterosexuality and Lesbian Existence," in *Blood, Bread, and Poetry: Selected Prose, 1979–1985* (New York: Norton, 1986), p. 31.

[5]Dinnerstein thanked Joan Herrmann for collaborating on this chapter.

MOST MEN—EVEN MOST MEN WHO BELIEVE in principle that this "right" is unfounded—cling hard to their right to rule the world. And most women—including many who are ashamed of the feeling—feel deep down a certain willingness to let them go on ruling it. People balk, brazenly or sheepishly, candidly or with fancy rationalizations, at any concrete step that is taken to break the male monopoly of formal, overt power. They have immediate practical reasons for balking. (Both the rulers and the ruled enjoy familiar privileges, and feel committed to familiar responsibilities, on which their sense of worth, safety, and competence rests; they shrink from novelty that could endanger, overtax, and humiliate them.) But they have older, longer-standing reasons as well.

Men's balking, I think, could hardly matter now if women were not balking too. Without substantial female compliance, male rule would at this point be a pushover. And what makes woman comply—indeed, what has doubtless always made her comply, apart from habit and tradition—is something more than the obvious physical fact of her procreative burden, which, together with man's greater muscular strength, has usually, until now, made her look to him for protection and put him in a position to demand her obedience. As modern technology undermines his sheer biologically given power to bully her, the importance of this something more becomes clearer and clearer.

The crucial psychological fact is that all of us, female as well as male, fear the will of woman. Man's dominion over what we think of as the world rests on a terror that we all feel: the terror of sinking back wholly into the helplessness of infancy. As the folk saying insists, there is another realm that interpenetrates all too intimately with what is formally recognized as the world: a realm already ruled, despotically enough, by the hand that rocks the cradle.

Female will is embedded in female power, which is under present conditions the earliest and profoundest prototype of absolute power. It emanates, at the outset, from a boundless, all-embracing presence. We live by its grace while our lives are most fragile. We grow human within its aura. Its reign is total, all-pervasive, throughout our most vulnerable, our most fatefully impressionable, years. *Power of this kind, concentrated in one sex and exerted at the outset over both, is far too potent and dangerous a force to be allowed free sway in adult life. To contain it, to keep it under control and harness it to chosen purposes, is a vital need, a vital task, for every mother-raised human.*

The weight of this emotional fact is so familiar to us, we carry it so universally and its pressure is so numbing, that to be vividly aware of how it crushes us—or to imagine not being crushed by it—is almost impossible. We can refer to it with the elliptical offhand intensity of that folk saying, or describe it with the sustained poetic lucidity of de Beauvoir, and still never focus on how the possibility of living free of it can be concretely realized.

Pre-Christian goddesses, de Beauvoir says, "were cruel, capricious, lustful; in giving birth to men they made men their slaves. Under Christianity, life and death depend only on God, and man, once out of the maternal body, has escaped that body forever. For the destiny of his soul is played out in regions where the mother's powers are abolished. . . ." But having said this (and she says it in many ways), de Beauvoir rests her case. Her implication is that in the very act of recognizing its truth, we will have started to surmount it, and of course she is right. What I am adding is that, having started, we must carry through what we have begun; and that to do so we must look hard at what is very hard to look at: the precise feature of childhood whose existence makes the adult situation de Beauvoir describes inevitable, and the consequent necessity for female abdication of unilateral rule over childhood, which she stopped short of facing. . . .

The Nature of Maternal Authority

Maternal will emanates, first of all, *from a subjectivity that we encounter before our own sense of subjectivity is at all clearly established. It is the first separate subjectivity of which we be-*

come aware, and its separateness . . . is a fact to which most of us are never fully reconciled. To recognize the actuality of any subjectivity outside our own—which means recognizing the actuality of our own as well—is a momentous intellectual step. It would be a huge, difficult step in any case: the discovery that any fellow creature exists revolutionizes the nature of existence. And the difficulty is immensely complicated by the difference between the mother's adult sentience and our own infant one, and by our grief at the separation, at the cutting off of our initial sense of fusion with her, that this step involves. We necessarily take this step so far as we must. But few of us carry it to its logical conclusion, which is a matter of coming to see in retrospect that the first parent was after all no more and no less than a fellow creature. To come to see this is not a task wholly beyond human strength, even under present conditions. But it is a task that is rarely taken on, since it is arduous and our male-female arrangements make it easy to shirk.

Female sentience, for this reason, carries permanently for most of us the atmosphere of that unbounded, shadowy presence toward which all our needs were originally directed. And the intentionality that resides in female sentience comes in this way to carry an atmosphere of the rampant and limitless, the alien and unknowable. It is an intentionality that needs to be conquered and tamed, corralled and subjugated, if we (men most urgently, but women too) are to feel at all safe in its neighborhood.

It needs to be corralled, controlled, not only because its boundaries are unclear but also because its wrath is all-potent and the riches it can offer or refuse us bottomless. *What makes female intentionality so formidable—so terrifying and at the same time so alluring—is the mother's life-and-death control over helpless infancy:* an intimately carnal control exerted at a time when mind and body—upon whose at least partial separability it later becomes a matter of human dignity to insist—are still subjectively inseparable. This *power* that the mother exerts is felt before the existence of her *will* can be perceived. When the child, in the process of coming to know itself as a center of will, starts to be aware of hers, it faces the will of a being at whose touch its flesh has shuddered with joy, a being the sound of whose footsteps has flooded its senses with a relief more total than it can ever know again. For a long time to come, her kiss will still make bumps and bruises better; her voice will still dispel terror. Yet she is a being who on other occasions has mysteriously withheld food, who has mysteriously allowed loneliness, terror, and pain to continue. She is still—and will be for years to come—a being whose moods of inattention or indifference cast an ominous shadow over existence, a being whose displeasure is exile from warmth and light.

But *what makes female intentionality formidable* is something more than the mother's power to give and withhold while we are passive. It *is also the mother's power to foster or forbid, to humble or respect, our first steps toward autonomous activity.* . . .

Woman is the will's first, overwhelming adversary. She teaches us that our intentions can be thwarted . . . by the opposed intentions of other living creatures. In our first real contests of will, we find ourselves, more often than not, defeated:[6] The defeat is always intimately carnal; and the victor is always female. Through woman's jurisdiction over child's passionate body, through her control over what goes into it and what comes out of it, through her right to restrict its movements and invade its orifices, to withhold pleasure or inflict pain until it obeys her wishes, each human being first discovers the peculiarly angry, bittersweet experience of conscious surrender to conscious, determined outside rule. It is against this background that child's occasional victories over woman are experienced, and its future attitude toward contact with her formed.

Mothers vary enormously, to be sure, in their use of force; some use it in only the gentlest and subtlest way, and some deny that they use it at all. But inescapably, they do use it: the adult must act to ensure the infant's survival, and to protect its growth, without applying beforehand for the infant's consent.

[6]This not to say that infants have no power, or negligible power, over their mothers: they are as a rule highly persuasive little creatures. It is only to say that since they want everything, most of what they want they do not get; and this fact they perceive—often wrongly, but often rightly too—as willed by the mother.

At the same time, it is not only through force that female will is imposed. Even without setting herself to secure the child's surrender, the mother, because she loves the child, prevails through the happiness that she is able to bestow. In gratitude for this happiness, and out of the wish to cause, to call up, expressions of this vital love—to exert some control over its flow—the child voluntarily undertakes to do what will please her. It takes the initiative, anticipating her wishes and making them its own. In this way it changes submission into mastery, is ruled at its own behest, ruled by a powerful and loved creature whose power and love it thereby incorporates within itself.

But the victor we go out halfway to embrace is still a victor. Some core of voluntariness in the self is still violated. Voluntary surrender is still surrender. Inside the toddler who hugs the woman's knees—living cheerfully within the framework of each day as she defines it, eating what she sets out and handling the objects she leaves within reach, moving inside the safety barriers she provides, learning to keep in and let out at times and places of her designation the excrement that is so continuous with its innards and so symbolic of all control and possession, releasing its hold on life to sink into sleep at her soothing command—inside this toddler, some center of will is suspended, tensed for a necessary confrontation. (As de Beauvoir puts it, the being whom you are responsible, as a mother, to nurture is at the same time "an independent stranger who is defined and confirmed only in revolting against you.") The child feels confidence within the predictable, customary shape of the life over which she presides; it feels power in joining forces with her power; it feels pride in acquiring the self-command (control over its muscles and its sphincters, ability to contain its own angry or grabby or otherwise importunate impulses) that will win her approval. But all of these feelings of strength are inseparable from the sense of obeying, or collaborating with, her female will. It may be a gentle or a harsh will, a sympathetic or an overbearing or a woundingly indifferent will, but it is in any case a uniquely potent will. And the vital strengths that are developed under its auspices must be tested out against it; otherwise they remain the mother's strengths, not the child's.

The child's will, then, is poised, for dear life's sake, to confront and resist the will of woman. But to live up to this challenge is to contend with appalling complications. For woman is not merely the first, permanently nebulous, outside "I" and the first, all-giving, provider, not merely the first, all-mighty, adversary and protector, lover and ruler. *She is also the first "you,"* and this "you"ness of hers contributes in a number of ways to the lifelong emotional impact of female intentionality.

It means, first of all, that her weight as an adversary rests not just on her strength in contrast with the child's puniness but also on the child's realization that she is consciously aware—and aware of the child's awareness—of this contrast. *In confronting her the child faces an old, devastatingly knowledgeable witness. . . .* Woman, de Beauvoir says, "knows everything about man that attacks his pride and humiliates his self-will."

But woman is also the audience who has acclaimed our first triumphs. . . . What we feel, along with vulnerability in the face of woman's old awareness of our weakness, is a deep sense of need, rooted in her old support of our nascent strength. *It is woman's will that nurtures*—celebrates, stimulates, shelters—*the growth of the child's own will.*

The child . . . in purposefully opposing the mother, takes a double risk. On the one hand she can retaliate by crushing her opponent's pride as only she is in a position to do: she can point up, dwell upon, the child's early failures instead of minimizing and smoothing them over; she can make the child knuckle under again as it has done before instead of acknowledging its growing strength, and its right to win sometimes, by compromising with its wishes. But on the other hand she can give way too far: she can leave the child in possession of an empty field; she can abandon it to a hollow victory, bereft of its mighty sponsor. Faced with this double risk, a naturally keen childhood fantasy-wish (lived out widely by adult men with the women whom they rule) is to keep female will in live captivity, obediently energetic, fiercely protective of its captor's pride, ready always to vitalize his projects with its magic maternal blessing and to support them with its concrete, self-abnegating maternal help. . . .

Woman is the first teacher. She is our first guide into the realm of socially pooled experience that constitutes the human world. As the small child becomes more mobile, active in a wider sphere, it becomes more aware of depending on the mother for second-hand information, experienced advice, to guide its activities and protect them from unpleasant outcomes. ("Watch out, you'll spill it!" "Careful, you'll fall!" "That will give you a bellyache." "If you don't go to the bathroom now, you'll wet yourself in the car.") . . .

The first "you," then, in addition to its other vital functions, is the original wellspring of pooled, stored, communicable experience upon which each child draws for its fundamental orientation to communally tested and communally created human reality, for its fundamental leap into civilization. The child must balance against each other two considerations vital to its success in making this leap. On the one hand, to ensure steady access to the content of the social environment that its body and its nervous system are built to inhabit, it needs harmony with the first "you." On the other hand, to assume active membership in the human species—to play a living part in this social realm that . . . is constructed out of the give-and-take between differing points of view—it must assert itself against, challenge the supremacy of, this archetypal female "you."

In this challenge there is an inevitable strain of vindictiveness: to insist on the validity of our own perspective, of our own feelings, we must vent the rage that we feel in the face of early parental power. And under present conditions, the vindictiveness does not have to be—and therefore typically never is—outgrown. If we are men, we are invited by the world's ways to express it directly, in arrogance toward everything female. If we are women, we are encouraged to express it both directly and indirectly: directly in distrust and disrespect toward other women; and indirectly by offering ourselves up to male vindictiveness, the satisfaction of which we can then vicariously share. In either case, we go on all our lives asserting ourselves against the first parent—with a vengeance.

The vengeance throws us, male and female alike, upon the mercies of male tyranny. . . . Patriarchal despotism is a booby trap into which humans must keep jumping until female monopoly of early child care—the arrangement that keeps us all childish—is abolished. . . .

The Nature of Paternal Authority

To mother-raised humans, male authority is bound to look like a reasonable refuge from female authority. We come eventually, of course, to resent male authority too: regardless of its gender, or of our gender, authority generates resentment. But the primitive swing between need and rage described just above is oriented originally, and stays oriented mainly, toward the will behind the hand that rocks the cradle. On the whole, our attitudes toward the second parent—the parent who ordinarily orbits, at the beginning, outside the enchanted mother-infant pair, and who then enters it so gradually that it remains for a long time a very lopsided triangle indeed—are far less infantile, far less inchoate, than our attitudes toward the first.

We do, needless to say, both love and fear a father's strength, both need and resent his feeling of responsibility for us. But his strength and his feeling of responsibility do not ordinarily become tangible to us until after the world has started to lose its initial magic. His presence is apt to be relatively peripheral until after we have started to organize the realm of inner feeling into reasonably discrete regions or units, and to recognize that a creature can have multiple aspects, shifting moods, and still be a permanent, unitary individual. For this reason he is perceived from the beginning (unless, of course, he is an abnormally rejecting or frightening person) as a more *human* being than the mother, more like an adult version of oneself, less engulfing, less nebulously overwhelming.

Even if a father inflicts corporal punishment, it is punishment endured by a body that we perceive as clearly separate from his. We experience opposition between his will and ours, even if he is autocratic and even though he easily wins, through an awareness that we have come to recognize as uniquely our own; and he experiences this opposition through an awareness on which we do not centrally depend to keep us oriented to the environment. What he mainly inspires is not so much ambivalence as a mixture of sentiments. The mixture can be disturbing, but the disturbance cannot come as close to the heart of our sense of existence itself as the ambivalence of the earlier, more vital, maternal tie.

A father can be quite tyrannical, then, and still be felt as in some sense a refreshing presence. His power is more distinct and clearly defined than the mother's, his wisdom less eerily clairvoyant. Because he is a creature more separate from ourselves, our resentment of him is less deeply tinged with anxiety and guilt. And our love for him, like our anger at him, lies outside the shadowy maternal realm from which all children, to grow up, must escape.

The father, as de Beauvoir has pointed out, is respected for an achievement to which every child, with some part of itself, aspires: he moves in a world that lies safely outside the maternal aura. His spirit eludes, and even partly controls, that wilderness of forces which is both nature and feminine. Even if his work in the world is menial, he has the status of a participant in history, because he is above female authority: he has identity outside the immediate family circle.

So the essential fact about paternal authority, the fact that makes both sexes accept it as a model for the ruling of the world, is that it is under prevailing conditions a sanctuary from maternal authority. It is a sanctuary passionately cherished by the essential part of a person's self that wants to come up (like Andersen's mermaid) out of the drowning sweetness of early childhood into the bright dry light of open day, the light of the adult realm in which human reason and human will—not the boundless and mysterious intentionality, the terrible uncanny omniscience, of the nursery goddess—can be expected, at least ideally, to prevail.

Adult Male Dominion

In sum, then, male rule of the world is not a conspiracy imposed by bad, physically strong and mobile, men on good, physically weak and burdened, women. Male rule has grown out of biotechnological conditions which we are just now, as a species, surmounting, and out of the psychological impulses that inevitably develop under those conditions. In an outer, objective sense, given the practical pressures that have until now enforced female care of the young, predominantly male responsibility for extra-domestic endeavors has been a matter of sheer economic necessity. And in an inner, subjective sense, given the feelings of adults who have been young under female care, male dominion (the position of men as the main representatives of societal will; the main managers—as Margaret Mead points out—of whatever the community sees as its central concerns; the main wielders of overt power in their private relations with women) has been an inexorable emotional necessity.

Male dominion violates some basic human inclinations; it has been a chronic strain on both sexes, a chronic drain on our species' energies: but on balance—even if the balance does fail for most people some of the time and for some people most of the time—it has met for both sexes some urgently felt needs. These needs are pathological, but the pathology is built into the prevailing division of labor between men and women; and the structure of this division has been mandatory, given our physical past . . . , just as its dissolution is now mandatory if we are to have a physical future. Male dominion after early childhood is on balance psychologically essential so long—but only so long—as female dominion during early childhood is bio-technologically essential. The problem we now face is a problem of transition.

At present, our concrete situation is that the right to be straightforwardly bossy—the right to exercise will head-on, in collision with or frank guidance of the will of another adult— cannot reside as comfortably in a woman as in a man. This is as true on the level of world politics as it is across the breakfast table.

MICHELE WALLACE

Black Macho and the Myth
of the Superwoman

Michele Wallace (b. 1952) wrote the brash, opinionated, brave polemic about sexual politics in the African-American community that one would expect from an author still in her twenties, with the audacity to take on this complex, challenging subject. *Black Macho and the Myth of the Superwoman,* published in 1978, is a book that can best be understood as a cry from the heart rather than as a reasoned argument. Wallace expressed her anger at black men with a frankness that shocked many readers. Charging that "misogyny was an integral part of Black Macho," she lashed out at the male chauvinism of the sixties Black Power movement. The prevalent belief that the black woman was a "superwoman" who had no need for feminism was, in her view, a myth. And she spoke of "a growing distrust, even hatred, between black men and black women." Recalling the upsurge of interracial dating she had observed as a teenager in Harlem during the sixties—black men with white women—she described black women's feelings of puzzlement and betrayal.

Even black feminist readers disagreed as to the book's significance: Poet June Jordan was highly critical, but novelist Toni Cade Bambara described it as "serious, well written . . . effective in its demystification."[1] In a thoughtful appraisal in *The Nation,* writer Julius Lester said, "Occasionally a book appears that can be criticized in several ways, and yet the work is so important that criticism slides off it like rain down a window.

---

[1]June Jordan, in *New York Times Book Review,* March 18, 1979, p. 15; Toni Cade Bambara, in *Washington Post Book World,* February 18, 1979, p. 1.

Black Macho and the Myth of the Superwoman is like that, a powerful though flawed work."[2]

Since 1978 Wallace has been studying; teaching English, creative writing, African-American literature, and black studies; and writing—her *Invisibility Blues* appeared in 1990 and *Black Popular Culture* in 1992. An essay in which she talked about her first book—"How I Saw It Then, How I See It Now"—was published in 1990.[3]

The following selection is excerpted from an adaptation of *Black Macho and the Myth of the Superwoman* that the author prepared for *Ms.* magazine.

SAPPHIRE, MAMMY. TRAGIC MULATTO WENCH. *Workhorse, can swing an ax, lift a load, pick cotton with any man. A wonderful housekeeper. Excellent with children. Very clean. Very religious. A terrific mother. A great little singer and dancer and a devoted teacher and social worker. She's always had more opportunities than the black man because she was no threat to the white man so he made it easy for her. Curiously enough, she frequently ends up on welfare. Not beautiful, rather hard-looking unless she has white blood, but then very beautiful. The black ones are exotic though, great in bed, tigers. And very fertile. If she is middle-class, she tends to be uptight about sex, prudish. She is unsupportive of black men, domineering, castrating. Very strong. Sorrow rolls right of her brow like so much rain. Tough, unfeminine. Opposed to women's rights movements, considers herself already liberated.*

From the intricate web of mythology that surrounds the black woman a fundamental image emerges. It is of a woman of

[2]Julius Lester, "Brothers and Sisters," *Nation*, February 17,1979, p. 181.
[3]The essay is an introduction to a new edition of *Black Macho and the Myth of the Superwoman* (London: Verso, 1990).

inordinate strength, who does not have the same fears, weaknesses, and insecurities as other women, but believes herself to be and is, in fact, stronger emotionally than most men. In other words, she is a superwoman.

Through the years this image has remained basically intact. Right now, I can imagine my reader thinking, *Of course she's stronger. Look what she's been through.* Even for me, it continues to be difficult to let the myth go.

I remember once I was watching a news show with a black male friend of mine who had a Ph.D. in psychology. We were looking at some footage of a black woman who seemed barely able to speak English, though at least six generations of her family before her had certainly claimed it as their first language. She was in bed wrapped in blankets, her numerous small, poorly clothed children huddled around her. Her apartment looked rat-infested, cramped, and dirty. She had not, she said, had heat and hot water for days. My friend, a solid member of the middle class now but surely no stranger to poverty in his childhood, felt obliged to comment—in order to assuage his guilt, I can think of no other reason—"That's a *strong* sister," as he bowed his head in reverence.

By the time I was fifteen, there was nothing I dreaded more than being like the women in my family. Their sharp tongues were able to disassemble any human ego in five minutes flat. Nearly all had been divorced at least once. They all worked. Never as domestics and none had ever been on welfare. "Too proud," they said. . . .

I can't remember when I first learned that my family expected me to work, but it had been drilled into me that the best and only sure support was self-support.

The fact that my family expected me to have a career should have made the things I wanted different from what little white girls wanted, according to the popular sociological view. But I don't believe any sociologist took into account a man like my stepfather. My stepfather gave me "housewife lessons." It was he who taught me how to clean house and how I should act around men. "Don't be like your mother," he told me. "She's a nice lady but she's a bad wife. She was just lucky with me. I want you to get a *good* husband."

Although he never managed to fully domesticate me, it was him I finally listened to because he was saying essentially the same things I read in the magazines, saw in the movies, gaped at on television. Growing up in Harlem, I listened to these messages no less intently than the little white girls who grew up on Park Avenue, in Scarsdale, or on Long Island. In a way I needed to hear them even more than they did. Their alternative was not eternal Aunt Jemimahood, Porgy-'n'-Besshood. Mine was.

Then in 1968, the year I turned sixteen, blackness came to Harlem. Black artists, musicians, writers, poets, many of them fresh from the East Village, began to gather in response to the cries of "black power" and "kill whitey" that had echoed in the streets during the recent riots. And Harlemites, who had always been divided into two distinct categories—the black bourgeoisie and the poor—now began to split into more factions.

The black bourgeoisie became the "knee-grows" and the poor became the "lumpen" or the "grass roots." The two new factions were the "militants" and the "nationalists." The militants had no patience with the singing, dancing, incense, and poetry-reading of the black nationalists; [or] with the black bourgeoisie's appeals for restraint; or the inertia of the poor. The nationalists could not abide the militants' insistence that everyone "hit the streets" or their Marxist rhetoric; the black bourgeoisie's loyalty to European culture; and the frequent cultural obtuseness of the poor about everything but rock, blues, and gospel. The black bourgeoisie was temporarily, but thoroughly, intimidated by everyone. And the poor thought they were *all* crazy. But all parties managed to agree on at least one issue: the black woman's act needed intensive cleaning up. She was one of the main reasons the black man had never been properly able to take hold of his situation in this country.

I was fascinated by all of this. Not by the political implications of a black movement in a white America. I quickly realized that was a male responsibility. But by how it would affect my narrow universe. To me and many other black women the Black Movement seemed to guarantee that our secret dreams of being male-dominated and supported women were that much more attainable. If black men had power, as in black power, then we would become the women of the powerful.

But first we had a hell of a history to live down. We had been rolling around in bed with the slave master while the black man was having his penis cut off; we had never been able to close our legs to a white man nor deny our breast to a white child; we had been too eagerly loyal to our white male employer, taking the job he offered when he would give none to our man, cleaning his house with love and attention while our man was being lynched by white men in white hoods. We had not allowed the black man to be a man in his own house. We had driven him to alcohol, to drugs, to crime, to every bad thing he had ever done to harm himself or his family because our eyes had not reflected his manhood.

I felt shocked by this history. My mother had done her best to keep all of it from me. I did know that the men in my family had seemed to be very sweet, very intelligent, but a bit ineffectual and spineless. And the women had seemed to be relentless achievers, often providers. At sixteen I had no use for para-doxes. The women in my family could not be both strong and weak, both victimizers and victimized. It was much easier just to believe these women were the bloodless monsters the Black Movement said they were, and to reckon with my share in that sin. What must I do, I wondered, to atone for my errors and make myself more palatable? I must be, black men told me, more feminine, more attractive, and above all more submissive, in other words a "natural woman."

Never realizing how imaginary my "strength" really was, I swore never to use it. But that didn't seem to be enough. I was not terribly convincing as a passive woman. The men seemed to go right through my fingers. I was overeager, too impatient, and somehow I could not stop getting angry from time to time. . . .

In 1967, the streets of New York had witnessed the grand coming out of all time of black male/white female couples. Frankly, I found this confusing. I was enough of a slave to white liberal fashions around me to believe that two people who wanted each other had a right to each other, but was that what this was about? It all seemed strangely inappropriate, poorly timed. Black was angry, anywhere from vaguely to militantly antiwhite; black was sexy and had unlimited potential. What did the black man want with a white woman now?

What convinced me that this situation had a broader meaning was the amazing way people were taking it. Educated middle-class white liberals seemed to feel it was their duty to condone relationships between white women and black men because that would mean they weren't racist. Black men often could not separate their interest in white women from their hostility toward black women: "I can't stand that black bitch." Some black men argued that white women gave them money, didn't put them down, made them feel like men. And black women made no attempt to disguise their anger and disgust, to the point of verbal, if not physical, assaults in the streets—on the white woman or the black man or on both. . . .

[By 1968] brothers, with softly beating drums in the background, were talking about beautiful black Queens of the Nile and beautiful full lips and black skin and big asses. Yet the "problem" with the white sisters downtown persisted.

Some of the more militant sisters uptown would tell you that the "problem" was that white women were *throwing* themselves at black men and that if they would just let the man be, he'd come home. And, furthermore, there was this matter of a black matriarchy. Everybody wanted to cut Daniel Moynihan's heart out and feed it to the dogs, but he did have a point after all.[4] The black woman had gotten out of hand. She got all the jobs, all the everything. The black man had never had a chance. No wonder he wanted a white woman. The black woman should keep her big, black mouth shut.

And the black woman started to do just that. The Women's Movement came along, and she went right on trimming her 'fro,

---

[4]Daniel Patrick Moynihan, *The Negro Family: The Case for National Action* (Washington, DC: Office of Policy Planning and Research, U.S. Department of Labor, 1965). Moynihan, then a Harvard sociologist, had blamed female-headed families for pathology in the black community.—*Ed.*

having her babies for the revolution. Admirably thorough about not allowing a word of feminist rhetoric to penetrate their minds, some black women even attacked the Women's Movement out of their feelings of inadequacy, shame, and hatred for white women. Others cleaned house and fried chicken. They just knew that their man, the black man, would not stand for no back talk from no white girl. He was on his way home for sure. But they were wrong.

There was between the black man and the black woman a misunderstanding as old as slavery. The push toward black liberation caused this accumulation of rage to explode upon the heads of black women. The black woman did not, could not, effectively fight back. It was a man's world.

Now that freedom, equality, rights, wealth, power were assumed to be on their way, she had to understand that manhood was essential to revolution. Could you imagine Che Guevara with breasts? Mao with a vagina? She had had her day. Womanhood was not essential to revolution. Or so everyone thought by the beginning of the 1970s.

I am saying, among other things, that for perhaps the last fifty years there has been a growing distrust, even hatred, between black men and black women. It has been nursed along not only by racism on the part of whites, but also by an almost deliberate ignorance on the part of blacks about the sexual politics of their experience in this country. It is from this perspective that the black man and woman faced the challenge of the Black Revolution—a revolution subsequently dissipated and distorted by their inability to see each other clearly through the fog of sexual myths and fallacies. This has cost us a great deal. It has cost us unity, for one thing.

Though I am a black feminist, and that label rightly suggests that I feel black men could stand substantial improvement, I still find it difficult to blame them alone. Black men have had no greater part than black women in perpetuating the ignorance with which they view one another. The black man, however, particularly since the Black Movement, has been in the position to define the black woman. He is the one who tells her whether or not she is a woman and what it is to be a woman. And therefore, whether he wishes or not, he determines her destiny as well as his own.

Though originally it was the white man who was responsible for the black woman's grief, a multiplicity of forces act upon her life now, and the black man is one of the most important. The white man is downtown. The black man lives with her. He's the head of her church and may be the principal of her local school or even the mayor of the city in which she lives.

She is the workhorse that keeps his house functioning, she is the foundation of his community, she raises his children, and she faithfully votes for him in elections, goes to his movies, reads his books, watches him on television, buys in his stores, solicits his services as doctor, lawyer, accountant.

The black man has not really kept his part of the bargain they made in the sixties. When she stood by silently as he became a "man," she assumed that he would finally glorify and dignify black womanhood just as the white man had done for the white woman. But he did not. He refused her. His involvement with white women was only the most dramatic form that refusal took. He refused her because the assertion of his manhood required something quite different of him. He refused her because it was too late to carbon-copy the male/female relationships of the Victorian era. And he refused her because he felt justified in his anger that she had betrayed him. She believed that, even as she denied it. She too was angry, but paralyzed by the feeling that she had no right to be.

Therefore her strange numbness, her determination, spoken or unspoken, to remain basically unquestioning of the black man's authority and thereby supportive of all he has done, even that which has been abusive of her. She is in the grip of Black Macho and it has created within her inestimable emotional devastation.

The black woman's silence is a new silence. She knows that. There has been from slavery until the civil rights movement a thin but continuous line of black women who have prodded their sisters to self-improvement, to education, to an industrious and active position in the affairs of their communities. In their

time a woman's interest in herself was not automatically
interpreted as hostile to men and their progress, at least not by
black people. Day by day these women, like most women, devoted their energies to their husbands and children. When they
found time, they worked on reforms in education, medicine,
housing, and their communities, through their organizations
and churches. Besides their other pursuits they took particular
interest in the problems of their fellow beings, black women.
Little did they know that one day their activities would be used
as proof that the black woman has never known her place and
has mightily battled the black man for his male prerogative as
head of the household.

The American black woman is haunted by the mythology
that surrounds the American black man. It is a mythology based
upon the real persecution of black men: castrated black men
hanging by their necks from trees; black men shining shoes;
black men behind bars, whipped raw by prison guards and police; black men with needles in their arms, with wine bottles in
their hip pockets; jobless black men on street corners; black men
being pushed out in front to catch the enemy's bullets in every
American war since the Revolution of 1776—these ghosts, rendered all the more gruesome by their increasing absence of detail, are crouched in the black woman's brain. Every time she
starts to wonder about her own misery, to think about recon-
structing her life, the ghosts pounce. "*You* crippled the black
man. *You* worked against him. *You* betrayed him. *You* laughed
at him. *You* scorned him. *You* and the white man."

Not only does the black woman continue to see the black
man historically as a cripple; she refuses to take seriously the
various ways he's been able to assert his manhood and capabilities in recent years. Granted that many of his gains of the past
decade have been temporary and illusory, he is, nevertheless, no
longer a pathetic, beaten-down slave (if indeed he ever was only
that). But whether he is cast as America's latest sex object, king
of virility and violence, master of the ghetto art of cool, or a
Mickey Mouse copy of a white capitalist, the black woman
pities him. She sees only the masses of unemployed black men,

junkies, winos, prison inmates. She does not really see the masses of impoverished, unemployed black women, their numerous children pulling at their skirts; or, if she does, she sees these women and children only as a further humiliation and burden to that poor, downtrodden black man.

She sees only the myth. In fact what most people see when they look at the black man is the myth.

American slavery was a dehumanizing experience for everyone involved. Yet somehow the story goes that the black man suffered a special denigration as the constant victim of an unholy alliance between his woman and the enemy, the white man. The facts are a good deal more complicated and ambiguous.

The slave family was constantly subject to disruption by sales of children, of father, and mother. Many black women did have sex with and did bear children for their white masters. Many slave fathers did lack traditional authority over their family. But to accept these features of slavery as the entire picture is to accept that the character of life in the black slave community was solely a product of white oppression.

Despite the obstacles, the slave family was often a stable entity. Most black families were headed by a stable male/female partnership, by a husband and a wife. Slaves were not usually required by their masters to form such permanent unions, but these unions did, nevertheless, exist in great quantities. That fact suggests that blacks, both males and females, took traditional marriage and all it entailed, including male authority, quite seriously.

That so many slave narratives show evidence of attachment for fathers would indicate that the father/child relationship was not taken lightly.

Yes, black men were called boys. Black women were also called girls. But the slaves thought of themselves as "mens and womens." There were cases of black women who were raped as their husbands looked on, powerless. There were also cases of men who fought to the death to prevent such things. Most of the women engaged in interracial unions were probably single; many were unwilling, some were not. There was also some sexual contact between black male slaves and white women. White men did not seem to become obsessed with preventing such relations until much later. In fact, before the American Revolution free blacks in the colonies were usually the products of unions between black male slaves and indentured white women. . . .

Viewing American slavery with any kind of objectivity is extremely difficult, mostly because the record was unevenly and inconsistently kept. Nevertheless, to suggest that the black man was emasculated by slavery is to suggest that the black man and the black woman were creatures without will, as well as that a black woman could not be equally humiliated. Slave men and women formed a coherent and, as much as possible, a beneficial code of behavior and values, based upon the amalgamation of their African past and the forced realities of their American experience—in other words, an African-American culture.

Yet the myth of the black man's castration in slavery has been nurtured over a century. The presumed dominance of the black female during slavery would not be quite enough to explain the full extent of black male anger, especially since it was more untrue than not, and at some point the black man must have known that. Rather his actual gripe must be that the black woman, his woman, was not *his* slave, that his right to expect her complete service and devotion was usurped. She *was*, after all, the white man's slave.

Nevertheless, the record shows that black men and black women emerged from slavery in twos, husbands and wives. It was mostly after slavery that the fear white men had of black men began to take some of its more lascivious forms. It was then that the myth of the black man's sexuality as a threat to pure white womanhood began to gain force.

Sacred white womanhood had been an economically necessary assumption under the slavery system. It had also been necessary to assume that black women were promiscuous and fickle and gave no more thought to their offsping than pigs did to their litter. Therefore whites might sell black children with impunity and do with them what they pleased. But the white woman would be the mother of the little man who would inherit the white man's fortune. One had to be certain of the child's origin. Thus the white woman's purity, like the black female's promiscuity, was based upon her status as property. After the ill-fated Reconstruction period came the rise of the Ku Klux Klan, the thousands of lynchings and the group effort on the part of white men to sever the black man's penis from his body and render him economically unable to provide for his family, despite his legal freedom.

How did the black family respond to this pressure? For the most part it continued the tradition of adaptation that had marked the evolution of the Afro-American family from slavery. There was the pressure of the American white standard but there was also the standard that black Americans had set for themselves. Slave rule provided for trial marriage, for pregnancy followed by marriage, for some degree of sexual experimentation prior to settling down. All of which had precedents in African societies, as well as in most precapitalist agrarian societies. After marriage, however, adultery was considered intolerable. If possible, the man worked and provided for all. If not, the woman also worked. But at no point in American history have more black women been employed than black men.

Only as American blacks began to accept the standards of family life, as well as manhood and womanhood, embraced by American whites, did black men and women begin to resent one another.

Americanization for the black man in particular meant more than coming to view the deviation of his woman from the American ideal as an affront to his manhood. It also meant that the inaccessibility of the white woman represented a severe limitation of that manhood. Furthermore, the experience of the civil rights movement would teach him that nonviolence did not work, nor did restraint, cleverness, wittiness, or patience. America, he thought, respected bravado, violence, and macho.

Around the time that Shirley Chisholm was running for President in 1972, a black comedian and television star made an infamous joke about her. He said that he would prefer Raquel Welch to Shirley Chisholm any day. The joke was widely publicized, particularly in the black community, and thought quite funny. It expressed the comparisons black men were making between black women and white women: responsibility, always tiresome, versus the illusion of liberation and freedom. But this joke had yet another level of meaning as well. We black men, the comedian's joke seemed to say, are more interested in going to bed with Raquel Welch than we are in having a black President.

Shirley Chisholm was the first black woman to run for President of the United States, and be taken seriously. However, almost none of the black political forces in existence at the time—in other words, the black male political forces—supported her. In fact, they actively opposed her nomination. The black man in the street seemed either outraged that she dared to run or simply indifferent. The campaign was composed largely of black and white women.

Ever since then it has really baffled me to hear black men say that black women have no time for feminism because being black comes first. For them, when it came to Shirley Chisholm, being black no longer came first at all. It turned out that what they really meant all along was that the black man came before the black woman.

The reaction of black men to Chisholm's campaign marked the point at which the Black Movement breathed its last as a viable entity. Black male hostility to Chisholm exploded any illusion that blacks might actually be able to sustain a notion of themselves apart from America's racist, sexist influence, a notion essential to their autonomy and inner direction. Misogyny was an integral part of Black Macho.

Meanwhile, the Women's Movement was redefining womanhood for white women in a manner that allowed them to work, to be manless, but still women. White women replaced some of their traditional activities with new ones—consciousness-raising, feminist meetings and demonstrations, political campaigns, antidiscrimination suits against employers, and the pursuit of an entirely new range of careers. And some white women dragged their men right along with them, not to mention a good many black men.

But the black woman, who had pooh-poohed the Women's

Movement, was left with only one activity that was not considered suspect: motherhood. A baby could counteract the damaging effect a career might have upon her feminine image. A baby clarified a woman's course for at least the next five years. No need for her to bother with difficult decisions about whether or not she ought to pursue promotion or return to school for an advanced degree, both of which might attract even more hostility from black men. If she didn't find a man, she might just decide to have a baby anyway.

Although black women have been having babies outside of marriage since slavery, there are several unusual things about the current trend. Whereas unmarried black women with babies have usually lived with extended families, these women tend to brave it alone. Whereas black women of previous generations generally married soon after the baby was born, these women may not and often say they do not wish to marry. Whereas the practice of having babies out of wedlock was generally confined to the poorer classes, it is now not uncommon among middle-class, moderately successful black women. While I don't believe that anything like a majority of black women are going in for this, it is worth finding out why so many of us have.

I am inclined to believe it is because the black woman has no legitimate way of coming together with other black women, no means of self-affirmation—in other words, no Women's Movement, and therefore no collective ideology. Career and success are still the social and emotional disadvantages to her that they were to white women in the fifties. There is little in the black community to reinforce a young black woman who does not have a man or a child and who wishes to pursue a career. She is still considered against nature.

Some young black women are beginning to be honest about seeing themselves as victims rather than superwomen. An alarming number go one disastrous step further. They become angry with black men, black people, blackness; it is simply a new way of blaming someone else for their underdevelopment. . . .

I believe that the black woman thinks of her history and condition as a wound that makes her different and therefore special and therefore exempt from human responsibility. The impartial observer may look at her and see a beautiful, healthy, glowing, vigorous woman, but none of that matters. What matters is that inside she feels powerless to do anything about her condition or anyone else's. Her solution is to simply not participate, or to participate on her own limited basis.

Yes, it is very important that we never forget the tragedy of our history or how racist white people have been or how the black man has let us down. But all of that must be set in its proper perspective. It belongs to the past and we must belong to the future. The future is something we can control.

Lately I've noticed the appearance of a number of black women's organizations and conferences. The organizations break up quickly and yet they keep forming. Every now and then, someone still mentions that white women are going to rip them off if they join the Women's Movement—that is, white women will use their support to make gains and then not share with the black women. Unfortunately, this is probably true. It would be true of any movement the black woman joined in her present condition, that is, without some clear understanding of her own priorities.

In February 1978, there was a series of articles in *The New York Times* on the changes in the black community since 1968. It covered the civil rights movement, the Black Movement, the economic and social situation for blacks today. Never once did it mention the contribution black women made to the civil rights movement. The articles spoke of three Americas: one white, one middle-class black, one poor black. No particular notice was given to the fact that poor black America consists largely of black women and children. It was as if these women and children did not exist.

History has been written without us. The imperative is clear: either we will make history or remain the victims of it.

ADRIENNE RICH

Compulsory Heterosexuality and Lesbian Existence

In 1974 Adrienne Rich (b. 1929) won the prestigious National Book Award for poetry.[1] At the awards ceremony she made the extraordinary gesture of accepting the prize not only on her own behalf but also for the two other women who had been poetry nominees. Their collective statement said, "We, Audre Lorde, Adrienne Rich, and Alice Walker, together accept this award in the name of all the women whose voices have gone and still go unheard in a patriarchal world, and in the name of those who, like us, have been tolerated as token women in this culture, often at great cost and in great pain. . . . none of us could accept this money for herself, nor could she let go unquestioned the terms on which poets are given or denied honor and livelihood in this world, especially when they are women. We dedicate this occasion to the struggle for self-determination of all women."

Rich's first volume of poetry was published in 1951, and she continued through the following decades to publish regularly—chronicling the radical changes in her own life through periods of radical social change. She wrote, said a *New York Times* reviewer, "through youth, fame, marriage, motherhood, separation, solitude, political rage, [and] feminist awakening. In its broad outlines . . . her progress through the decades has paralleled that of her generation of women."[2] Among Rich's poetry collections are *Snapshots of a Daughter-in-law* (1963, rev.

---

[1]Rich was recognized for *Diving into the Wreck: Poems, 1971–1972*. She shared the prize with poet Allen Ginsberg.

[2]Le Anne Schreiber, *New York Times Book Review*, December 9, 1981, p. 29.

1967), *Diving into the Wreck* (1973), *The Dream of a Common Language* (1978), *A Wild Patience Has Taken Me This Far* (1981), and *An Atlas of the Difficult World* (1991). Her prose works include *Of Woman Born: Motherhood as Experience and Institution* (1976) and *On Lies, Secrets, and Silence: Selected Prose, 1966–1978.*

Rich's essay "Compulsory Heterosexuality and Lesbian Existence" was written in 1978 for the journal *Signs,* where it was published in 1980. It was created, she later explained, "to challenge the erasure of lesbian existence from so much of scholarly feminist literature" and "to encourage heterosexual feminists to examine heterosexuality as a political institution."[3]

The following excerpt is taken from the 1986 reprint of the essay in Rich's collection *Blood, Bread, and Poetry.* Only a few of the author's extensive footnotes have been retained.

One

Biologically men have only one innate orientation—a sexual one that draws them to women,—while women have two innate orientations, sexual toward men and reproductive toward their young.[4]

I was a woman terribly vulnerable, critical, using femaleness as a sort of standard or yardstick to measure and discard men. Yes—something like that. I was an Anna who invited defeat from men without ever being conscious of it. (But I am conscious of it. And being conscious of it means I shall leave it all behind me and become—but what?) I was stuck fast in an emotion common to

[3]Adrienne Rich, *Blood, Bread, and Poetry: Selected Prose, 1979–1985* (New York: Norton, 1986), p. 23.
[4]Alice Rossi, "Children and Work in the Lives of Women," paper delivered at the University of Arizona, Tucson, February 1976.

women of our time, that can turn them bitter, or Lesbian, or solitary. Yes, that Anna during that time was . . .
[Another blank line across the page:][5]

The bias of compulsory heterosexuality, through which lesbian experience is perceived on a scale ranging from deviant to abhorrent or simply rendered invisible, could be illustrated from many texts other than the two just preceding. The assumption made by Rossi, that women are "innately" sexually oriented only toward men, and that made by Lessing, that the lesbian is simply acting out of her bitterness toward men, are by no means theirs alone; these assumptions are widely current in literature and in the social sciences.

I am concerned here with two other matters as well: first, how and why women's choice of women as passionate comrades, life partners, co-workers, lovers, community has been crushed, invalidated, forced into hiding and disguise; and second, the virtual or total neglect of lesbian existence in a wide range of writings, including feminist scholarship. Obviously there is a connection here. I believe that much feminist theory and criticism is stranded on this shoal.

My organizing impulse is the belief that it is not enough for feminist thought that specifically lesbian texts exist. Any theory or cultural/political creation that treats lesbian existence as a marginal or less "natural" phenomenon, as mere "sexual preference," or as the mirror image of either heterosexual or male homosexual relations is profoundly weakened thereby, whatever its other contributions. Feminist theory can no longer afford merely to voice a toleration of "lesbianism" as an "alternative life style" or make token allusion to lesbians. A feminist critique of compulsory heterosexual orientation for women is long overdue. . . .

This assumption of female heterosexuality seems to me in itself remarkable: it is an enormous assumption to have glided so silently into the foundations of our thought.

[5]Doris Lessing, *The Golden Notebook,* 1962 (New York: Bantam, 1977), p. 480.

The extension of this assumption is the frequently heard assertion that in a world of genuine equality, where men are nonoppressive and nurturing, everyone would be bisexual. Such a notion blurs and sentimentalizes the actualities within which women have experienced sexuality; it is a liberal leap across the tasks and struggles of here and now, the continuing process of sexual definition which will generate its own possibilities and choices. (It also assumes that women who have chosen women have done so simply because men are oppressive and emotionally unavailable, which still fails to account for women who continue to pursue relationships with oppressive and/or emotionally unsatisfying men.) I am suggesting that heterosexuality, like motherhood, needs to be recognized and studied as a *political institution*—even, or especially, by those individuals who feel they are, in their personal experience, the precursors of a new social relation between the sexes.

Two

IF WOMEN ARE THE EARLIEST SOURCES of emotional caring and physical nurture for both female and male children, it would seem logical, from a feminist perspective at least, to pose the following questions: whether the search for love and tenderness in both sexes does not originally lead toward women; *why in fact women would ever redirect that search;* why species survival, the means of impregnation, and emotional/erotic relationships should ever have become so rigidly identified with each other; and why such violent strictures should be found necessary to enforce women's total emotional, erotic loyalty and subservience to men. I doubt that enough feminist scholars and theorists have taken the pains to acknowledge the societal forces which wrench women's emotional and erotic energies away from themselves and other women and from woman-identified values. These forces, as I shall try to show, range from literal physical enslavement to the disguising and distorting of possible options.

I do not assume that mothering by women is a "sufficient

cause" of lesbian existence. But the issue of mothering by women has been much in the air of late, usually accompanied by the view that increased parenting by men would minimize antagonism between the sexes and equalize the sexual imbalance of power of males over females. These discussions are carried on without reference to compulsory heterosexuality as a phenomenon, let alone as an ideology. I do not wish to psychologize here, but rather to identify sources of male power. I believe large numbers of men could, in fact, undertake child care on a large scale without radically altering the balance of male power in a male-identified society.

In her essay "The Origin of the Family," Kathleen Gough lists eight characteristics of male power in archaic and contemporary societies which I would like to use as a framework. . . .[6] (Gough does not perceive these power characteristics as specifically enforcing heterosexuality, only as producing sexual inequality.) Below, Gough's words appear in italics; the elaboration of each of her categories, in brackets, is my own.

Characteristics of male power include *the power of men*

1. *to deny women* [their own] *sexuality*—[by means of clitoridectomy and infibulation; chastity belts; punishment, including death, for female adultery; punishment, including death, for lesbian sexuality; psychoanalytic denial of the clitoris; strictures against masturbation; denial of maternal and postmenopausal sensuality; unnecessary hysterectomy; pseudolesbian images in the media and literature; closing of archives and destruction of documents relating to lesbian existence]

2. *or to force it* [male sexuality] *upon them*—[by means of rape (including marital rape) and wife beating; father-daughter, brother-sister incest; the socialization of women to feel that male sexual "drive" amounts to a right; idealization of heterosexual romance in art, literature, the media, advertising, etc.; child marriage; arranged marriage; prostitution; the harem; psychoanalytic doctrines of frigidity and vaginal orgasm; porno-

[6]Kathleen Gough, "The Origin of the Family," in *Toward an Anthropology of Women*, ed. Rayna [Rapp] Reiter (New York: Monthly Review Press, 1975), pp. 69–70.

graphic depictions of women responding pleasurably to sexual violence and humiliation (a subliminal message being that sadistic heterosexuality is more "normal" than sensuality between women)]

3. *to command or exploit their labor to control their produce*—[by means of the institutions of marriage and motherhood as unpaid production; the horizontal segregation of women in paid employment; the decoy of the upwardly mobile token woman; male control of abortion, contraception, sterilization, and childbirth; pimping; female infanticide, which robs mothers of daughters and contributes to generalized devaluation of women]

4. *to control or rob them of their children*—[by means of father right and "legal kidnaping"; enforced sterilization; systematized infanticide; seizure of children from lesbian mothers by the courts; the malpractice of male obstetrics; use of the mother as "token torturer" in genital mutilation or in binding the daughter's feet (or mind) to fit her for marriage]

5. *to confine them physically and prevent their movement*—[by means of rape as terrorism, keeping women off the streets; purdah; foot binding; atrophying of women's athletic capabilities; high heels and "feminine" dress codes in fashion; the veil, sexual harassment on the streets, horizontal segregation of women in employment; prescriptions for "full-time" mothering at home; enforced economic dependence of wives]

6. *to use them as objects in male transactions*—[use of women as "gifts"; bride price; pimping; arranged marriage; use of women as entertainers to facilitate male deals—e.g., wife-hostess, cocktail waitress required to dress for male sexual titillation, call girls, "bunnies," geisha, *kisaeng* prostitutes, secretaries]

7. *to cramp their creativeness*—[witch persecutions as campaigns against midwives and female healers, and as pogrom against independent, "unassimilated" women; definition of male pursuits as more valuable than female within any culture, so that cultural values become the embodiment of male subjectivity; restriction of female self-fulfillment to marriage and motherhood; sexual exploitation of women by male artists and

teachers; the social and economic disruption of women's creative aspirations; erasure of female tradition]

8. *to withhold from them large areas of the society's knowledge and cultural attainments*—[by means of noneducation of females; the "Great Silence" regarding women and particularly lesbian existence in history and culture; sex-role tracking which deflects women from science, technology, and other "masculine" pursuits; male social/professional bonding which excludes women; discrimination against women in the professions]

These are some of the methods by which male power is manifested and maintained. Looking at the schema, what surely impresses itself is the fact that we are confronting not a simple maintenance of inequality and property possession, but a pervasive cluster of forces, ranging from physical brutality to control of consciousness, which suggests that an enormous potential counterforce is having to be restrained.

Some of the forms by which male power manifests itself are more easily recognizable as enforcing heterosexuality on women than are others. Yet each one I have listed adds to the cluster of forces within which women have been convinced that marriage and sexual orientation toward men are inevitable—even if unsatisfying or oppressive—components of their lives. . . .

When we look hard and clearly at the extent and elaboration of measures designed to keep women within a male sexual purlieu, it becomes an inescapable question whether the issue feminists have to address is not simple "gender inequality" nor the domination of culture by males nor mere "taboos against homosexuality," but the enforcement of heterosexuality for women as a means of assuring male right of physical, economic, and emotional access. One of many means of enforcement is, of course, the rendering invisible of the lesbian possibility, an engulfed continent which rises fragmentedly into view from time to time only to become submerged again. Feminist research and theory that contribute to lesbian invisibility or marginality are actually working against the liberation and empowerment of women as a group.

The assumption that "most women are innately heterosexual" stands as a theoretical and political stumbling block for feminism. It remains a tenable assumption partly because lesbian existence has been written out of history or cataloged under disease, partly because it has been treated as exceptional rather than intrinsic, partly because to acknowledge that for women heterosexuality may not be a "preference" at all but something that has had to be imposed, managed, organized, propagandized, and maintained by force is an immense step to take if you consider yourself freely and "innately" heterosexual. Yet the failure to examine heterosexuality as an institution is like failing to admit that the economic system called capitalism or the caste system of racism is maintained by a variety of forces, including both physical violence and false consciousness. To take the step of questioning heterosexuality as a "preference" or "choice" for women—and to do the intellectual and emotional work that follows—will call for a special quality of courage in heterosexually identified feminists, but I think the rewards will be great: a freeing-up of thinking, the exploring of new paths, the shattering of another great silence, new clarity in personal relationships.

Three

I HAVE CHOSEN TO USE THE TERMS *lesbian existence* and *lesbian continuum* because the word *lesbianism* has a clinical and limiting ring. *Lesbian existence* suggests both the fact of the historical presence of lesbians and our continuing creation of the meaning of that existence. I mean the term *lesbian continuum* to include a range—through each woman's life and throughout history—of woman-identified experience, not simply the fact that a woman has had or consciously desired genital sexual experience with another woman. If we expand it to embrace many more forms of primary intensity between and among women, including the sharing of a rich inner life, the bonding against male tyranny, the giving and receiving of practical and political support, if we can also hear it in such associations as *marriage resistance* and the "haggard" behavior identified by Mary Daly (obsolete meanings: "intractable," "willful," "wanton," and "unchaste," "a woman reluctant to yield to wooing"),[7] we begin to grasp breadths of female history and psychology which have lain out of reach as a consequence of limited, mostly clinical, definitions of *lesbianism*.

Lesbian existence comprises both the breaking of a taboo and the rejection of a compulsory way of life. It is also a direct or indirect attack on male right of access to women. But it is more than these, although we may first begin to perceive it as a form of naysaying to patriarchy, an act of resistance. It has, of course, included isolation, self-hatred, breakdown, alcoholism, suicide, and intrawoman violence; we romanticize at our peril what it means to love and act against the grain, and under heavy penalties; and lesbian existence has been lived (unlike, say, Jewish or Catholic existence) without access to any knowledge of a tradition, a continuity, a social underpinning. The destruction of records and memorabilia and letters documenting the realities of lesbian existence must be taken very seriously as a means of keeping heterosexuality compulsory for women, since what has been kept from our knowledge is joy, sensuality, courage, and community, as well as guilt, self-betrayal, and pain.

Lesbians have historically been deprived of a political existence through "inclusion" as female versions of male homosexuality. To equate lesbian existence with male homosexuality because each is stigmatized is to erase female reality once again. Part of the history of lesbian existence is, obviously, to be found where lesbians, lacking a coherent female community, have shared a kind of social life and common cause with homosexual men. But there are differences: women's lack of economic and cultural privilege relative to men; qualitative differences in female and male relationships—for example, the patterns of anonymous sex among male homosexuals, and the pronounced ageism in male homosexual standards of sexual attractiveness. I perceive the lesbian experience as being, like motherhood, a profoundly *female* experience, with particular oppressions, meanings, and potentialities we cannot comprehend as long as

[7]Mary Daly, *Gyn/Ecology: The Metaethics of Radical Feminism* (Boston: Beacon Press, 1978), p. 15.

we simply bracket it with other sexually stigmatized existences. Just as the term *parenting* serves to conceal the particular and significant reality of being a parent who is actually a mother, the term *gay* may serve the purpose of blurring the very outlines we need to discern, which are of crucial value for feminism and for the freedom of women as a group.

As the term *lesbian* has been held to limiting, clinical associations in its patriarchal definition, female friendship and comradeship have been set apart from the erotic, thus limiting the erotic itself. But as we deepen and broaden the range of what we define as lesbian existence, as we delineate a lesbian continuum, we begin to discover the erotic in female terms: as that which is unconfined to any single part of the body or solely to the body itself; as an energy not only diffuse but, as Audre Lorde has described it, omnipresent in "the sharing of joy, whether physical, emotional, psychic," and in the sharing of work; as the empowering joy which "makes us less willing to accept powerlessness, or those other supplied states of being which are not native to me, such as resignation, despair, self-effacement, depression, self-denial."[8] . . .

If we consider the possibility that all women—from the infant suckling at her mother's breast, to the grown woman experiencing orgasmic sensations while suckling her own child, perhaps recalling her mother's milk smell in her own, to two women, like Virginia Woolf's Chloe and Olivia, who share a laboratory,[9] to the woman dying at ninety, touched and handled by women—exist on a lesbian continuum, we can see ourselves as moving in and out of this continuum, whether we identify ourselves as lesbian or not.

We can then connect aspects of woman identification as diverse as the impudent, intimate girl friendships of eight or nine year olds and the banding together of those women of the twelfth and fifteenth centuries known as Beguines who . . .

[8] Audre Lorde, "Uses of the Erotic: The Erotic as Power," in *Sister Outsider* (Trumansburg, NY: Crossing Press, 1984).

[9] Virginia Woolf, *A Room of One's Own* (London: Hogarth Press, 1929), p. 126.

earned their livings as spinsters, bakers, nurses, or ran schools for young girls, and who managed—until the Church forced them to disperse—to live independent both of marriage and of conventual restrictions. It allows us to connect these women with the more celebrated "Lesbians" of the women's school around Sappho of the seventh century B.C., with the secret sororities and economic networks reported among African women, and with the Chinese marriage-resistance sisterhoods— communities of women who refused marriage or who, if married, often refused to consummate their marriages and soon left their husbands, the only women in China who were not foot-bound and who, Agnes Smedley tells us, welcomed the births of daughters and organized successful women's strikes in the silk mills.[10] It allows us to connect and compare disparate individual instances of marriage resistance: for example, the strategies available to Emily Dickinson, a nineteenth-century white woman genius, with the strategies available to Zora Neale Hurston, a twentieth-century Black woman genius. Dickinson never married, had tenuous intellectual friendships with men, lived self-convented in her genteel father's house in Amherst, and wrote a lifetime of passionate letters to her sister-in-law Sue Gilbert and a smaller group of such letters to her friend Kate Scott Anthon. Hurston married twice but soon left each husband, scrambled her way from Florida to Harlem to Columbia University to Haiti and finally back to Florida, moved in and out of white patronage and poverty, professional success, and failure; her survival relationships were all with women, beginning with her mother. Both of these women in their vastly different circumstances were marriage resisters, committed to their own work and selfhood, and were later characterized as "apolitical." Both

[10]See Denise Paulmé, ed., *Women of Tropical Africa* (Berkeley: University of California Press, 1963); . . . Marjorie Topley, "Marriage Resistance in Rural Kwangtung," in *Women in Chinese Society,* ed. M. Wolf and R. Witke (Stanford, CA: Stanford University Press, 1978); Agnes Smedley, *Portraits of Chinese Women in Revolution,* ed. J. MacKinnon and S. MacKinnon (Old Westbury, NY: Feminist Press, 1976).

were drawn to men of intellectual quality; for both of them women provided the ongoing fascination and sustenance of life.

If we think of heterosexuality as *the* natural emotional and sensual inclination for women, lives such as these are seen as deviant, as pathological, or as emotionally and sensually deprived. Or, in more recent and permissive jargon, they are banalized as "life styles." And the work of such women, whether merely the daily work of individual or collective survival and resistance or the work of the writer, the activist, the reformer, the anthropologist, or the artist—the work of self-creation—is undervalued, or seen as the bitter fruit of "penis envy" or the sublimation of repressed eroticism or the meaningless rant of a "man-hater." But when we turn the lens of vision and consider the degree to which and the methods whereby heterosexual "preference" has actually been imposed on women, not only can we understand differently the meaning of individual lives and work, but we can begin to recognize a central fact of women's history: that women have always resisted male tyranny. A feminism of action, often though not always without a theory, has constantly re-emerged in every culture and in every period. We can then begin to study women's struggle against powerlessness, women's radical rebellion, not just in male-defined "concrete revolutionary situations" but in all the situations male ideologies have not perceived as revolutionary—for example, the refusal of some women to produce children, aided at great risk by other women; the refusal to produce a higher standard of living and leisure for men. . . . We can no longer have patience with Dinnerstein's view that women have simply collaborated with men in the "sexual arrangements" of history. We begin to observe behavior, both in history and in individual biography, that has hitherto been invisible or misnamed, behavior which often constitutes, given the limits of the counterforce exerted in a given time and place, radical rebellion. And we can connect these rebellions and the necessity for them with the physical passion of woman for woman which is central to lesbian existence: the erotic sensuality which has been, precisely, the most violently erased fact of female experience.

Heterosexuality has been both forcibly and subliminally imposed on women. Yet everywhere women have resisted it, often at the cost of physical torture, imprisonment, psychosurgery, social ostracism, and extreme poverty. "Compulsory heterosexuality" was named as one of the "crimes against women" by the Brussels International Tribunal on Crimes against Women in 1976. . . .

Nor can it be assumed that women . . . who married, stayed married, yet dwelt in a profoundly female emotional and passional world, "preferred" or "chose" heterosexuality. Women have married because it was necessary, in order to survive economically, in order to have children who would not suffer economic deprivation or social ostracism, in order to remain respectable, in order to do what was expected of women, because, coming out of "abnormal" childhoods, they wanted to feel "normal" and because heterosexual romance has been represented as the great female adventure, duty, and fulfillment. We may faithfully or ambivalently have obeyed the institution, but our feelings—and our sensuality— have not been tamed or contained within it. There is no statistical documentation of the numbers of lesbians who have remained in heterosexual marriages for most of their lives. . . .

This *double life*—this apparent acquiescence to an institution founded on male interest and prerogative—has been characteristic of female experience: in motherhood and in many kinds of heterosexual behavior, including the rituals of courtship; the pretense of asexuality by the nineteenth-century wife; the simulation of orgasm by the prostitute, the courtesan, the twentieth-century "sexually liberated" woman. . . .

Four

WOMAN IDENTIFICATION IS A SOURCE OF ENERGY, a potential springhead of female power, curtailed and contained under the institution of heterosexuality. The denial of reality and visibility to women's passion for women, women's choice of women as allies, life companions, and community, the forcing of such relationships into dissimulation and their disintegration under intense pressure have meant an incalculable loss to the power of all women *to change the social relations of the sexes, to liberate ourselves and each other.* The lie of compulsory female heterosexuality today afflicts not just feminist scholarship, but every profession, every reference work, every curriculum, every organizing attempt, every relationship or conversation over which it hovers. It creates, specifically, a profound falseness, hypocrisy, and hysteria in the heterosexual dialogue, for every heterosexual relationship is lived in the queasy strobe light of that lie. However we choose to identify ourselves, however we find ourselves labeled, it flickers across and distorts our lives.

The lie keeps numberless women psychologically trapped, trying to fit mind, spirit, and sexuality into a prescribed script because they cannot look beyond the parameters of the acceptable. It pulls on the energy of such women even as it drains the energy of "closeted" lesbians—the energy exhausted in the double life. The lesbian trapped in the "closet," the woman imprisoned in prescriptive ideas of the "normal" share the pain of blocked options, broken connections, lost access to self-definition freely and powerfully assumed.

The lie is many-layered. In Western tradition, one layer—the romantic—asserts that women are inevitably, even if rashly and tragically, drawn to men; that even when that attraction is suicidal (e.g., *Tristan and Isolde,* Kate Chopin's *The Awakening*), it is still an organic imperative. In the tradition of the social sciences it asserts that primary love between the sexes is "normal"; that women *need* men as social and economic protectors, for adult sexuality, and for psychological completion; that the heterosexually constituted family is the basic social unit; that women who do not attach their primary intensity to men must be, in functional terms, condemned to an even more devastating outsiderhood than their outsiderhood as women. Small wonder that lesbians are reported to be a more hidden population than male homosexuals. The Black lesbian-feminist critic Lorraine Bethel, writing on Zora Neale Hurston, remarks that for a Black woman—already twice an outsider—to choose to assume still another "hated identity" is problematic indeed. Yet the lesbian continuum has been a life line for Black women both in Africa and the United States. . . .

Another layer of the lie is the frequently encountered implication that women turn to women out of hatred for men. Profound skepticism, caution, and righteous paranoia about men may indeed be part of any healthy woman's response to the misogyny of male-dominated culture, to the forms assumed by "normal" male sexuality, and to *the failure even of "sensitive" or "political" men to perceive or find these troubling.* Lesbian existence is also represented as mere refuge from male abuses, rather than as an electric and empowering charge between women. One of the most frequently quoted literary passages on lesbian relationship is that in which Colette's Renée, in *The Vagabond,* describes "the melancholy and touching image of two weak creatures who have perhaps found shelter in each other's arms, there to sleep and weep, safe from man who is often cruel, and there to taste *better than any pleasure, the bitter happiness of feeling themselves akin, frail and forgotten* [emphasis added]." Colette is often considered a lesbian writer. Her popular reputation has, I think, much to do with the fact that she writes about lesbian existence as if for a male audience; her earliest "lesbian" novels, the Claudine series, were written under compulsion for her husband and published under both their names. At all events, except for her writings on her mother, Colette is a less reliable source on the lesbian continuum than, I would think, Charlotte Brontë, who understood that while women may, indeed must, be one another's allies, mentors, and comforters in the female struggle for survival, there is quite extraneous delight in each other's company and attraction to each other's minds and character, which attend a recognition of each other's strengths.

By the same token, we can say that there is a *nascent* feminist political content in the act of choosing a woman lover or life partner in the face of institutionalized heterosexuality. But for lesbian existence to realize this political content in an ultimately liberating form, the erotic choice must deepen and expand into conscious woman identification—into lesbian feminism.

The work that lies ahead, of unearthing and describing what

I call here "lesbian existence," is potentially liberating for all women. It is work that must assuredly move beyond the limits of white and middle-class Western Women's Studies to examine women's lives, work, and groupings within every racial, ethnic, and political structure. There are differences, moreover, between "lesbian existence" and the "lesbian continuum," differences we can discern even in the movement of our own lives. The lesbian continuum, I suggest, needs delineation in light of the "double life" of women, not only women self-described as heterosexual but also of self-described lesbians. We need a far more exhaustive account of the forms the double life has assumed. Historians need to ask at every point how heterosexuality as institution has been organized and maintained through the female wage scale, the enforcement of middle-class women's "leisure," the glamorization of so-called sexual liberation, the withholding of education from women, the imagery of "high art" and popular culture, the mystification of the "personal" sphere, and much else. We need an economics which comprehends the institution of heterosexuality, with its doubled workload for women and its sexual divisions of labor, as the most idealized of economic relations.

The question inevitably will arise: Are we then to condemn all heterosexual relationships, including those which are least oppressive? I believe this question, though often heartfelt, is the wrong question here. We have been stalled in a maze of false dichotomies, which prevents our apprehending the institution as a whole: "good" versus "bad" marriages; "marriage for love" versus arranged marriage; "liberated" sex versus prostitution; heterosexual intercourse versus rape; *Liebeschmerz* versus humiliation and dependency. Within the institution exist, of course, qualitative differences of experience; but the absence of choice remains the great unacknowledged reality, and in the absence of choice, women will remain dependent upon the chance or luck of particular relationships and will have no collective power to determine the meaning and place of sexuality in their lives. As we address the institution itself, moreover, we begin to perceive a history of female resistance which has never fully understood itself because it has been so fragmented, miscalled, erased. It will require a courageous grasp of the politics and economics, as well as the cultural propaganda, of heterosexuality to carry us beyond the individual cases or diversified group situations into the complex kind of overview needed to undo the power men everywhere wield over women, power which has become a model for every other form of exploitation and illegitimate control.

V

Our Bodies

ANNE SEXTON

In Celebration of My Uterus

In a preface to the collected poems of Anne Sexton (1928–1974), poet Maxine Kumin said that women poets owe Sexton a debt, because in her choice of subject matter she "broke new ground, shattered taboos, and endured a barrage of attacks along the way." Sexton was one of the first who dared to create poetry about breasts and wombs, about abortion, menstruation, masturbation, incest, adultery. One male critic who attacked her, Kumin recalled, singled out her "Menstruation at Forty" as particularly unacceptable, and another, writing in *The New York Times Book Review*, "excoriated the poems in *All My Pretty Ones* [1962], saying, 'It would be hard to find a writer who dwells more insistently on the pathetic and disgusting aspects of bodily experience.'"[1]

But from the start Sexton was popular with young women, who flocked to her poetry readings. And as times changed and her work lost some of its shock effect, a broader audience came to appreciate her poetry. She was awarded the Pulitzer Prize for her third volume of poetry, *Live or Die* (1966).

The poem reprinted here, "In Celebration of My Uterus," was included in Sexton's 1969 collection *Love Poems*. As interpreted by Alicia Ostriker, herself a poet and a perceptive critic, this poem "finds unity where the culture propagates division: between a woman's sexuality and her spirituality, her creativity and her procreativity, herself and other women, her private and her public self." It opens with the discovery of a medical misdiagnosis, in a mood "euphoric, buoyant, hyperbolic." The

---

[1]"How It Was: Maxine Kumin on Anne Sexton," foreword to Anne Sexton, *The Complete Poems* (Boston: Houghton Mifflin, 1981), pp. xix–xx, xxxiv.

middle section compares the fecundity of the poet's healthy uterus with the earth's ability to nurture plants. And as the poem closes, the fertility of the poet's imagination—which can conjure women of many nations and occupations—is equated with her life-producing womb.[2]

Sexton once again was ahead of her time. De Beauvoir and many of her devotees in the women's movement—one thinks especially of Shulamith Firestone, whose book came out just after this poem appeared—regarded biology as an impediment, the primal cause for the subjection of women. But Sexton struck a note of joy and transcendence in celebrating woman's physical nature—a note many future feminist writings would echo. Ten years later, for example, Ntozake Shange would write defiantly:

I've decided to wear my ovaries on my sleeve
raise my poems on my milk
& count my days by the flow of my mensis.[3]

Everyone in me is a bird.
I am beating all my wings.
They wanted to cut you out
but they will not.
They said you were immeasurably empty
but you are not.
They said you were sick unto dying
but they were wrong.
You are singing like a school girl.
You are not torn.

[2]Alicia Suskin Ostriker, *Stealing the Language: The Emergence of Women's Poetry in America* (Boston: Beacon Press, 1986), p. 111.

[3]Ntozake Shange, "wow . . . yr just like a man," in *nappy edges* (New York: St. Martin's, 1978), p. 16.

Sweet weight,
in celebration of the woman I am
and of the soul of the woman I am
and of the central creature and its delight
I sing for you. I dare to live.
Hello, spirit. Hello, cup.
Fasten, cover. Cover that does contain.
Hello to the soil of the fields.
Welcome, roots.

Each cell has a life.
There is enough here to please a nation.
It is enough that the populace own these goods.
Any person, any commonwealth would say of it,
"It is good this year that we may plant again
and think forward to a harvest.
A blight had been forecast and has been cast out."
Many women are singing together of this:
one is in a shoe factory cursing the machine,
one is at the aquarium tending a seal,
one is dull at the wheel of her Ford,
one is at the toll gate collecting,
one is tying the cord of a calf in Arizona,
one is straddling a cello in Russia,
one is shifting pots on the stove in Egypt,
one is painting her bedroom walls moon color,
one is dying but remembering a breakfast,
one is stretching on her mat in Thailand,
one is wiping the ass of her child,
one is staring out the window of a train
in the middle of Wyoming and one is
anywhere and some are everywhere and all
seem to be singing, although some can not
sing a note.

Sweet weight,
in celebration of the woman I am
let me carry a ten-foot scarf,
let me drum for the nineteen-year-olds,
let me carry bowls for the offering
(if that is my part).
Let me study the cardiovascular tissue,
let me examine the angular distance of meteors,
let me suck on the stems of flowers
(if that is my part).
Let me make certain tribal figures
(if that is my part).
For this thing the body needs
let me sing
for the supper,
for the kissing,
for the correct
yes.

ANNE KOEDT

The Myth of
the Vaginal Orgasm

In his 1910 work, *Three Essays on the Theory of Sexuality,* Sigmund Freud postulated that females have two distinct types of orgasms—a clitoral and a vaginal—and that the latter was preferable to, more mature than, the former. Well-adjusted women, he indicated, repressed clitoral sexuality at puberty and thereafter experienced vaginal orgasms exclusively. Although Freud offered no proof of this theory, it was spread by his disciples and by Freudian popularizers over the next few decades. Those women who admitted that they did not experience the approved (vaginal) sexual response were often labeled frigid neurotics who were denying their femininity and were in need of psychiatric assistance. Many women suffered deeply from a presumed failure to accept their feminine nature.

In 1968, feminist activist, artist, and writer Anne Koedt wrote a four-paragraph statement titled "The Myth of the Vaginal Orgasm: A Thesis for Future Study" and published it in the mimeographed feminist paper *Notes from the First Year.* The brief article had a stunning impact on readers. The vaginal orgasm, Koedt said, does not exist; the clitoris is the center of female sexual pleasure. It was not so much that her message was news, for Koedt was essentially reiterating the widely publicized research findings of Masters and Johnson, which had been published two years earlier.[1] It was just that the full implications of these discoveries had yet to be assimilated by women.

Even before Masters and Johnson, doubts about Freud's theory had surfaced. The pioneer of sex research, Alfred Kinsey,

[1] William H. Masters and Virginia E. Johnson, *Human Sexual Response* (Boston: Little, Brown, 1966).

reported as early as 1953 that "the vaginal walls are quite insensitive," and he bluntly termed the vaginal orgasm a "biologic impossibility."[2] Earlier still, Ruth Herschberger wrote in her delightful and amusing feminist book, *Adam's Rib*, "In the symphony of love, the lost chord is a small organ lying somewhat north of the vagina."[3]

But such was the prestige of Freud that most people had simply accepted the reality of the vaginal orgasm. For example, one of Doris Lessing's "free women" in *The Golden Notebook* (1962) speaks of the "real"—that is, vaginal—orgasm as opposed to "the sharp violence of the exterior orgasm." And in Mary McCarthy's *The Group* (1963), the character Dotty remarks that a clitoral climax "seemed to her almost perverted."

Anne Koedt expanded her essay for *Notes from the Second Year* (1970). She analyzed the social context in which a false, harmful account of female sexual development was produced and perpetuated over decades. Why did men maintain the fiction? Koedt asked. Why did women accept it? How would the truth affect the future of male-female sexual relations? "Koedt's classic essay," declared the authors of a 1986 book on changing sexual practices, "was no less than a declaration of sexual independence."[4]

The following selection is excerpted from *Notes from the Second Year*.

---

[2]Alfred Kinsey, et al., *Sexual Behavior in the Human Female* (Philadelphia: Saunders, 1953), pp. 580, 584.

[3]Ruth Herschberger, *Adam's Rib* (1948; reprint, New York: Harper & Row, 1970), p. 30.

[4]Barbara Ehrenreich, Elizabeth Hess, and Gloria Jacobs, *Re-making Love* (Garden City, NY: Anchor Press/Doubleday, 1986), p. 70.

WHENEVER FEMALE ORGASM AND FRIGIDITY IS DISCUSSED, a false distinction is made between the vaginal and the clitoral orgasm. Frigidity has generally been defined by men as the failure of women to have vaginal orgasms. Actually the vagina is not a highly sensitive area and is not constructed to achieve orgasm. It is the clitoris which is the center of sexual sensitivity and which is the female equivalent of the penis.

I think this explains a great many things: First of all, the fact that the so-called frigidity rate among women is phenomenally high. Rather than tracing female frigidity to the false assumptions about female anatomy, our "experts" have declared frigidity a psychological problem of women. Those women who complained about it were recommended psychiatrists, so that they might discover their "problem"—diagnosed generally as a failure to adjust to their role as women.

The facts of female anatomy and sexual response tell a different story. There is only one area for sexual climax, although there are many areas for sexual arousal; that area is the clitoris. All orgasms are extensions of sensation from this area. Since the clitoris is not necessarily stimulated sufficiently in the conventional sexual positions, we are left "frigid."

Aside from physical stimulation, which is the common cause of orgasm for most people, there is also stimulation through primarily mental processes. Some women, for example, may achieve orgasm thorugh sexual fantasies or through fetishes. However, while the stimulation may be psychological, the orgasm manifests itself physically. Thus, while the cause is psychological, the *effect* is still physical, and the orgasm necessarily takes place in the sexual organ equipped for sexual climax—the clitoris. The orgasm experience may also differ in degree of intensity—some more localized, and some more diffuse and sensitive. But they are all clitoral orgasms.

All this leads to some interesting questions about conventional sex and our role in it. Men have orgasms essentially by friction with the vagina, not the clitoral area, which is external and not able to cause friction the way penetration does. Women have thus been defined sexually in terms of what pleases men; our own biology has not been properly analyzed. Instead, we are fed the myth of the liberated woman and her vaginal orgasm—an orgasm which in fact does not exist.

What we must do is redefine our sexuality. We must discard the "normal" concepts of sex and create new guidelines which take into account mutual sexual enjoyment. While the idea of mutual enjoyment is liberally applauded in marriage manuals, it is not followed to its logical conclusion. We must begin to demand that if certain sexual positions now defined as "standard" are not mutually conducive to orgasm, they no longer be defined as standard. New techniques must be used or devised which transform this particular aspect of our current sexual exploitation.

Freud—A Father of the Vaginal Orgasm

FREUD CONTENDED THAT THE CLITORAL ORGASM was adolescent, and that upon puberty, when women began having intercourse with men, women should transfer the center of orgasm to the vagina. The vagina, it was assumed, was able to produce a parallel, but more mature, orgasm than the clitoris. Much work was done to elaborate on this theory, but little was done to challenge the basic assumptions. . . .

Once having laid down the law about the nature of our sexuality, Freud not so strangely discovered a tremendous problem of frigidity in women. His recommended cure for a woman who was frigid was psychiatric care. She was suffering from failure to mentally adjust to her "natural" role as a woman. Frank S. Caprio, a contemporary follower of these ideas, states: ". . . whenever a woman is incapable of achieving an orgasm via coitus, provided her husband is an adequate partner, and prefers clitoral stimulation to any other form of sexual activity, she can be regarded as suffering from frigidity and requires psychiatric assistance."[5] The explanation given was that women were envi-

[5] *The Sexually Adequate Female* (Greenwich, CT: Fawcett, 1953, 1966), p. 64.

ous of men—"renunciation of womanhood." Thus it was diagnosed as an anti-male phenomenon.

It is important to emphasize that Freud did not base his theory upon a study of woman's anatomy, but rather upon his assumptions of woman as an inferior appendage to man, and her consequent social and psychological role. In their attempts to deal with the ensuing problem of mass frigidity, Freudians created elaborate mental gymnastics. Marie Bonaparte, in *Female Sexuality,* goes so far as to suggest surgery to help women back on their rightful path. Having discovered a strange connection between the nonfrigid woman and the location of the clitoris near the vagina,

> it then occurred to me that where, in certain women, this gap was excessive, and clitoridal fixation obdurate, a clitoridal-vaginal reconciliation might be effected by surgical means, which would then benefit the normal erotic function. Professor Halban, of Vienna, as much a biologist as surgeon, became interested in the problem and worked out a simple operative technique. In this, the suspensory ligament of the clitoris was severed and the clitoris secured to the underlying structures, thus fixing it in a lower position, with eventual reduction of the labia minora."[6]

But the severest damage was not in the area of surgery, where Freudians ran around absurdly trying to change female anatomy to fit their basic assumptions. The worst damage was done to the mental health of women, who either suffered silently with self-blame, or flocked to the psychiatrists looking desperately for the hidden and terrible repression that kept from them their vaginal destiny.

[6]*Female Sexuality* (New York: Grove Press), p. 148.

Lack of Evidence?

ONE MAY PERHAPS AT FIRST CLAIM that these are unknown and unexplored areas, but upon closer examination this is certainly not true today, nor was it true even in the past. For example, men have known that women suffered from frigidity often during intercourse. So the problem was there. Also, there is much specific evidence. Men knew that the clitoris was and is the essential organ for masturbation, whether in children or adult women. So obviously women made it clear where *they* thought their sexuality was located. Men also seem suspiciously aware of the clitoral powers during "foreplay," when they want to arouse women and produce the necessary lubrication for penetration. Foreplay is a concept created for male purposes, but works to the disadvantage of many women, since as soon as the woman is aroused the man changes to vaginal stimulation, leaving her both aroused and unsatisfied.

It has also been known that women need no anesthesia inside the vagina during surgery, thus pointing to the fact that the vagina is in fact not a highly sensitive area.

Today, with extensive knowledge of anatomy, with Kinsey, and Masters and Johnson, to mention just a few sources, there is no ignorance on the subject. There are, however, social reasons why this knowledge has not been popularized. We are living in a male society which has not sought change in women's role. . . .

Women Who Say They Have
Vaginal Orgasms

Confusion

Because of the lack of knowledge of their own anatomy, some women accept the idea that an orgasm felt during "normal" intercourse was vaginally caused. This confusion is caused by a combination of two factors. One, failing to locate the center of the orgasm, and two, by a desire to fit her experience to the male-defined idea of sexual normalcy. Considering that women know little about their anatomy, it is easy to be confused.

Deception

The vast majority of women who pretend vaginal orgasm to their men are faking it to, as Ti-Grace Atkinson says, "get the job." In a new best-selling Danish book, *I Accuse* (my own translation), Mette Ejlersen specifically deals with this common problem, which she calls the "sex comedy." This comedy has many causes. First of all, the man brings a great deal of pressure to bear on the woman, because he considers his ability as a lover at stake. So as not to offend his ego, the woman will comply with the prescribed role and go through simulated ecstasy. In some of the other Danish women mentioned, women who were left frigid were turned off to sex, and pretended vaginal orgasm to hurry up the sex act. Others admitted that they had faked vaginal orgasm to catch a man. In one case, the woman pretended vaginal orgasm to get him to leave his first wife, who admitted being vaginally frigid. Later she was forced to continue the deception, since obviously she couldn't tell him to stimulate her clitorally.

Many more women were simply afraid to establish their right to equal enjoyment, seeing the sexual act as being primarily for the man's benefit, and any pleasure that the woman got as an added extra.

Other women, with just enough ego to reject the man's idea that they needed psychiatric care, refused to admit their frigidity. They wouldn't accept self-blame, but they didn't know how to solve the problem, not knowing the physiological facts about themselves. So they were left in a peculiar limbo.

Again, perhaps one of the most infuriating and damaging results of this whole charade has been that women who were perfectly healthy sexually were taught that they were not. So in addition to being sexually deprived, these women were told to blame themselves, when they deserved no blame. Looking for a cure to a problem that has none can lead a woman on an endless path of self-hatred and insecurity. For she is told by her analyst that not even in her one role allowed in a male society—the role of a woman—is she successful. She is put on the defensive, with phony data as evidence that she better try to be even more feminine, think more feminine, and reject her envy of men. That is, shuffle even harder, baby.

Why Men Maintain the Myth

1. Sexual Penetration Is Preferred

The best stimulant for the penis is the woman's vagina. It supplies the necessary friction and lubrication. From a strictly technical point of view this position offers the best physical conditions, even though the man may try other positions for variation.

2. The Invisible Woman

One of the elements of male chauvinism is the refusal or inability to see women as total, separate human beings. Rather, men have chosen to define women only in terms of how they benefited men's lives Sexually, a woman was not seen as an individual wanting to share equally in the sexual act, any more than she was seen as a person with independent desires when she did anything else in society. Thus, it was easy to make up what was convenient about women; for on top of that, society has been a function of male interests, and women were not organized to form even a vocal opposition to the male experts.

3. The Penis as Epitome of Masculinity

. . . To the extent that men try to rationalize and justify male superiority through physical differentiation, masculinity may be symbolized by being the *most* muscular, the most hairy, the deepest voice, and the biggest penis. Women, on the other hand, are approved of (i.e., called feminine) if they are weak, petite, shave their legs, have high soft voices, and no penis.

Since the clitoris is almost identical to the penis, one finds a great deal of evidence of men in various societies trying to either ignore the clitoris and emphasize the vagina (as did Freud), or, as in some places . . . , actually performing clitoridectomy. Freud saw this ancient and still practiced custom as a way of further "feminizing" the female by removing this cardinal vestige of her masculinity. . . .

4. Sexually Expendable Male

Men fear that they will become sexually expendable if the clitoris is substituted for the vagina as the center of pleasure for women. Actually this has a great deal of validity if one considers *only* the anatomy. The position of the penis inside the vagina, while perfect for reproduction, does not necessarily stimulate an orgasm in women because the clitoris is located externally and higher up. Women must rely upon indirect stimulation in the "normal" position.

Lesbian sexuality could make an excellent case, based upon anatomical data, for the extinction of the male organ. Albert Ellis says something to the effect that a man without a penis can make a woman an excellent lover.

Considering that the vagina is very desirable from a man's point of view, purely on physical grounds, one begins to see the dilemma for men. And it forces us as well to discard many "physical" arguments explaining why women go to bed with men. What is left, it seems to me, are primarily psychological reasons why women select men at the exclusion of women as sexual partners.

5. Control of Women

One reason given to explain the . . . practice of clitoridectomy is that it will keep the women from straying. By removing the sexual organ capable of orgasm, it must be assumed that her sexual drive will diminish. Considering how men look upon their women as property, particularly in very backward nations, we should begin to consider a great deal more why it is not in the men's interest to have women totally free sexually. The double standard, as practiced for example in Latin America, is set up to keep the woman as total property of the husband, while he is free to have affairs as he wishes.

6. Lesbianism and Bisexuality

Aside from the strictly anatomical reasons why women might equally seek other women as lovers, there is a fear on men's part that women will seek the company of other women on a full, human basis. The establishment of clitoral orgasm as fact would threaten the heterosexual *institution*. For it would indicate that sexual pleasure was obtainable from either men *or* women, thus making heterosexuality not an absolute, but an option. It would thus open up the whole question of *human* sexual relationships beyond the confines of the present male-female role system.

GERMAINE GREER

The Female Eunuch

ermaine Greer (b. 1939) announced in the opening sentence of *The Female Eunuch,* "This book is a part of the second feminist wave." But others riding that same wave were curiously reluctant to welcome her to their company. It did not help that, at a time when many feminists saw men as the enemy, *Life* magazine called Greer the "saucy feminist that even men like." Nor did her celebration of the delights of heterosexual intercourse endear her to those feminists who were counseling separation from men. One American movement activist, evidently irked by the Australia-born author's star status, described Greer as "pretty, predictable, aggressively heterosexual, media-wise, clever, foreign, and exotic," and chided her for believing that "feminism equals free love"[1]—clearly a simplistic rendering of the author's message.

The Female Eunuch was a best-seller both in Great Britain, where it was published in 1970, and in the United States. Its author, a Shakespeare scholar, was a university professor in England and had also worked as an actress and a journalist. If her book was thoroughly outrageous—and it was—that was exactly her intention. Her barbed comments were aimed even at other feminists. She ridiculed Betty Friedan for seeking "admission to the world of the ulcer and the coronary" for women. As for the socialist feminists—among whom she regarded Juliet Mitchell as "the most coherent"—Greer thought they left women stranded, waiting in the wings for world revolution. In

---

[1]Claudia Dreifus, "The Selling of a Feminist," in *Radical Feminism,* ed. Anne Koedt, Ellen Levine, and Anita Rapone (New York: Quadrangle, 1973), p. 358.

fact, Greer seemed to regard herself as a committee of one, the only feminist with a feasible program for the liberation of her sex. What that program amounted to was a kind of bootstrap feminism: an insistence that it is up to the individual woman to transform herself.

Greer's approach to understanding women was founded on de Beauvoir's insight that the model of "woman" is a social construct devised by the dominant sex. Although women and men are not very different in most respects, argued Greer, society forces women to behave in ways that emphasize and exaggerate the differences. Women accordingly distort and suppress their human qualities in order to fit a fantasy stereotype created by men.

The stereotypical female is a "Sexual Object . . . a doll." Her facial expression must betray no humor or intelligence but wear a continuous smile; she "absolutely must be young, her body hairless, her flesh buoyant, and *she must not have a sexual organ.*" Her desexualization also involves her mind and feelings—she must be *"without libido."* In short, the ideal woman has become the nearest thing to a castrated creature: a female eunuch.

How can women reclaim human qualities, including sexuality? Greer offered no specific formula, but she was an apostle of female physicality, energy, daring, experimentation, independence, vigor. "Take possession of your body and glory in its power," she urged, "accepting its own laws of loveliness." Eschew clothing or makeup, such as false eyelashes, that is designed to bolster the synthetic image of womanhood. Refuse to marry or live in a monogamous relationship. It was the golden age of sexual emancipation—the birth control pill was new and AIDS was unknown. "Love can exist outside marriage," Greer insisted. "Why must it be exclusive?"

Fourteen years later, with the publication of her book *Sex and Destiny,* Greer seemed to many readers to have abandoned her liberationist ideas and become more conservative. However, she herself denied that interpretation. She told a reporter that women had exchanged "fidelity" for "promiscuity," trading one type of restriction of freedom for another.[2] And in a later interview, she said she remained convinced that monogamy is no more natural for the female sex than for the male.[3]

Other books by Greer include *The Obstacle Race: The Fortunes of Women Painters and Their Works* (1979), *The Madwoman's Underclothes: Essays and Occasional Writings* (1986), and *The Change: Women, Ageing and the Menopause* (1991).

The following selection from *The Female Eunuch* is composed of excerpts from the introduction and from the chapter "Sex."

FEMALE SEXUALITY HAS ALWAYS BEEN A FASCINATING TOPIC; this discussion of it attempts to show how female sexuality has been masked and deformed by most observers, and never more so than in our own time. . . . The female is considered as a sexual object for the use and appreciation of other sexual beings, men. Her sexuality is both denied and misrepresented by being identified as passivity. The vagina is obliterated from the imagery of femininity in the same way that the signs of independence and vigor in the rest of her body are suppressed. The characteristics that are praised and rewarded are those of the castrate—timidity, plumpness, languor, delicacy, and preciosity. . . .

Women's sexual organs are shrouded in mystery.

It is assumed that most of them are internal and hidden, but even the ones that are external are relatively shady. When little girls begin to ask questions, their mothers provide them, if they

---

[2]Cited by Barbara Ehrenreich, Elizabeth Hess, and Gloria Jacobs, in *Remaking Love* (Garden City, NY: Anchor Books/Doubleday, 1986), p. 178.

[3]Germaine Greer, " 'Anon' Got It Wrong. It's Not My Change," in *New York Observer,* August 10–17, 1992, p. 1.

are lucky, with crude diagrams of the sexual apparatus, in which the organs of pleasure feature much less prominently than the intricacies of tubes and ovaries. I myself did not realize that the tissues of my vagina were quite normal until I saw a meticulously engraved dissection in an eighteenth-century anatomy textbook. The little girl is not encouraged to explore her own genitals or to identify the tissues of which they are composed, or to understand the mechanism of lubrication and erection. The very idea is distasteful. Because of this strange modesty, which a young woman will find extends even into the doctor's office, where the doctor is loath to examine her, and loath to expatiate on what he finds, female orgasm has become more and more of a mystery, at the same time as it has been exalted as a duty. Its actual nature has become a matter for metaphysical speculation. All kinds of false ideas are still in circulation about women, although they were disproved years ago; many men refuse to relinquish the notion of female ejaculation, which, although it has a long and prestigious history, is utterly fanciful.

Part of the modesty about the female genitalia stems from actual distaste. The worst name anyone can be called is *cunt*. The best thing a cunt can be is small and unobtrusive: the anxiety about the bigness of the penis is only equaled by anxiety about the smallness of the cunt. No woman wants to find out that she has a twat like a horse-collar: she hopes she is not sloppy or smelly, and obligingly obliterates all signs of her menstruation in the cause of public decency. Women were not always so reticent: in ballad literature we can find lovely examples of women vaunting their genitals, like the lusty wench who admonished a timid tailor in round terms because he did not dare measure her fringed purse with his yard:

> You'l find the purse so deep,
> You'l hardly come to the treasure.

. . . Early gynecology was entirely in the hands of men, some of whom, like Samuel Collins, described the vagina so lovingly that any woman who read his words would have been greatly cheered. Of course such books were not meant to be seen by women at all. He speaks of the vagina as the Temple of Venus and the *mons veneris* as Venus's cushion. . . .

Collins's description is an active one: the vagina *speaks, throws,* is *tense* and *vigorous.* He and his contemporaries assumed that young women were even more eager for intercourse than young men. Some of the terms they used to describe the tissues of the female genitalia in action are very informative and exact, although unscientific. The vagina is said to be lined "with tunicles like the petals of a full-blown rose," with "Wrinckle on wrinckle" which "do give delight in Copulations." The vagina was classified as "sensitive enough," which is an exact description. They were aware of the special role of the clitoris, in causing the "sweetness of love" and the "fury of venery."

The notion that healthy and well-adjusted women would have orgasms originating in the vagina was a metaphysical interpolation in the empirical observations of these pioneers. Collins took the clitoris for granted, as a dear part of a beloved organ; he did not underemphasize the role of the vagina in creating pleasure, as we have seen. Unhappily we have accepted, along with the reinstatement of the clitoris after its proscription by the Freudians, a notion of the utter passivity and even irrelevance of the vagina. Love-making has become another male skill, of which women are the judges. The skills that the Wife of Bath used to make her husbands swink, the athletic sphincters of the Tahitian girls who can keep their men inside them all night, are alike unknown to us. All the vulgar linguistic emphasis is placed upon the *poking* element; *fucking, screwing, rooting, shagging* are all acts performed upon the passive female: the names for the penis are all *tool* names. . . .

Serious attempts have been made to increase women's participation in copulation. A. H. Kegel, teaching women how to overcome the bladder weakness that often afflicts women, showed them how to exercise the pubococcygeal muscles and found inadvertently that this increased their sexual enjoyment. What their mates thought of it is not on record. The incontinence resulted from the same suppression of activity that inhibited sexual pleasure; we might find that if we restored women's competence in managing their own musculature many of their pelvic disturbances would cease, and their sexual enjoyment might correspondingly grow. Of course we cannot do this until we find out how the pelvis ought to operate: as long as women cannot operate it, we cannot observe its action, and so the circle perpetuates itself. If the right chain reaction could happen, women might find that the clitoris was more directly involved in intercourse, and could be brought to climax by a less pompous and deliberate way than digital massage. In any case, women will have to accept part of the responsibility for their own and their partners' enjoyment, and this involves a measure of control and conscious cooperation. Part of the battle will be won if they can change their attitude towards sex, and embrace and stimulate the penis instead of *taking* it. Enlightened women have long sung the praises of the female superior position, because they are not weighted down by the heavier male body, and can respond more spontaneously. It is after all a question of communication, and communication is not advanced by the *he talk, me listen* formula.

The banishment of the fantasy of the vaginal orgasm is ultimately a service, but the substitution of the clitoral spasm for genuine gratification may turn out to be a disaster for sexuality. Masters and Johnson's conclusions have produced some unlooked for side-effects, like the veritable clitoromania which infects Mette Ejlersen's book, *I accuse!* While speaking of women's orgasms as resulting from the "right touches on the button," she condemns sexologists who

> recommend . . . the stimulation of the clitoris as part of the prelude to intercourse, to that which most men consider to be the "real thing." What is in fact the "real thing" for them is *completely devoid of sensation* for the woman.
>
> This is the heart of the matter! Concealed for hundreds of years by humble, shy and subservient women.

Not all the women in history have been humble and subservient to such an extent. It is nonsense to say that a woman feels nothing when a man is moving his penis in her vagina: the orgasm is qualitatively different when the vagina can undulate around the penis instead of vacancy. The differentiation between the simple inevitable pleasure of men and the tricky responses of women is not altogether valid. If ejaculation meant release for all men, given the constant manufacture of sperm and the resultant pressure to have intercourse, men could copulate without transport or disappointment with anyone. The process described by the experts, in which man dutifully does the rounds of the erogenous zones, spends an equal amount of time on each nipple, turns his attention to the clitoris (usually too directly), leads through the stages of digital or lingual stimulation, and then politely lets himself into the vagina, perhaps waiting until the retraction of the clitoris tells him that he is welcome, is laborious and inhumanly computerized. The implication that there is a statistically ideal fuck which will always result in satisfaction if the right procedures are followed is depressing and misleading. There is no substitute for excitement: not all the massage in the world will insure satisfaction, for it is a matter of psychosexual release. Real satisfaction is not enshrined in a tiny cluster of nerves but in the sexual involvement of the whole person. Women's continued high enjoyment of sex, which continues after orgasm, observed by men with wonder, is not based on the clitoris, which does not respond particularly well to continued stimulus, but in a general sensual response. If we localize female response in the clitoris we impose upon women the same limitation of sex which has stunted the male's response. The male sexual idea of virility without languor or amorousness is profoundly desolating: when the release is expressed in mechanical terms it is sought mechanically. Sex becomes masturbation in the vagina.

Many women who greeted the conclusions of Masters and Johnson with cries of "I told you so!" and "I am normal!" will feel that this criticism is a betrayal. They have discovered sexual pleasure after being denied it but the fact that they have only ever experienced gratification from clitoral stimulation is evidence for my case, because it is the index of the desexualization of the whole body, the substitution of genitality for sexuality. The ideal marriage as measured by the electronic equipment in the Reproductive Biology Research Foundation laboratories is enfeebled—dull sex for dull people. The sexual personality is basically antiauthoritarian. If the system wishes to enforce complete suggestibility in its subjects, it will have to tame sex. Masters and Johnson supplied the blueprint for standard, low-agitation, cool-out monogamy. If women are to avoid this last reduction of their humanity, they must hold out not just for orgasm but for ecstasy.

BOSTON WOMEN'S HEALTH BOOK COLLECTIVE

Our Bodies, Ourselves

A women's health movement developed in the 1970s in response to overwhelming dissatisfaction with the traditional health care system. One knowledgeable estimate is that there were about 1,200 women's health groups nationwide by 1973.[1] Believing that control over women's bodies had been usurped by the male-dominated, profit-oriented health establishment, the groups' overall goal was for women to reclaim the power to define their own physical needs and wishes. The table of contents of the 1978 anthology *Seizing Our Bodies* exemplifies this goal; it includes articles titled "The Theft of Childbirth," "The Epidemic in Unnecessary Hysterectomy," "What Doctors Won't Tell You About Menopause," and "The Dangers of Oral Contraception."[2]

Before long, women had created a thriving alternative health network offering education, care, and support services of all sorts. A few groups helped to arrange for and even performed illegal abortions. The collective "Jane," in Chicago, the most active in this field, assisted in terminating some 11,000 pregnancies over a four-year period before the legalization of abortion—with an excellent safety record.[3]

The women's health movement also brought a burgeoning of interest in internal self-examination. Writer Ellen Frankfort de-

[1] Linda Gordon, *Woman's Body, Woman's Right* (1976; rev. ed., New York: Penguin, 1990), p. 442.

[2] Claudia Dreifus, ed., *Seizing Our Bodies: The Politics of Women's Health* (New York: Vintage, 1978). The articles referred to were written, respectively, by Adrienne Rich, Deborah Larned, Rosetta Reitz, and Barbara Seaman.

[3] Gordon, *Woman's Body*, p. 410.

scribed a session in a church basement conducted by members of the Los Angeles Feminist Women's Health Clinic and attended by some fifty women. One woman undressed, inserted a speculum into her vagina, and invited those present to view her cervix, instructing them in how to recognize pregnancy, infection, or other changes. "Once we became tuned in to our uterus," she said, "we saw we had great control." Commented Frankfort, "It was a little like having a blind person see for the first time—for what woman is not blind to her own insides?"[4]

But no project of the women's health movement was as influential as the phenomenally popular book produced by the twelve-member Boston Women's Health Book Collective, *Our Bodies, Ourselves*. Part how-to manual, part political action memo, part textbook, part inspirational literature—this book was simply one of a kind. Its publishing history tells the story: In 1970 it was issued by a New Left publishing firm, the New England Free Press, and with a minimum of promotion and a minuscule ad budget, it sold a quarter of a million copies by 1973. The collective then agreed to let Simon & Schuster publish the book on condition that the authors would retain editorial control and that nonprofit health centers could purchase copies at a substantial discount. The collective has remained nearly unchanged over the decades and regularly revises the book. Sales to date exceed 3 million copies internationally, and profits go to a variety of women's health ventures.

The first edition of *Our Bodies, Ourselves* presented down-to-earth information on heterosexuality, lesbian experience, nutrition, sports and exercise, venereal disease, birth control, abortion, childbearing, and menopause. It discussed overcoming low self-esteem, rediscovering anger, living in a marriage and as a single woman. It gave advice on how to maneuver the American health care system, with subsections called "The Power and Role of Male Doctors," "The Profit Motive in Health Care," "Women as Health Care Workers," and "Hospitals."

---

[4]Ellen Frankfort, *Vaginal Politics* (New York: Quadrangle, 1972), p. xii.

The selection here is from the preface and the chapter on childbearing in the first Simon & Schuster edition (1973).

Preface

THE HISTORY OF THIS BOOK, *Our Bodies, Ourselves,* is lengthy and satisfying.

It began at a small discussion group on "women and their bodies" which was part of a women's conference held in Boston in the spring of 1969. These were the early days of the women's movement, one of the first gatherings of women meeting specifically to talk with other women. For many of us it was the very first time we got together with other women to talk and think about our lives and what we could do about them. Before the conference was over some of us decided to keep on meeting as a group to continue the discussion, and so we did.

In the beginning we called the group "the doctor's group." We had all experienced similar feelings of frustration and anger toward specific doctors and the medical maze in general, and initially we wanted to do something about those doctors who were condescending, paternalistic, judgmental, and non-informative. As we talked and shared our experiences with one another, we realized just how much we had to learn about our bodies. So we decided on a summer project—to research those topics which we felt were particularly pertinent to learning about our bodies, to discuss in the group what we had learned, then to write papers individually or in small groups of two or three, and finally to present the results in the fall as a course for women on women and their bodies.

As we developed the course we realized more and more that we were really capable of collecting, understanding, and evaluating medical information. Together we evaluated our reading of books and journals, our talks with doctors and friends who were medical students. We found we could discuss, question, and argue with each other in a new spirit of cooperation rather than competition. We were equally struck by how important it was for us to be able to open up with one another and share our feelings about our bodies. The process of talking was as crucial as the facts themselves. Over time the facts and feelings melted together in ways that touched us very deeply, and that is re-flected in the changing titles of the course and then the book—from *Women and Their Bodies* to *Women and Our Bodies* to, finally, *Our Bodies, Ourselves*.

When we gave the course we met in any available free space we could get—in day schools, in nursery schools, in churches, in our homes. We expected the course to stimulate the same kind of talking and sharing that we who had prepared the course had experienced. We had something to say, but we had a lot to learn as well; we did not want a traditional teacher-student relation-ship. At the end of ten to twelve sesions—which roughly cov-ered the material in the current book—we found that many women felt both eager and competent to get together in small groups and share what they had learned with other women. We saw it as a never-ending process always involving more and more women.

After the first teaching of the course, we decided to revise our initial papers and mimeograph them so that other women could have copies as the course expanded. Eventually we got them printed and bound together in an inexpensive edition published by the New England Free Press. It was fascinating and very ex-citing for us to see what a constant demand there was for our book. It came out in several editions, a larger number being printed each time, and the time from one printing to the next becoming shorter. The growing volume of requests began to strain the staff of the New England Free Press. Since our book was clearly speaking to many people, we wanted to reach be-yond the audience who lived in the area or who were acquainted with the New England Free Press. For wider distribution it made sense to publish our book commercially.

You may want to know who we are. We are white, our ages range from twenty-four to forty, most of us are from middle-class backgrounds and have had at least some college education, and some of us have professional degrees. Some of us are married, some of us are separated, and some of us are single. Some of us have children of our own, some of us like spending time with children, and others of us are not sure we want to be with children. In short, we are both a very ordinary and a very special group, as women are everywhere. We are white middle-class women, and as such can describe only what life has been for us. But we do realize that poor women and non-white women have suffered far more from the kinds of misinformation and mistreatment that we are describing in this book. In some ways, learning about our womanhood from the inside out has allowed us to cross over the socially created barriers of race, color, income, and class, and to feel a sense of identity with all women in the experience of being female.

We are twelve individuals and we are a group. (The group has been ongoing for three years and some of us have been together since the beginning. Others came in at later points. Our current collective has been together for one year.) We know each other well—our weaknesses as well as our strengths. We have learned through good times and bad how to work together (and how not to as well). We recognize our similarities and differences and are learning to respect each person for her uniqueness. We love each other.

Many, many other women have worked with us on the book. A group of gay women got together specifically to do the chapter on lesbianism. Other papers were done still differently. For instance, along with some friends the mother of one woman in the group volunteered to work on menopause with some of us who have not gone through that experience ourselves. Other women contributed thoughts, feelings and comments as they passed through town or passed through our kitchens or workrooms. There are still other voices from letters, phone conversations, a variety of discussions, etc., that are included in the chapters as excerpts of personal experiences. Many women have spoken for themselves in this book, though we in the collective do not agree with all that has been written. Some of us are even uncomfortable with part of the material. We have included it anyway, because we give more weight to accepting that we differ than to our uneasiness. We have been asked why this is exclusively a book about women, why we have restricted our course to women. Our answer is that we are women and, as women, do not consider ourselves experts on men (as men through the centuries have presumed to be experts on us). We are not implying that we think most twentieth-century men are much less alienated from their bodies than women are. But we know it is up to men to explore that for themselves, to come together and share their sense of themselves as we have done. We would like to read a book about men and their bodies.

We are offering a book that can be used in many different ways—individually, in a group, for a course. Our book contains real material about our bodies and ourselves that isn't available elsewhere, and we have tried to present it in a new way—an honest, humane, and powerful way of thinking about ourselves and our lives. We want to share the knowledge and power that comes with this way of thinking and we want to share the feelings we have for each other—supportive and loving feelings that show we can indeed help one another grow.

From the very beginning of working together, first on the course that led to this book and then on the book itself, we have felt exhilarated and energized by our new knowledge. Finding out about our bodies and our bodies' needs, starting to take control over that area of our lives, has released for us an energy that has overflowed into our work, our friendships, our relationships with men and women, for some of us our marriages and our parenthood. In trying to figure out why this has had such a life-changing effect on us, we have come up with several important ways in which this kind of body education has been liberating for us and may be a starting point for the liberation of many other women.

First, we learned what we learned equally from professional sources—textbooks, medical journals, doctors, nurses—and from our own experiences. The facts were important, and we did careful research to get the information we had not had in the past. As we brought the facts to one another we learned a good deal, but in sharing our personal experiences relating to those facts we learned still more. Once we had learned what the "experts" had to tell us, we found that we still had a lot to teach and to learn from one another. For instance, many of us had "learned" about the menstrual cycle in science or biology classes—we had perhaps even memorized the names of the menstrual hormones and what they did. But most of us did not remember much of what we had learned. This time when we read in a text that the onset of menstruation is a normal and universal occurrence in young girls from ages ten to eighteen, we started to talk about our first menstrual periods. We found that, for many of us, beginning to menstruate had not felt normal at all, but scary, embarrassing, mysterious. We realized that what we had been told about menstruation and what we had not been told, even the tone of voice it had been told in—all had had an effect on our feelings about being female. Similarly, the information from enlightened texts describing masturbation as a normal, common sexual activity did not really become our own until we began to pull up from inside ourselves and share what we had never before expressed—the confusion and shame we had been made to feel, and often still felt, about touching our bodies in a sexual way.

Learning about our bodies in this way really turned us on. This is an exciting kind of learning, where information and feelings are allowed to interact. It has made the difference between rote memorization and relevant learning, between fragmented pieces of a puzzle and the integrated picture, between abstractions and real knowledge. We discovered that you don't learn very much when you are just a passive recipient of information. We found that each individual's response to information is valid and useful, and that by sharing our responses we can develop a base on which to be critical of what the experts tell us. Whatever we need to learn now, in whatever area of our life, we know more how to go about it.

A second important result of this kind of learning has been that we are better prepared to evaluate the institutions that are supposed to meet our health needs—the hospitals, clinics, doctors, medical schools, nursing schools, public health departments, Medicaid bureaucracies, and so on. For some of us it was the first time we had looked critically, and with strength, at the existing institutions serving us. The experience of learning just how little control we had over our lives and bodies, the coming together out of isolation to learn from each other in order to define what we needed, and the experience of supporting one another in demanding the changes that grew out of our developing critique—all were crucial and formative political experiences for us. We have felt our potential power as a force for political and social change.

The learning we have done while working on *Our Bodies, Ourselves* has been such a good basis for growth in other areas of life for still another reason. For women throughout the centuries, ignorance about our bodies has had one major consequence—pregnancy. Until very recently pregnancies were all but inevitable, biology *was* our destiny—that is, because our bodies are designed to get pregnant and give birth and lactate, that is what all or most of us did. The courageous and dedicated work of people like Margaret Sanger started in the early twentieth century to spread and make available birth control methods that women could use, thereby freeing us from the traditional lifetime of pregnancies. But the societal expectation that a woman above all else will have babies does not die easily. When we first started talking to each other about this we found that that old expectation had nudged most of us into a fairly rigid role of wife and motherhood from the moment we were born female. Even in 1969, when we first started the work that led to this book, we found that many of us were still getting pregnant when we didn't want to. It was not until we researched carefully and learned more about our reproductive systems, about birth-control methods and abortion, about laws governing birth-control and abortion, not until we put all this information together with what it meant to us to be female, did we begin to feel that we could truly set out to control whether and when we would have babies.

This knowledge has freed us to a certain extent from the constant, energy-draining anxiety about becoming pregnant. It has made our pregnancies better, because they no longer happen to us; we actively choose them and enthusiastically participate in them. It has made our parenthood better, because it is our choice rather than our destiny. This knowledge has freed us from playing the role of mother if it is not a role that fits us. It has given us a sense of a larger life space to work in, an invigorating and challenging sense of time and room to discover the energies and talents that are in us, to do the work we want to do. And one of the things we most want to do is to help make this freedom of choice, this life space, available to every woman. That is why people in the women's movement have been so active in fighting against the inhumane legal restrictions, the imperfections of available contraceptives, the poor sex education, the highly priced and poorly administered health care that keeps too many women from having this crucial control over their bodies.

There is a fourth reason why knowledge about our bodies has generated so much new energy. For us, body education is core education. Our bodies are the physical bases from which we move out into the world; ignorance, uncertainty—even, at worst, shame—about our physical selves create in us an alienation from ourselves that keeps us from being the whole people that we could be. Picture a woman trying to do work and to enter into equal and satisfying relationships with other people—when she feels physically weak because she has never tried to be strong; when she drains her energy trying to change her face, her figure, her hair, her smells, to match some ideal norm set by magazines, movies, and TV; when she feels confused and ashamed of the menstrual blood that every month appears from some dark place in her body; when her internal body processes are a mystery to her and surface only to cause her trouble (an unplanned pregnancy, or cervical cancer); when she does not understand nor enjoy sex and concentrates her sexual drives into aimless romantic fantasies, perverting and misusing a potential energy because she has been brought up to deny it. Learning to understand, accept, and be responsible for our physical selves, we are freed of some of these preoccupations and can start to use our untapped energies. Our image of ourselves is on a firmer base, we can be better friends and better lovers, better *people*, more self-confident, more autonomous, stronger, and more whole.

Childbearing

WE WANT TO UNDERSTAND our childbearing experience. We literally have been kept in the dark about what we can expect physically and emotionally when we conceive and give birth to our children.

We have needs that are not being met. One great need we have is to experience our childbearing year as a continuum. This continuum begins with conception and our decision to carry our child to term. It includes pregnancy, labor, and delivery, the period immediately after our child is born and the postpartum period. (Adjustments may last up to a year or more after birth.) We have a great need for knowledgeable medical care, which begins early in pregnancy and sometimes continues for several months after our child is born. And we need personal support, one or more people to be with us and support us throughout the whole cycle.

The present medical system doesn't provide for these needs. Pretending to help us, it tends to interfere with natural processes. For instance, doctors and hospitals have set what to us are artificial boundaries. Each period of childbearing is handled by a different set of "experts." During our pregnancy we see one private doctor or a series of doctors or nurses in a clinic. We might deliver our baby with someone we know or with someone we've never seen before. After the birth we're cared for by a new set of attendants and nurses, while our baby will have his or her own doctor. When we come home we don't have a doctor anymore, and we care for ourselves or depend on family or friends. So an experience that could be a unified one is all broken up. We begin to rely on one person or set of people, then we are shunted to another set.

In this country we are denied control over our own very personal childbearing experience. Childbirth, which could be as much a part of our everyday lives as pregnancy and child care, is removed to an unfamiliar place for sick people. There we are separated at a crucial time from family and friends. We and our present children suffer from this sudden removal; to our children it's a mysterious absence. In the hospital we are depersonalized; usually our clothes and personal effects, down to glasses and hairpins, are taken away. We lose our identity. We are expected to be passive and acquiescent and to make no trouble. (Passivity is considered a sign of maturity.) We are expected to depend not on ourselves but on doctors. Most often for the doctor's convenience, we are given drugs to "ease" our labor. (We have let ourselves be convinced by doctors who have never experienced labor and by our unprepared frightened forebears that our labor will be too painful to bear.) After our baby is born s/he is taken away for an hour, for a day, or longer. We pay a lot of money for our hospital space, sometimes more than we can afford.

Our obstetricians are trained mainly to deal with complications of childbirth. "Well," we say, "you never know. Something might happen. We need our doctor." We are afraid on many levels. We have been taught to have very little confidence in ourselves, our bodies, in other women's experience. In fact, 95 percent of our deliveries are normal. Most of us could very easily give birth with the experience and help of a trained midwife, either in a hospital, a special maternity house, or at home among family and friends. However, emergency equipment must be present or ready.

We want to improve maternity care for ourselves and all women by calling into question the present care we receive. This care interferes with the rhythm of our lives. It turns us into objects. We want to be able to choose where and how we have our babies. We want adequate flexible medical institutions that correspond to our needs. . . .

Childbirth preparation means educating ourselves about what is likely to happen to our bodies, our minds, and our lives during the childbirth experience. It also means finding someone—husband, friend, or relative—to share this period with us.

It is certainly not impossible to go through pregnancy, child-birth, and motherhood alone and unprepared, but it is difficult and unnecessary.

Above all, we must try not to be alone during labor. The companion we choose (early in our pregnancy) should be read-ing the same books, attending the same classes, and learning the same exercises and breathing techniques as we are. This person will serve as our coach during labor, and will stay with us throughout the entire birth process. Often the baby's father will be our coach. Sharing the labor experience and witnessing the birth with him is an important beginning to sharing the respon-sibilities and joys of parenthood. Some of us want to be with an-other woman during labor. We will find it most helpful to have as coach a woman who has already given birth. She will be able to support us with her firsthand knowledge, and her presence is a witness to the fact that it can be done . . .

However, there are hospitals that will allow only a registered nurse to be with you during labor, and many hospitals will not allow any outsider into the delivery room. We must work to change these rules, but until they are eliminated, search around until you find a doctor and a hospital that meet your require-ments. Be particular, and make all the demands you feel are nec-essary to your best interests and your baby's security.

Prepared childbirth is often called natural childbirth. The only thing natural is that a woman's body is biologically equipped to bear and give birth to children. This doesn't mean that we have to have children or that we shouldn't be able to choose when we want to have children. It also doesn't mean that we should go through childbirth without preparation. Although much of our society considers it normal for us to have our ba-bies while heavily drugged, in helpless ignorance and pain, and totally dependent on the medical profession, we believe it is much more natural for us to want to know what is happening to our bodies during labor. We want to give birth to our babies with confidence.

We are trying to find a way to have our babies safely and with dignity. The concept of dignity in labor was made popular in the West by two obstetricians. In 1932 Dr. Grantly Dick-Read, an Englishman, first introduced a method of concentrated relaxation during labor with the publication of his book *Childbirth Without Fear*. He understood that fear causes tension, and tension causes pain. Thus his approach was to try to eliminate the fear of labor through education and exercise. A French doctor, Fernand Lamaze, offered a different idea, called the psychoprophylactic method for childbirth. Lamaze asked that women respond actively to labor contractions with a set of prelearned, controlled breathing techniques. As the intensity of the contraction increased, so would the woman's rate of breathing. As a result, the laboring woman's posture and attitude changed. She was no longer flat on her back, to be pitied by all onlookers: now she was active, changing positions and breathing patterns as she knew she must. The onlookers cheered.

Marjorie Karmel introduced the Lamaze method of childbirth to the United States with her book *Thank You, Dr. Lamaze,* published in 1959. She had had her first child delivered in Paris by Dr. Lamaze, and when she returned to the States and tried to have her second child delivered by the same method, she ran into tremendous opposition and a great deal of ignorance on the part of doctors here. Mrs. Karmel finally joined with Elisabeth Bing, a physical therapist from Berlin, and founded the American Society for Psychoprophylaxis in Obstetrics (ASPO). The purpose of this society was to train doctors, nurses, and expectant parents in prepared childbirth techniques.

Now there are childbirth-preparation classes in every major city in the United States . . . There are also many books, articles, and films on the subject. . . . Yet, as with everything else in our impersonal society, neither the classes nor the books will meet our very individual needs unless we demand that they do. Many of the classes are too large, sometimes with ten to twenty couples attending at a time. So it's often difficult to learn more than just the fundamentals, such as basic anatomy and routine breathing techniques. These are essential to a prepared delivery, but they are sometimes not enough. If you look for them, you can usually find smaller, more personal classes, and the fee is generally the same as the fee for the larger, group classes. However, in either case the fee is higher than many women or couples can afford.

Furthermore, although physical preparation is necessary, psychological and emotional preparation can sometimes be more important. Often large classes are not conducive to discussions of personal problems. People should have the opportunity to talk to each other about all phases of childbearing, from the original decision to conceive a child to the all-too-neglected fears and feelings about child raising. Ideally there should be voluntary, free classes open to anyone who feels the need to talk to other people about any aspect of pregnancy and parenthood. Since these classes are nonexistent in most communities, we must organize ourselves to get them started if we want them.

It's up to us to seek the support we need. Until the time when we can persuade the medical profession to give us less mechanized care, we will have to find all the help we need from each other. But it's often hard to find each other! One way is to ask doctors and hospitals to provide us with the names of the pregnant women they are seeing. They cooperate with diaper services, so why shouldn't they cooperate with us? A way to find the names of women in your area who have just delivered babies is to check the town and state registries of births.

Once we have the people, we must have a place to meet. Hospitals and community centers can provide us with meeting rooms. As for books and teachers, one source is the department of public education. Information about pregnancy and childbirth is so vitally important to so many of us that we have the right to ask that it be supported by public funds. Surely if the state department of education can pay the salary of a person who teaches cake decorating in an adult education class, we might expect it to pay a teacher to prepare us for childbirth.

So far we haven't said anything about avoiding the hospital altogether by having our babies at home . . . In the United States almost all of us are hospitalized for delivery. In England there is an extensive system of midwives and traveling emergency units which makes home delivery routine, and it is often only the special case that is delivered in a hospital with an attending obstetrician. In the United States we have no such system, and thus home delivery can indeed be very risky. We feel that one of our demands must be to make home delivery feasible here in America. Many women have already experienced successful home deliveries, some with their doctor's help, and many without it. In northern California there is apparently a movement afoot to convince doctors to participate in deliveries at home. Some doctors themselves are behind this movement. However, until our society is willing to break up the hospital's monopoly on safe deliveries by financing small traveling oxygen and emergency-equipment units for use at home, every woman must decide between hospital and home with . . . eyes wide open to the dangers as well as the joys.

VI

Working for Change

EQUAL RIGHTS AMENDMENT

An Equal Rights Amendment (ERA) to the U.S. Constitution was proposed in 1923 by members of the National Woman's Party, originally a militant suffrage organization. It was first introduced in Congress that year, and the seemingly indefatigable ex-suffragists caused the amendment to be reintroduced every succeeding year—through the twenties, thirties, forties, fifties, and sixties—without success. Even the 1963 report of the President's Commission on the Status of Women did not back the ERA, because organized labor—a strong voice on the commission—considered the measure a threat to various state laws meant to protect the health and safety of women workers.

Shortly after the founding of NOW, Betty Friedan proposed that the fledgling organization endorse the ERA. But when she broached the issue at NOW's national convention in 1967, some of those present warned that supporting the ERA might cost NOW the aid of labor unions, which it could ill afford to lose. However, Friedan stood firm. She was convinced that in backing the ERA, NOW would forge "the crucial generational links between the century-long battle for women's rights that was our past and the young women who were the future." She later observed that when "those very old suffragettes sitting in the front row" addressed the NOW meeting in support of the ERA, "they *spoke to* those very young women who had never heard of it before."[1] The NOW convention voted to take a pro-ERA stand, and the director of the Women's Department of the

---

[1]Betty Friedan, *It Changed My Life: Writings on the Women's Movement* (New York: Norton, 1976), pp. 104–105.

United Auto Workers, Caroline Davis, promptly resigned as secretary-treasurer of NOW.

A series of successful NOW actions in Washington in behalf of the ERA in early 1970 helped persuade Representative Martha Griffiths, Democrat of Michigan, to attempt to pry the amendment out of the Judiciary Committee and onto the floor of the House—a maneuver that required Griffiths's considerable tactical skill and the assistance of feminist cadre around the country. By this time federal courts had voided many state protective labor laws as discriminatory under the terms of Title VII, clearing the way for labor to drop its long opposition to the amendment. The United Auto Workers became the first major national union to endorse the ERA. Labor's support plus a tremendous volume of telephone calls and telegrams from female constituents encouraged the House to pass the measure handily, 350 to 15, but it was subsequently defeated in the Senate. The House reconsidered in 1971 and again overwhelmingly approved the amendment, 354 to 23. As the Senate prepared to vote in 1972, feminists mounted a nationwide campaign of impressive dimension—"Capitol Hill veterans were gasping, 'I've never seen anything like it in all my years here,' " wrote one reporter[2]—and the amendment was approved 84 to 8.

Final adoption of a constitutional amendment required one more step: ratification by a minimum of thirty-eight states. But as June 30, 1982—the ultimate deadline for the ERA—approached, only thirty-five states had ratified. Proponents had put together a powerful coalition of pro-ERA organizations, and polls showed that a majority of Americans favored the amendment. But opponents—mainly religious and political conservatives—had managed to convince many people that the measure threatened traditional lifestyles. Their scare tactics included warnings that the ERA would force housewives to provide half of the family income, would draft women into the armed forces and put them into combat, would deny divorced women alimony and child support, and would bring about single-

[2]Isabelle Shelton in the Washington *Star;* quoted in Flora Davis, *Moving the Mountain* (New York: Simon & Schuster, 1991), p. 134.

sex toilets. In the end, the holdout state legislatures could not be turned around, and the ERA went down to defeat.

Why was the ERA important enough to several generations of American feminists to warrant the immense effort expended on it? Up until the time the amendment was passed by the Senate in 1972, feminists believed that a constitutional guarantee of equality to women would eliminate in a single stroke a host of discriminatory laws and practices. However, by the end of the bitterly disappointing decade-long fight for the ERA's ratification, most of the objectionable statutes had already been struck down one by one. The amendment then represented a need that was more symbolic than practical: To most women it seemed a matter of simple justice and self-respect that the keystone of the nation's legal edifice should extend to female citizens the same protection and rights as it offered to male citizens.

The text of the amendment passed by Congress in 1972 follows.

Section I: Equality of Rights under the law shall not be denied or abridged by the United States or any state on account of sex.

Section II: The Congress shall have the power to enforce, by appropriate legislation, the provisions of this article.

Section III: This amendment shall take effect two years after the date of ratification.

NEW YORK CITY COMMISSION ON HUMAN RIGHTS

Hearings on Women's Rights

ELEANOR HOLMES NORTON

A Strategy for Change

For five days in late September 1970, the chair of the New York City Commission on Human Rights, attorney Eleanor Holmes Norton (b. 1937), conducted an exceptional event: municipal hearings on the rights of women at which people from all walks of life testified. Over 150 individuals were heard, including such well-known figures as Kate Millett, lawyer Florynce Kennedy, anthropologist Margaret Mead, educators Florence Howe, Cynthia Fuchs Epstein, Ann Scott, and Mirra Komarovsky, Representative Shirley Chisholm (who would campaign in 1972 for the Democratic presidential nomination), and Pauli Murray—as well as dozens of ordinary citizens.

In her opening-day speech at the hearings—excerpted here—Norton delivered some straight talk about political strategies for women. Her comments on the Equal Rights Amendment were amazingly accurate; the possibility she envisaged—that the amendment would be defeated by "reactionary state legislators"—is exactly what occurred twelve years hence. The women's political coalition she urged was realized in 1972 with the formation of the National Women's Political Caucus.

Norton's subsequent political career included four years as President Jimmy Carter's appointee to head the Equal Employment Opportunity Commission (EEOC) and participation on the committee that drafted the 1988 Democratic Party platform.

In both these positions Norton was a staunch advocate for women. In her first bid for elective office, in 1990, Norton won a seat in Congress as the nonvoting delegate from the District of Columbia.

IF THESE HEARINGS ARE IMPORTANT for their attempt to be a comprehensive governmental inquiry into a subject not yet taken fully seriously by the public, they are nevertheless no occasion for either government or women to indulge in self-congratulation. The blame for the status of women has been laid almost everywhere in society—on government, on education, on employers, on men, indeed on women themselves. But in my view, the blame laid has been far too unspecific and rhetorical to ensure the kind of critique necessary to produce a strategy for change.

Women have done an unprecedented job in rapidly raising the issue of women's rights to that of a major issue of our time. It may be too much to expect that so indispensable and brilliant a job of consciousness-raising should be accompanied by an organized, rather than a hit-and-miss, strategy for change. But if change is to come, it must be pursued not in general but in its hard specifics and with the clarity of strategies that is all-required when a group seeks profound change.

As a city official most specifically charged with eliminating bias, and indeed as a woman participating in the women's struggle, I feel something of a duty to leave off celebrating the rise of this newly discovered issue today. Instead, I would like to use this occasion to offer a few suggested trial balloons regarding the critique and strategy I believe are missing from the women's-rights issue.

If we are to fully appreciate the need for a clear strategy, we must attempt to discern the tenacity of the problem. To underestimate its depth, to assume its evils have a self-evident quality, as I believe some of us have, is to lay the way for devastating failure.

No change in society has ever been seen or envisioned [that is] as deep as the prospect of equality of the sexes. None of the great revolutions has altered the most fundamental relationship of all, that between man and woman—not the abolition of classes envisioned by the great political and economic revolutionaries; not the spread of the great religions of the world; not the eradication of racial prejudice, for which we still toil. To alter the economic and political order, to be sure, is to change society very profoundly indeed. To erase the blight of racial bigotry is to rediscover the principles of both humanism and Judeo-Christian ethics. But basic as would be the changes, they would change society, not civilization, as sexual equality would. For the inequality of the sexes is the oldest inequality of all, preceding both class and racial discrimination and tapping us at our most vulnerable sources.

Thus, if we demand rapid changes in the status of women—and we most certainly do demand—we must nevertheless not misjudge the difficulty, thereby failing to develop real and lasting cures. Yet I believe we have already shown that we are new and tentative to the uses and ways of power. We have, to be sure, demonstrated the potential for awesome strength, as witnessed in the way we engendered the 350 to 15 vote in the House in favor of the women's [Equal] Rights Amendment. The leadership of Representative Martha Griffiths in that fight gave her colleagues a firsthand lesson in the proposition that political action knows no sex. . . .

But that victory is impressive precisely because it stands in such dramatic isolation. If we are serious and if we are to be taken seriously, we must demonstrate that the House Equal Rights Amendment vote was not merely an election-year quirk, or worse, a piece of political cynicism which congressmen and senators would be safe in supporting today because the reactionary state legislators, to whom the amendment must also go, would be more willing executioners tomorrow. I am afraid that, whatever happens, the Equal Rights Amendment will stand as inconclusive proof of our strength.

But there is a set of bills in Congress that can make the point of female strength unequivocally, expressly. Correlatively, the failure to pass these bills will make just the opposite point: that feminist power is a bluff, that we are still one more blunderbuss lobby, long on talking, short on truths. These bills include one that would give enforcement powers to the Equal Employment Opportunity Commission, the federal agency charged with regulating job opportunity based on sex, but lacking the muscle for cease and desist orders or enforcement in court which would make the EEOC more than the conciliation agency it has been ever since it was created under the 1964 Civil Rights Act. What 10 percent of the population cannot do by itself can surely be done by that much larger group who are women. Or can it? Those who are astute at judging political strength will be looking to see.

The same can be said of our attempt to cover teachers and professors now exempted from the federal job discrimination law. This is a crucial test for us because teachers are overwhelmingly female and administrators overwhelmingly male in a field where job discrimination based on sex appears clear.

And there are other important bills that we must get through, or admit to being something less than a full-fledged movement. We have demanded universal free child care, but we have not been able to get a bill that will extend a child care service to all classes.

Further, Congresswoman Griffiths's bill to eliminate discrimination against working wives under Social Security has yet to garner real support. And that formidable lobby, the American Legion, has let die—if it ever noticed—the bill to grant equality of treatment to married women who are members of the armed forces.

I do not cite these bills simply to be informative. I cite them because I believe that together they constitute a critical test of strength for women. I would be less than frank if I simply urged us to work for these and other bills instead of acknowledging what I believe to be the truth: that we are not fully equipped to meet this or any other notable legislative challenge. I am prepared to admit that having been for so long denied access to power, women have used power haphazardly, clumsily, or, more often, not at all.

For example, women slept through the critical issue of tax reform in 1969 when every petty corporation and vested interest was lobbying in Washington for tax advantages. In an economy in which free child care facilities for all are surely not just around the corner, women should have sought and could have gotten a tax deduction for child care expenses comparable to the business expense deduction that constitutes an often-abused tax break for men who work.

It is scandalous that the law would afford lavish, liberal tax breaks for most expenses incurred by businessmen while denying businesswomen, except for a small number in the lowest income brackets, any tax break for child care expenses. It is equally scandalous that women would abide such treatment. A business deal may well go through without the endless martinis which the federal government allows businessmen to write off. But a woman can consummate no deal, indeed she cannot even work, unless she also can find a means to pay for the care of her children. Our call for job equality and our laws affording us that right are empty frills if we fail to get a tax break and child care facilities, without which working is impossible for millions of women.

What do women need to do to avoid mistakes such as our tax blunders? How can we establish ourselves as a force in American politics?

I believe we must forge a women's political coalition equal in its competence, professionalism, and drive to any lobby the Congress has ever seen. . . . The difference between a women's political coalition and our present lobbying efforts is simple. Such a coalition would signal the inauguration of a unified strategy for achieving women's announced goals. It is unfair to leave the achievement of these goals to a few valiant sisters who labor at hard political tasks while the rest of us rap away at consciousness-raising sessions. Rap sessions are critical, and they must continue if we are to undo thousands of years of damage to ourselves. But it is too late to neatly divide our thrust into compartments—so many years to raise our collective consciousness, so many years to pursue our goals. If women do not demand concrete results simultaneously with ideological conversion, they will be the first exploited group I know to be so patient or so foolish.

It may seem strange that I, as an appointed rather than an elected official, should stress a women's political coalition. And after all, I am in an administrative agency, enforcing the law, not in the political area where the law is made. But it is precisely this experience that led me to believe that women must move politically in a better-organized, more systematic, and more knowledgeable fashion. . . .

The Commission on Human Rights has had only about forty cases alleging sex discrimination in the last twelve months, and this despite women's efforts at consciousness-raising and a multitude of other activities that should have spurred complaints. When a law is so clearly underused, the conclusion is inescapable—the law in many respects is ahead of women's consciousness, at least in this city.

I can but challenge women to come forward just as blacks and Puerto Ricans have come forward. Identify yourselves as a discriminated-against group and pursue your rights with vigor. I call for the women's political coalition because much of the law I administer will be incapable of vigorous enforcement if women do not achieve other political gains unrelated to the city's human rights law.

For example, women must be freed from constant child care if the law against discrimination based on sex is to be a truly effective instrument of equality. We have sought to dramatize this point by opening a drop-in child care center here during this week of hearings, with the certain knowledge that many women would be unable to come to learn of their role in contemporary American society without such a facility available, just as millions cannot work for lack of such facilities. Only a women's political coalition will be able to marshal the effort to convince a skeptical public that women are a uniquely exploited group in this and so many other ways.

It is time we left off decrying the ignorant myths that surround our status and organize to defeat them. Eight million women heads of families need to join the struggle for women's rights, to take to task that large segment of the public who believe women work for pin money; so do the 84 percent of mothers who, though living with their husbands, must work to supplement low male wages; so do the one-third of working mothers who go to work, though they have children under six years of age and no adequate child care facilities.

Working and union women who have won millions of dollars in back pay for unequal wages received for doing the same work as men need to tell it and join the women's struggle to banish wage inequality. And trade union sisters who have sued to nullify weight-lifting and overtime laws aimed at women need to challenge the unions to represent them equally with men. The union movement I was taught to revere—the movement of Debs, Reuther, of Randolph—is surely ashamed that so many unions have been joined as defendants with employers who denied women equal advancement opportunities.

Another deadly myth that traps us, or sometimes fulfills its own prophecy, is that job turnover of women's work is greater than men's. A recent study revealed that sex and job turnover are not related; rather, the correlation is between low status and turnover. Compared by job level, women leave their jobs less frequently than men. And I am sure it will astound many women to learn that women have fewer absences than men, even counting absences for pregnancies and absences to take care of children. Only by organizing women can we break the hold of these old myths.

There is one myth that troubles me personally as much as all the rest, and that is the myth that somehow black women are not a part of the struggle for women's rights but belong exclusively to the movement for black liberation. That cannot be. For black women are preeminently working women who have borne double oppression. Without day care facilities, almost half of all black mothers with preschool children work, compared with 28 percent of white mothers with preschool children. And once their children go to school, nearly 70 percent of black mothers go to work. Theirs are the lowest of wages. Fully 64 percent of women reporting their jobs as day workers or hourly workers—maids and laundresses—are black. These women need to join the struggle for women's rights and demand that part of our effort go to making women's work a dignified and well-paid work. . . .

We who are black have failed to develop our own issues in this struggle. Black sisters need to stop criticizing the white woman's struggle for being white, for it will only take on color if we who are black join it. It is hypocritical for us who are black to insist upon speaking for ourselves but to blame white women for articulating their needs, not ours.

Finally, black women need to spurn the rhetoric of those who would divide blacks from women, and who talk about whose cause has priority. No person's oppression has priority over another's. And I believe this to be the case, although it is clearly true that America reserved for black people a special form of oppression she kept from others. Slavery and its attendant racial prejudice is too awful a state of oppression to afford comparison. Yet those who insist upon meaningless talk of priorities of oppression are caught in a philosophical dilemma deeper than they appear to understand.

For example, using the logic of a comparative oppression, would they have black people compare their oppression in this country with the American Indians' to see who comes out first?—or last, whichever you prefer. How do you compare slavery with genocide? If we are to debate blacks versus women, perhaps we should also debate blacks versus Puerto Ricans, with Puerto Ricans citing their worse statistics as to unemployment and education, and blacks citing their history as slaves. What an antihuman debate! How foreign to the humanism, mutual respect, and decency that must undergird every movement for justice. . . .

I realize that a broad and well-coordinated political coalition is not the answer to all women's problems. But surely it is a beginning. Women have raised profound, complex issues by striving to change women's status. We have thus made inevitable the necessity to work on every front, for no major area of life has remained untouched by sexual stereotypes.

If there is reason for blacks to join with women, there is reason for men to join as well. Our roles are no more rigid than yours; oppressive female stereotypes have their correlative in previous male stereotypes. We are none of us free.

BETTY FRIEDAN

Women's Rights and the Revolution of Rising Expectations

The hearings of the Human Rights Commission followed directly on the heels of the Women's Strike for Equality, the brainchild of Betty Friedan, who had called for it in her farewell address as president of NOW.

The strike was scheduled for a historic date—August 26, 1970, the fiftieth anniversary of the granting of the vote to women in the United States. In New York City, demonstrators with arms linked marched down Fifth Avenue, filling the broad thoroughfare from sidewalk to sidewalk. As seen by writer-activist Jo Freeman, the strike "marked a turning point for the whole women's liberation movement. It was the first time that the potential power of the movement became publicly apparent . . . Women turned out by the thousands in cities all over the country. The sheer numbers shocked everyone—including the organizers."[1]

Friedan's comments on the demonstration reprinted here are from her testimony before the New York City Commission.

---

[1]Jo Freeman, *The Politics of Women's Liberation* (New York: McKay, 1975), p. 84.

I SPEAK TO THE REVOLUTION OF RISING EXPECTATIONS of American women and of the women of New York as evidenced on Fifth Avenue, and in the streets of the city on August twenty-sixth, and in the streets of cities throughout the nation.

I think it is very important that in this city, which has pioneered in so many areas of vital social progress, that the truly revolutionary nature of the rising expectations of women will not be turned off or in any way met by the hiring of a token few—one or two women in a Wall Street office, the advancement of one or two token women to an executive position in any insurance company, publishing company, or corporation office in the city. The revolution of rising expectations of women of this city and country will only be met by full equality—full equality of opportunity in employment, in education, and in the restructuring of all institutions and professions in the world outside the home that have up until now been fully structured as man's world. This means, of course, also a restructuring of the home and of marriage and of childbearing. But we will table that for the moment.

These are not empty words. I think that you saw by the absolutely unexpected taking to the streets of women of this city— old women, young women, middle-class women, working women, mothers with babies—so many mothers with babies—the determination of women and the unity of women behind their demand for full equality of education and employment opportunities and for child care centers and for the right of control of their own bodies and reproductive processes. I think this spirit surprised everyone.

I would like to tell you a little of what I pieced together, not only from our own underground of women, which now I think stretches through every office in New York, but through what sort-of-amazed male employers have told me of some of the things that went on on that day and that show that we are in an absolutely different place now, where women are concerned.

One of the major magazines whose headquarters are in the city told me that in the three days before August twenty-sixth, for the first time women who worked the telephone and switch-boards, receptionists, secretaries, and a few editorial assistants began to talk to each other about their common grievances, began to realize that they all had a lot of unfinished business of equality and would leave together on the twenty-sixth to take to the streets for it. He said that at night the cleaning women came in, and suddenly he realized the cleaning women were people, too, and they began to talk in a completely different way about the wages they were paid and the jobs they were expected to do.

A man who is a director of another major institution in this city told me that on the morning of the twenty-sixth he was dic-tating a letter to his secretary, and his secretary looked at him, and she said, "I am taking dictation from you now, but that doesn't mean that this is all I can do or will do for the rest of my life. And I want you to understand that today."

And this is the spirit that I think we are going to have and must have from now on in the future of women. . . .

BERNICE SANDLER

Patterns of Discrimination and Discouragement in Higher Education

One of the more egregious shortcomings of Title VII of the Civil Rights Act of 1964 was the specific exclusion of educa-tional institutions from the law's provisions. This exclusion left female faculty members without any way of fighting employ-ment bias—at least until Bernice Sandler entered the fray.

Sandler, a psychologist teaching at the University of Mary-land in 1969, encountered problems in her own career that seemed attributable to gender discrimination. Searching for a means of seeking redress, she perused a federal executive order that President Lyndon Johnson had issued to eliminate discrimi-natory practices by federal contractors. From a footnote, she discovered that the order had been amended, effective October 1968—and that the little-known amendment forbade government contractors from discriminating on the basis of sex. Since most colleges and universities received federal funds, and since the executive order did not exempt educational institutions, Sandler thought it might be just what she needed.

When Sandler testified before the New York City Commission on Human Rights, she had already filed, under the auspices of the Women's Equity Action League (WEAL), a historic class action suit against all the colleges and universities in the nation holding federal contracts.

Hundreds of other complaints followed, brought by WEAL, NOW, individual women, and various women's organizations on campuses. Through Sandler's tireless political and legal efforts, the issue of sex discrimination became a central concern in institutions of higher education throughout the country. In 1971 the University of Michigan became the first university to adopt a detailed affirmative action plan for female faculty. Finally, in 1972, Title VII was amended to include educational institutions.

Excerpts from Sandler's testimony before the New York City Commission follow.

I AM CHAIRMAN of the Action Committee for Federal Contract Compliance in Education of the Women's Equity Action League (WEAL). I am also a psychologist and a former visiting lecturer in the Department of Counseling and Personnel Services at the University of Maryland. . . .

Since January 31, 1970, the Women's Equity Action League has initiated formal charges of sex discrimination under the Federal Executive Order 11246, as amended, against more than one hundred universities and colleges. This executive order forbids federal contractors from discriminating against race, creed, color, national origin, and sex. As federal contractors receiving more than 3.3 billion dollars of federal contract money yearly, universities and colleges are subject to the provisions of that order. Among the institutions charged are the entire state university and college systems of the states of Florida, California, New Jersey, and the entire city university system of New York (CUNY). And just a few months ago the National Organization for Women filed similar charges of sex discrimination against the entire State University of New York (SUNY).

In WEAL's initial complaint, WEAL charged an industry-wide pattern of sex discrimination and asked for a class action and compliance review of all universities and colleges holding federal contracts. At that time WEAL submitted to the Secretary of Labor more than eighty pages of documents substantiating its charges of sex discrimination in the academic community.

Half of the brightest people in our country—half of the most talented people with the potential for the highest intellectual endeavor—are women. Yet these gifted women will find it very difficult to obtain the same kind of quality education that is so readily available to their brothers. These women will encounter discrimination after discrimination—not once, not twice, but time after time in the very academic institutions which claim to preach the tenets of democracy and fair play.

These gifted women will face official and unofficial quotas at both the undergraduate and graduate levels. They will face discrimination when they apply for scholarship aid and financial assistance. When they graduate, their own university placement service will discriminate against them in helping them to find jobs. They will be discriminated against in hiring for the faculty. If hired at all, they will be promoted far more slowly than their male counterparts, and in all likelihood, they will receive far less money than their colleagues of the opposite sex.

Contrary to popular mythology, the position of women in higher education is *worsening;* women are slowly being pushed out of the university world. For example, in 1870, women were one-third of the faculty in our nation's institutions of higher learning; one hundred years later women hold less than one-fourth of these positions. In the prestigious Big Ten universities, they hold 10 percent or less of the faculty positions. The proportion of women graduate students *is less now* than it was in 1930. The University of Chicago, for example, has a *lower* proportion of women on its faculty *now* than it did in 1899.

Let me give you some more examples. Women are 22 percent of the graduate students in the Graduate School of Arts and Sciences at Harvard University. But last year, of the 411 tenured professors at the Graduate School of Arts and Sciences, *not one* was a woman. At the University of Connecticut, women are 33 percent of the instructors but only 4.8 percent of the full professors. At the University of Massachusetts campus at Boston, there were sixty-five women faculty, but *only two* of them have tenure. . . .

Academic women are promoted far more slowly than their male colleagues, and are most often found in the low-paying, low-prestige university jobs of lecturer, teaching assistant, and the like. One study which equated the qualifications of men and women found that 90 percent of the men with a Ph.D. and twenty years of teaching experience were likely to be full professors; for women with the *same* qualifications, barely half will be full professors. In other words, women have about half the chance that men have to become a full professor. In some of the more prestigious universities the promotion rate is even slower: at Stanford University, 50 percent of the men have the rank of associate or full professor; only 10 percent of the women are at these ranks. Somehow, women who are "qualified" enough to be hired are not "qualified" enough to be promoted. . . .

Salary discrepancies abound. Deans of men make far more money than deans of women, even in the same institution. Numerous national studies have documented the pay differences between men and women with the same academic positions. Women instructors earn less than men instructors; women assistant professors earn less than men assistant professors; and women full professors earn less than men full professors. . . .

At the administrative level women are most conspicuous by their absence. The number of women college presidents is decreasing even at women's colleges. Women rarely head departments. In fields where one would expect women to be, such as in education, they do not move to the top. In many schools the only administrative posts held by women are the heads of nursing and home economics schools.

Even in the placement services provided for their own graduates, universities and colleges discriminate. The College Placement Council (to which over 1,000 major colleges and universities subscribe, including the City College in New York, Brooklyn College, Hunter College, other members of the CUNY system, and numerous private institutions in New York) publishes a thick *College Placement Annual,* listing corporate and governmental employers who recruit college graduates. The *Annual*'s lists of employers are used by college placement officers, despite the blatant discriminatory advertisements within it, such as "sales personnel, male only," "personnel for executive development program, male only," "engineer, male only," "social worker, male only," "geologist, male only," and of course, "secretary, women only." Such advertising is a violation of both Title VII of the Civil Rights Act—educational institutions are *not* exempt in placement activities but only in their educational activities—and Executive Order 11246, as amended. University administrators who would be horrified if a placement bulletin for students listed job openings for "whites only" apparently see little or nothing wrong with job openings that read "male only." . . .

When I first started exploring sex discrimination in higher education I naïvely thought that there were merely isolated individual instances of discrimination, and that where such discrimination existed it was merely a matter of a particular department or a particular individual chairman or administrator. Certainly every professional woman has anecdotes about discrimination, but there has been little that has been written or documented in terms of the *total* picture within the university community. As WEAL's activities and filings have become known, women and men from all over the country, from small and large colleges and universities, from public and private institutions, from institutions of all sorts, have contacted WEAL, sending statistical data and asking WEAL to file on their behalf against their college or university. Let me add here that none of WEAL's filings has been based on anecdotal material; about twenty, including the one at Lehman College (CUNY), have been based on discriminatory advertising; the remainder and majority of the complaints have been based on hard statistical data. As more and more information has been collected, there is no question whatsoever that there is a *massive, consistent, and vicious pattern* of sex discrimination in our universities and colleges. On campus after campus, women are almost always restricted to the lower academic ranks, and in some instances they are not hired at all. Whether by design or accident, women are *second class citizens on the campus.*

PATRICIA JONES
Women in Household Employment

Writing some months after the New York Commission on Human Rights hearings had ended, Chair Eleanor Holmes Norton referred back to the testimony of "a young black woman named Patricia Jones, who had come to New York from the South for a job as a domestic worker." Jones had "held the hearings spellbound with her story of being picked from a 'slave market' lineup." Her presentation of the plight of those who labor in other people's kitchens had led to a successful campaign in the New York State legislature for a mandatory minimum wage for household employees—the majority of whom were black women over the age of forty. This legislative victory, Norton contended, indicated the type of action the women's movement should undertake in the future.[1]

The testimony of Patricia Jones is reprinted here.

---

[1] Eleanor Holmes Norton, "Introduction," *Women's Role in Contemporary Society: The Report of the New York City Commission on Human Rights* (New York: Avon, 1972), p. 22.

I AM EMPLOYED at Public School 225 in Brooklyn as an educational assistant, and I am currently the UFT [United Federation of Teachers] borough coordinator for paraprofessionals.

I am grateful for this opportunity to speak about a part of my life, which is not only an important part of my past but the everyday experience of all too many young black women such as I was at seventeen, when I read in a North Carolina daily the most impressive ad that I had ever read.

It said, "Come to New York City! Fifty dollars per week. Your own room. High school diploma preferred." At the time I saw the ad, I was making about twenty dollars a week for a seven-day week, so of course I jumped at the opportunity.

I lived on a farm with eleven other children. I was never a part of the family. I had been sent away by my father after the death of my mother when I was twelve years old. I was well cared for, under the circumstances, by relatives while I attended school. I felt that if I didn't graduate from high school, farming would be the only way of life for me. (By the way, there are no educational requirements in the fields.)

Therefore, you can see why this ad held my attention.

My ticket arrived a few weeks later. I arrived in the city with the ticket, high school diploma, and eagerness for the new job. Not knowing any better and being used to the slave labor practices of the South, I assumed that the way domestics were being traded and abused was normal, or at least a part of getting a job.

I remember the scene quite well. There were about twenty black girls and women sitting in the agency (just off the bus), and about ten well-married white women walking back and forth, making remarks such as, "She can't speak proper English." "Can't they get better help than this?" and one that stuck with me all these years. There was a lady sitting there and she was, I guess, about in her late forties, and she had just gotten off the bus as I had, and one of the well-married white women said, "She's too dirty. I don't want her around my children. They have never seen a pig."

In this day of enlightened labor practices, when even farm workers are beginning to come off the slavery of low wages and poor working conditions, I am sorry to report that the same tactics are being used today by employment agencies for domestic workers *in this city.* Let me explain.

Since the jobs of many paraprofessionals in the city school system were up in the air until the board found some of the additional funds needed to pay a living wage to school aides and educational assistants, I spent the latter part of the summer going to various agencies and seeking other employment. I wanted to be prepared, just in case. I was shocked to find that the same abuse and slave wages and working conditions that I had found twelve years ago are still in effect. Women are still being lured here with the promise of a better future, but now they promise you $140 a week.

While in these various agencies, I talked to other women who convinced me that I was right in referring to the situation of domestic workers as slave conditions.

There was a lady I knew, Mrs. J., from South Carolina. She is about twenty-three, with little or no education. She was paid fifty dollars per week to care for an eleven-room apartment on Park Avenue, and she was told that she could work her way up to a higher salary.

There was also a Mrs. M. from another southern state. She was paid fifty-five dollars a week for a sleep-in job on [Long] Island, approximately fourteen hours a day for five and a half days.

There was a Mrs. C., who had just stepped off the bus from North Carolina, her worldly possessions tucked into a small overnight case. Looking to better herself at age forty-five and earn more money to support nine children back home, the offer to come to New York was very attractive. She was paid fifty dollars a week to take care of a ten-room house. The job required her to work fifteen hours a day and to be available for parties.

My best offer was seventy-five dollars a week working five and a half days, fourteen hours a day. I was to take care of a ten-room split-level house, two children under age eight, and a dog whose room had to be scrubbed daily with the rest of the house.

Now, I ask you, is this human dignity for women, black, white, or domestic?

PHYLLIS GRABER
Discrimination in High School Sports

High school student Phyllis Graber formally complained to the New York City Commission on Human Rights that she was not permitted to play tennis at her school because she was a girl, and there was no girls' team. In 1970 education authorities were legally within their rights in preventing Graber from competing on a team with boys. But the following year the New York City Board of Education voted to allow high school girls to compete with boys in noncontact sports. And a year after that, a federal bill prohibiting discrimination on the basis of sex in any educational program or activity receiving federal financial assistance—Title IX of the Education Amendments of 1972—was skillfully shepherded through Congress by Representative Edith Green, Democrat of Oregon.

Although Title IX had broad applicability, it was in the area of athletics that the public felt its impact most forcefully. A storm of outrage accompanied the realization that funds would have to be diverted from high-profile male intercollegiate sports competitions to establish equity for women's sports programs. Schools were under pressure to offer more athletic scholarships to women, upgrade women's teams, and in general recast the face of physical education in U.S. high schools and colleges. The agency charged with enforcement of Title IX, the Office of Civil Rights (OCR), was at first every bit as recalcitrant as the EEOC had been in complying with the sex provisions of Title VII. However, the demands of individual women and girls within their own schools and communities eventually forced substantial progress.

The record of women's sports at Syracuse University, a New York State school that regularly fields strong men's football and basketball teams, is illustrative. The school had had a Women's Athletic Association since 1905, but not until 1971 did it inaugurate an intercollegiate athletic program for women. Initially there were five varsity women's teams, with a total budget of $7,500. Twenty years later, the university was supporting nine varsity women's sports—each team with a full-time head coach and assistant, and funds allotted for travel and scholarships. However, around the nation, full compliance with Title IX is still evaded: The average ratio of men to women participating in sports remains a lopsided 70 percent to 30 percent.[1]

Excerpts from Graber's spirited testimony follow.

I ATTEND JAMAICA HIGH SCHOOL [in New York City] as a junior. I entered Jamaica High School as a sophomore and I have a great interest in tennis. I have been playing tennis since I was nine years old, and I have been taking lessons for some time.

Upon entering Jamaica, I immediately inquired about a girls' tennis team and I was told there was no girls' team, but there was a girls' club. I found out that the girls' club consisted mostly of beginners and I was not interested in helping beginners, which was what the club primarily did. I was interested in competition to improve my own game.

I found out about a boys' team and I was told that the team started tryouts in March. I then met Mr. Ron Ettus [the coach] and asked him if I could try out for the team. I was aware that it would be difficult because of my sex. Mr. Ettus wasn't sure of the Public School Athletic League rules, but he said yes, I could try out, and he would proceed to find out the rulings. I made the team, but he also found out that the PSAL rules would not allow girls to compete with boys in any kind of school teams. Thus I was completely prevented from competition because of my sex.

[1]Andrea C. Marsh, "Fair Play," *Syracuse University Magazine,* December 1992, p. 46.

This is the same kind of ridiculous discrimination as if I were not allowed to play because I was black or had red hair. I was completely prohibited from playing. . . .

Granted the Board of Education has its rules, but it hasn't given me any legitimate reasons for the rules, and I have not received one bit of evidence for my ineligibility for the team. And Mr. Ettus . . . and the New York Civil Liberties Union have inquired and their inquiries have been answered with the most ambiguous reasons.

As to my ability, there is no question of it, and I quote from Mr. Ettus, "Phyllis Graber cannot play on the Jamaica High School tennis team because she is a girl. Phyllis has the ability to qualify for the team, and I am sure she would do well in competition."

The New York City Board of Education responded that I might be good enough to make the team, but once I reached the top, the cream of the crop in the boys' competition, I might fall out. Well, I might fall out but it would be because I was beaten by a better player, not because I was a girl. There is no educational reason for girls not being allowed to play in non-contact sports. . . . I quote the *New York Post* of September 14, 1970: "The State Education Department says preliminary results show its experimental integration of women into high school interscholastic sports was a success. The department said yesterday that educators and medical authorities agree that girls can compete with men in many non-contact sports where they were previously barred. The department's experiments consisted of entering women students in such sport events as tennis, golf and bowling in selected school districts last semester. The results to date showed negative results only in the area of social acceptance of the idea." . . .

At this point I have been trying for five or six months to change the policy of the Board of Education with the help of the New York Civil Liberties Union, and all of these efforts have been in vain. And I would like to file a formal complaint with the Commission against the Board of Education for arbitrary and gross discrimination because of sex.

I think that the Board of Education's sexist policies are only one of many discriminations that women and girls must encounter in society today, and I came here to speak about the tennis team matter. I don't want to use this as a rhetorical spring-board, but I detest having my rights as a human being stepped on because of my sex and specifically I don't see why the Board of Education should have the right to impose its judgment upon me without offering any legal or valid arguments for its opinion.

BELLA ABZUG
Women in Elective Office

Only two women were elected to seats in the U.S. Senate in the forty years after women won the vote, and no woman was elected governor of a state on her own merits in all that time.[1] Moreover, no independent "women's vote" on any issue had emerged. The dream of a distinct female voice in politics had inspired the suffragists; and with the revival of feminism in the sixties, the dream revived. But political power for women was still only a gleam in feminists' eyes in 1970, when attorney and peace activist Bella Abzug (b. 1920) spoke at the New York City Commission on Human Rights hearings.

By the next year, Abzug herself was one of those who had begun to effect hopeful changes in the political scene. Elected to the U.S. House of Representatives from New York City, she was one of fourteen winning women candidates. She was returned to the House three times by her constituents and afterward served in appointive positions, most notably as presiding officer of the national commission for International Women's Year, which staged the historic Houston, Texas, conference in November 1977.

In the 1980s, there developed at long last a significant sepa-rate women's vote on specific issues and candidates—tagged the

---

[1]The senators were Hattie W. Caraway of Arkansas and Margaret Chase Smith of Maine. The first woman elected governor of a state in her own right (not the widow of a former governor, for example) was Ella Grasso, Democrat of Connecticut, in 1974.

"gender gap." The women's movement became a force in main-stream politics: Representative Geraldine Ferraro of New York was nominated as the Democratic Party's candidate for vice president of the United States in 1984. To help finance women's campaigns, Emily's List (*Emily* is an acronym for Early Money Is Like Yeast) was founded in 1985. Several years later, the Fund for the Feminist Majority became another source of contributions to spur "the feminization of power." In 1990, three women governors were elected. And the year 1993 saw a sudden jump in the number of women in Congress—from 6 percent to nearly 10 percent, including six senators and forty-seven representatives (plus nonvoting delegate Eleanor Holmes Norton).

Bella Abzug is the coauthor, with Mim Kelber, of *Gender Gap* (1984). In the speech reprinted here, Abzug took a long view, looking back to the American Revolution and ahead to a time when women as voters and lawmakers would reshape national priorities.

FOR MOST OF THIS COUNTRY'S HISTORY, women have lived without visible political power, and they have been excluded from all levels of government of American society. The momentous decisions of war and peace, as well as the everyday decisions that affect how all people live, have been made by a minority of individuals who happen to be born as white males. In reality, they are still making the decisions, despite some token gestures toward representation of women and minority groups.

Nor is this exclusion of women from political power any less deliberate than exclusion of black people and other minorities. Nearly 200 years ago when our founding fathers were drawing up the Constitution of our new nation, John Adams received a letter from his wife, Abigail, which said, "My dear John, By the way, in the new code of laws . . . I desire you would remember the ladies, and be more generous and favorable to them than your ancestors. Do not put such unlimited power in the hands of husbands. Remember all men would be tyrants if they could. Your loving wife, Abigail." Mr. Adams' reply came right to the point. "Depend upon it, my dear wife," he wrote, "we know better than to repeal our masculine systems." Just as, of course, they knew better than to repeal the system of slavery that inexorably warped the democratic development of our nation and condemned millions to misery, servitude, and repression.

So it was up to the women to repeal the "masculine systems" and it took a heartbreaking and backbreaking struggle of almost a century—a political struggle—to win the right to vote for women in 1920. In the course of that struggle, women developed and mastered every political technique that is now taken for granted in American politics—checking voting records, compiling lists by election districts, doorbell ringing, leafleting, lobbying, parading, demonstrating by the thousands, and even getting arrested.

Yes, our political skills are now very highly valued. We are allowed to do most of the drudgery and the dirty work and the detail work of politics. I would venture to say that there is no political party in the United States that could survive were it not for the fact that the women are holding up those structures on their backs. But for the most part, women are still excluded from the political power they create. Women are a majority of the population. They are also a majority in every racial and ethnic group. But they are almost invisible in government.

Out of 435 members in the House of Representatives in the Ninety-first Congress, only ten are women, including just one black woman, a great black woman, Shirley Chisholm, but just one. Of course, there are no Puerto Ricans, Mexican-Americans, or Indians in Congress, women or men. Out of 100 Senators, only one is a woman and she got there initially as a replacement for her husband, who died in office.[2] There are no women on the Supreme Court, no women governors, no women mayors in big cities, and right here in New York City, Mayor Lindsay confessed the other day that only a few women hold

[2] Senator Margaret Chase Smith, Republican of Maine, replaced her husband in the House of Representatives, then was reelected four times. She also served in the Senate, from 1949 to 1973.—*Ed.*

top city jobs. Some of them are good women. In Washington, as of December 1969, of more than 300 administration posts filled by President Nixon, only thirteen have gone to women, and three of those are White House secretaries.

This is merely one aspect of the discrimination against women that blights all parts of our society—economically, legally, and socially, as well as politically. But in this year of women's liberation movements, in this year when passage of the Equal Rights Amendment has finally come within sight, women are speaking up more militantly than ever for equality, and they are determined—and we shall get what is our due.

In the process we are finding out that although the daily reality of woman's role has been totally revolutionized in the past two centuries, some men's thinking has not changed very much from the time of John Adams. Just last month when the Equal Rights Amendment was being debated in the House, Congressman Emanuel Celler stood up and in all seriousness said, and I quote: "Ever since Adam," that is the first Adam, "gave up his rib to make a woman, throughout the ages we have learned that physical, emotional, psychological, and social differences exist and dare not be disregarded." And then, with the condescending flattery that passes for chivalry, Mr. Celler went on to say, "Neither the National Woman's Party nor the delightful, delectable, and dedicated gentlelady from Michigan" (he was referring to Congresswoman Martha Griffiths) "can change nature. They cannot do it."

There is one thing women can change—and that is the Congress of the United States and the political power structure of our country. And we are not going to wait another fifty years to do so. If some men complain that we are "boisterous and aggressive" instead of "delightful and delectable"—and I enjoy saying this in particular—that's all right with us. We cannot all be Shirley Temples, nor do we want to be.

Women are going to set political goals of full representation in government, not just tokenism. Within the next few years—let us say by the 200th birthday of our nation's founding—women must fight for and win a political structure that mirrors reality. And along the way, they will find many allies among men and political organizations who recognize that a society which, at long last, gives full scope to the abilities and creativity of half its population can only gain in health, wisdom, and strength.

I am not suggesting here that women are the repository of all good, or that they have a single cohesive viewpoint. Women—whether they are conservative, liberal, or radical—should be fully represented in the political power structure simply as a matter of right, nor should they be expected to perform like superwomen. But perhaps just because they have been excluded from the governmental process, they have, on the whole, a clearer view of what our nation's priorities should be and a more direct, less encumbered approach to solving human problems.

Suppose, for example, that instead of just eleven women in the House and Senate, we had several hundred—and I am not talking about just middle-class professional women, but about representatives of America's 30 million working women, women from the garment factories of midtown Manhattan, the auto plants of Detroit, from the great vineyards of California and the cotton fields of the South, from laundries, schools, and hospitals, and women who work at home—shopping, cooking, cleaning, raising kids, and performing the hundreds of thousands of volunteer jobs that keep our society functioning.

Needless to say, such a Congress would not tolerate the countless laws on the books that discriminate against women in all phases of their lives. But more than that. Does anyone think that with that kind of representation we would have reached the twilight of the twentieth century without a national health care system for all Americans? Would we rank fourteenth in infant mortality among the developed nations of the world? Would we allow a situation in which thousands of kids grow up without decent care because their mothers have to work for a living and have no place to leave their children, or else that condemns women to stay at home when they want to work, because there are no facilities for their children? Would a Congress with large numbers of women condone the continued murdering of young girls and mothers in amateur abortion mills, or would it guarantee that the right to free abortions belonged in all parts of the country? Would women allow the fraudulent packaging and cheating of consumers that they find every time they shop? Would they consent to the perverted sense of priorities that has dominated our government for the past few decades, appropriating billions of dollars for war and plunging our cities into crises of neglect? Would they vote for ABMs instead of schools, MIRVs[3] instead of decent housing or health centers? And does anyone think they would have allowed the war in Vietnam to go on for so many years, slaughtering and maiming our young men and the people of Indochina?

This may all sound like wishful thinking: the thought that someday we may have a Fannie Lou Hamer instead of a James Eastland in the Senate may seem too absurd. Indeed, even the suggestion that we should have ten or twenty times as many women in Congress as we now have, or that there should be women on the Supreme Court, or in the White House, will no doubt provoke haughty editorial lectures about exaggerated demands, or psychological tomes about the castration complexes of women or, at the very least, keep the gag writers for *Laugh-In*[4] busy for weeks.

But I suggest that what is really ludicrous is a political structure that denies representation to a majority of its population and then winds up fingering the victims of this situation as somehow responsible for it because of their personal inadequacies.

This is the same historic game of one-upmanship that is being so magnificently rejected by black Americans, and women now are recognizing that they too will have to join in militant action for their rights. I am not going to lecture women about the responsibilities of citizenship, or the need to get out and vote—but do it anyhow—or to join political movements. Women are *in* politics. They know *how* to organize. They recognize their needs. But they are going to have to upgrade their demands and seek a full share in political power and leadership. And I submit that what is good for women will turn out to be good for the entire country.

---

[3]Antiballistic missiles and multiheaded guided missiles.—*Ed.*
[4]A television series featuring topical satire.—*Ed.*

JANE ROE V. HENRY WADE

Opinion of the Court

In 1965 a nineteen-year-old named Sarah Ragle entered the University of Texas Law School, one of about 40 women in a student body of 1,600. When she graduated in 1967, she received no job offer from any law firm, though she was in the top quarter of her class. The young lawyer, who had recently married and was now known as Sarah Weddington, was friendly with a group of women connected with a counter-culture newspaper in Austin, *The Rag*. The group obtained a prepublication mimeographed copy of *Our Bodies, Ourselves* and held meetings to talk about the book. They discussed the overall status of women in society but focused frequently on the need for more access to reliable contraception and safe abortion. Abortion in Texas—as in the majority of states—was illegal except to save the life of the pregnant woman.

Before long some of the group were running an informal abortion-referral service—the Women's Liberation Birth Control Information Center—one of scores of such projects all over the United States. Those involved in the Austin center were worried about the legality of their activities and asked their attorney friend Sarah Weddington to research the matter. She began studying abortion law.

Soon after, Weddington and a former law school classmate, Linda Coffee, met Norma McCorvey, age twenty-one, a high school dropout who was working as a waitress in a bar. Separated from her drifter husband and with no permanent residence, McCorvey had a five-year-old daughter whom her mother was raising. The common interest that brought the three women together was the fact that McCorvey was pregnant and wanted an abortion, while Weddington and Coffee were looking for the right woman to be a plaintiff in an abortion lawsuit.[1]

Restrictive abortion laws had lately been successfully attacked in a number of state courts, notably California's. But Weddington and Coffee decided to take a bolder approach. They bypassed the Texas courts and in early 1970 filed a federal suit challenging the constitutionality of Texas's antiabortion statute and, by inference, similar abortion laws of other states as well.

Thus began one of the most famous and important court cases of our time: *Roe v. Wade*. Weddington and Coffee fought successfully in federal courts against Henry Wade, district attorney of Dallas County, on behalf of Norma McCorvey, alias Jane Roe.

Finally, the case was considered by the U.S. Supreme Court, with Weddington herself conducting oral argument. On January 22, 1973, the high court by a vote of 7 to 2 struck down all state laws that restricted a woman's right to an abortion during the first trimester of pregnancy, and granted to the states only very limited regulatory rights in the second trimester. The decision was based on the right of privacy founded in the Fourteenth Amendment's concept of personal freedom. *The New York Times* called the decision "a historic resolution of a fiercely controversial issue" and characterized it editorially as "a major contribution to the preservation of individual liberties."[2]

However, the right to an abortion did not guarantee a woman access to one. Opponents of *Roe* immediately mobilized against it (after 1980, with increasing effect), while supporters were forced to wage a twenty-year struggle to preserve reproductive freedoms. Justice Harry A. Blackmun, author of the majority opinion in *Roe v. Wade*, spoke in 1989 of his "fear for the liberty and equality of the millions of women who have lived and come of age in the sixteen years since Roe was decided."[3] However, with the election of a pro-choice president in 1992, and the 1993 appointment of a feminist judge, Ruth Bader Ginsburg, to the Supreme Court, the threat to *Roe* receded.

[1] As related by Sarah Weddington in her memoir, *A Question of Choice* (New York: Putnam, 1992).
[2] *New York Times*, January 23, 1973, p. 1, and January 24, 1973, editorial.
[3] In *Webster v. Reproductive Health Services*, 492 U.S. 490 (1989).

Excerpts from Justice Blackmun's opinion in *Roe v. Wade* are reprinted here. Concurring were Chief Justice Warren Burger and Justices William Douglas, William Brennan, Potter Stewart, Thurgood Marshall, and Lewis Powell. Dissenting were Justices Byron White and William Rehnquist.

MR. JUSTICE BLACKMUN DELIVERED THE OPINION.of the Court.

This Texas federal appeal . . . present[s] constitutional challenges to state criminal abortion legislation. The Texas statutes under attack here are typical of those that have been in effect in many States for approximately a century. . . .

We forthwith acknowledge our awareness of the sensitive and emotional nature of the abortion controversy, of the vigorous opposing views, even among physicians, and of the deep and seemingly absolute convictions that the subject inspires. One's philosophy, one's experiences, one's exposure to the raw edges of human existence, one's religious training, one's attitudes toward life and family and their values, and the moral standards one establishes and seeks to observe, are all likely to influence and to color one's thinking and conclusions about abortion.

In addition, population growth, pollution, poverty, and racial overtones tend to complicate and not simplify the problem.

Our task, of course, is to resolve the issue by constitutional measurement, free of emotion and of predilection. We seek earnestly to do this. . . .

The Texas statutes that concern us here . . . make it a crime to "procure an abortion," as therein defined, or to attempt one, except with respect to "an abortion procured or attempted by medical advice for the purpose of saving the life of the mother." Similar statutes are in existence in a majority of the States.

Texas first enacted a criminal abortion statute in 1854. This was soon modified into language that has remained substantially unchanged to the present time. . . .

• • •

Jane Roe,[4] a single woman who was residing in Dallas County, Texas, instituted this federal action in March 1970 against the District Attorney of the county. She sought a declaratory judgment that the Texas criminal abortion statutes were unconstitutional on their face, and an injunction restraining the defendant from enforcing the statutes.

Roe alleged that she was unmarried and pregnant; that she wished to terminate her pregnancy by an abortion "performed by a competent, licensed physician, under safe, clinical conditions"; that she was unable to get a "legal" abortion in Texas because her life did not appear to be threatened by the continuation of her pregnancy; and that she could not afford to travel to another jurisdiction in order to secure a legal abortion under safe conditions. She claimed that the Texas statutes were unconstitutionally vague and that they abridged her right of personal privacy, protected by the First, Fourth, Fifth, Ninth, and Fourteenth Amendments. By an amendment to her complaint Roe purported to sue "on behalf of herself and all other women" similarly situated. . . .

It perhaps is not generally appreciated that the restrictive criminal abortion laws in effect in a majority of States today are of relatively recent vintage. Those laws, generally proscribing abortion or its attempt at any time during pregnancy except when necessary to preserve the pregnant woman's life, are not of ancient or even of common-law origin. Instead, they derive from statutory changes effected, for the most part, in the latter half of the nineteenth century. . . .

Three reasons have been advanced to explain historically the enactment of criminal abortion laws in the nineteenth century and to justify their continued existence. It has been argued occasionally that these laws were the product of a Victorian social concern to discourage illicit sexual conduct. Texas, however, does not advance this justification in the present case, and it appears that no court or commentator has taken the argument

[4]The name is a pseudonym.

seriously. The appellants and *amici* contend, moreover, that this is not a proper state purpose at all and suggest that, if it were, the Texas statutes are overbroad in protecting it since the law fails to distinguish between married and unwed mothers.

A second reason is concerned with abortion as a medical procedure. When most criminal abortion laws were first enacted, the procedure was a hazardous one for the woman. . . . Abortion mortality was high. Even after 1900, and perhaps until as late as the development of antibiotics in the 1940s, standard modern techniques such as dilation and curettage were not nearly so safe as they are today. Thus, it has been argued that a State's real concern in enacting a criminal abortion law was to protect the pregnant woman, that is, to restrain her from submitting to a procedure that placed her life in serious jeopardy.

Modern medical techniques have altered this situation. Appellants and various *amici* refer to medical data indicating that abortion in early pregnancy, that is, prior to the end of the first trimester, although not without its risk, is now relatively safe. Mortality rates for women undergoing early abortions, where the procedure is legal, appear to be as low as or lower than the rates for normal childbirth. Consequently, any interest of the State in protecting the woman from an inherently hazardous procedure . . . has largely disappeared. . . .

The third reason is the State's interest—some phrase it in terms of duty—in protecting prenatal life. Some of the argument for this justification rests on the theory that a new human life is present from the moment of conception. The State's interest and general obligation to protect life then extends, it is argued, to prenatal life. Only when the life of the pregnant mother herself is at stake, balanced against the life she carries within her, should the interest of the embryo or fetus not prevail. . . .

The Constitution does not explicitly mention any right of privacy. In a line of decisions, however, going back perhaps as far as . . . 1891, the Court has recognized that a right of personal privacy, or a guarantee of certain areas or zones of privacy, does exist under the Constitution. . . . These decisions make it clear that only personal rights that can be deemed "fundamental" or "implicit in the concept of ordered liberty" are included in this guarantee of personal privacy. They also make it clear that the right has some extension to activities relating to marriage, procreation, family relationships, and child rearing and education.

This right of privacy, whether it be founded in the Fourteenth Amendment's concept of personal liberty and restrictions upon state action, as we feel it is, or, as the District Court determined, in the Ninth Amendment's reservation of rights to the people, is broad enough to encompass a woman's decision whether or not to terminate her pregnancy. The detriment that the State would impose upon the pregnant woman by denying this choice altogether is apparent. Specific and direct harm medically diagnosable even in early pregnancy may be involved. Maternity, or additional offspring, may force upon the woman a distressful life and future. Psychological harm may be imminent. Mental and physical health may be taxed by child care. There is also the distress, for all concerned, associated with the unwanted child, and there is the problem of bringing a child into a family already unable, psychologically and otherwise, to care for it. In other cases, as in this one, the additional difficulties and continuing stigma of unwed motherhood may be involved. All these are factors the woman and her responsible physician necessarily will consider in consultation.

On the basis of elements such as these, appellant and some *amici* argue that the woman's right is absolute and that she is entitled to terminate her pregnancy at whatever time, in whatever way, and for whatever reason she alone chooses. With this we do not agree. Appellant's arguments that Texas either has no valid interest at all in regulating the abortion decision, or no interest strong enough to support any limitation upon the woman's sole determination, are unpersuasive. The Court's decisions recognizing a right of privacy also acknowledge that some state regulation in areas protected by that right is appropriate. . . . A State may properly assert important interests in safeguarding health, in maintaining medical standards, and in protecting potential life. At some point in pregnancy, these respective interests become sufficiently compelling to sustain regulation of the factors that govern the abortion decision. The privacy right involved, therefore, cannot be said to be absolute. In fact, it is not clear to us that the claim asserted by some *amici* that one has an unlimited right to do with one's body as one pleases bears a close relationship to the right of privacy previously articulated in the Court's decisions. The Court has refused to recognize an unlimited right of this kind in the past.

We, therefore, conclude that the right of personal privacy includes the abortion decision, but that this right is not unqualified and must be considered against important state interests in regulation. . . .

Appellant, as has been indicated, claims an absolute right that bars any state imposition of criminal penalties in the area. Appellee argues that the State's determination to recognize and protect prenatal life from and after conception constitutes a compelling state interest. . . . We do not agree fully with either formulation.

A. The appellee and certain *amici* argue that the fetus is a "person" within the language and meaning of the Fourteenth Amendment. In support of this, they outline at length and in detail the well-known facts of fetal development. If this suggestion of personhood is established, the appellant's case, of course, collapses, for the fetus' right to life would then be guaranteed specifically by the Amendment. . . .

The Constitution does not define "person" in so many words. . . . But in nearly all [references to "person"], the use of the word is such that it has application only postnatally. None indicates, with any assurance, that it has any possible prenatal application.

All this, together with our observation, *supra,* that throughout the major portion of the nineteenth century prevailing legal abortion practices were far freer than they are today, persuades us that the word "person," as used in the Fourteenth Amendment, does not include the unborn. . . .

B. The pregnant woman cannot be isolated in her privacy. She carries an embryo and, later, a fetus. . . . The situation therefore is inherently different from marital intimacy, or bedroom possession of obscene material, or marriage, or procreation, or education. . . . As we have intimated above, it is reasonable and appropriate for a State to decide that at some point in time another interest, that of health of the mother or that of potential human life, becomes significantly involved. The woman's privacy is no longer sole and any right of privacy she possesses must be measured accordingly.

Texas urges that, apart from the Fourteenth Amendment, life begins at conception and is present throughout pregnancy, and that, therefore, the State has a compelling interest in protecting that life from and after conception. We need not resolve the difficult question of when life begins. When those trained in the respective disciplines of medicine, philosophy, and theology are unable to arrive at any consensus, the judiciary, at this point in the development of man's knowledge, is not in a position to speculate as to the answer. . . .

In areas other than criminal abortion, the law has been reluctant to endorse any theory that life, as we recognize it, begins before live birth or to accord legal rights to the unborn except in narrowly defined situations and except when the rights are contingent upon live birth. . . . The unborn have never been recognized in the law as persons in the whole sense.

In view of all this, we do not agree that, by adopting one theory of life, Texas may override the rights of the pregnant woman that are at stake. We repeat, however, that the State does have an important and legitimate interest in preserving and protecting the health of the pregnant woman . . . and that it has still *another* important and legitimate interest in protecting the potentiality of human life. These interests are separate and distinct. Each grows in substantiality as the woman approaches term and, at a point during pregnancy, each becomes "compelling."

With respect to the State's important and legitimate interest in the health of the mother, the "compelling" point, in the light of present medical knowledge, is at approximately the end of the first trimester. This is so because of the now-established medical fact . . . that until the end of the first trimester mortality in abortion may be less than mortality in normal childbirth. It follows that, from and after this point, a State may regulate the abortion procedure to the extent that the regulation reasonably relates to the preservation and protection of maternal health. Examples of permissible state regulation in this area are requirements as to the qualifications of the person who is to perform the abortion; as to the licensure of that person; as to the facility in which the procedure is to be performed; . . . and the like.

This means, on the other hand, that, for the period of pregnancy prior to this "compelling" point, the attending physician, in consultation with his patient, is free to determine, without regulation by the State, that, in his medical judgment, the patient's pregnancy should be terminated. If that decision is reached, the judgment may be effectuated by an abortion free of interference by the State.

With respect to the State's important and legitimate interest in potential life, the "compelling" point is at viability. This is so because the fetus then presumably has the capability of meaningful life outside the mother's womb. State regulation protective of fetal life after viability thus has both logical and biological justifications. If the State is interested in protecting fetal life after viability, it may go so far as to proscribe abortion during that period, except when it is necessary to preserve the life or health of the mother.

Measured against these standards, Art. 1196 of the Texas Penal Code, in restricting legal abortions to those "procured or attempted by medical advice for the purpose of saving the life of the mother," sweeps too broadly. The statute makes no distinction between abortions performed early in pregnancy and those performed later, and it limits to a single reason, "saving" the mother's life, the legal justification for the procedure. The statute, therefore, cannot survive the constitutional attack made upon it here.

GLORIA STEINEM

The Way We Were—
And Will Be

Gloria Steinem (b. 1934) has been to the second wave of American feminism what Susan B. Anthony was to the first. Like Anthony, Steinem devoted decades of her life to empowering women. She organized protests, recruited supporters, raised money, founded new pressure groups, and made speeches—the latter despite what she has described as her "almost pathological fear of speaking in public."[1] Anthony, too, overcame severe stage fright—"It is a terrible martyrdom for me to speak," she wrote in 1860—and went on to become a great movement organizer and leader.

The idea of sisterhood is a key element of Steinem's feminism. For about five years she toured the country with one of several black feminist partners; they shared the speaker's platform at hundreds of meetings, with the aim of promoting racial diversity in the women's movement.[2] Propelled by the wish to unite women around common needs, in 1972 Steinem became a co-founder of *Ms.* magazine—the first mass-market periodical addressed to the new feminist woman. Even when she faced bitter attacks by other feminists, Steinem held fast to trust in sisterhood.

Although Steinem had a flourishing career as a journalist before becoming a feminist organizer and editor, her first book to be published in the United States did not appear until 1983. Called *Outrageous Acts and Everyday Rebellions,* it is mainly a

---

[1] Gloria Steinem, *Outrageous Acts and Everyday Rebellions* (New York: Holt, Rinehart & Winston, 1983), p. 9.

[2] Steinem's speaking partners were Dorothy Pitman Hughes, Florynce Kennedy, and Margaret Sloan.

compilation of her articles previously printed in *Ms.* "There have been days in the last ten or twelve years," she wrote in the introduction, "when I thought my collected works would consist entirely of fund-raising letters, scribbled outlines of speeches, statements hammered out at the birth of some new coalition, and introductions to other people's books."[3] However, she has over time produced several books of her own, including a feminist interpretation of Marilyn Monroe and a highly successful guide to enhancing one's self-esteem, *Revolution from Within* (1992). In 1994 another book—*Moving Beyond Words*—was published.

Steinem's writings display her clarity, honesty, and fairness; her ability to poke fun at herself; and her skill in combining the personal and the political without trivializing either. The article excerpted here was first printed in the December 1979 issue of *Ms.*, alongside a chronology of women's achievements through the seventies. In it, Steinem took note of an incipient antifeminist "backlash" but was optimistic about the long-term future of feminism. Her concern proved justified. Even as she penned this survey of women's growing power, Ronald Reagan was preparing to enter the White House, where he and his successor, George Bush, would pursue an antifeminist social agenda for the next twelve years.

THINK FOR A MINUTE. Who were you before the seventies began?

Trying to remember our way back into past realities, past rooms, past beliefs is a first step toward measuring the depth of change in ourselves and the world. It's also a reminder that the progress we may now take for granted is the result of many major accomplishments of the past and just the beginning of more changes to come.

Sharing these past measures of change—in the same way we

[3]Steinem, *Outrageous Acts*, p. 1.

have learned to personally share current problems and solutions in consciousness-raising groups—is probably the most accurate, bias-proof, and feminist way of identifying and recording our own history. After all, if women of diverse experience and age and background and even nationality can begin to see patterns of similarity emerge from the telling of past learning-moments and milestones, then we are probably on the track of an accurate historical pattern. And if we can accomplish this sharing, then history may cease to be limited mainly to the documented acts of national leaders, or to the interpretations of scholars proving a particular theory. We can begin to create a women's history—and finally a people's history—that is accurate, nourishing, and accessible.

Of course, massive change proceeds more as a spiral than a straight line. We repeat similar patterns over and over again, each time in a slightly different circumstance, so experiences that appear to be circular and discouraging in the short run may turn out to be moving in a clear direction in the long run. Those of us who were taught the cheerful American notion that progress is linear and hierarchical, for instance, may have had to learn with pain in the seventies that no worthwhile battle can be fought and won only once. Whether the struggle is as clear-cut as an individual woman's right to equal pay—and to decide for herself when and whether she will have a child—or as complex as the cross-cultural principles of economic equity and reproductive freedom, the issues still repeat themselves in different ways and in constantly shifting arenas. The process goes on and on—until the spiral has passed through the superficiality of official phrases or newspaper reports and moved into the deeper regions of everyday acceptance and culture. In fact, truly successful politics are probably definable simply as "culture."

Our own personal spirals of growth blend in with the larger one wherever it touches most directly on our experience.

My memory tells me, for instance, that I was certainly old enough to understand these well-educated, white, upper-middle-class housewives who began to rebel in the sixties against a feminine mystique that had kept them and their sisters locked out of professions and into the suburbs. Nonetheless, I not only felt little personal connection between their words and my own life, but was often put off by their emphasis on getting a piece of the existing professional pie: on bringing women, as the National Organization for Women put it in 1966, "into full participation in the mainstream of American society," and on becoming "a civil rights movement to speak for women, as there has been for Negroes"—this last seeming to imply either that all women were white, or that Negro women didn't suffer from sex discrimination.

As a journalist, I was already near the mainstream of my profession and very far from the suburbs; yet I was still suffering from a world in which I was assumed to be far less "serious" (and to need far less money) than my male colleagues, and where the highest praise I could earn was "You write like a man." I felt alienated among the powerful men of that "mainstream," and attracted to the farm-worker meetings or black-run community centers about which I chose to write; yet those early reformers couldn't help me to understand why. They seemed to want to become the "token woman" I already was.

Only in the late sixties when many women who had grown up in the peace or civil rights movements began to propose feminism—that is, an analysis that included all women as a caste and called for a transformation of patriarchy, not just integration into it by a few women—did my own feelings of recognition, empathy, and hope begin to explode. Many of these feminists had rejected their own hard-won but subordinate places inside male-run professions or political groups. Some had the courage to expose the real sexual caste systems inside movements that were supposed to be about social justice, but whose revolutionary sons treated women the same or with less equality than their conservative fathers had done. A few took on both political and literary heroes by occupying a prestigious publishing house that was actually supporting itself with sadomasochistic pornography, or by writing well-documented attacks on the sexual politics of male cultural heroes.

In each case, there was some odd echo of an experience that I had thought was idiosyncratic and mine alone. One woman told of the years she had spent doing much of the research and background work for radical male colleagues, for instance, but her major reward was to be called "a real brother." I had been doing free-lance editing jobs for the male editor of a national women's magazine who always handed me manuscripts with the instruction (intended as praise, since he had such contempt for his readers), "Pretend you're a woman and read this." Furthermore, I had always felt resentful or depressed when reading much-admired literary works in which women were humiliated, yet I assumed I had no right to criticize.

Instead of demonstrating outside posh "men only" lunch havens, as some of the reformers were then doing, these feminists were declaring their common bonds with women as a group, and holding public speak-outs on such populist and still illegal issues as abortion. For the first time, I understood that the abortion I had kept so shamefully quiet about for years was an experience I had probably shared with at least one out of four American women.

And for the first time, I realized that our bodies, much less the rest of our lives, could never be entirely our own as long as we were viewed and controlled by society as the most basic means of production: the means of *re*production. . . .

On the other hand, thousands of women [were] strengthened and started on paths of lifelong change by hearing their experiences as wives, mothers, and frustrated professionals accurately described by those reformers of the sixties. They then went on to discover that success in the mainstream simply wasn't possible through the efforts of one group of women alone, or through changing only our work lives. By the seventies, almost all the early reformers became feminists through realizing that they were strengthened by alliances with women of different races and classes, women who were welfare mothers or employed in traditional "women's work," women who were lesbians or who had chosen unconventional lifestyles. After all, a woman might start out identifying "upward" with her male boss and not "downward" with another secretary, but both often realized that they shared problems as women, and they needed to support each other to have any power at all. As for rights of sexual expression and reproductive freedom, women finally discovered that all of us were endangered when one group was denied.

At the same time, most of the early feminists were learning the importance of being inside as well as outside those structures that need change; of legislative lobbying and electoral politics; in short, of the skills that their reformist sisters often possessed. We have even admitted the degree to which stylistic differences kept us from seeing that shared issues had been there all along. In retrospect, for instance, I realize that NOW had made a dignified and courageous demand for "repealing penal laws governing abortion" in 1967, almost two years before so many of us experienced the more dramatic revelation of hearing women demand the same repeal by speaking out publicly about their experiences of illegal abortions. If I had been willing to look beyond the superficial style differences of women who picketed against employers in their mink coats (in order to prove, as one of them now ruefully recalls, "that we were demonstrating out of principle, not need"), I might have started to work on the vital issue of abortion two years earlier. And if more of the early reformers had been willing to look beyond the boots-and-jeans uniform and impersonal rhetoric with which some of us emerged from the male-dominated Left, they might have realized that we were neither so far from them on issues nor such a political liability as we seemed.

This personal note on two different paths to feminism is only a hint at the diversity of experience that each of us would count as vital in summing up the seventies: the first full decade of the second wave of feminism in America. Each of us would probably choose a different way of measuring how far the revolution has come.

If we are sociologists or reporters, for instance, we might explain that every major issue raised by the Women's Movement now has majority support in national public opinion polls: from the supposedly "easy" ones like equal pay, women in political office, and equal access to education to the supposedly "controversial" ones like the Equal Rights Amendment, a woman's right to choose abortion, and "would-you-work-for-a-woman?"

That represents major change from the early seventies, when most such issues were supported by only a minority; and an even bigger change from the sixties, when they weren't included in public opinion polls at all.

If we are history buffs or students of revolution, we might see the seventies as a time of massive consciousness-raising: of breaking the conspiracy of silence on the depth of sex-based inequities, both nationally and internationally, and of achieving token victories that raised women's hopes. Having forged a majority change in consciousness, we are now ready for more institutional, systematic change in the eighties. A redistribution of power in families, a revolution in the way children are raised and by whom, flexible work schedules outside the home, recognition of work done by women (and men) in the home, a lessening of the violence that is rooted in the cult of masculinity, the redistribution of wealth that would begin if we actually got comparable pay: all these structural changes are possible because hopes were raised in the seventies.

If, on the other hand, we are simply among the millions of women struggling to survive the double burden of working outside the home, yet carrying the major responsibility for homemaking and raising children, we might describe the seventies as the decade in which we advanced *half* the battle. We've learned that women can and should do "men's jobs," for instance, and we've won the principle (if not the fact) of getting equal pay. But we haven't yet established the principle (much less the fact) that men can and should do "women's jobs": that homemaking and child-rearing are as much a man's responsibility, too, and that those jobs in which women are concentrated outside the home would probably be better paid if more men became secretaries, file clerks, and nurses, too.

Obviously, society in general and women in particular will have to make more demands on men as equal parents in the eighties. Job patterns must allow both fathers and mothers of young children to arrange shorter workdays or shorter workweeks. (We'll also have to return to the battle for quality child care that we lost at the beginning of the seventies; this time with a clear statement that free child-care centers are not for the benefit of "working mothers," any more than free schools are. They are simply the right of every child.) Existing affirmative action measures will have to be used to integrate men into "women's jobs," and not just the other way around, especially where large employers can be forced to pay decent salaries to *all* workers in order to attract men. Yet this integration *must* retain its first stage. If men become flight attendants but women don't become pilots and airline executives, for instance, women will still be on the losing end.

Politicians and organizers would surely measure the success of the seventies—and the danger of the eighties—by the force of the right-wing backlash against all of these majority changes in hopes and values. Representatives of a social order that depends mostly on sex, race, and class privilege for its power, and is often justified by the mythic and economic force of patriarchal religions, are feeling endangered. They have paid this feminism the honor of opposing it very seriously indeed. . . .

The seventies were a decade in which women reached out to each other: first in consciousness-raising groups that allowed us to create a psychic turf (for women have not even a neighborhood of our own); then in movement meetings and a women's culture that created more psychic territory; and finally across national and cultural boundaries. The eighties can build on these beginnings.

We are all part of the spiral of history.

VII

Themes of the Eighties and Nineties

ANDREA DWORKIN

Pornography: Men Possessing Women

Laws banning material with explicit sexual content—what used to be called antiobscenity laws—were not widespread in the United States until the late nineteenth century, when Congress, responding to pressure groups such as the Society for the Suppression of Vice, enacted legislation prohibiting dissemination of "obscene, lewd, or lascivious" matter. This legislation, like many similar laws later passed by states and cities, hit a wide range of targets. For example, in 1914 the U.S. Post Office invoked the federal antiobscenity statute in declaring that issues of Margaret Sanger's *Woman Rebel* that discussed birth control were unmailable. Later, the Supreme Court judged obscene a number of great works of literature and barred them from sale in the United States; no U.S. publisher was permitted to issue James Joyce's *Ulysses* until 1933, eleven years after the novel was published in France.

During the sixties and seventies many legal restraints on the contents of magazines, books, and movies were reversed in accord with Supreme Court guidelines that held material obscene only if it depicted sexual behavior that offended contemporary community standards *and* was without redeeming social or artistic value. With liberalization of the law and the advent of new technology—especially home videos—pornography entered a boom period, growing into a multibillion-dollar industry. There were insistent protests from religious groups and the political right, but the most innovative legal foray against pornography came in the eighties from two improbable modern-day moral crusaders. One was feminist attorney Catharine MacKinnon; the other, Andrea Dworkin, was a radical feminist writer.

Andrea Dworkin (b. 1946) published two books by the time she was thirty: *Woman Hating* (1974) and *Our Blood: Prophecies and Discourses on Sexual Politics* (1976). However, it was with her book *Pornography: Men Possessing Women* (1981) that she found the subject that engaged her deepest feelings and most profound commitment, and with which she is still most strongly identified. To Dworkin, pornography is a prime means by which men assert their power over women. She argues that, like rape, porn is more about domination and violence than about sex. Through reading Dworkin, many women came to understand pornography for the first time as an agent in the oppression of women. Pornography became a feminist issue—to the eventual dismay of many feminists.

In 1983 Dworkin and MacKinnon—then jointly teaching a course on pornography at the University of Minnesota—were invited by a group of Minneapolis residents to assist their efforts to limit the traffic in pornography in their city. Discarding the "community standards" yardstick, the two feminists drafted an antipornography ordinance based instead on the novel argument that porn is harmful to women and violates their civil rights. The Minneapolis City Council passed the ordinance twice, only to have the mayor veto it each time. Similar legislation in Indianapolis was struck down in 1985 by the U.S. Court of Appeals as an infringement of the First Amendment right to free speech. But at the same time, the court apparently accepted the concept that porn harms women. "Depictions of subordination tend to perpetuate subordination," the court's written opinion stated. "The subordinate status of women, in turn, leads to affront and lower pay at work, insult and injury at home, battery and rape on the streets."[1]

The drive to suppress pornography enlisted many supporters among feminists but also precipitated tremendous debate. Susan Brownmiller and Robin Morgan, for example, backed the Dworkin-MacKinnon initiative; in fact, years before Dworkin's book was published, Morgan had argued that "pornography is

---

[1]Opinion of Judge Frank H. Easterbrook, for the U.S. Court of Appeals for the Seventh Circuit. *American Booksellers v. Hudnut*, 771 F.2d 329 (1985).

the theory, and rape the practice."[2] Betty Friedan, Adrienne Rich, and Kate Millett opposed court-imposed limitations on free speech. Novelist Erica Jong wrote that much as she shared Andrea Dworkin's outrage over pornography, she feared even more the hand of the state censor. "I remain a strict free-speech advocate," she asserted.[3]

In the nineties, the focus of the pornography debate shifted to Canada when a pornography shop owner named Donald Butler challenged the constitutionality of that nation's longstanding criminal obscenity law. A group of Canadian women assisted by Catharine MacKinnon intervened in the case; they presented a new rationale for upholding the obscenity law, based on the theory that pornography is harmful to women. Their argument was successful: On February 27, 1992, the Supreme Court of Canada outlawed sexually explicit pornography that is violent or degrading, asserting that it exploits women and negatively affects their right to equality and security. MacKinnon declared that Canada was the first place in the world where "what is obscene is what harms women, not what offends our values."[4] There followed heated disagreement about the impact of the *Butler* decision. According to *The New York Times,* Canadian bookstore owners reported that since *Butler,* customs agents had been emboldened "to seize books that are mainstream and serious, as well as sexually explicit pornography."[5] Among the hundreds of items detained after *Butler* were a novella by Marguerite Duras, much gay and lesbian literature, and even some books by Andrea Dworkin. But Canadian customs had frequently stopped allegedly obscene materials at the border in the years before *Butler.* Pointing this out, Dworkin and MacKinnon insisted that the agents were simply carrying on

[2]Robin Morgan, "Theory and Practice: Pornography and Rape," 1974; in *The Word of a Woman: Feminist Dispatches, 1968–1992* (New York: Norton, 1992), p. 88.

[3]Erica Jong, "Changing My Mind About Andrea Dworkin," *Ms.,* June 1988, p. 64.

[4]*New York Times,* February 28, 1992, p. B–7. Andrea Dworkin, who believes that no criminal obscenity law should be supported, declined to participate in the Canadian effort.

[5]*New York Times,* December 13, 1993, p. A–8.

business as usual, and that no cause-and-effect relationship be-tween *Butler* and subsequent border seizures had been demon-strated.[6]

Andrea Dworkin is a controversial writer. Her blunt, hard-hitting prose is anything but temperate or judicious, and she condemns men en masse for the evil of pornography. Her recent work includes several novels and the nonfiction volumes *Intercourse* (1987) and *Letters from a War Zone: Writings, 1976–1989*.

In the following selection from Chapter 1, "Power," of her book *Pornography*, Dworkin outlines seven ways in which male power is expressed through pornography.

THE MAJOR THEME OF PORNOGRAPHY as a genre is male power, its nature, its magnitude, its use, its meaning. Male power, as ex-pressed in and through pornography, is discernible in discrete but interwoven, reinforcing strains: the power of self, physical power over and against others, the power of terror, the power of naming, the power of owning, the power of money, and the power of sex. These strains of male power are instrinsic to both the substance and production of pornography; and the ways and means of pornography are the ways and means of male power. The harmony and coherence of hateful values, perceived by men as normal and neutral values when applied to women, distinguish pornography as message, thing, and experience. The strains of male power are embodied in pornography's form and content, in economic control of and distribution of wealth within the industry, in the picture or story as thing, in the pho-tographer or writer as aggressor, in the critic or intellectual who through naming assigns value, in the actual use of models, in the application of the material in what is called real life (which

[6] "Statement by Catharine A. MacKinnon and Andrea Dworkin Regarding Canadian Customs and Legal Approaches to Pornography," August 26, 1994.

women are commanded to regard as distinct from fantasy). A saber penetrating a vagina is a weapon; so is the camera or pen that renders it; so is the penis for which it substitutes (vagina literally means "sheath"). The persons who produce the image are also weapons as men deployed in war become in their persons weapons. Those who defend or protect the image are, in this same sense, weapons. The values in the pornographic work are also manifest in everything surrounding the work. The valuation of women in pornography is a secondary theme in that the degradation of women exists in order to postulate, exercise, and celebrate male power. Male power, in degrading women, is first concerned with itself, its perpetuation, expansion, intensification, and elevation. . . . Male power is the raison d'être of pornography; the degradation of the female is the means of achieving this power.

The photograph is captioned "BEAVER HUNTERS." Two white men, dressed as hunters, sit in a black Jeep. The Jeep occupies almost the whole frame of the picture. The two men carry rifles. The rifles extend above the frame of the photograph into the white space surrounding it. The men and the Jeep face into the camera. Tied onto the hood of the black Jeep is a white woman. She is tied with thick rope. She is spread-eagle. Her pubic hair and crotch are the dead center of the car hood and the photograph. Her head is turned to one side, tied down by rope that is pulled taut across her neck, extended to and wrapped several times around her wrists, tied around the rearview mirrors of the Jeep, brought back around her arms, crisscrossed under her breasts and over her thighs, drawn down and wrapped around the bumper of the Jeep, tied around her ankles. Between her feet on the car bumper, in orange with black print, is a sticker that reads: I brake for Billy Carter. The text under the photograph reads: "Western sportsmen report beaver hunting was particularly good throughout the Rocky Mountain region during the past season. These two hunters easily bagged their limit in the high country. They told HUSTLER that they stuffed and mounted their trophy as soon as they got her home."

The men in the photograph are self-possessed; that is, they possess the power of self. This power radiates from the photograph. They are armed: first, in the sense that they are fully clothed; second, because they carry rifles, which are made more prominent, suggesting erection, by extending outside the frame of the photograph; third, because they are shielded by being inside the vehicle, framed by the windshield; fourth, because only the top parts of their bodies are shown. The woman is possessed; that is, she has no self. A captured animal, she is naked, bound, exposed on the hood of the car outdoors, her features not distinguishable because of the way her head is twisted and tied down. The men sit, supremely still and confident, displaying the captured prey for the camera. The stillness of the woman is like the stillness of death, underlined by the evocation of taxidermy in the caption. He is, he takes; she is not, she is taken.

The photograph celebrates the physical power of men over women. They are hunters, use guns. They have captured and bound a woman. They will stuff and mount her. She is a trophy. While one could argue that the victory of two armed men over a woman is no evidence of physical superiority, the argument is impossible as one experiences (or remembers) the photograph. The superior strength of men is irrefutably established by the fact of the photograph and the knowledge that one brings to it: that it expresses an authentic and commonplace relationship of the male strong to the female weak, wherein the hunt—the targeting, tracking down, pursuing, the chase, the overpowering of, the immobilizing of, even the wounding of—is common practice, whether called sexual pursuit, seduction, or romance. The photograph exists in an immediate context that supports the assertion of this physical power; and in the society that is the larger context, there is no viable and meaningful reality to contradict the physical power of male over female expressed in the photograph.

In the photograph, the power of terror is basic. The men are hunters with guns. Their prey is women. They have caught a woman and tied her onto the hood of a car. The terror is implicit in the content of the photograph, but beyond that the photograph strikes the female viewer dumb with fear. One perceives that the bound woman must be in pain. The very power to make the photograph (to use the model, to tie her in that way) and the fact of the photograph (the fact that someone did use the model, did tie her in that way, that the photograph is published in a magazine and seen by millions of men who buy it specifically to see such photographs) evoke fear in the female observer unless she entirely dissociates herself from the photograph: refuses to believe or understand that real persons posed for it, refuses to see the bound person as a woman like herself. Terror is finally the content of the photograph, and it is also its effect on the female observer. That men have the power and desire to make, publish, and profit from the photograph engenders fear. That millions more men enjoy the photograph makes the fear palpable. That men who in general champion civil rights defend the photograph without experiencing it as an assault on women intensifies the fear, because if the horror of the photograph does not resonate with these men, that horror is not validated as horror in male culture, and women are left without apparent recourse. . . .

The threat in the language accompanying the photograph is also fierce and frightening. She is an animal, think of deer fleeing the hunter, think of seals clubbed to death, think of species nearly extinct. The men will stuff and mount her as a trophy: think of killing displayed proudly as triumph.

Here is the power of naming. Here she is named beaver. In the naming she is diminished to the point of annihilation; her humanity is canceled out. Instead of turning to the American Civil Liberties Union for help, she should perhaps turn to a group that tries to prevent cruelty to animals—beaver, bird, chick, bitch, dog, pussy, and so forth. The words that transform her into an animal have permanence: the male has done the naming. The power of naming includes the freedom to joke. The hunters will brake for Billy Carter. The ridicule is not deadly; they will let him live. The real target of the ridicule is the fool who brakes for animals, here equated with women. The language on the bumper sticker suggests the idea of the car in motion, which would otherwise be lacking. The car becomes a weapon, a source of death, its actual character as males use it.

One is reminded of the animal run over on the road, a haunting image of blood and death. One visualizes the car, with the woman tied onto its hood, in motion crashing into something or someone.

Owning is expressed in every aspect of the photograph. These hunters are sportsmen, wealth suggested in hunting as a leisure-time pursuit of pleasure. They are equipped and outfitted. Their car shines. They have weapons: guns, a can They have a woman, bound and powerless, to do with as they like. They will stuff and mount hen Their possession of her extends over time, even into (her) death. She is owned as a thing, a trophy, or as something dead, a dead bird, a dead deer; she is dead beaver. The camera and the photographer behind it also own the woman. The camera uses and keeps her. The photographer uses her and keeps the image of her. The publisher of the photograph can also claim her as a trophy. He has already mounted her and put her on display. Hunting as a sport suggests that these hunters have hunted before and will hunt again, that each captured woman will be used and owned, stuffed and mounted, that this right to own inheres in man's relationship to nature, that this right to own is so natural and basic that it can be taken entirely for granted, that is, expressed as play or sport.

Wealth is implicit in owning. The woman is likened to food (a dead animal), the hunter's most immediate form of wealth. As a trophy, she is wealth displayed. She is a commodity, part of the measure of male wealth. Man as hunter owns the earth, the things of it, its natural resources. She is part of the wildlife to be plundered for profit and pleasure, collected, used. That they "bagged their limit," then used what they had caught, is congruent with the idea of economy as a sign of mature masculinity.

The fact of the photograph signifies the wealth of men as a class. One class simply does not so use another class unless that usage is maintained in the distribution of wealth. The female model's job is the job of one who is economically imperiled, a sign of economic degradation. The relationship of the men to the woman in the photograph is not fantasy; it is symbol, meaningful because it is rooted in reality. The photograph shows a relationship of rich to poor that is actual in the larger society. The

fact of the photograph in relation to its context—an i[...]
that generates wealth by producing images of women ab[...]
used, a society in which women cannot adequately earn mo[...]
because women are valued precisely as the woman in the phot[...]
graph is valued—both proves and perpetuates the real connection between masculinity and wealth. The sexual-economic
significance of the photograph is so simple that it is easily overlooked: the photograph could not exist as a type of photograph
that produces wealth without the wealth of men to produce and
consume it.

Sex as power is the most explicit meaning of the photograph.
The power of sex unambiguously resides in the male, though the
characterization of the female as a wild animal suggests that the
sexuality of the untamed female is dangerous to men. But
the triumph of the hunters is the nearly universal triumph of
men over women, a triumph ultimately expressed in the stuffing
and mounting. The hunters are figures of virility. Their penises
are hidden but their guns are emphasized. The car, beloved ally
of men in the larger culture, also indicates virility, especially
when a woman is tied to it naked instead of draped over it wearing an evening gown. The pornographic image explicates the
advertising image, and the advertising image echoes the pornographic image.

The power of sex is ultimately defined as the power of conquest. They hunted her down, captured, tied, stuffed, and
mounted her. The excitement is precisely in the nonconsensual
character of the event. The hunt, the ropes, the guns, show that
anything done to her was or will be done against her will. Here
again, the valuation of conquest as being natural—of nature, of
man in nature, of natural man—is implicit in the visual and linguistic imagery.

The power of sex, in male terms, is also funereal. Death per-
meates it. The male erotic trinity—sex, violence, and death—
reigns supreme. She will be or is dead. They did or will kill her.
Everything that they do to or with her is violence. Especially
evocative is the phrase "stuffed and mounted her," suggesting as
it does both sexual violation and embalming.

Different Voice

In a Different Voice: Psychological Theory and Women's Development, by Harvard psychologist Carol Gilligan (b. 1936), was hailed from the time of its publication in 1982 as a feminist classic. *Ms.* magazine featured the author's picture on a cover, declaring her "The *Ms.* Woman of the Year." Gilligan, said *Ms.,* had initiated "a revolution in values" based on female sensibility.[1] However, some women saw troubling implications in Gilligan's message: It seemed that she was a feminist with a different voice—one who claimed the sexes were *unlike* in mind as well as body.

In the introduction to her book, Gilligan explained that after a decade of interviewing males and females about morality and identity, she had begun to discern two voices: "two ways of speaking about moral problems, two modes of describing the relationship between other and self." Females generally sought closeness to others and feared separation; they defined themselves primarily in terms of their relationships (as mother, for instance, or daughter); they based their judgments of people on how much care and consideration was shown to others rather than on personal achievements; they were more concerned with responsibilities than with rights. Because psychologists had failed to include sufficient numbers of females in their research samples, Gilligan argued, most theories of human development were flawed.

Citing the work of Nancy Chodorow, Gilligan suggested that the root of differences between women and men lay in early

---

[1]Lindsy Van Gelder, "Carol Gilligan: Leader for a Different Kind of Future," *Ms.,* January 1984, p. 37.

childhood. Very briefly, Chodorow had indicated that because a little girl's primary caregiver is a person of the same gender, her development of female identity is consistent with her closeness to her mother. Boys, by contrast, must separate from the mother in order to acquire masculine identity. Thus, as adults, men often feel threatened by intimacy, while women require it.[2]

Gilligan's analysis was quickly adopted as part of the intellectual underpinning for "cultural feminism," a movement that had arisen in the seventies. Cultural feminism stemmed from the view that the values, interests, and priorities of women are different from, and often superior to, those of men. It was accompanied by the establishment of a kind of women's counterculture, with feminist communes, publishing houses, bookstores, art galleries, film collectives, restaurants, therapy groups, and health clinics. All-female spiritual circles were formed, many of which involved goddess religions or witchcraft.

Gilligan's ideas apparently penetrated even into corporate boardrooms. An article in the *Harvard Business Review,* for example, declared that the leadership styles of businessmen and businesswomen were dissimilar: Men prefer to "command and control," while women tend to relate to subordinates "interactively." This conclusion was disputed by several researchers, one of whom criticized its premises as "old superstitions." He said, "We know there is a huge range of male leadership styles. There is no reason to believe that women are not just as complicated."[3]

In a special symposium on the Gilligan thesis that ran in the scholarly journal *Signs,* historian Linda Kerber wrote that she was "haunted by the sense that we have heard this argument before, vested in different language." As far back as the ancient Greeks, Kerber noted, "reason" was ascribed to men and "feeling" to women, while the Victorians thought men and women

---

[2]Nancy Chodorow, *The Reproduction of Mothering: Psychoanalysis and the Sociology of Gender* (Berkeley: University of California Press, 1978).

[3]Judy Rosener, "The Ways Women Lead," *Harvard Business Review,* 1990; and Jeffrey Sonnenfelt, lead author of a study conducted by Emory University and Andersen Consulting; both quoted in *New York Times,* August 15, 1993, p. 6.

were so different they should inhabit separate "spheres." Other contributors to the *Signs* symposium challenged Gilligan's methodology—for example, the small size and lack of diversity of her sample population—as well as her conclusions. Responding, Gilligan defended her research, interpretations, and goals. "I am well aware that reports of sex differences can be used to rationalize oppression," she wrote, "and I deplore any use of my work for this purpose."[4]

In her book *Deceptive Distinctions,* sociologist Cynthia Fuchs Epstein examined the Gilligan debate and cautioned that belief in gender stereotypes can be self-fulfilling. Her thorough review of recent research led her to conclude that men and women are more alike than unlike both mentally and emotionally. However, she argued, widespread acceptance of Gilligan's theory could actually increase gender inequality, since social beliefs tend to bring about social realities.[5]

The following excerpt, from Chapter 2 of *In a Different Voice,* "Images of Relationship," presents Gilligan's best-known example of the different approaches of males and females to the same moral dilemma.

TWO CHILDREN WERE IN THE SAME SIXTH-GRADE CLASS at school and were participants in the rights and responsibilities study,[6] designed to explore different conceptions of morality and self. The sample selected for this study was chosen to focus the variables of gender and age while maximizing developmental potential by holding constant, at a high level, the factors of in-

[4]*Signs: Journal of Women in Culture and Society,* vol. 11, no. 2, Winter 1986, pp. 304–333.

[5]Cynthia Fuchs Epstein, *Deceptive Distinctions: Sex, Gender, and the Social Order* (New Haven, CT: Yale University Press, 1988).

[6]A study involving 144 males and females ranging in age from six to sixty —*Ed.*

telligence, education, and social class that have been associated with moral development, at least as measured by existing scales. The two children in question, Amy and Jake, were both bright and articulate and, at least in their eleven-year-old aspirations, resisted easy categories of sex-role stereotyping, since Amy aspired to become a scientist while Jake preferred English to math. Yet their moral judgments seem initially to confirm familiar notions about differences between the sexes, suggesting that the edge girls have on moral development during the early school years gives way at puberty with the ascendance of formal logical thought in boys.

The dilemma that these eleven-year-olds were asked to resolve was one in the series devised by [Lawrence] Kohlberg to measure moral development in adolescence by presenting a conflict between moral norms and exploring the logic of its resolution. In this particular dilemma, a man named Heinz considers whether or not to steal a drug which he cannot afford to buy in order to save the life of his wife. In the standard format of Kohlberg's intervewing procedure, the description of the dilemma itself—Heinz's predicament, the wife's disease, the druggist's refusal to lower his price—is followed by the question, "Should Heinz steal the drug?" The reasons for and against stealing are then explored through a series of questions that vary and extend the parameters of the dilemma in a way designed to reveal the underlying structure of moral thought.

Jake, at eleven, is clear from the outset that Heinz should steal the drug. Costructing the dilemma, as Kohlberg did, as a conflict between the values of property and life, he discerns the logical priority of life and uses that logic to justify his choice:

For one thing, a human life is worth more than money, and if the druggist only makes $1,000, he is still going to live, but if Heinz doesn't steal the drug, his wife is going to die. (*Why is life worth more than money?*) Because the druggist can get a thousand dollars later from rich people with cancer, but Heinz can't get his wife again. (*Why not?*) Because people are all different and so you couldn't get Heinz's wife again.

Asked whether Heinz should steal the drug if he does not love his wife, Jake replies that he should, saying that not only is there "a difference between hating and killing," but also, if Heinz were caught, "the judge would probably think it was the right thing to do." Asked about the fact that, in stealing, Heinz would be breaking the law, he says that "the laws have mistakes, and you can't go writing up a law for everything that you can imagine."

Thus, while taking the law into account and recognizing its function in maintaining social order (the judge, Jake says, "should give Heinz the lightest possible sentence"), he also sees the law as man-made and therefore subject to error and change. Yet his judgment that Heinz should steal the drug, like his view of the law as having mistakes, rests on the assumption of agreement, a societal consensus around moral values that allows one to know and expect others to recognize what is "the right thing to do."

Fascinated by the power of logic, this eleven-year-old boy locates truth in math, which, he says, is "the only thing that is totally logical." Considering the moral dilemma to be "sort of like a math problem with humans," he sets it up as an equation and proceeds to work out the solution. Since his solution is rationally derived, he assumes that anyone following reason would arrive at the same conclusion and thus that a judge would also consider stealing to be the right thing for Heinz to do. Yet he is also aware of the limits of logic. Asked whether there is a right answer to moral problems, Jake replies that "there can only be right and wrong in judgment," since the parameters of action are variable and complex. Illustrating how actions undertaken with the best of intentions can eventuate in the most disastrous of consequences, he says, "like if you give an old lady your seat on the trolley, if you are in a trolley crash and that seat goes through the window, it might be that reason that the old lady dies."

Theories of developmental psychology illuminate well the position of this child, standing at the juncture of childhood and adolescence, at what Piaget describes as the pinnacle of childhood intelligence, and beginning through thought to discover a wider universe of possibility. The moment of preadolescence is caught by the conjunction of formal operational thought with a description of self still anchored in the factual parameters of his childhood world—his age, his town, his father's occupation, the substance of his likes, dislikes, and beliefs. Yet as his self-description radiates the self-confidence of a child who has arrived, in Erikson's terms, at a favorable balance of industry over inferiority—competent, sure of himself, and knowing well the rules of the game—so his emergent capacity for formal thought, his abililty to think about thinking and to reason things out in a logical way, frees him from dependence on authority and allows him to find solutions to problems by himself.

This emergent autonomy follows the trajectory that Kohlberg's six stages of moral development trace, a three-level progression from an egocentric understanding of fairness based on individual need (stages one and two), to a conception of fairness anchored in the shared conventions of societal agreement (stages three and four), and finally to a principled understanding of fairness that rests on the free-standing logic of equality and reciprocity (stages five and six). While this boy's judgments at eleven are scored as conventional on Kohlberg's scale, a mixture of stages three and four, his abililty to bring deductive logic to bear on the solution of moral dilemmas, to differentiate morality from law, and to see how laws can be considered to have mistakes points toward the principled conception of justice that Kohlberg equates with moral maturity.

In contrast, Amy's respose to the dilemma conveys a very different impression, an image of development stunted by a failure of logic, an inability to think for herself. Asked if Heinz should steal the drug, she replies in a way that seems evasive and unsure:

> Well, I don't think so. I think there might be other ways besides stealing it, like if he could borrow the money or make a loan or something, but he really shouldn't steal the drug—but his wife shouldn't die either.

Asked why he should not steal the drug, she considers neither property nor law but rather the effect that theft could have on the relationship between Heinz and his wife:

> If he stole the drug, he might save his wife then, but if he did, he might have to go to jail, and then his wife might get sicker again, and he couldn't get more of the drug, and it might not be good. So, they should really just talk it out and find some other way to make the money.

Seeing in the dilemma not a math problem with humans but a narrative of relationships that extends over time, Amy envisions the wife's continuing need for her husband and the husband's continuing concern for his wife and seeks to respond to the druggist's need in a way that would sustain rather than sever connection. Just as she ties the wife's survival to the preservation of relationships, so she considers the value of the wife's life in a context of relationships, saying that it would be wrong to let her die because, "if she died, it hurts a lot of people and it hurts her." Since Amy's moral judgment is grounded in the belief that, "if somebody has something that would keep somebody alive, then it's not right not to give it to them," she considers the problem in the dilemma to arise not from the druggist's assertion of rights but from his failure of response.

As the interviewer proceeds with the series of questions that follow from Kohlberg's construction of the dilemma, Amy's answers remain essentially unchanged, the various probes serving neither to elucidate nor to modify her initial response. Whether or not Heinz loves his wife, he still shouldn't steal or let her die; if it were a stranger dying instead, Amy says that "if the stranger didn't have anybody near or anyone she knew," then Heinz should try to save her life, but he should not steal the drug. But as the interviewer conveys through the repetition of questions that the answers she gave were not heard or not right, Amy's confidence begins to diminish, and her replies become more constrained and unsure. Asked again why Heinz should not steal the drug, she simply repeats, "Because it's not right." Asked again to explain why, she states again that theft would not be a good solution, adding lamely, "if he took it, he might not know how to give it to his wife, and so his wife might still die." Failing to see the dilemma as a self-contained problem in moral logic, she does not discern the internal structure of its resolution; as she constructs the problem differently herself, Kohlberg's conception completely evades her.

Instead, seeing a world comprised of relationships rather than of people standing alone, a world that coheres through human connection rather than through systems of rules, she finds the puzzle in the dilemma to lie in the failure of the druggist to respond to the wife. Saying that "it is not right for someone to die when their life could be saved," she assumes that if the druggist were to see the consequences of his refusal to lower his price, he would realize that "he should just give it to the wife and then have the husband pay back the money later." Thus she considers the solution to the dilemma to lie in making the wife's condition more salient to the druggist or, that failing, in appealing to others who are in a position to help.

Just as Jake is confident the judge would agree that stealing is the right thing for Heinz to do, so Amy is confident that, "if Heinz and the druggest had talked it out long enough, they could reach something besides stealing." As he considers the law to "have mistakes," so she sees this drama as a mistake, believing that "the world should just share things more and then people wouldn't have to steal." Both children thus recognize the need for agreement but see it as mediated in different ways—he, impersonally through systems of logic and law, she, personally through communication in relationship. Just as he relies on the conventions of logic to deduce the solution to this dilemma, assuming these conventions to be shared, so she relies on a process of communication, assuming connection and believing that her voice will be heard. Yet while his assumptions about agreement are confirmed by the convergence in logic between his answers and the questions posed, her assumptions are belied by the failure of communication, the interviewer's inability to understand her response.

Although the frustration of the interview with Amy is apparent in the repetition of questions and its ultimate circularity, the problem of interpretation is focused by the assessment of her response. When considered in the light of Kohlberg's definition of the stages and sequence of moral development, her moral judgments appear to be a full stage lower in maturity than those of the boy. Scored as a mixture of stages two and three, her responses seem to reveal a feeling of powerlessness in the world, an inability to think systematically about the concepts of morality or law, a reluctance to challenge authority or to examine the logic of received moral truths, a failure even to conceive of acting directly to save a life or to consider that such action, if taken, could possibly have an effect. As her reliance on relationships seems to reveal a continuing dependence and vulnerability, so her belief in communication as the mode through which to resolve moral dilemmas appears naive and cognitively immature.

Yet Amy's description of herself conveys a markedly different impression. Once again, the hallmarks of the preadolescent child depict a child secure in her sense of herself, confident in the substance of her beliefs, and sure of her ability to do something of value in the world. Describing herself at eleven as "growing and changing," she says that she "sees some things differently now, just because I know myself really well now, and I know a lot more about the world." Yet the world she knows is a different world from that refracted by Kohlberg's construction of Heinz's dilemma. Her world is a world of relationships and psychological truths where an awareness of the connection between people gives rise to a recognition of responsibility for one another, a perception of the need for response. Seen in this light, her understanding of morality as arising from the recognition of relationship, her belief in communication as the mode of conflict resolution, and her conviction that the solution to the dilemma will follow from its compelling representation seem far from naive or cognitively immature. Instead, Amy's judgments contain the insights central to an ethic of care, just as Jake's judgments reflect the logic of the justice approach. Her incipient awareness of the "method of truth," the central tenet of nonviolent conflict resolution, and her belief in the restorative activity of care, lead her to see the actors in the dilemma arrayed not as opponents in a contest of rights but as members of a network of relationships on whose continuation they all depend. Consequently her solution to the dilemma lies in activating the network by communication, securing the inclusion of the wife by strengthening rather than severing connections.

But the different logic of Amy's response calls attention to the interpretation of the interview itself. Conceived as an interrogation, it appears instead as a dialogue, which takes on moral dimensions of its own, pertaining to the interviewer's uses of power and to the manifestations of respect. With this shift in the conception of the interview, it immediately becomes clear that the interviewer's problem in understanding Amy's response stems from the fact that Amy is answering a different question from the one the interviewer thought had been posed. Amy is considering not *whether* Heinz should act in this situation ("*should* Heinz steal the drug?") but rather *how* Heinz should act in response to his awareness of his wife's need ("Should Heinz *steal* the drug?"). The interviewer takes the mode of action for granted, presuming it to be a matter of fact; Amy assumes the necessity for action and considers what form it should take. In the interviewer's failure to imagine a response not dreamt of in Kohlberg's moral philosophy lies the failure to hear Amy's question and to see the logic in her response, to discern that what appears, from one perspective, to be an evasion of the dilemma signifies in other terms a recognition of the problem and a search for a more adequate solution.

Thus in Heinz's dilemma these two children see two very different moral problems—Jake a conflict between life and property that can be resolved by logical deduction, Amy a fracture of human relationship that must be mended with its own thread. Asking different questions that arise from different conceptions of the moral domain, the children arrive at answers that fundamentally diverge, and the arrangement of these answers as successive stages on a scale of increasing moral maturity calibrated by the logic of the boy's response misses the different truth revealed in the judgment of the girl. To the question, "What does he see that she does not?" Kohlberg's theory provides a ready response, manifest in the scoring of Jake's judgments a full stage higher than Amy's in moral maturity; to the question, "What does she see that he does not?" Kohlberg's theory has nothing to say. Since most of her responses fall through the sieve of Kohlberg's scoring system, her responses appear from his perspective to lie outside the moral domain.

Yet just as Jake reveals a sophisticated understanding of the logic of justification, so Amy is equally sophisticated in her understanding of the nature of choice. Recognizing that "if both the roads went in totally separate ways, if you pick one, you'll never know what would happen if you went the other way," she explains that "that's the chance you have to take, and like I said, it's just really a guess." To illustrate her point "in a simple way," she describes her choice to spend the summer at camp:

> I will never know what would have happened if I had stayed here, and if something goes wrong at camp, I'll never know if I stayed here if it would have been better. There's really no way around it because there's no way you can do both at once, so you've got to decide, but you'll never know.

In this way, these two eleven-year-old children, both highly intelligent and perceptive about life, though in different ways, display different modes of moral understanding, different ways of thinking about conflict and choice. In resolving Heinz's dilemma, Jake relies on theft to avoid confrontation and turns to the law to mediate the dispute. Transposing a hierarchy of power into a hierarchy of values, he defuses a potentially explosive conflict between people by casting it as an impersonal conflict of claims. In this way, he abstracts the moral problem from the interpersonal situation, finding in the logic of fairness an objective way to decide who will win the dispute. But this hierarchical ordering, with its imagery of winning and losing and the potential for violence which it contains, gives way in Amy's construction of the dilemma to a network of connection, a web of relationships that is sustained by a process of communication. With this shift, the moral problem changes from one of unfair domination, the imposition of property over life, to one of unnecessary exclusion, the failure of the druggist to respond to the wife.

The Chalice and the Blade:
Our History, Our Future

During the summer of 1993 two American bishops had an audience with Pope John Paul II, in the course of which the Pope urged the Americans to combat the "bitter, ideological" feminism practiced by Catholic women in the United States who were worshiping an earth goddess.[1]

Goddess worship did indeed capture the interest of many feminists in the eighties and nineties. Relatively few women were actual practitioners, but women of all religious backgrounds were enthusiastically reading and discussing the spate of goddess literature. The topic was not new to feminism. In 1891, at the age of seventy-five, Elizabeth Cady Stanton made a speech entitled "The Matriarchate, or Mother-Age," in which she embraced the theories about goddesses and ancient matriarchal civilizations that were then being advanced by some anthropologists.[2] Women, Stanton said, could gain "a new sense of dignity and self-respect" from the knowledge "that our mothers, during some periods in the long past, have been the ruling power."[3]

The Chalice and the Blade (1987) by Riane Eisler is the best-known volume on the goddess bookshelf. It is an interpretative study of new archaeological discoveries that reveal a period of human history—in the Paleolithic and Neolithic ages—when men and women worshiped goddesses and celebrated fertility.

[1] *New York Times,* August 3, 1993, p. 1.

[2] Johann Bachofen's *Das Mutterrecht* was published in 1861, and Lewis Henry Morgan's studies of matrilineal descent in native American Indian societies appeared in the 1870s.

[3] Elizabeth Cady Stanton, "The Matriarchate, or Mother-Age," in Aileen S. Kraditor, ed., *Up from the Pedestal* (Chicago: Quadrangle, 1970), pp. 140–147.

During this era, said Eisler, there was "an exceptionally long period of peace and prosperity." The arts of civilization were developed in societies that were not violent or hierarchic but woman-centered and matrilineal, and whose residents venerated the creative forces of nature.

In Eisler's narrative of human history, warlike people from hunter-based cultures invaded the goddess-worshiping cultures and, over millennia, gradually shattered their way of life. The new rulers transformed society into the male-dominant, violence-prone, ecologically unbalanced system of today. They attempted, sometimes ruthlessly, to eradicate every last vestige of the goddess. Eisler believes we have now come to another period of potential cultural transformation, when conditions are favorable for the replacement of patriarchy with a "partnership way." She envisions vast social change characterized by a new era of peace, equality, respect for the earth, and cooperation between women and men.

The new goddess literature has been criticized for its speculativeness, its tendency to ignore contrary data, and its oversimplification of evidence. An analysis by Wellesley professor Mary Lefkowitz found another major flaw: its reduction of all womankind to a genital identity. "What, after all, could women in wildly different societies . . . have in common with each other, except for the most rudimentary biological characteristics?" she asked.[4] By contrast, historian Gerda Lerner, while recognizing that the theory of a woman-centered past is unprovable, commented that by providing an alternative to male-centered interpretations of prehistory, it can "challenge, inspire and fascinate."[5]

Eisler based her conclusions primarily on work by Marija Gimbutas, professor emerita of European archaeology at the University of California, Los Angeles—especially Gimbutas's books *The Goddesses and Gods of Old Europe 7000–3500 B.C.: Myths and Cult Images* (1982) and *The Language of the*

[4]Mary Lefkowitz, "The Twilight of the Goddess," *New Republic*, August 3, 1992, p. 33.
[5]Quoted in *New York Times*, February 13, 1990, p. C-1.

Goddess (1989)—as well as on James Mellaart's description of the archaeological dig at Catal Huyuk, in Turkey, and Nicolas Platon's writings on Minoan Crete. The selection here is excerpted from Chapter 2 of *The Chalice and the Blade,* "Messages from the Past: The World of the Goddess."

WHAT KIND OF PEOPLE were our prehistoric ancestors who worshiped the Goddess? What was life like during the millennia of our cultural evolution before recorded or written history? And what can we learn from those times that is relevant to our own?

Because they left us no written accounts, we can only infer, like Sherlock Holmes turned scientist, how the people of the Paleolithic and of the later, more advanced Neolithic thought, felt, and behaved. But almost everything we have been taught about antiquity is based on conjecture. Even the records we have from early historic cultures, such as Sumer, Babylon, and Crete, are at best scanty and fragmentary and largely concerned with inventories of goods and other mercantile matters. And the more detailed later written accounts about both prehistory and early history from classical Greek, Roman, Hebrew, and Christian times are also mainly based on inferences—made without even the aid of modern archaeological methods.

Indeed, most of what we have learned to think of as our cultural evolution has in fact been interpretation. . . . It has consisted of conclusions drawn from fragmentary data interpreted to conform to the traditional model of our cultural evolution as a linear progression from "primitive man" to so-called "civilized man," who, despite their many differences, shared a common preoccupation with conquering, killing, and dominating.

Through scientific excavations of ancient sites, archaelogists have in recent years obtained a great deal of primary information about prehistory, particularly about the Neolithic, when our ancestors first settled in communities sustained by farming and the breeding of stock. Analyzed from a fresh perspective, these excavations provide the data base for a re-evaluation, and reconstruction, of our past.

One important source of data is excavations of buildings and their contents—including clothing, jewelry, food, furniture, containers, tools, and other objects used in daily life. Another is the excavation of burial sites, which tell us not only about people's attitudes about death but also about their lives. And overlapping both of these data sources is our richest source of information about prehistory: art.

Even when there is a written as well as an oral literary tradition, art is a form of symbolic communication. The extensive art of the Neolithic—be it wall paintings about daily life or about important myths, statuary of religious images, friezes depicting rituals, or simply vase decorations, pictures on seals, or engravings on jewelry—tells us a great deal about how these people lived and died. It also tells us a great deal about how they thought, for in a very real sense Neolithic art is a kind of language or shorthand symbolically expressing how people in that time experienced, and in turn shaped, what we call reality. And if we let this language speak for itself, without projecting on it prevailing models of reality, it tells a fascinating—and in comparison to the stereotype, a far more hopeful—story of our cultural origins.

Neolithic Art

One of the most striking things about Neolithic art is what it does *not* depict. For what people do not depict in their art can tell us as much about them as what they do.

In sharp contrast to later art, a theme notable for its absence from Neolithic art is imagery idealizing armed might, cruelty, and violence-based power. There are here no images of "noble warriors" or scenes of battles. Nor are there any signs of "heroic conquerors" dragging captives around in chains or other evidences of slavery.

Also in sharp contrast to the remains of even their earliest and most primitive male-dominant invaders, what is notable in these Neolithic Goddess-worshiping societies is the absence of lavish "chieftain" burials. And in marked contrast to later male-dominant civilizations like that of Egypt, there is here no sign of mighty rulers who take with them into the afterlife less powerful humans sacrificed at their death.

Nor do we here find, again in contrast to later dominator societies, large caches of weapons or any other sign of the intensive application of material technology and natural resources to arms. The inference that this was a much more, and indeed characteristically, peaceful era is further reinforced by another absence: military fortifications. Only gradually do these begin to appear, apparently as a response to pressures from the warlike nomadic bands coming from the fringe areas of the globe. . . .

In Neolithic art, neither the Goddess nor her son-consort carries the emblems we have learned to associate with might—spears, swords, or thunderbolts, the symbols of an earthly sovereign and/or deity who exacts obedience by killing and maiming. Even beyond this, the art of this period is strikingly devoid of the ruler-ruled, master-subject imagery so characteristic of dominator societies.

What we do find everywhere—in shrines and houses, on wall paintings, in the decorative motifs on vases, in sculptures in the round, clay figurines, and bas reliefs—is a rich array of symbols from nature. Associated with the worship of the Goddess, these attest to awe and wonder at the beauty and mystery of life.

There are the life-sustaining elements of sun and water, for instance, the geometric patterns of wavy forms called meanders (which symbolized flowing waters) incised on an Old European altar from about 5000 B.C.E. in Hungary. There are the giant stone heads of bulls with enormous curled horns painted on the walls of Catal Huyuk shrines, terra-cotta hedgehogs from southern Romania, ritual vases in the form of does from Bulgaria, egg-shaped stone sculptures with the faces of fish, and cult vases in the form of birds.

There are serpents and butterflies (symbols of metamorphosis) which are in historic times still identified with the transformative powers of the Goddess, as in the seal impression from Zakro, in eastern Crete, portraying the Goddess with the wings of an eyed butterfly. Even the later Cretan double axe, reminiscent of the hoe axes used to clear farm lands, was a stylization of the butterfly. Like the serpent, which sheds its skin and is "reborn," it was part of the Goddess's epiphany, yet another symbol of her powers of regeneration.

And everywhere—in murals, statues, and votive figurines—we find images of the Goddess. In the various incarnations of Maiden, Ancestress, or Creatrix, she is the Lady of the waters, the birds, and the underworld, or simply the divine Mother cradling her divine child in her arms. . . .

The unity of all things in nature, as personified by the Goddess, seems to permeate Neolithic art. For here the supreme power governing the universe is a divine Mother who gives her people life, provides them with material and spiritual nurturance, and who even in death can be counted on to take her children back into her cosmic womb.

For instance, in the shrines of Catal Huyuk we find representations of the Goddess both pregnant and giving birth. Often she is accompanied by powerful animals such as leopards and particularly bulls. As a symbol of the unity of all life in nature, in some of her representations she is herself part human and part animal. Even in her darker aspects, in what scholars call the chthonic, or earthy, she is still portrayed as part of the natural order. Just as all life is born from her, it also returns to her at death to be once again reborn.

It could be said that what scholars term the chthonic aspect of the Goddess—her portrayal in surrealistic and sometimes grotesque form—represented our forebears' attempt to deal with the darker aspects of reality by giving our human fears of the shadowy unknown a name and shape. These chthonic images—masks, wall paintings, and statuettes symbolizing death in fantastic and sometimes also humorous forms—would also be designed to impart to the religious initiate a sense of mystical unity with both the dangerous as well as the benign forces governing the world.

Thus, in the same way that life was celebrated in religious imagery and ritual, the destructive processes of nature were also recognized and respected. At the same time that religious rites and ceremonies were designed to give the individual and the community a sense of participation in and control over the life-giving and preserving processes of nature, other rites and ceremonies attempted to keep the more fearful processes at bay.

But with all of this, the many images of the Goddess in her dual aspect of life and death seem to express a view of the world in which the primary purpose of art, and of life, was not to conquer, pillage, and loot but to cultivate the earth and provide the material and spiritual wherewithal for a satisfying life. And on the whole, Neolithic art, and even more so the more developed Minoan art, seems to express a view in which the primary function of the mysterious powers governing the universe is not to exact obedience, punish, and destroy but rather to give.

We know that art, particularly religious or mythical art, reflects not only peoples' attitudes but also their particular form of culture and social organization. The Goddess-centered art we have been examining, with its striking absence of images of male domination or warfare, seems to have reflected a social order in which women, first as heads of clans and priestesses and later on in other important roles, played a central part, and in which both men and women worked together in equal partnership for the common good. If there was here no glorification of wrathful male deities or rulers carrying thunderbolts or arms, or of great conquerors dragging abject slaves about in chains, it is not unreasonable to infer it was because there were no counterparts for those images in real life. And if the central religious image was a woman giving birth and not, as in our time, a man dying on a cross, it would not be unreasonable to infer that life and the love of life—rather than death and the fear of death—were dominant in society as well as art.

The Worship of the Goddess

. . . Although this . . . is rarely included in what we are taught about our cultural evolution, much of what evolved in the millennia of Neolithic history is still with us today. As [James] Mellaart writes, "it formed the basis on which all later cultures and civilizations have built." Or as [Marija] Gimbutas put it, even after the world they represented was destroyed, the mythic images of our Goddess-worshiping Neolithic forebears "lingered in the substratum which nourished further European cultural developments," enormously enriching the European psyche.

Indeed, if we look closely at the art of the Neolithic, it is truly astonishing how much of its Goddess imagery has survived—and that most standard works on the history of religion fail to bring out this fascinating fact. Just as the Neolithic pregnant Goddess was a direct descendant of the full-bellied Paleolithic "Venuses," this same image survives in the pregnant Mary of medieval Christian iconography. The Neolithic image of the young Goddess or Maiden is also still worshiped in the aspect of Mary as the Holy Virgin. And of course the Neolithic figure of the Mother-Goddess holding her divine child is still everywhere dramatically in evidence as the Christian Madonna and Child.

Images traditionally associated with the Goddess, such as the bull and the bucranium, or horns of the bull, as symbols of the power of nature, also survived well into classical, and later Christian, times. The bull was appropriated as a central symbol of later "pagan" patriarchal mythology. Still later, the horned bull god was in Christian iconography converted from a symbol of male power to a symbol of Satan or evil. But in Neolithic times, the bull horns we now routinely associate with the devil had a very different meaning. Images of bull horns have been excavated in both houses and shrines at Catal Huyuk, where horns of consecration sometimes form rows or altars under representations of the Goddess. And the bull itself is here also still a manifestation of the ultimate power of the Goddess. It is a symbol of the male principle, but it is one that, like all else, issues from an all-giving divine womb—as graphically depicted in a Catal Huyuk shrine where the Goddess is shown giving birth to a young bull.

Even the Neolithic imagery of the Goddess in two simultaneous forms—such as the twin Goddesses excavated in Catal Huyuk—survived into historic times, as in the classical Greek images of Demeter and Kore as the two aspects of the Goddess: Mother and Maid as symbols of the cyclical regeneration of nature. Indeed, the children of the Goddess are all integrally connected with the themes of birth, death, and resurrection. Her daughter survived into classical Greek times as Persephone, or Kore. And her son-lover/husband likewise survived well into historic times under such diverse names as Adonis, Tammutz, Attis—and finally, Jesus Christ.

This seemingly remarkable continuity of religious symbolism becomes more understandable if we consider that in both the Neolithic-Chalcolithic of Old Europe and the later Minoan-Mycenaean Bronze Age civilization the religion of the Great Goddess appears to have been the single most prominent and important feature of life. In the Anatolian site of Catal Huyuk the worship of the Goddess appears to permeate all aspects of life. For example, out of 139 rooms excavated between 1961 and 1963, more than 40 appear to have served as shrines.

This same pattern prevails in Neolithic and Chalcolithic Europe. In addition to all the shrines dedicated to various aspects of the Goddess, the houses had sacred corners with ovens, altars (benches), and offering places. And the same holds true for the later civilization of Crete, where, as Gimbutas writes, "shrines of one kind or another are so numerous that there is reason to believe that not only every palace but every private house was put to some such use. . . . To judge by the frequency of shrines, horns of consecration, and the symbol of the double-axe, the whole palace of Knossos must have resembled a sanctuary. Wherever you turn, pillars and symbols remind one of the presence of the Great Goddess."

To say the people who worshiped the Goddess were deeply religious would be to understate, and largely miss, the point. For here there was no separation between the secular and the sacred. As religious historians point out, in prehistoric and, to a large extent, well into historic times, religion was life, and life was religion.

One reason this point is obscured is that scholars have in the past routinely referred to the worship of the Goddess, not as a religion, but as a "fertility cult," and to the Goddess as an "earth mother." But though the fecundity of women and of the earth was, and still is, a requisite for species survival, this characterization is far too simplistic. It would be comparable, for example, to characterizing Christianity as just a death cult because the central image in its art is the Crucifixion.

Neolithic religion—like present-day religious and secular ideologies—expressed the worldview of its time. How different this worldview was from ours is dramatically illustrated if we contrast the Neolithic religious pantheon with the Christian one. In the Neolithic, the head of the holy family was a woman: the Great Mother, the Queen of Heaven, or the Goddess in her various aspects and forms. The male members of this pantheon— her consort, brother, and/or son—were also divine. By contrast, the head of the Christian holy family is an all-powerful Father. The second male in the pantheon—Jesus Christ—is another aspect of the godhead. But though father and son are immortal and divine, Mary, the only woman in this religious facsimile of patriarchal family organization, is merely mortal—clearly, like her earthly counterparts, of an inferior order.

Religions in which the most powerful or only deity is male tend to reflect a social order in which descent is patrilinear (traced through the father) and domicile is patrilocal (the wife goes to live with the family or clan of her husband). Conversely, religions in which the most powerful or sole deity is female tend to reflect a social order in which descent is matrilinear (traced through the mother) and domicile is likewise matrilocal (a husband goes to live with his wife's family or clan). Moreover, a male-dominated and generally hierarchic social structure has historically been reflected and maintained by a male-dominated religious pantheon and by religious doctrines in which the subordination of women is said to be divinely ordained.

If It Isn't Patriarchy It Must Be Matriarchy

Applying these principles to the mounting evidence that for millennia of human history the supreme deity had been female, a number of nineteenth- and early twentieth-century scholars came to a seemingly earthshaking conclusion. If prehistory was not patriarchal, it must have been matriarchal. In other words, if men did not dominate women, women must have dominated men.

Then, when the evidence did not seem to support this conclusion of female dominance, many scholars returned to the more conventionally accepted view. If there never was a matriarchate, they reasoned, male-dominance must, after all, always have been the human norm.

The evidence, however, supports neither one of these conclusions. To begin with, the archaeological data we now have indicate that in its general structure prepatriarchal society was, by any contemporary standard, remarkably equalitarian. In the second place, although in these societies descent appears to have been traced through the mother, and women as priestesses and heads of clans seem to have played leading roles in all aspects of life, there is little indication that the position of men in this social system was in any sense comparable to the subordination and suppression of women characteristic of the male-dominant system that replaced it.

From his excavations of Catal Huyuk, where the systematic reconstruction of the life of the city's inhabitants was the primary archaeological goal, Mellaart concluded that though some social inequality is suggested by sizes of buildings, equipment, and burial gifts, this was "never a glaring one." For example, there are in Catal Huyuk no major differences between houses, most of which show a standardized rectangular plan covering about twenty-five square meters of floor space. Even shrines are not structurally different from houses, nor are they necessarily larger in size. Moreoever, they are intermingled with the houses in considerable numbers, once again indicating a communally based rather than a centralized, hierarchic social and religious structure.

The same general picture emerges from an analysis of Catal Huyuk burial customs. Unlike the later graves of Indo-European chieftains, which clearly bespeak a pyramidal social structure ruled by a feared and fearful strongman on the top, those of Catal Huyuk indicate no glaring social inequalities.

As for the relationship between men and women, it is true, as Mellaart points out, that the divine family of Catal Huyuk is represented "in order of importance as mother, daughter, son, and father," and that this probably mirrored the human families of the city's inhabitants, which were evidently matrilineal and matrilocal. It is also true that in Catal Huyuk and other Neolithic societies the anthropomorphic representations of the Goddess—the young Maid, the mature Mother, and the old Grandmother or Ancestress, all the way back to the original Creatrix—are, as the Greek philosopher Pythagoras later noted, projections of the various stages of the life of woman. Also suggesting a matrilineal and matrilocal social organization is that in Catal Huyuk the sleeping platform where the woman's personal possessions and her bed or divan were located is always found in the same place, on the east side of the living quarters. That of the man shifts, and is also somewhat smaller.

But despite such evidence of the preeminence of women in both religion and life, there are no indications of glaring inequality between women and men. Nor are there any signs that women subjugated or oppressed men.

In sharp contrast to the male-dominated religions of our time, in which in almost all cases until quite recently only men could become members of the religious hierarchy, there is here evidence of both priestesses and priests. For instance, Mellaart points out that although it seems likely that it was primarily priestesses who officiated at the worship of the Goddess in Catal Huyuk, there is also evidence pointing to the participation of priests. He reports that two groups of objects found only in burials in shrines were mirrors of obsidian and fine bone belt fasteners. The former were found only with the bodies of women, the latter only with men. This led Mellaart to conclude that these were "attributes of certain priestesses and priests, which would explain both their rarity and their discovery in shrines."

It is also revealing that sculptures of elderly men, sometimes fashioned in a position reminiscent of Rodin's famous *The Thinker,* suggest that old men as well as old women had important and respected roles. Equally revealing is that the bull and the bucranium, or horns of consecration, which have a central place in the shrines of Neolithic Anatolia, Asia Minor, and Old Europe and later in Minoan and Mycenaean imagery, are symbols of the male principle, as are the images of phalluses and boars, which make their appearance in the later Neolithic, particularly in Europe. Moreoever, some of the earlier Goddess figurines are not only hybrids of human and animal features, but often also have features, such as exaggerated long necks, that can be interpreted as androgynous. And of course the young god, the son-consort of the Goddess, plays a recurring part in the central miracle of prepatriarchal religion, the mystery of regeneration and rebirth.

Clearly, then, while the feminine principle as the primary symbol of the miracle of life permeated Neolithic art and ideology, the male principle also played an important role. The fusion of these two principles through the myths and rituals of the Sacred Marriage was in fact still celebrated in the ancient world well into patriarchal times. For example, in Hittite Anatolia, the great shrine of Yazilikaya was dedicated to this purpose. And even later, in Greece and Rome, the ceremony survived as the *hieros gamos.*

It is interesting in this connection that there is Neolithic imagery indicating an understanding of the joint roles of women and men in procreation. For example, a small stone plaque from Catal Huyuk shows a woman and man in a tender embrace; immediately next to them is the relief of a mother holding a child, the offspring of their union.

All this imagery reflects the markedly different attitudes prevailing in the Neolithic about the relationship between women and men—attitudes in which linking rather than ranking appears to have been predominant. As Gimbutas writes, here "the world of myth was not polarized into female and male as it was among the Indo-Europeans and many other nomadic and pastoral peoples of the steppes. Both principles were manifest side by side. The male divinity in the shape of a young man or male animal appears to affirm and strengthen the forces of the creative and active female. Neither is subordinate to the other: by complementing one another, their power is doubled."

Again and again we find that the debate about whether there once was or was not a matriarchate, which still periodically erupts in academic and popular works, seems to be more a function of our prevailing paradigm than of any archaeological evidence. That is, in our culture built on the ideas of hierarchy and ranking and in-group versus out-group thinking, rigid differences or polarities are emphasized. Ours is characteristically the kind of if-it-isn't-this-it-has-to-be-that, dichotomized, either/or thinking that philosophers from earliest times have cautioned can lead to a simplistic misreading of realilty. And, indeed, psychologists today have discovered it is the mark of a *lower* or less psychologically evolved stage of cognitive and emotional development.

Mellaart apparently tried to ovecome this either/or, if-it-isn't-patriarchy-it-has-to-be-matriarchy tangle when he wrote the following passage: "If the Goddess presided over all the various activities of the life and death of the Neolithic population of Catal Huyuk, so in a way did her son. Even if his role is strictly subordinate to hers, the males' role in life seems to have been fully realized." But in the contradiction between a "fully realized" and a "strictly subordinate" role we again find ourselves tangled up in the cultural and linguistic assumptions inherent in a dominator paradigm: that human relations must fit into some kind of superior-inferior pecking order.

However, looked at from a strictly analytical or logical viewpoint, the primacy of the Goddess—and with this the centrality of the values symbolized by the nurturing and regenerating powers incarnated in the female body—does not justify the inference that women here dominated men. This becomes more apparent if we begin by analogizing from the one human relationship that even in male-dominant societies is not generally conceptualized in superiority-inferiority terms. This is the relationship between mother and child—and the way we perceive it may actually be a remnant of the prepatriarchal conception of the world. The larger, stronger adult mother is clearly, in hierarchic terms, superior to the smaller, weaker child. But this does not mean we normally think of the child as inferior or less valued.

Analogizing from this different conceptual framework, we can see that the fact that women played a central and vigorous role in prehistoric religion and life does not have to mean that men were perceived and treated as subservient. For here both men and women were the children of the Goddess, as they were the children of the women who headed the families and clans. And while this certainly gave women a great deal of power, analogizing from our present-day mother-child relationship, it seems to have been a power that was more equated with responsibility and love than with oppression, privilege, and fear.

In sum, in contrast to the still prevailing view of power as the power symbolized by the Blade—the power to take away or to dominate—a very different view of power seems to have been the norm in these Neolithic Goddess-worshiping societies. This view of power as the "feminine" power to nurture and give was undoubtedly not always adhered to, for these were societies of real flesh-and-blood people, not make-believe utopias. But it was still the normative ideal, the model to be emulated by both women and men.

The view of power symbolized by the Chalice . . . obviously reflects a very different type of social organization from the one we are accustomed to. We may conclude from the evidence of the past examined so far that it cannot be called matriarchal. As it cannot be called patriarchal either, it does not fit into the conventional dominator paradigm of social organization. However . . . it does fit the other alternative for human organization: a partnership society in which neither half of humanity is ranked over the other and diversity is not equated with inferiority or superiority.

SUSAN FALUDI

Backlash

Pulitzer Prize–winning newspaper reporter Susan Faludi documented a decade of intensified resistance to feminism in her book *Backlash: The Undeclared War Against American Women* (1991). Employing the techniques of investigative journalism, she exposed instances of misinformation and outright deception that fed an antifeminist reaction in the 1980s.

For Faludi, periods of backlash are primarily caused by the anxiety men feel when women begin to make initial modest advances toward gender equality. In other words, antifeminism in the eighties—as in previous historical periods when society seemed to turn against women's progress—was the outgrowth of an ongoing struggle for supremacy between men and women. Since men dominate the major institutions of society, the contest is heavily weighted in their favor.

Faludi asserted that the American women's movement scored important successes in the seventies, particularly in the areas of control of reproduction and fairness in employment. Although women were still a long way from equality, the changes that had taken place were resented by many men, who longed to return to a media-evoked, romanticized version of gender relations in the fifties. The repercussions for women were extensive, among them: retreat in public support for such institutions as rape crisis centers, women's health facilities, and shelters for battered women; retraction of federal funding of abortions for the poor; threatened repeal of *Roe v. Wade* by a newly conservative Supreme Court; bombing of abortion clinics by right-to-life zealots; failure of the ERA when the last few required endorsements were lost in state legislatures; and inaction by the EEOC and other agencies on complaints of sex discrimination. Yet,

Faludi said, "women never really surrendered"; through all the negative propaganda, most kept faith with the primary goals of the movement. In fact, feminists even managed to win some victories during the eighties.

The selection here describes how the media invented a season of discontent among "liberated women." It is excerpted from Chapter 1 of *Backlash*, "Introduction: Blame It on Feminism."

TO BE A WOMAN IN AMERICA at the close of the twentieth century—what good fortune. That's what we keep hearing, anyway. The barricades have fallen, politicians assure us. Women have "made it," Madison Avenue cheers. Women's fight for equality has "largely been won," *Time* magazine announces. Enroll at any university, join any law firm, apply for credit at any bank. Women have so many opportunities now, corporate leaders say, that we don't really need equal opportunity policies. Women are so equal now, lawmakers say, that we no longer need an Equal Rights Amendment. Women have "so much," former President Ronald Reagan says, that the White House no longer needs to appoint them to higher office. Even American Express ads are saluting a woman's freedom to charge it. At last, women have received their full citizenship papers.

And yet . . .

Behind this celebration of the American woman's victory, behind the news, cheerfully and endlessly repeated, that the struggle for women's rights is won, another message flashes. You may be free and equal now, it says to women, but you have never been more miserable.

This bulletin of despair is posted everywhere—at the newsstand, on the TV set, at the movies, in advertisements and doctors' offices and academic journals. Professional women are suffering "burnout" and succumbing to an "infertility epidemic." Single women are grieving from a "man shortage." *The New York Times* reports: Childless women are "depressed and confused" and their ranks are swelling. *Newsweek* says: Unwed women are "hysterical" and crumbling under a "profound crisis of confidence." The health advice manuals inform: High-powered career women are stricken with unprecedented out-breaks of "stress-induced disorders," hair loss, bad nerves, alcoholism, and even heart attacks. The psychology books advise: Independent women's loneliness represents "a major mental health problem today." Even founding feminist Betty Friedan has been spreading the word: she warns that women now suffer from a new identity crisis and "new 'problems that have no name.'"[1]

How can American women be in so much trouble at the same time that they are supposed to be so blessed? If the status of women has never been higher, why is their emotional state so low? If women got what they asked for, what could possibly be the matter now?

The prevailing wisdom of the past decade has supported one, and only one, answer to this riddle: it must be all that equality that's causing all that pain. Women are unhappy precisely *because* they are free. Women are enslaved by their own liberation. They have grabbed at the gold ring of independence, only to miss the one ring that really matters. They have gained control of their fertility, only to destroy it. They have pursued their own professional dreams—and lost out on the greatest female adventure. The women's movement, as we are told time and again, has proved women's own worst enemy. . . .

But what "equality" are all these authorities talking about?

If American women are so equal, why do they represent two-thirds of all poor adults? Why are nearly 75 percent of full-time working women making less than $20,000 a year, nearly double the male rate? Why are they still far more likely than men to live in poor housing and receive no health insurance, and twice as likely to draw no pension? Why does the average working woman's salary still lag as far behind the average man's as it did twenty years ago? Why does the average female college graduate

---

[1] Betty Friedan, *The Second Stage* (New York: Summit, 1981), p. 9.

today earn less than a man with no more than a high school diploma (just as she did in the fifties)—and why does the average female high school graduate today earn less than a male high school dropout? Why do American women, in fact, face one of the worst gender-based pay gaps in the developed world?

If women have "made it," then why are nearly 80 percent of working women still stuck in traditional "female" jobs—as secretaries, administrative "support" workers, and salesclerks? And, conversely, why are they less than 8 percent of all federal and state judges, less than 6 percent of all law partners, and less than one-half of 1 percent of top corporate managers? Why are there only three female state governors, two female U.S. senators, and two Fortune 500 chief executives? Why are only 19 of the 4,000 corporate officers and directors women—and why do more than half the boards of Fortune companies still lack even one female member?

If women "have it all," then why don't they have the most basic requirements to achieve equality in the work force? Unlike virtually all other industrialized nations, the U.S. government still has no family-leave and child care programs—and more than 99 percent of American private employers don't offer child care either. Though business leaders say they are aware of and deplore sex discrimination, corporate America has yet to make an honest effort toward eradicating it. In a 1990 national poll of chief executives at Fortune 1000 companies, more than 80 percent acknowledged that discrimination impedes female employees' progress—yet, less than 1 percent of these same companies regarded *remedying* sex discrimination as a goal that their personnel departments should pursue. In fact, when the companies' human resource officers were asked to rate their department's priorities, women's advancement ranked last.

If women are so "free," why are their reproductive freedoms in greater jeopardy today than a decade earlier? Why do women who want to postpone childbearing now have fewer options than ten years ago? The availability of different forms of contraception has declined, research for new birth control has virtually halted, new laws restricting abortion—or even *information* about abortion—for young and poor women have been passed, and the U.S. Supreme Court has shown little ardor in defending the right it granted in 1973.

Nor is women's struggle for equal education over; as a 1989 study found, three-fourths of all high schools still violate the federal law banning sex discrimination in education. In colleges, undergraduate women receive only 70 percent of the aid undergraduate men get in grants and work-study jobs—and women's sports programs receive a pittance compared with men's. A review of state equal-education laws in the late eighties found that only thirteen states had adopted the minimum provisions required by the federal Title IX law—and only seven states had antidiscrimination regulations that covered all education levels.

Nor do women enjoy equality in their own homes, where they still shoulder 70 percent of the household duties—and the only major change in the last fifteen years is that now middle-class men *think* they do more around the house. (In fact, a national poll finds the ranks of women saying their husbands share equally in child care shrunk to 31 percent in 1987 from 40 percent three years earlier.) Furthermore, in thirty states, it is still generally legal for husbands to rape their wives; and only ten states have laws mandating arrest for domestic violence—even though battering was the leading cause of injury to women in the late eighties. Women who have no other option but to flee find that isn't much of an alternative either. Federal funding for battered women's shelters has been withheld and one-third of the 1 million battered women who seek emergency shelter each year can find none. Blows from men contributed far more to the rising numbers of "bag ladies" than the ill effects of feminism. In the eighties, almost half of all homeless women (the fastest growing segment of the homeless) were refugees of domestic violence.

The word may be that women have been "liberated," but women themselves seem to feel otherwise. Repeatedly in national surveys, majorities of women say they are still far from equality. Nearly 70 percent of women polled by *The New York Times* in 1989 said the movement for women's rights had only just begun. Most women in the 1990 Virginia Slims opinion poll agreed with the statement that conditions for their sex in American society had improved "a little, not a lot." In poll after poll in the decade, overwhelming majorities of women said they needed equal pay and equal job opportunities, they needed an Equal Rights Amendment, they needed the right to an abortion without government interference, they needed a federal law guaranteeing maternity leave, they needed decent child care services. They have none of these. So how exactly have we "won" the war for women's rights? . . .

Women themselves don't single out the women's movement as the source of their misery. To the contrary, in national surveys 75 to 95 percent of women credit the feminist campaign with *improving* their lives, and a similar proportion say that the women's movement should keep pushing for change. Less than 8 percent think the women's movement might have actually made their lot worse.

What actually IS troubling the American female population, then? If the many ponderers of the Woman Question really wanted to know, they might have asked their subjects. In public opinion surveys, women consistently rank their own *inequality,* at work and at home, among their most urgent concerns. Over and over, women complain to pollsters about a lack of economic, not marital, opportunities; they protest that working men, not working women, fail to spend time in the nursery and the kitchen. The Roper Organization's survey analysts find that men's opposition to equality is "a major cause of resentment and stress" and "a major irritant for most women today." It is justice for their gender, not wedding rings and bassinets, that women believe to be in desperately short supply. When *The New York Times* polled women in 1989 about "the most important problem facing women today," job discrimination was the overwhelming winner; none of the crises the media and popular culture had so assiduously promoted even made the charts. In the 1990 Virginia Slims poll, women were most upset by their lack of money, followed by the refusal of their men to shoulder child care and domestic duties. By contrast, when the women were asked where the quest for a husband or the desire to hold a "less pressured" job or to stay at home ranked on their list of concerns, they placed them at the bottom.

As the last decade ran its course, women's unhappiness with inequality only mounted. In national polls, the ranks of women protesting discriminatory treatment in business, political, and personal life climbed sharply. The proportion of women complaining of unequal employment opportunities jumped more than ten points from the seventies, and the number of women complaining of unequal barriers to job advancement climbed even higher. By the end of the decade, 80 percent to 95 percent of women said they suffered from job discrimination and unequal pay. Sex discrimination charges filed with the Equal Employment Opportunity Commission rose nearly 25 percent in the Reagan years, and charges of general harassment directed at working women more than doubled. In the decade, complaints of sexual harassment nearly doubled. At home, a much increased proportion of women complained to pollsters of male mistreatment, unequal relationships, and male efforts to, in the words of the Virginia Slims poll, "keep women down." The share of women in the Roper surveys who agreed that men were "basically kind, gentle, and thoughtful" fell from almost 70 percent in 1970 to 50 percent by 1990. And outside their homes, women felt more threatened, too: in the 1990 Virginia Slims poll, 72 percent of women said they felt "more afraid and uneasy on the streets today" than they did a few years ago. Lest this be attributed only to a general rise in criminal activity, by contrast only 49 percent of men felt this way.

While the women's movement has certainly made women more cognizant of their own inequality, the rising chorus of female protest shouldn't be written off as feminist-induced "oversensitivity." The monitors that serve to track slippage in women's status have been working overtime since the early eighties. Government and private surveys are showing that women's already vast representation in the lowliest occupations is rising, their tiny presence in higher-paying trade and craft jobs stalled or backsliding, their minuscule representation in upper management posts stagnant or falling, and their pay dropping in the very occupations where they have made the most "progress."

The status of women lowest on the income ladder has plunged most perilously; government budget cuts in the first four years of the Reagan administration alone pushed nearly 2 million female-headed families and nearly 5 million women below the poverty line. And the prime target of government rollbacks has been one sex only: one-third of the Reagan budget cuts, for example, came out of programs that predominantly serve women—even more extraordinary when one considers that all these programs combined represent only 10 percent of the federal budget.

The alarms aren't just going off in the work force. In national politics, the already small numbers of women in both elective posts and political appointments fell during the eighties. In private life, the average amount that a divorced man paid in child support fell by about 25 percent from the late seventies to the mid-eighties (to a mere $140 a month). Domestic-violence shelters recorded a more than 100 percent increase in the numbers of women taking refuge in their quarters between 1983 and 1987. And government records chronicled a spectacular rise in sexual violence against women. Reported rapes more than doubled from the early seventies—at nearly twice the rate of all other violent crimes and four times the overall crime rate in the United States. While the homicide rate declined, sex-related murders rose 160 percent between 1976 and 1984. And these murders weren't simply the random, impersonal by-product of a violent society; at least one-third of the women were killed by their husbands or boyfriends, and the majority of that group were murdered just after declaring their independence in the most intimate manner—by filing for divorce and leaving home. . . .

Some women began to piece the picture together. In the 1989 *New York Times* poll, more than half of black women and one-fourth of white women put it into words. They told pollsters they believed men were now trying to retract the gains women had made in the last twenty years. "I wanted more autonomy," was how one woman, a thirty-seven-year-old nurse, put it. And her estranged husband "wanted to take it away."

The truth is that the last decade has seen a powerful counterassault on women's rights, a backlash, an attempt to retract the handful of small and hard-won victories that the feminist movement did manage to win for women. This counterassault is largely insidious: in a kind of pop-culture version of the Big Lie, it stands the truth boldly on its head and proclaims that the very steps that have elevated women's position have actually led to their downfall.

The backlash is at once sophisticated and banal, deceptively "progressive" and proudly backward. It deploys both the "new" findings of "scientific research" and the dime-store moralism of yesteryear; it turns into media sound bites both the glib pronouncements of pop-psych trend-watchers and the frenzied rhetoric of New Right preachers. The backlash has succeeded in framing virtually the whole issue of women's rights in its own language. Just as Reaganism shifted political discourse far to the right and demonized liberalism, so the backlash convinced the public that women's "liberation" was the true contemporary American scourge—the source of an endless laundry list of personal, social, and economic problems.

But what has made women unhappy in the last decade is not their "equality"—which they don't yet have—but the rising pressure to halt, and even reverse, women's quest for that equality. The "man shortage" and the "infertility epidemic" are not the price of liberation; in fact, they do not even exist. But these chimeras are the chisels of a society-wide backlash. They are part of a relentless whittling-down process—much of it amounting to outright propaganda—that has served to stir women's private anxieties and break their political wills. Identifying feminism as women's enemy only furthers the ends of a backlash against women's equality, simultaneously deflecting attention from the backlash's central role and recruiting women to attack their own cause.

Some social observers may well ask whether the current pressures on women actually constitute a backlash—or just a continuation of American society's long-standing resistance to women's rights. Certainly hostility to female independence has always been with us. But if fear and loathing of feminism is a sort of perpetual viral condition in our culture, it is not always

in an acute stage; its symptoms subside and resurface periodically. And it is these episodes of resurgence, such as the one we
face now, that can accurately be termed "backlashes" to wom-
en's advancement. If we trace these occurrences in American history . . . , we find such flare-ups are hardly random; they have
always been triggered by the perception—accurate or not—that
women are making great strides. These outbreaks are backlashes because they have always arisen in reaction to women's
"progress," caused not simply by a bedrock of misogyny but by
the specific efforts of contemporary women to improve their status, efforts that have been interpreted time and again by men—
especially men grappling with real threats to their economic and
social well-being on other fronts—as spelling their own masculine doom.

The most recent round of backlash first surfaced in the late
seventies on the fringes, among the evangelical right. By the
early eighties, the fundamentalist ideology had shouldered its
way into the White House. By the mid-eighties, as resistance to
women's rights acquired political and social acceptability, it
passed into the popular culture. And in every case, the timing
coincided with signs that women were believed to be on the
verge of breakthrough.

Just when women's quest for equal rights seemed closest to
achieving its objectives, the backlash struck it down. Just when
a "gender gap" at the voting booth surfaced in 1980, and
women in politics began to talk of capitalizing on it, the
Republican party elevated Ronald Reagan and both political
parties began to shunt women's rights off their platforms. Just
when support for feminism and the Equal Rights Amendment
reached a record high in 1981, the amendment was defeated the
following year. Just when women were starting to mobilize
against battering and sexual assaults, the federal government
stalled funding for battered-women's programs, defeated bills to
fund shelters, and shut down its Office of Domestic Violence—
only two years after opening it in 1979. Just when record numbers of younger women were supporting feminist goals in the
mid-eighties (more of them, in fact, than older women) and a
majority of all women were calling themselves feminists, the

media declared the advent of a younger "postfeminist genera-tion" that supposedly reviled the women's movement. Just when women racked up their largest percentage ever supporting the right to abortion, the U.S. Supreme Court moved toward recon-sidering it.

In other words, the antifeminist backlash has been set off not by women's achievement of full equality but by the increased possibility that they might win it. It is a preemptive strike that stops women long before they reach the finish line. "A backlash may be an indication that women really have had an effect," feminist psychologist Dr. Jean Baker Miller has written, "but backlashes occur when advances have been small, before changes are sufficient to help many people. . . . It is almost as if the leaders of backlashes use the fear of change as a threat be-fore major change has occurred."[2] In the last decade, some women did make substantial advances before the backlash hit, but millions of others were left behind, stranded. Some women now enjoy the right to legal abortion—but not the 44 million women, from the indigent to the military work force, who de-pend on the federal government for their medical care. Some women can now walk into high-paying professional careers—but not the more than 19 million still in the typing pools or be-hind the department store sales counters. (Contrary to popular myth about the "have-it-all" baby-boom women, the largest percentage of women in this generation remain typists and clerks.)

As the backlash has gathered force, it has cut off the few from the many—and the few women who have advanced seek to prove, as a social survival tactic, that they aren't so interested in advancement after all. Some of them parade their defection from the women's movement, while their working-class peers founder and cling to the splintered remains of the feminist cause. While a very few affluent and celebrity women who are showcased in news articles boast about having "found my niche as Mrs. Andy Mill" and going home to "bake bread," the many

---

[2]Jean Baker Miller, *Toward a New Psychology of Women* (Boston: Beacon Press, 1976), pp. xv–xvi.

working-class women appeal for their economic rights—flocking to unions in record numbers, striking on their own for pay equity and establishing their own fledgling groups for working women's rights. In 1986, while 41 percent of upper-income women were claiming in the Gallup poll that they were not feminists, only 26 percent of low-income women were making the same claim.

Women's advances and retreats are generally described in military terms: battles won, battles lost, points and territory gained and surrendered. The metaphor of combat is not without its merits in this context and, clearly, the same sort of martial accounting and vocabulary is already surfacing here. But by imagining the conflict as two battalions neatly arrayed on either side of the line, we miss the entangled nature, the locked embrace, of a "war" between women and the male culture they inhabit. We miss the reactive nature of a backlash, which, by definition, can exist only in response to another force.

In times when feminism is at a low ebb, women assume the reactive role—privately and most often covertly struggling to assert themselves against the dominant cultural tide. But when feminism itself becomes the tide, the opposition doesn't simply go along with the reversal: it digs in its heels, brandishes its fists, builds walls and dams. And its resistance creates countercurrents and treacherous undertows.

The force and furor of the backlash churn beneath the surface, largely invisible to the public eye. On occasion in the last decade, they have burst into view. We have seen New Right politicians condemn women's independence, antiabortion protesters firebomb women's clinics, fundamentalist preachers damn feminists as "whores" and "witches." Other signs of the backlash's wrath, by their sheer brutality, can push their way into public consciousness for a time—the sharp increase in rape, for example, or the rise in pornography that depicts extreme violence against women.

More subtle indicators in popular culture may receive momentary, and often bemused, media notice, then quickly slip from social awareness: a report, for instance, that the image of women on prime-time TV shows has suddenly degenerated. A survey of mystery fiction finding the numbers of female characters tortured and mutilated mysteriously multiplying. The puzzling news that, as one commentator put it, "So many hit songs have the B-word [bitch] to refer to women that some rap music seems to be veering toward rape music."[3] The ascendancy of virulently misogynist comics like Andrew Dice Clay—who called women "pigs" and "sluts" and strutted in films in which women were beaten, tortured, and blown up—or radio hosts like Rush Limbaugh, whose broadsides against "femi-Nazi" feminists made his syndicated program the most popular radio talk show in the nation. Or word that in 1987, the American Women in Radio & Television couldn't award its annual prize for ads that feature women positively: it could find no ad that qualified.

These phenomena are all related, but that doesn't mean they are somehow coordinated. The backlash is not a conspiracy, with a council dispatching agents from some central control room, nor are the people who serve its ends often aware of their role; some even consider themselves feminists. For the most part, its workings are encoded and internalized, diffuse and chameleonic. Not all of the manifestations of the backlash are of equal weight or significance either; some are mere ephemera, generated by a culture machine that is always scrounging for a "fresh" angle. Taken as a whole, however, these codes and cajolings, these whispers and threats and myths, move overwhelmingly in one direction: they try to push women back into their "acceptable" roles—whether as Daddy's girl or fluttery romantic, active nester or passive love object.

Although the backlash is not an organized movement, that doesn't make it any less destructive. In fact, the lack of orchestration, the absence of a single string-puller, only makes it harder to see—and perhaps more effective. A backlash against women's rights succeeds to the degree that it appears *not* to be political, that it appears not to be a struggle at all. It is most

[3]Alice Kahn, "Macho—The Second Wave," *San Francisco Chronicle,* September 16, 1990, Sunday Punch section, p. 2.

powerful when it goes private, when it lodges inside a woman's mind and turns her vision inward, until she imagines the pressure is all in her head, until she begins to enforce the backlash, too—on herself.

In the last decade, the backlash has moved through the culture's secret chambers, traveling through passageways of flattery and fear. Along the way, it has adopted disguises: a mask of mild derision or the painted face of deep "concern." Its lips profess pity for any woman who won't fit the mold, while it tries to clamp the mold around her ears. It pursues a divide-and-conquer strategy: single versus married women, working women versus homemakers, middle- versus working-class. It manipulates a system of rewards and punishments, elevating women who follow its rules, isolating those who don't. The backlash remarkets old myths about women as new facts and ignores all appeals to reason. Cornered, it denies its own existence, points an accusatory finger at feminism, and burrows deeper underground.

Backlash happens to be the title of a 1947 Hollywood movie in which a man frames his wife for a murder he's committed. The backlash against women's rights works in much the same way: its rhetoric charges feminists with all the crimes it perpetrates. The backlash line blames the women's movement for the "feminization of poverty"— while the backlash's own instigators in Washington pushed through the budget cuts that helped impoverish millions of women, fought pay equity proposals, and undermined equal opportunity laws. The backlash line claims the women's movement cares nothing for children's rights—while its own representatives in the capital and state legislatures have blocked one bill after another to improve child care, slashed billions of dollars in federal aid for children, and relaxed state licensing standards for day care centers. The backlash line accuses the women's movement of creating a generation of unhappy single and childless women—but its purveyors in the media are the ones guilty of making single and childless women feel like circus freaks.

To blame feminism for women's "lesser life" is to miss entirely the point of feminism, which is to win women a wider range of experience. Feminism remains a pretty simple concept, despite repeated—and enormously effective—efforts to dress it up in greasepaint and turn its proponents into gargoyles. As Rebecca West wrote sardonically in 1913, "I myself have never been able to find out precisely what feminism is: I only know that people call me a feminist whenever I express sentiments that differentiate me from a doormat."[4]

The meaning of the word "feminist" has not really changed since it first appeared in a book review in the *Athenaeum* of April 27, 1895, describing a woman who "has in her the capacity of fighting her way back to independence." It is the basic proposition that, as Nora put it in Ibsen's *A Doll's House* a century ago, "Before everything else I'm a human being." It is the simply worded sign hoisted by a little girl in the 1970 Women's Strike for Equality: I AM NOT A BARBIE DOLL. Feminism asks the world to recognize at long last that women aren't decorative ornaments, worthy vessels, members of a "special-interest group." They are half (in fact, now more than half) of the national population, and just as deserving of rights and opportunities, just as capable of participating in the world's events, as the other half. Feminism's agenda is basic: It asks that women not be forced to "choose" between public justice and private happiness. It asks that women be free to define themselves—instead of having their identity defined for them, time and again, by their culture and their men.

The fact that these are still such incendiary notions should tell us that American women have a way to go before they enter the promised land of equality.

⁴Rebecca West, *The Clarion*, November 14, 1913, cited in Cheris Kramarae and Paula A. Treichler, eds., *A Feminist Dictionary* (London: Pandora, 1985), p. 160.

ANITA HILL

Statement to the Senate
Judiciary Committee

In the years before the modern women's movement, sexual harassment was not a crime. In fact, it was hardly an event at all, since it did not even have a name. Nonetheless, it was a common occurrence—a detestable but more or less inevitable experience for nearly every woman at some time or other, whether at school, on the public streets, or at work.

Sexual harassment was first placed on the feminist agenda in 1974, in Ithaca, New York, when Carmita Wood, a forty-four-year-old mother of four, quit her job because of unwanted sexual advances by her boss. Wood filed for unemployment benefits, claiming that she had, in effect, been forced to resign. Several feminist activists at Cornell University stepped in to assist Wood, and while preparing a speak-out on the problem, they thought up the phrase *sexual harassment.*

Although Wood's claim eventually was rejected, the issue itself snowballed. Appellate courts ruled in other cases that sexual harassment in the workplace violated Title VII of the 1964 Civil Rights Act—the federal statute prohibiting sex discrimination on the job. The Equal Employment Opportunity Commission (EEOC) received an increasing number of complaints from women who wished to sue their employers, and under EEOC chair Eleanor Holmes Norton—President Jimmy Carter's appointee to the position—the agency took a strong stand against sexual harassment.

In 1986, the U.S Supreme Court heard its first-ever sexual harassment case, *Meritor Savings Bank v. Vinson.* Co-counsel for bank employee Mechelle Vinson, the plaintiff, was Catharine MacKinnon, author of the pathbreaking book *Sexual Harassment of Working Women* (1979). The Supreme Court's decision was a unanimous ratification of the argument by MacKinnon and others that sexual harassment of an employee by her supervisor violates Title VII. Furthermore, the Court agreed that behavior that produces "a hostile or abusive work environment" for women can itself constitute sexual harassment, even if no job-related threat or reward is involved.

In the fall of 1991, confirmation hearings for a Supreme Court Justice became the unlikely forum for the airing of charges of sexual harassment in the workplace—as well as for the enactment of a painful drama that explored the intersecting worlds of sexism and racism. In July, President George Bush had nominated Clarence Thomas, then a federal appeals court judge, to fill the seat vacated by retiring Justice Thurgood Marshall. Thomas, an African American, had served for eight years as chair of the EEOC, where, according to attorney Margaret A. Burnham, he was "Reagan's hatchet man" who "sat by while his agency's budget was chopped in half and its caseload jettisoned."[1]

During gentlemanly questioning by members of the Senate Judiciary Committee, Thomas skirted queries concerning his views on issues like abortion rights and employment discrimination. But despite his conservative record, he had considerable support among African Americans. Poet Maya Angelou spoke for many in the black community when she announced that she backed Thomas, while acknowledging that his actions as EEOC chair had been "anti–affirmative action, anti-busing and anti-other opportunities to redress inequality in our country."[2]

As the final Senate vote on the Thomas confirmation approached, the matter was suddenly returned to the Judiciary Committee for reconsideration because of startling charges that had become public. These involved alleged sexual harassment of an African-American woman, a former Justice Department employee, by her boss, Clarence Thomas. Professor Anita Hill,

---

[1]Margaret A. Burnham, "The Supreme Court Appointment Process and the Politics of Race and Sex," in *Race-ing Justice, En-gendering Power*, ed. Toni Morrison (New York: Pantheon, 1992), p. 302.

[2]*New York Times*, August 25, 1991, Section 4, p. 15.

who had left government employment and was now teaching law at the University of Oklahoma, had lodged the charges when she was questioned about Thomas by a committee aide.

The Senate committee rehearing opened on October 11, 1991, with Thomas's denial. "For almost a decade," Thomas said, "my responsibilities included enforcing the rights of victims of sexual harassment. . . . I have never had such an allegation leveled against me." Next Hill's detailed and specific story of sexual harassment was presented to the committee and—via live television coverage—to a spellbound nation. Thomas's brief and bitter rejoinder followed; in it he said, "unequivocally, uncategorically . . . I deny each and every single allegation against me today." Calling the proceedings "a circus" and "a national disgrace," he added, "And from my standpoint, as a black American, it is a high-tech lynching for uppity blacks."

The confirmation process was instantly transformed into a mesmerizing national teach-in on sexual harassment. All over the United States, women identified with Anita Hill and relived their own unhappy workplace experiences. As they watched the fourteen-member all-male Senate committee at work, it was difficult to avoid the perception that the U.S. Congress was a men's club with little sensitivity to the real problems of women. Immediately after Hill's testimony, support for Thomas among women dropped to 43 percent.

The Senate confirmed Clarence Thomas as the second African American ever to serve on the Supreme Court. But the Hill-Thomas controversy was far from ended, for this was one of those emblematic events with consequences far larger than the occasion itself. Thus, in 1992 NOW reported a surge in membership. More women than ever before entered election campaigns: 150 women nationwide ran for seats in the House of Representatives and eleven entered Senate races. *The New York Times* reported that most of the organizations assisting women in politics "saw membership and contributions rise dramatically after Anita Hill's testimony."[3] The EEOC received over 50 percent more sexual harassment complaints than in the previous

[3]*New York Times,* October 21, 1992, p. D-21.

year, an increase clearly attributable to the Hill-Thomas hearings, according to an EEOC spokeswoman.[4] A huge throng of from 500,000 to 750,000 people marched in Washington for reproductive rights, perhaps the largest demonstration ever held in the capital. It seemed that the dignified, religious, sexually reticent, politically conservative law professor from Oklahoma had been a catalyst for the revivification of American feminism.

Excerpts from Anita Hill's statement alleging sexual harassment appear here.

MR. CHAIRMAN, SENATOR THURMOND, members of the committee:

My name is Anita F. Hill, and I am a professor of law at the University of Oklahoma. I was born on a farm in Okmulgee County, Oklahoma, in 1956. I am the youngest of thirteen children.

I had my early education in Okmulgee County. My father, Albert Hill, is a farmer in that area. My mother's name is Erma Hill. She is also a farmer and a housewife.

My childhood was one of a lot of hard work and not much money, but it was one of solid family affection as represented by my parents. I was reared in a religious atmosphere in the Baptist faith, and I have been a member of the Antioch Baptist Church in Tulsa, Oklahoma, since 1983. It is a very warm part of my life at the present time.

For my undergraduate work, I went to Oklahoma State University and graduated from there in 1977. I am attaching to this statement a copy of my resume for further details of my education. . . .

I graduated from the university with academic honors, and proceeded to the Yale Law School, where I received my J.D. degree in 1980.

---

[4]Nicole Spiegelthal, quoted in *Ms.,* July–August 1993, p. 87.

Upon graduation from law school, I became a practicing lawyer with the Washington, DC, firm of Wald, Harkrader & Ross. In 1981 I was introduced to now Judge Thomas by a mutual friend.

Judge Thomas told me that he was anticipating a political appointment, and asked if I would be interested in working with him.

He was in fact appointed as assistant secretary of education for civil rights. After he had taken that post, he asked if I would become his assistant, and I accepted that position.

In my early period there, I had two major projects. First was an article I wrote for Judge Thomas's signature on the education of minority students. The second was the organization of a seminar on high-risk students, which was abandoned because Judge Thomas transferred to the EEOC, where he became the chairman of that office.

During this period at the Department of Education my working relationship with Judge Thomas was positive. I had a good deal of responsibility and independence. I thought he respected my work, and that he trusted my judgment.

After approximately three months of working there, he asked me to go out socially with him. What happened next, and telling the world about it, are the two most difficult things—experiences of my life.

It is only after a great deal of agonizing consideration, and a number of sleepless nights, that I am able to talk of these unpleasant matters to anyone but my close friends.

I declined the invitation to go out socially with him, and explained to him that I thought it would jeopardize what at the time I considered to be a very good working relationship. I had a normal social life with other men outside the office. I believed then, as now, that having a social relationship with a person who was supervising my work would be ill advised. I was very uncomfortable with the idea and told him so.

I thought that by saying no and explaining my reasons, my employer would abandon his social suggestions. However, to my regret, in the following few weeks, he continued to ask me out on several occasions.

He pressed me to justify my reasons for saying no to him. These incidents took place in his office, or mine. They were in the form of private conversations, which would not have been overheard by anyone else.

My working relationship became even more strained when Judge Thomas began to use work situations to discuss sex. On these occasions he would call me into his office for a course on education issues and projects, or he might suggest that because of the time pressures of his schedule we go to lunch to a government cafeteria.

After a brief discussion of work, he would turn the conversation to a discussion of sexual matters. His conversations were very vivid. He spoke about acts that he had seen in pornographic films involving such matters as women having sex with animals, and films showing group sex or rape scenes.

He talked about pornographic materials depicting individuals with large penises or large breasts, involving various sex acts.

On several occasions, Thomas told me graphically of his own sexual prowess.

Because I was extremely uncomfortable talking about sex with him at all, and particularly in such a graphic way, I told him that I did not want to talk about these subjects. I would also try to change the subject to education matters or to nonsexual personal matters, such as his background or his beliefs.

My efforts to change the subject were rarely successful.

Throughout the period of these conversations, he also from time to time asked me for social engagements. My reaction to these conversations was to avoid them by limiting opportunities for us to engage in extended conversations.

This was difficult because, at the time, I was his only assistant at the office of education—or office for civil rights. During the latter part of my time at the Department of Education, the social pressures, and any conversation of his offensive behavior, ended. I began both to believe and hope that our working relationship could be a proper, cordial, and professional one.

When Judge Thomas was made chair of the EEOC, I needed to face the question of whether to go with him. I was asked to do so, and I did.

The work itself was interesting, and at that time it appeared that the sexual overtures which had so troubled me had ended.

I also faced the realistic fact that I had no alternative job. While I might have gone back to private practice, perhaps in my old firm or at another, I was dedicated to civil rights work and my first choice was to be in that field. Moreover, at that time, the Department of Education itself was a dubious venture. President Reagan was seeking to abolish the entire department.

For my first months at the EEOC, where I continued to be an assistant to Judge Thomas, there were no sexual conversations or overtures. However, during the fall and winter of 1982 these began again. The comments were random and ranged from pressing me about why I didn't go out with him to remarks about my personal appearance. I remember his saying that some day I would have to tell him the real reason that I wouldn't go out with him.

He began to show displeasure in his tone and voice and his demeanor and his continued pressure for an explanation. He commented on what I was wearing in terms of whether it made me more or less sexually attractive. The incidents occurred in his inner office at the EEOC.

One of the oddest episodes I remember was an occasion in which Thomas was drinking a Coke in his office. He got up from the table at which we were working, went over to his desk to get the Coke, looked at the can, and asked, "Who has put pubic hair on my Coke?"

On other occasions, he referred to the size of his own penis as being larger than normal and he also spoke on some occasions of the pleasures he had given to women with oral sex. At this point, late 1982, I began to be concerned that Clarence Thomas might take out his anger with me by degrading me or not giving me important assignments. I also thought that he might find an excuse for dismissing me.

In January of 1983, I began looking for another job. I was handicapped because I feared that if he found out, he might make it difficult for me to find other employment and I might be dismissed from the job I had. Another factor that made my search more difficult was that this was during a period of a hiring freeze in the government.

In February 1983 I was hospitalized for five days on an emergency basis for acute stomach pain, which I attributed to stress on the job. Once out of the hospital I became more committed to find other employment and sought further to minimize my contact with Thomas. This became easier when Allyson Duncan became office director because most of my work was then funneled through her and I had contact with Clarence Thomas mostly in staff meetings.

In the spring of 1983, an opportunity to teach at Oral Roberts University opened up. I participated in a seminar, taught an afternoon session in a seminar at Oral Roberts University. The dean of the university saw me teaching and inquired as to whether I would be interested in further pursuing a career in teaching beginning at Oral Roberts University.

I agreed to take the job, in large part because of my desire to escape the pressures I felt at the EEOC due to Judge Thomas.

When I informed him that I was leaving in July, I recall that his response was that now I would no longer have an excuse for not going out with him. I told him that I still preferred not to do so. At some time after that meeting, he asked if he could take me to dinner at the end of the term. When I declined, he assured me that the dinner was a professional courtesy only and not a social invitation. I reluctantly agreed to accept that invitation but only if it was at the very end of a working day.

On, as I recall, the last day of my employment at the EEOC in the summer of 1983, I did have dinner with Clarence Thomas. We went directly from work to a restaurant near the office. We talked about the work I had done, both at Education and at the EEOC. He told me that he was pleased with all of it except for an article and speech that I had done for him while we were at the Office for Civil Rights. Finally he made a comment that I will vividly remember. He said that if I ever told anyone of his behavior that it would ruin his career. This was not an apology; nor was it an explanation. That was his last remark about the possibility of our going out or reference to his behavior.

In July of 1983 I left the Washington, DC, area and I've had miminal contacts with Judge Clarence Thomas since. . . .

It is only after a great deal of agonizing consideration that I am able to talk of these unpleasant matters to anyone except my closest friends, as I've said before. These last few days have been very trying and very hard for me and it hasn't just been the last few days this week.

It has actually been over a month now that I have been under the strain of this issue.

Telling the world is the most difficult experience of my life, but it is very close to having to live through the experience that occasioned this meeting.

I may have used poor judgment early on in my relationship with this issue. I was aware, however, that telling at any point in my career could adversely affect my future career, and I did not want, early on, to burn all the bridges to the EEOC.

As I said, I may have used poor judgment. Perhaps I should have taken angry or even militant steps, both when I was in the agency or after I had left it. But I must confess to the world that the course that I took seemed the better as well as the easier approach.

I declined any comment to newspapers, but later, when Senate staff asked me about these matters, I felt that I had a duty to report.

I have no personal vendetta against Clarence Thomas. I seek only to provide the committee with information which it may regard as relevant.

It would have been more comfortable to remain silent. I took no initiative to inform anyone. But when I was asked by a representative of this committee to report my experience, I felt that I had to tell the truth. I could not keep silent.

AFRICAN AMERICAN WOMEN
IN DEFENSE OF OURSELVES

For African-American women, the Hill-Thomas hearing was an event with special relevance—one that reflected in a profound way the reality of their own experience. The hearing was, according to one woman, a trauma. To another, it was "like a hurricane that whipped across the landscape of our lives." Yet, she added, it had left a "rainbow in its wake," because afterward a number of previously suppressed problems, including sexual harassment, were suddenly opened up for public discussion. The most important benefit for black women, though, she said, was that Hill, in speaking out, had helped break "generations of black women's silence on and denial of their differences with black men."[1]

Within a few days of the hearing, an ad hoc group called African American Women in Defense of Ourselves circulated a statement protesting the Senate Committee's treatment of Anita Hill and expressing solidarity with her.[2] It was signed by 1,603 women of African descent, most of them academics. The text, wrote Barbara Smith, a founding member of the Combahee River Collective, "marks a watershed in Black feminist organizing. Never have so many Black women publicly stated their refusal to pit racial oppression against sexual oppression."[3]

[1]Nellie Y. McKay, "Remembering Anita Hill and Clarence Thomas: What Really Happened When One Black Woman Spoke Out," in *Race-ing Justice, Engendering Power*, ed. Toni Morrison (New York: Pantheon, 1992), pp. 269, 277.

[2]Deborah K. King, professor of sociology at Dartmouth College, identified Elsa Barkley Brown, Barbara Ransby, and herself as the authors of the statement.

[3]Barbara Smith, "Ain't Gonna Let Nobody Turn Me Around," in *Court of Appeal*, ed. Robert Chrisman and Robert L. Allen (New York: Ballantine, 1992), p. 188.

The document was published as a nearly full-page ad in *The New York Times* on November 17, 1991, and also in half a dozen black newspapers around the country. It is reprinted in full here.

AS WOMEN OF AFRICAN DESCENT, we are deeply troubled by the recent nomination, confirmation, and seating of Clarence Thomas as an Associate Justice of the U.S. Supreme Court. We know that the presence of Clarence Thomas on the Court will be continually used to divert attention from historic struggles for social justice through suggestions that the presence of a Black man on the Supreme Court constitutes an assurance that the rights of African Americans will be protected. Clarence Thomas's public record is ample evidence this will not be true. Further, the consolidation of a conservative majority on the Supreme Court seriously endangers the rights of all women, poor and working class people and the elderly. The seating of Clarence Thomas is an affront not only to African American women and men, but to all people concerned with social justice.

We are particularly outraged by the racist and sexist treatment of Professor Anita Hill, an African American woman who was maligned and castigated for daring to speak publicly of her own experience of sexual abuse. The malicious defamation of Professor Hill insulted all women of African descent and sent a dangerous message to any woman who might contemplate a sexual harassment complaint.

We speak here because we recognize that the media are now portraying the Black community as prepared to tolerate both the dismantling of affirmative action and the evil of sexual harassment in order to have any Black man on the Supreme Court. We want to make clear that the media have ignored or distorted many African American voices. We will not be silenced.

Many have erroneously portrayed the allegations against Clarence Thomas as an issue of either gender or race. As women of African descent, we understand sexual harassment as both. We further understand that Clarence Thomas outrageously manipulated the legacy of lynching in order to shelter himself from Anita Hill's allegations. To deflect attention away from the reality of sexual abuse in African American women's lives, he trivialized and misrepresented this painful part of African American people's history. This country, which has a long legacy of racism and sexism, has never taken the sexual abuse of Black women seriously. Throughout U.S. history Black women have been sexually stereotyped as immoral, insatiable, perverse; the initiators in all sexual contacts—abusive or otherwise. The common assumption in legal proceedings as well as in the larger society has been that Black women cannot be raped or otherwise sexually abused. As Anita Hill's experience demonstrates, Black women who speak of these matters are not likely to be believed.

In 1991, we cannot tolerate this type of dismissal of any one Black woman's experience or this attack upon our collective character without protest, outrage, and resistance.

As women of African descent, we express our vehement opposition to the policies represented by the placement of Clarence Thomas on the Supreme Court. The Bush administration, having obstructed the passage of civil rights legislation, impeded the extension of unemployment compensation, cut student aid and dismantled social welfare programs, has continually demonstrated that it is not operating in our best interests. Nor is this appointee. We pledge ourselves to continue to speak out in defense of one another, in defense of the African American community and against those who are hostile to social justice, no matter what color they are. No one will speak for us but ourselves.

RUTH BADER GINSBURG

On Being Nominated to the Supreme Court

On June 14, 1993, President Bill Clinton nominated Judge Ruth Bader Ginsburg (b. 1933) to fill a vacancy on the Supreme Court. The president declared, "She is to the women's movement what former Supreme Court Justice Thurgood Marshall was to the movement for the rights of African Americans. I can think of no greater compliment to bestow on an American lawyer."

Clinton's high praise of his nominee referred to her pioneering legal work as an advocate for women. In the early seventies Ginsburg founded and was director of the Women's Rights Project of the American Civil Liberties Union, for which she argued six women's-rights cases before the Supreme Court—winning five of them. These cases established precedents that profoundly altered the law as it pertained to women.

In her appearances before the High Court, Ginsburg maintained that laws that treat females and males differently violate the equal-protection clause of the Fourteenth Amendment. She attempted to persuade the justices that such laws were based on gender stereotypes that are harmful to both sexes. In *Frontiero v. Richardson* (1973), for example, she argued successfully against the unequal treatment accorded by the government to a female air force lieutenant and her husband, a student. Lieutenant Sharron Frontiero had been denied benefits ordinarily granted without question to married service*men*—whose spouses were automatically assumed to be financial dependents.

In the fifties, Ginsburg did not consider herself a feminist— "The subject never even came up," she has said. Not until she spent time in Sweden in the sixties and had an opportunity to observe the more egalitarian society there did she begin to think about women's rights. Reading de Beauvoir's *The Second Sex* in the late sixties further stirred her interest. Finally, while teaching law at Rutgers University, she read everything available on legal aspects of sex discrimination. "My consciousness was awakened," she later wrote. "I began to wonder: 'How have people been putting up with such arbitrary distinctions? How have I been putting up with them?' "[1]

Ginsburg's nomination to the Supreme Court came while she was serving on the U.S. Court of Appeals in Washington, DC. At her Supreme Court confirmation hearing before the Senate Judiciary Committee, she was introduced by her friend and colleague Eleanor Holmes Norton. Ginsburg spoke movingly of the path that had brought her to that place. "I surely would not be in this room today," she reflected, "without the determined efforts of men and women who kept dreams alive—dreams of equal citizenship in the days when few would listen—people like Susan B. Anthony, Elizabeth Cady Stanton, and Harriet Tubman come to mind.

"I stand on the shoulders of those brave people."

Excerpts from Ginsburg's response to her Supreme Court nomination appear here.

---

[1]Quoted in *New York Times,* June 25, 1993, p. A-19.

THE ANNOUNCEMENT THE PRESIDENT JUST MADE is significant, I believe, because it contributes to the end of the days when women, at least half the talent pool in our society, appear in high places only as one-at-a-time performers. Recall that when President Carter took office in 1976, no woman ever served on the Supreme Court, and only one woman . . . then served at the next Federal court level, the United States Court of Appeals.

Today Justice Sandra Day O'Connor graces the Supreme Court bench, and close to twenty-five women serve at the Federal Court of Appeals level, two as chief judges. I am confident that more will soon join them. That seems to me inevitable, given the change in law school enrollment.

My law school class in the late 1950s numbered over 500. That class included less than 10 women. . . . Not a law firm in the entire city of New York bid for my employment as a lawyer when I earned my degree. Today few law schools have female enrollment under 40 percent, and several have reached or passed the 50 percent mark. And thanks to Title VII, no entry doors are barred. . . .

I am indebted to so many for this extraordinary chance and challenge: to a revived women's movement in the 1970s that opened doors for people like me, to the civil rights movement of the 1960s from which the women's movement drew inspiration. . . .

I have a last thank you. It is to my mother, Celia Amster Bader, the bravest and strongest person I have ever known, who was taken from me much too soon. I pray that I may be all that she would have been had she lived in an age when women could aspire and achieve and daughters are cherished as much as sons. I look forward to stimulating weeks this summer and, if I am confirmed, to working at a neighboring court to the best of my ability for the advancement of the law in the service of society. Thank you.

SOURCES OF SELECTIONS

The first source cited for each selection is the one from which the reading was taken. For selections not printed in full in this volume, a second source is provided whenever possible.

African American Women in Defense of Ourselves, *New York Times,* November 17, 1991, p. A-53.

Simone de Beauvoir, *The Second Sex* (New York: Alfred A. Knopf, 1953). Reprint, Vintage, 1989.

Boston Women's Health Book Collective, *Our Bodies, Ourselves* (New York: Simon & Schuster, 1973). Also available, *The New Our Bodies, Ourselves* (New York: Simon & Schuster, 1992).

Susan Brownmiller, *Against Our Will: Men, Women, and Rape* (New York: Simon & Schuster, 1975). Reprint, Fawcett, 1993.

Civil Rights Act of 1964, Title VII: Equal Employment Opportunity Discrimination Because of Race, Color, Religion, Sex, or National Origin, 78 Stat. 25.3; 42 *U.S.C.,* 20008 et seq.

The Combahee River Collective Statement, in Zillah Eisenstein, ed., *Capitalist Patriarchy and the Case for Socialist Feminism* (New York: Monthly Review Press, 1978). Also available in *Home Girls: A Black Feminist Anthology,* ed. Barbara Smith (Latham, NY: Kitchen Table: Women of Color Press, 1983), pp. 272–282.

Mary Daly, "After the Death of God the Father: Women's Liberation and the Transformation of Christian Consciousness," *Commonweal,* March 12, 1971, pp. 7–11.

Dorothy Dinnerstein, *The Mermaid and the Minotaur: Sexual Arrangements and Human Malaise* (New York: Harper & Row, 1976). Reprint, Harper Perennial, 1991.

Andrea Dworkin, *Pornography: Men Possessing Women* (New York: Putnam, 1981). Reprint, NAL-Dutton, 1989.

Riane Eisler, *The Chalice and the Blade: Our History, Our Future*

(San Francisco: Harper & Row, 1987). Reprint, Harper San Francisco, 1988.

Susan Faludi, *Backlash: The Undeclared War Against American Women* (New York: Crown, 1991). Reprint, Anchor/Doubleday, 1992.

Shulamith Firestone, *The Dialectic of Sex: The Case for Feminist Revolution* (New York: Morrow, 1970). Reprint, Quill/Morrow, 1993.

Betty Friedan, *The Feminine Mystique* (New York: W. W. Norton, 1963). Reprint, Dell, 1984.

Carol Gilligan, *In a Different Voice: Psychological Theory and Women's Development* (Cambridge, MA: Harvard University Press, 1982). Reprint, Harvard University Press, 1993.

Ruth Bader Ginsburg, On Being Nominated to the Supreme Court, in press release from the White House Office of the Press Secretary, June 14, 1993. Also available in *New York Times,* June 15, 1993, p. A-24.

Germaine Greer, *The Female Eunuch* (New York: McGraw-Hill, 1970). Reprint, Bantam, 1972.

Casey Hayden and Mary King, "A Kind of Memo from Casey Hayden and Mary King to a Number of Other Women in the Peace and Freedom Movements," *Liberation,* vol. 11, no. 2, April 1966, p. 35.

Anita Hill, Statement to the Senate Judiciary Committee in Hearings before the Committee on the Judiciary, U.S. Senate, 102nd Congress, 1st Session; Nomination of Judge Clarence Thomas To Be Associate Justice of the Supreme Court of the United States (Washington, DC: U.S. Government Printing Office, 1993), part 4, pp. 36–40. Also available in *Court of Appeal,* ed. Robert Chrisman and Robert L. Allen (New York: Ballantine, 1992), pp. 15–21.

Beverly Jones, "Toward a Female Liberation Movement," mimeographed copy. Full text available from Redstockings Women's Liberation Archives Distribution Project, P.O. Box 2625, Gainesville, FL 32602, $5.50. Also available in Leslie B. Tanner, ed., *Voices from Women's Liberation* (New York: Signet, 1970), pp. 362–415.

Anne Koedt, "The Myth of the Vaginal Orgasm," *Notes from the Second Year: Women's Liberation—Major Writings of the Radical Feminists,* April 1970, pp. 37–41. Also available in Anne Koedt, Ellen Levine, Anita Rapone, eds., *Radical Feminism* (New York: Quadrangle, 1973).

Doris Lessing, *The Golden Notebook* (New York: Simon & Schuster, 1962). Reprint, Bantam, 1981.

Audre Lorde, "Who Said It Was Simple," *Undersong: Chosen Poems Old and New, Revised* (New York: W. W. Norton, 1992).

Kathy McAfee and Myrna Wood, "Bread and Roses," *Leviathan* 3, June 1969, pp. 8–11, 43–44. Also available in Leslie B. Tanner, ed., *Voices from Women's Liberation* (New York: Signet, 1970), pp. 415–433.

Kate Millett, *Sexual Politics* (New York: Doubleday, 1970). Reprint, Touchstone/Simon & Schuster, 1990.

Juliet Mitchell, "Women: The Longest Revolution," *New Left Review* 40, November–December 1966, pp. 11–37. Revised and expanded in Juliet Mitchell, *Woman's Estate* (New York: Pantheon, 1971).

Robin Morgan, "Goodbye to All That," *Rat Subterranean News,* February 6–23, 1970, pp. 6–7.

Pauli Murray and Mary O. Eastwood, "Jane Crow and the Law: Sex Discrimination and Title VII," *George Washington Law Review,* vol. 34, no. 2, December 1965.

National Black Feminist Organization Statement of Purpose, *Ms.,* May 1974, p. 99.

The National Organization for Women Statement of Purpose, distributed by National Organization for Women, New York City Chapter, 15 West 18 St., New York, NY 10011. Also available in Betty Friedan, *It Changed My Life* (New York: Random House, 1976), pp. 87–91.

New York City Commission on Human Rights Hearings on Women's Rights. Available in *Women's Role in Contemporary Society* (New York: Avon, 1972).

Sylvia Plath, "Purdah," in *Collected Poems,* ed. Ted Hughes (New York: Harper & Row, 1981).

Cynthia Ozick, "Previsions of the Demise of the Dancing Dog," *Art & Ardor* (New York: Knopf, 1983), pp. 263–283.

Radicalesbians, "The Woman-Identified Woman," pamphlet published by Gay Flames, 1972.

Redstockings Manifesto, *Notes from the Second Year: Women's Liberation—Major Writings of the Radical Feminists,* April 1970, pp. 112–113.

The Report of the President's Commission on the Status of Women, *American Women* (Washington, DC: U.S. Government Printing Office, 1963). Also available in *American Women,* The Report of the President's Commission on the Status of Women and Other Publications of the Commission (New York: Charles Scribner's Sons, 1965).

Adrienne Rich, "Compulsory Heterosexuality and Lesbian Existence," *Blood, Bread, and Poetry: Selected Prose, 1979–1985* (New York: W. W. Norton, 1986), pp. 23–68.

Jane Roe v. Henry Wade, Opinion of the Court, 410 U.S. 113, L. Ed. 2d 147, 93 Sup. Ct. 705 (1973).

Muriel Rukeyser, "The Poem as Mask," *Collected Poems* (New York: McGraw-Hill, 1978).

An SDS Statement on the Liberation of Women, *New Left Notes,* July 10, 1967, p. 4.

Anne Sexton, "In Celebration of My Uterus," *The Complete Poems* (Boston: Houghton Mifflin, 1981).

Gloria Steinem, "The Way We Were—And Will Be," *Ms.,* December 1979, pp. 60–94 (with photos). Also available in *The Decade of Women: A Ms. History of the Seventies in Words and Pictures* (New York: Putnam, 1980).

Michele Wallace, "Black Macho and the Myth of the Super-woman," *Ms.,* January 1979, pp. 45–48, 87–91, adapted by the author from *Black Macho and the Myth of the Superwoman* (New York: Dial, 1979). Reprint, Verso, 1990.

Naomi Weisstein, "Kinder, Küche, Kirche as Scientific Law: Psychology Constructs the Female," *Motive,* vol. 29, nos. 6–7, March–April 1969. Expanded and revised in *Social Education,* April 1971, pp. 363–373. Reprinted in Vivian Gornick and Barbara K. Moran, eds., *Woman in Sexist Society* (New York: Signet, 1972), pp. 207–224.

ACKNOWLEDGMENTS

Grateful acknowledgment is made

to Walter Schneir, for generous assistance with many aspects of this project.

to Louise Bernikow, Cynthia Fuchs Epstein, Anne Koedt, Jesse Lemisch, Robin Morgan, Barbara Smith, and Polly Thistlethwaite, each of whom shared expertise and/or research materials relating to a specific selection.

to the following for permission to reprint previously published material: *African American Women in Defense of Ourselves:* (New York Times, November 17, 1991). Reprinted by permission of Deborah K. King. *Georges Borchardt, Inc.:* Excerpts from *Sexual Politics* by Kate Millett, copyright © 1969 by Kate Millett. Reprinted by permission of Georges Borchardt, Inc., for the author. *The Boston Women's Health Book Collective:* Excerpts from *Our Bodies, Ourselves* by The Boston Women's Health Book Collective, 1973 edition, copyright © 1971, 1973 by The Boston Women's Health Book Collective. Reprinted by permission of The Boston Women's Health Book Collective. *Commonweal:* "After the Death of God the Father: Women's Liberation and the Transformation of Christian Consciousness" by Mary Daly (*Commonweal,* March 12, 1971), copyright © 1971 by Commonweal Publishing Company, Inc. Reprinted by permission of *Commonweal. Crown Publishers, Inc.:* Excerpts from *Backlash* by Susan Faludi, copyright © 1991 by Susan Faludi. Reprinted by permission of Crown Publishers, Inc. *The George Washington Law Review:* "Jane Crow and the Law" by Pauli Murray and Mary O. Eastwood (*The George Washington Law Review,* vol. 34, no. 2, December 1965). Reprinted by permission of *The George Washington Law Review* © 1965. *HarperCollins Publishers, Inc.:* Excerpts from *The Mermaid and the Minotaur* by Dorothy Dinnerstein, copyright © 1976 by Dorothy Dinnerstein; excerpts from Chapter 2 from *The Chalice and the Blade: Our History, Our Future* by Riane Eisler, copyright © 1987 by Riane Eisler. Reprinted by permission of HarperCollins Publishers, Inc. *HarperCollins Publishers, Inc. and Faber and Faber Limited:* "Purdah" from *Winter Trees* by Sylvia Plath, copyright © 1963 by Ted Hughes. Originally appeared in *Poetry.* Rights outside the U.S. from *Collected Poems* by Sylvia Plath, edited by Ted Hughes, administered by Faber and Faber Limited,

London. Reprinted by permission of HarperCollins Publishers, Inc., and Faber and Faber Limited. *Harvard University Press:* Excerpt from *In a Different Voice: Psychological Theory and Women's Development* by Carol Gilligan, copyright © 1982 by Carol Gilligan. Reprinted by permission of Cambridge, Mass.: Harvard University Press. *Houghton Mifflin Company:* "In Celebration of My Uterus" from *Love Poems* by Anne Sexton, copyright © 1967, 1968, 1969 by Anne Sexton. Reprinted by permission of Houghton Mifflin Company. All rights reserved. *Beverly Jones:* Excerpts from Part I, "Toward a Female Liberation Movement" by Beverly Jones (The Florida Paper on Women's Liberation, 1968). Reprinted by permission of Beverly Jones. *Alfred A. Knopf, Inc.:* Excerpts from *The Second Sex* by Simone de Beauvoir, translated by H. M. Parshley, copyright © 1952 by Alfred A. Knopf, Inc.; excerpts from "Previsions of the Demise of the Dancing Dog" from *Art and Ardor* by Cynthia Ozick, copyright © 1983 by Cynthia Ozick. Reprinted by permission of Alfred A. Knopf, Inc. *Anne Koedt:* Excerpts from "The Myth of the Vaginal Orgasm" by Anne Koedt from *Notes from the Second Year,* edited by Shulamith Firestone and Anne Koedt, copyright © 1970 by Anne Koedt. Reprinted by permission of Anne Koedt. *Liberation:* "Sex and Caste: A Kind of Memo" by Casey Hayden and Mary King (*Liberation,* April 1966). Reprinted by permission of *Liberation. Kathy McAfee:* Excerpts from "Bread and Roses" by Kathy McAfee and Myrna Wood (*Leviathan* 3, June 1969). Reprinted by permission of Kathy McAfee. *McGraw-Hill, Inc.,* and *Aitken, Stone & Wylie Ltd:* Excerpts from *The Female Eunuch* by Germaine Greer, copyright © 1971 by Germaine Greer. Rights in Canada administered by Aitken, Stone & Wylie Ltd, London. Reprinted by permission of McGraw-Hill, Inc., and Aitken, Stone & Wylie Ltd. *Elaine Markson Literary Agency, Inc.:* Excerpt from *Pornography: Men Possessing Women* by Andrea Dworkin (E. P. Dutton, 1989), copyright © 1981 by Andrea Dworkin. Reprinted by permission of Andrea Dworkin. *Monthly Review Foundation:* Excerpts from "The Combahee River Collective Statement" from *Capitalist Patriarchy and the Case for Socialist Feminism* by Zillah R. Eisenstein (*Monthly Review,* 1978), copyright © 1978 by Zillah R. Eisenstein. Reprinted by permission of Monthly Review Foundation. *Robin Morgan:* "Goodbye to All That" by Robin Morgan (*Rat,* Feb. 6–23, 1970 and subsequently in *The Word of a Woman: Feminist Dispatches 1969–1992,* W. W. Norton & Company), copyright © 1970 by Robin Morgan. Reprinted by permission of Robin Morgan. *William Morrow & Company, Inc.:* Excerpts from "Conclusion: The Ultimate Revolution" from *The Dialectic of Sex* by Shulamith Firestone, copyright © 1970 by Shulamith Firestone. Reprinted by permission of William Morrow & Company, Inc. *W. W. Norton & Company, Inc.:* "The Problem That Has No Name" from *The Feminine Mystique* by Betty Friedan, copyright © 1963 by Betty Friedan; "Who Said It Was Simple" from *Undersong, Chosen Poems Old and New, Revised Edition,* by Audre Lorde, copyright © 1968, 1970, 1973, 1974, 1976, 1982, 1992 by Audre Lorde. Reprinted by permission of W. W. Norton & Company, Inc. *W. W. Norton & Company, Inc.:* Excerpts from *Blood, Bread, and Poetry, Selected Prose 1979–1985,* by Adrienne Rich, copyright © 1986 by Adrienne Rich. Reprinted by permission of the author and W. W. Norton & Company, Inc. *Rogers, Coleridge & White Ltd.*: Excerpts from *Women: The Longest Revolution* by Juliet Mitchell (*New Left Review* 40, Nov.–Dec., 1966). Reprinted by permission of Rogers, Coleridge & White Ltd. *William L. Rukeyser:* "The Poem as Mask" by Muriel Rukeyser, from *Out of Silence* (TriQuarterly Books, Evanston, IL, 1992), copyright © William L. Rukeyser. Reprinted by permission of William L. Rukeyser. *Simon & Schuster, Inc.:* Excerpts from *Against Our Will* by Susan Brownmiller, copyright © 1975 by Susan Brownmiller. Reprinted by permission of Simon & Schuster, Inc. *Simon & Schuster, Inc.* and *Michael Joseph Ltd.*: Excerpts from *The Golden Notebook* by Doris Lessing, copyright © 1962 by Doris Lessing. Rights outside the U.S. administered by Michael Joseph Ltd., London. Reprinted by permission of Simon & Schuster, Inc., and Michael Joseph Ltd. *Gloria Steinem:* Excerpts from "The Way We Were—And Will Be" by Gloria Steinem (*Ms.,* December 1979), copyright © 1979 by Gloria Steinem. Reprinted by permission of Gloria Steinem. *Michele Wallace:* Excerpts from "Black Macho and the Myth of the Superwoman" by Michele Wallace. (*Ms.,* January 1979), copyright © 1978 by Michele Wallace. Reprinted by permission of Michele Wallace. *Naomi Weisstein:* Excerpts from "Kinder, Küche, Kirche as Scientific Law: Psychology Constructs the Female" by Naomi Weisstein (*Motive* 29, March–April 1969; expanded and revised in *Social Education,* April 1971), copyright © 1971 by Naomi Weisstein. Reprinted by permission of Naomi Weisstein.

INDEX

MIRIAM SCHNEIR is the editor of the anthology *Feminism: The Essential Historical Writings* (Vintage Books, 1972, 1994). She is a coauthor of *Remember the Ladies": Women in America, 1750–1815* (1976), and wrote with Walter Schneir *Invitation to an Inquest,* a study of the Rosenberg case (1965, 1983). Her articles have appeared in *Ms., The Nation, The New York Times Magazine,* and various other publications.

Under the auspices of Columbia University Teachers College, she prepared a critique of the coverage and treatment of women in a multivolume encyclopedia, which was the basis for revision of the encyclopedia. She was a research associate with Columbia University Center for the Social Sciences Program in Sex Roles and Social Change.

ALSO AVAILABLE

FEMINISM
The Essential Historical Writings

EDITED WITH AN INTRODUCTION
AND COMMENTARIES BY
MIRIAM SCHNEIR

Tracing women's struggle for self-determination from the time of the American Revolution to the first decades of the twentieth century, *Feminism: The Essential Historical Writings* is a landmark collection of richly diverse writings by authors ranging from Mary Wollstonecraft to Virginia Woolf. When this trailblazing work was originally published in 1972, it helped shape the modern women's movement, introducing young activists to their feminist forbears. The continued relevance of these feminist writings is a testament to the force of their authors' moral and political vision and the continuity of the quest of women to control their own destinies.

ISBN: 0-679-75381-8/Women's Studies/History